The Official RED BOOK®

A GUIDE BOOK OF
WASHINGTON AND
STATE QUARTER DOLLARS

Complete Source for
History, Grading, and Prices

Q. David Bowers

Foreword by
Garrett Burke

Valuations Editor
Lawrence Stack

Whitman Publishing, LLC
PUBLISHING SINCE 1934
Atlanta, Georgia

737.4973
BOWERS

Whitman
Publishing, LLC
PUBLISHING SINCE 1934
www.whitman**books**.com

The WCG™ pricing grid used throughout this publication is patent pending. THE OFFICIAL RED BOOK is a trademark of Whitman Publishing, LLC.

All rights reserved, including duplication of any kind and storage in electronic or visual retrieval systems. Permission is granted for writers to use a reasonable number of brief excerpts and quotations in printed reviews and articles, provided credit is given to the title of the work and the author. Written permission from the publisher is required for other uses of text, illustrations, and other content, including in books and electronic or other media.

Correspondence concerning this book may be directed to the publisher, at the address above.

10/12
19/12

ISBN: 079482059x
Printed in China

Disclaimer: Expert opinion should be sought in any significant numismatic purchase. This book is presented as a guide only. No warranty or representation of any kind is made concerning the completeness of the information presented. The author, a professional numismatist, regularly buys, sells, and sometimes holds certain of the items discussed in this book.

Caveat: The value estimates given are subject to variation and differences of opinion. Before making decisions to buy or sell, consult the latest information. Past performance of the rare coin market or any coin or series within that market is not necessarily an indication of future performance, as the future is unknown. Such factors as changing demand, popularity, grading interpretations, strength of the overall coin market, and economic conditions will continue to be influences.

Advertisements within this book: Whitman Publishing, LLC, does not endorse, warrant, or guarantee any of the products or services of its advertisers. All warranties and guarantees are the sole responsibility of the advertiser.

About the cover: The 1932 Washington quarter is the first in the series. It replaced the Standing Liberty quarter design, which had been minted since 1916. The Bicentennial reverse, struck in 1975 and 1976, honored the 200-year anniversary of the Declaration of Independence. Also pictured on the cover are the reverse design used from 1932 to 1998, and the obverse designs of several of the state quarters minted since 1999.

About the portrait on page xvi: Charles Daughtrey is an artist, photographer, and numismatic author who specializes in Lincoln cents. His *Portrait of John Flanagan* (pencil on Bristol board, 2006) is the fourth in a series of tributes to U.S. Mint designers and their coins. More of Daughtrey's limited-edition numismatic artwork can be seen at his Web site, www.cdaughtrey.com.

Other books in **The Official** RED BOOK® include: *A Guide Book of Morgan Silver Dollars; A Guide Book of Double Eagle Gold Coins; A Guide Book of United States Type Coins; A Guide Book of Modern United States Proof Coin Sets; A Guide Book of Shield and Liberty Head Nickels; A Guide Book of Buffalo and Jefferson Nickels; A Guide Book of Flying Eagle and Indian Head Cents; A Guide Book of Washington and State Quarters;* and *A Guide Book of United States Commemorative Coins.* Future titles include *A Guide Book of Barber Silver Coins* and *A Guide Book of Liberty Seated Coins.*

For a complete catalog of numismatic reference books, supplies, and storage products, visit Whitman Publishing online at **www.whitmanbooks.com**.

ABOUT THE AUTHOR

Q. David Bowers, numismatic director of Whitman Publishing, has been in the rare coin business since he was a teenager in 1953. He is also affiliated with American Numismatic Rarities, LLC, of Wolfeboro, New Hampshire.

Bowers is a recipient of the Pennsylvania State University College of Business Administration's Alumni Achievement Award (1976); he has served as president of the American Numismatic Association (1983–1985) and president of the Professional Numismatists Guild (1977–1979); he is a recipient of the highest honor bestowed by the ANA (the Farran Zerbe Award); he was the first ANA member to be named Numismatist of the Year (1995); and he has been inducted into the Numismatic Hall of Fame (at ANA Headquarters in Colorado Springs).

Bowers is a recipient of the highest honor given by the Professional Numismatists Guild (The Founders' Award) and has received more "Book of the Year Award" and "Best Columnist" honors given by the Numismatic Literary Guild than has any other writer. In 2000 he was the first annual recipient of the Burnett Anderson Memorial Award, an honor jointly sponsored by the American Numismatic Society, the American Numismatic Association, and the Numismatic Literary Guild. In July 1999, in a poll published in *COINage* ("Numismatists of the Century," by Ed Reiter), Bowers was recognized in this list of just 18 names.

He is the author of more than 50 books, hundreds of auction and other catalogs, and several thousand articles including columns in Coin World (now the longest-running by any author in numismatic history) and, in past years, The Numismatist. His past commercial affiliations have included Empire Coin Co., Bowers and Ruddy Galleries, and Bowers and Merena, among others.

Despite having handled a large share of major collections and just about every rarity in the book, Dave claims, "I have never worked a day in my life. I love what I do." His prime enjoyments in numismatics are knowing "coin people," from newcomers to old-timers, and studying the endless lore and history of coins, tokens, medals, and paper money.

ABOUT THE VALUATIONS EDITOR

Lawrence Stack is the CEO of Stack's Rare Coins, a family-owned firm that has been a leader in professional numismatics in America since 1935.

CREDITS AND ACKNOWLEDGMENTS

American Numismatic Rarities provided many illustrations (by Douglas Plasencia), helped with research, and assisted in other ways.

Casey Baeslack of ANACS made text suggestions and grading comments. **Becky Bailey** of the United States Mint helped with information and background on the state quarters. **Steven M. Bieda** discussed the creation of the Michigan state quarter and furnished an illustration. **Wynn Bowers** reviewed the text and made suggestions. **Roger W. Burdette** conducted research in the National Archives and furnished legislative, Treasury, Commission of Fine Arts, and other documents and correspondence relating to the background of the design, 1930 to 1932. **Garrett Burke,** designer of the 2005 California quarter dollar, wrote the foreword and also helped with copyediting the manuscript. **Greg Burns** helped with information on the California quarter.

Terry Campbell commented on the design selection process for the New York quarter. **G.C. Carnes** sent information concerning the Texas quarter dollar. **Daniel Carr,** artist for three of the state quarters, helped in several ways. The **Commission of Fine Arts,** Washington, DC, provided certain documents. **José Cortez** provided photos.

Beth Deisher, editor of *Coin World,* provided extensive information.

Gloria Eskridge of the United States Mint answered inquiries and helped in other ways.

Howard Feltham corresponded concerning state quarters. **C. John Ferreri** provided an illustration. **Bill Fivaz** gave recollections concerning the creation of the Georgia quarter design and made suggestions concerning die varieties. He also provided photographs and price information for certain issues. **Roberta A. French** worked on extensive research assignments and the transcription of comments and documents.

David L. Ganz reviewed portions of the book and made suggestions. He also supplied legislative information. **Jeff Garrett** provided major assistance and advice with the compilation of price data and also supplied coins for photography. **David Gladfelter** suggested a source for information.

Steve Hayden supplied classic Washingtoniana items. Former Mint director **Henrietta Holsman Fore** facilitated inquiries and helped in other ways. **Charles R. Hosch** shared notes he kept on state quarters.

Paul Jackson sent information concerning state-reverse quarters in general and his work on the Missouri design in particular. **Katherine Jaeger** reviewed the text and made suggestions. Former Mint director **Jay Johnson** gave reminiscences and comments concerning coinage. **R.W. Julian** provided historical and numismatic information on George Washington, the early years of the Washington quarter, and the Indiana state quarter.

Cathy LaPerle, of the United States Mint, answered inquiries and provided many images for selection. **Robert Leonard** reviewed the manuscript and made suggestions. **Brett Lothrop** discussed the weakly struck details of many 2001-D Michigan quarters.

Dwight N. Manley supplied an in-person report on the California quarter launch ceremony and an illustration of a rare early Washington medal. **Cynthia Meals** of the United States Mint helped with information and research. **John Mercanti,** sculptor-engraver at the United States Mint, helped in several ways. **Scott Miller** provided a portrait of John Flanagan. **Tom Mulvaney** took the majority of photographs of individual quarters in chapter 8 and elsewhere. **Michele Orzano** shared information and research gathered during the course of her writing for *Coin World* on the subject of state quarters. **Kathleen J. Oviatt** of ANACS made text suggestions and provided grading comments.

Jesse Patrick provided information about 1932 design proposals and reviewed the manuscript. **Bob Paul** sent information concerning "waffle coins." **Spencer Peck** shared information concerning the New Jersey quarter dollar design process. **Ken Potter** provided illustrations.

Alex Shagin corresponded about various state quarter designs. **Mark Smith** corresponded about the 2004-D Wisconsin quarter varieties. **Rick Snow** told the story of the 2004-D quarters with extra leaves. **Thomas Snyder** furnished a large file of clippings and news items relating to design and distribution of the 2004 Wisconsin coins. **J.T. Stanton** furnished manuscript pages of the new fourth edition, volume II, of the *Cherrypickers' Guide to Rare Die Varieties* (Bill Fivaz, co-author), enabling the revised Fivaz-Stanton numbering system to be included here together with related rarity information (on the Universal Rarity Scale). He also provided photographs. **Don K. Stout** corresponded about state quarters. **David M. Sundman** made suggestions. **Donald Sundman**, Mystic Stamp Company, provided illustrations.

Steve Tanenbaum supplied classic Washingtonia items. **Gar Travis** suggested several information sources for the Maine quarter and the history of the lighthouse depicted on it.

The United States Mint provided photographs of state-reverse quarters and launch ceremonies and helped in other ways.

Frank Van Valen did copyediting and made valuable suggestions. **Eric von Klinger** corresponded concerning aspects of state quarters.

Fred Weinberg provided information on Mint error coins. **Ben Weinstein** provided details about the first identification of "extra leaf" 2004-D Wisconsin quarters. **Stephanie Westover**, Littleton Coin Co., provided certain coin illustrations. **Frank Wight** discussed die characteristics of quarters.

In addition, news articles, letters, and other reports published in *Coin World*, *COINage*, *Coins* magazine, *Numismatic News*, and *Numismatist* were of great help.

Certain staff members of *Coin World*, particularly **Michele Orzano, Beth Deisher**, and **Paul Gilkes**, assisted with information on the state-reverse quarter dollars from 1999 to date; documents pertaining to the 2002 Ohio quarter were particularly important. Certain uncredited historical illustrations are from Q. David Bowers LLC.

In this age of the **Internet,** many obscure facts and points were checked on various Web sites, generally credited in the notes.

FREE $20 VALUE

NGC CERTIFIED GEM BRILLIANT UNCIRCULATED

2006 Silver Eagle

2006 EAGLE S$1
GEM BU
1944244-001

NUMISMATIC GUARANTY CORPORATION

Coin Image not to Scale

To Celebrate the 20th anniversary of the Silver American Eagles, Universal Coin & Bullion, Ltd. is offering brand new, Gem Brilliant Uncirculated (Gem BU) NGC certified, Year 2006 Silver American Eagle.

ABSOLUTELY FREE!*

- Guaranteed Gem Brilliant Uncirculated by the Numismatic Guaranty Corporation [NGC]
- Sonically Sealed in Tamper Evident Holder ($5 Value)
- One Full Ounce of Pure .999 Fine Silver
- NGC is a **preferred** independent grading and authentication service of Universal Coin & Bullion, Ltd.

Once our allotment is gone, this offer will be withdrawn.
*You pay only the cost of priority shipping & insurance.
Limit one per household • New Customers Only
No Dealers Please

Free Bonus Gift

Diamond Anniversary Issue of our, 40 page/full color, newsletter, Awarded "Best Dealer Publication" by the Numismatic Literary Guild

Universal Coin & Bullion

welcomes the opportunity to be your rare coin team.

Call toll free today...

(800) 459-2646

Vault Verification: **USQS506**

Est. 1994

Universal Coin & Bullion, Ltd.
7410 Phelan Blvd.
Beaumont, TX 77706

universalcoin.com

All customers will receive a five (5) year subscription to our 7-time NLG award-winning newsletter, Investor's Profit Advisory ($200 value) at no charge with order. We may contact you from time to time regarding items of interest in the newsletter. • Please allow 2-3 weeks for delivery after receipt of good funds • Once our allotment is gone, this offer will be withdrawn. *You pay only $10, the cost of priority shipping & insurance.

CONTENTS

FOREWORD

One inch of sculpted metal is just the right size to fit a big idea.

Liberty, courage, education, heritage, and innovation are some of the American ideals immortalized on Washington and state quarter dollars. First minted in 1932 to honor the 200th anniversary of George Washington's birth, this coin series celebrated America's own Bicentennial in 1976 and continues to delight with the innovative ten-year 50 State Quarters® Program.

Spanning colonial and depression eras to the present day, David Bowers' time-traveling investigations reveal the events and personalities behind these widely circulating coins. His engaging commentary, facts, and images detail the complex mechanisms that transform our collective identity into collectable history. Numismatists of all ages will benefit from this skilled analysis of values, mintages, grading standards, and tips on building a collection of Washington quarters from the first year of issue, 1932, down to the present day. The estimated 140,000,000 state quarter enthusiasts, many of whom began their interest with the first coin out of the Mint—the Delaware quarter of 1999— will enjoy this chronicle of the phenomenally popular commemorative series, particularly the spirited stories behind each state's quarter selection.

Washington quarters are the workhorse coin of everyday life, defining much of what we do in commerce, easy to take for granted until you're faced with a hungry parking meter. In 1999 George's noble obverse portrait catapulted into the realm of pop culture icon. Loose change started getting a second and third look. By that time the rare 1932-D and S coins of yesteryear were no longer to be found. A new panorama of interesting coins made its appearance. Now it's possible to see people examining handfuls of quarters, muttering "Ooh . . . a Connecticut, I need that one!" Coin collecting from pocket change is exciting again, receiving overdue and renewed attention.

Was inviting public participation to suggest themes for statehood quarters a brilliant marketing strategy or a Pandora's box of sometimes colliding expectations? The answer is "yes!" Though the end results may be debated, this gallery of pocket art features something for everyone to admire. Each quarter's minting and launch affords ten weeks of state identity in the nationwide spotlight. In the pages to follow, you will experience an "I was there when it happened!" feeling as you read the narrative of how each was created, often with unexpected twists and turns. Dave Bowers has captured the essence and spirit of the Washington quarter, preserving many scenes before they slip into history.

Thirty years ago while touring the United States Mint in Philadelphia on my elementary school field trip, I could never have imagined being selected as concept designer of the 2005 California state quarter. This book witnesses how more than 8,000 entries, three selection committees and two governors added up to 520,400,000 coins showcasing one of California's many big ideas: respect for nature—and this is just one scenario. Dozens of other state quarters have their own and often fascinating stories, to be revealed in the pages to follow.

My career designing visual communications for the unique worlds of Star Wars, James Bond, and Harry Potter was excellent preparation for navigating California's own universe of symbols. Submitting coin concepts stirred in me a deep sense of state pride and creative responsibility. I'm always thrilled to find a John Muir in Yosemite Valley state quarter and equally reluctant to spend one.

This is a lifetime honor that brings opportunities and unofficial obligations. People are fascinated with our family's unlikely state quarter journey. My wife, daughter, and I have spoken and signed autographs at coin shows, schools, colleges, museums, and the California State Fair. We hope sharing our story increases the quarter's value by inspiring people to make a positive difference for their community.

The top three questions I'm often asked:

Are you disappointed your initials don't appear on the coin?
No, because I never expected that to happen. However, several people suggested I change my name to Darrett Eurke. (Apologies to Don Everhart, the brilliant sculptor at the Mint whose initials do appear on the coin.)

Did you meet your famous governor, Arnold Schwarzenegger?
Yes, and we have the memories to prove it.

Did you get paid anything?
Yes, a quarter, one really great quarter.

Dive into David Bowers's definitive book and see how the art of celebrating America through its coinage is more alive today than ever. Now that's a big idea worth commemorating.

Garrett Burke
Los Angeles, California

PREFACE

About Washington quarters, minted from 1932 to date, everything is known. This is what I thought several years ago when I began keeping notes on the state-reverse quarters, adding these to my long-time files on earlier regular issues. I soon realized how much I did *not* know. There was a lot more to be learned about the past. As to the present, there has been a continuing flow of new information.

The 50 State Quarters Program®, as the United States Mint designated and registered it, has unfolded year by year—a dynamic, wonderful, and unprecedented panorama of new designs available for face value by the general public. The quarters have been released one at a time, five each year in the order of statehood. First out of the box was the 1999 Delaware quarter—a design that today many consider to be one of the best.

From the outset I kept careful notes of everything I read, saw, and heard. The United States Mint web site was and is a great source of *official* information. Excellently constructed, it has grown to include a tremendous amount of data. In addition, several past directors as well as the staff of the Mint have answered many questions and furnished insights.

Mint information is, however, *official.* For quite a few quarter designs, great controversy raged. Was the right design chosen? Was the sketch by the original artist altered too much by Mint staff when the models and dies were made? Is what was chosen what the people of the state wanted? Was the final design "pretty" or was it "ugly"?

Many of these questions have no single answer. I think the Maine, Rhode Island, and California quarters are appealing for their *scenic* aspects, I agree with just about everyone that the Delaware quarter with Caesar Rodney on horseback is compelling and dynamic. I could add more favorites to the list. In contrast, the Arkansas, Missouri, and Florida quarters seem to me to be a hodge-podge of items, with no unifying or "scenic" cohesion. As you review each of the state quarters, your opinions of aesthetic quality may be entirely different. After all, beauty is in the eye of the beholder.

To find more than the *official* information required a lot of delving into source material—correspondence with committee members of the various states, off-the-record conversations (for use in this book, but not for attribution) with government officials, local and regional newspapers, radio program transcripts, web sites posted by the various states, and more.

Two of the most widely circulating weekly publications, *Coin World* and *Numismatic News,* have followed each quarter dollar program from the beginning. Each has printed comments from collectors, as well as from artists whose work had either been chosen or rejected. Each features sketches of proposed designs, and more. These were prime sources for *unofficial* but real information. *COINage, Coins* magazine, and the *Numismatist,* each covered the new quarters as well.

While the credits page lists many who have helped, I believe if a gold medal were to be awarded for reporting on the state quarters, Michele Orzano would take it home. No doubt a book could be written simply by reprinting her columns. Equally important, in my opinion, is that she often added her insightful personal opinions, identifying them as such, as to the beauty of designs or lack thereof, or other subjective aspects.

In writing about the state quarters I have devoted a section to each of the 50 issues, most of which have already reached circulation. I have tried to give an objective view even with certain issues that swirled with hot controversy (Missouri and California are prime examples). I have no vested interest in the outcome, save that I enjoy my own collection of these quarters. I have simply tried to relate the facts as I see them. Some are quite fascinating. Did you know that a *frog* pushed the button on a coining press to launch the 2000 Connecticut quarter? This is the same quarter that has the wrong tree depicted on the reverse.

Two people can view the same set of circumstances differently. What do *you* think? In any event, you are welcome to take any of my remarks with a grain of salt. The key is to *enjoy* these quarters, as I do. Collectively, the coins are wonderful, and I congratulate the United States Mint on one of the finest programs in numismatic history. By now the sculptor-engravers at the Mint must feel like leading actors in a Broadway play—many plaudits mixed with comments from people who do not like the designs, applause and bouquets mixed with boos and tossed eggs. That goes with the territory—part of creativity. Occasionally, when I write a provocative column in *Coin World* I get my share of slings and arrows. Collectively, independent coin designers (a rare species nowadays), Mint sculptor-engravers, and Mint staff include some of the nicest people I have met. We are all fortunate that many of them are frequent attendees at coin conventions.

I have had close ties with the Mint as a researcher and writer for most of the time since the 1960s. The degree of closeness has varied with the warmth of the current director and his or her appreciation, or lack thereof, for numismatic scholarship. It has been a quid pro quo relationship—I've answered a lot of questions about Mint and coinage history, and the Mint has given me access to files, old coin models, visits to engraving and coining operations, and the like. Recently in my files I found a nice handwritten letter from Angela M. "Bay" Buchanan, treasurer of the United States from 1981 to 1983, thanking me for the assistance I had furnished the Treasury Department over a period of years. When on April 3, 1992, the Mint celebrated the 200th anniversary of the Mint Act of April 2, 1792, I was invited to be the keynote speaker.

As to Washington quarters *before* 1999, the regular issues, these have their own fascination as well, sprinkled with a few mysteries. In quite a few books and other sources it is stated that Secretary of the Treasury Andrew W. Mellon, who made the decision as to the final design for the 1932 Washington quarter, rejected the best one in favor of a poor substitute. The best, according to the Commission of Fine Arts at the time, was one done by Laura Gardin Fraser, a sculptor of great talent, who with her husband, James Earle Fraser, created many motifs. They did the 1926 Oregon Trail Memorial half dollar, the design voted the most beautiful of all by members of the Society for United States Commemoratives.

The reason for Mellon's rejection of Fraser's art? Not because of artistic quality or beauty, but supposedly because *she was a woman.* Mellon was a sexist, this per modern conventional wisdom, vastly expanded by this comment by Walter Breen (*Complete Encyclopedia of U.S. and Colonial Coins*, p. 7), which has achieved wide circulation: "His male chauvinism partly or wholly motivated his unwillingness to let a woman win." This 1988 statement has been picked up and repeated many times. The only problem with this is that in checking contemporary records, correspondence, Mint documents in the National Archives, and more, I find no such scenario. Further, Mellon, secretary of the Treasury since 1921, appointed Mary M. O'Reilly assistant director of the Mint in 1923, the first woman ever to serve in that post. Mellon worked closely with her on many matters. No record has been found of Mellon being sexist in the presidency of the Mellon National Bank, or anything else. Credit the whole story as a modern fairy tale.

Another discrepancy is this: Why are 1932-D quarters, with a mintage slightly higher than the 1932-S, several times rarer in choice Mint State grade? I have always wondered, and I do not know the answer.

Time was when numismatists collected Washington quarters in routine date and mint sequence. Then came recognition of the Light Motto variety of 1934. Then, through the efforts and publicity of the "Collectors' Clearinghouse" column in *Coin World*, the writing of Herbert Hicks, John Feigenbaum, James Wiles, and others, and the popularity of the *Cherrypickers' Guide to Die Varieties* by Bill Fivaz and J.T. Stanton, interest spread beyond dates and mintmarks. When the "Extra Leaf Low" and "Extra Leaf High" varieties of the 2004-D Wisconsin quarter made headlines and created a lot of excitement in January 2005, I was as thrilled as anyone—and, in fact, bought several, including one for my set of quarters. Bill Fivaz was excited as well. On the other hand, Ken Potter, popular columnist in *Coin World* and an occasional feature writer for *Numismatic News*, dismissed them as "die dents." This goes to show that in numismatics, for one action there is sometimes an opposite reaction. Such spice adds to the hobby. Again, what do *you* think about these curious quarters?

To the preceding aspects of enjoying the history of quarters can be added the quest for ultra-high grades. This, too, is a new aspect of Washington quarters. Time was when the 1932-D and S sold for premium prices because they were key dates, but not much attention was paid to the other varieties. Beginning in a large way with the popularity of the Professional Coin Grading Service (PCGS, launched in 1986), there has been a scramble to obtain the highest possible certified grades of various coins. If a high-mintage issue of the 1950s is as common as can be in, say, Mint State-65 grade, but only a few are known in the MS-69 category, the MS-69 can be worth thousands of dollars. These are called *condition rarities*, or coins that are worth a high price only if they are in an unusually high grade.

The aspect of attractive toning is another relatively new consideration. If a Washington quarter dollar in a nice high grade, say MS-65 or higher, but not necessarily the highest grade known, is attractively toned it can be worth a strong premium. Both condition rarity and attractive toning give a lot of collectors bragging rights, especially in registry sets and various commentaries on the Internet. There is something special about listening to two collectors discuss the merits of a gem 1940-D quarter, a coin that I sold years ago by the roll, never doing more than quickly glancing at the coins to be sure that in fact they were basically Uncirculated.

When I began collecting coins as a young teenager in 1952 and started dealing in them in 1953, Washington quarters were a routine series—not much to notice except that the 1932-D and S were rare. It puzzled me that choice Mint State 1932-S quarters were readily available, even in an occasional roll, but the slightly higher mintage 1932-D was hard to find. All the others were available in roll quantities, particularly those after 1934, although the 1936-D was not seen often. A few years later, Jim Ruddy and I noticed that the mintage of the 1937-S was low as was the price, and we spent a couple years or so hoarding them—finding a few dozen rolls. Today, Washington quarters comprise hundreds of date and mintmark varieties, with four mint and metal varieties of each state quarter adding to the panorama.

Certainly, today Washington quarters are the most diverse series in American numismatics and one of the most interesting, something that could not have been said before the parade of 50 state coins commenced. There are no impossible rarities from 1932 to date, although the 1932-D and S remain key issues. All are affordable, and most issues of recent generations are very inexpensive.

There are still some mysteries to unravel, including the origin of the extra leaves on the 2004-D Wisconsin quarter, the subject of an internal investigation by the Mint. You can be your own art critic. Which of the state quarters are gorgeous? Which are not? In any event, you will want one of each. This program is still history in the making, as new designs are created and new coins released.

Even before state quarters were dreamed of, a Washington quarter could nip someone with numismatic virus, for which there is no known cure. In 1955 in Dallas, Harry W. Bass, Jr., a bank director, heard that the low-mintage 1955-D quarters might become scarce, and bought a $10 roll for face value. This opened the door to his forming one of the greatest collections of United States *gold* coins ever gathered, plus many other series as well. The Harry W. Bass, Jr., Library at the American Numismatic Society in New York City bears his name, as does the incredible gallery of gold coins at the American Numismatic Association Headquarters in Colorado Springs. All because of a Washington quarter!

I enjoyed writing this book. I hope you will enjoy reading it.

Q. David Bowers
Wolfeboro, New Hampshire

How to Use This Book

Each Washington quarter date and mintmark has its own listing. I give general and specific comments concerning rarity, availability, and other aspects as a key to collecting each. For some issues, interesting repunchings or other die varieties are described, these being a few of my favorites—the ones I consider to be the most significant—from the latest edition of the Fivaz/Stanton *Cherrypickers' Guide to Rare Die Varieties*. FS numbers refer to this text. For even more varieties, refer to the *Cherrypickers' Guide* itself or the three books by James Wiles (see Selected Bibliography).

The population numbers represent the combined total certified by ANACS, NGC, and PCGS as of late 2005. Such numbers are in a constant state of flux, with new coins being added constantly. As a result, the numbers given here may be lower than the latest figures when you read this book. Also, such numbers may increase dramatically over a period of time. As explained in chapter 7, use these numbers with extreme caution.

The field population numbers are my ballpark estimates of how many coins are out there in the general wide categories of circulated, Mint State, and Proof. These too may change in a future edition, depending on new information and reader input.

The prices have been compiled by valuations editor Lawrence Stack, with suggestions from me and certain others of the Whitman staff and *Guide Book of United States Coins* editors. They represent the market as of early 2006. Prices change over a period of time and can move down as well as up. As explained in the four steps to being a smart buyer, chapter 7, check recent listings when you buy or bid.

In addition, I provide the Optimal Collecting Grade (OCG) for each issue from 1932 to 1998. The OCGs offer suggestions to the advanced collector desiring to put together a choice and gem Mint State or Proof set, in the 64 and 65 numerical categories. Generally, within these two grades, the OCG is the one that offers an exceptional value at current market prices in comparison to the next highest grade. For Washington quarters of the past several decades, generally MS-65 and Proof-65 have been suggested, although grades that are slightly lower are less expensive and often grades of 66 or 67 are not much more expensive. The OCG is not a hard-and-fast rule, but simply a quick guide for value. Use your individual preferences in any instance.

If budget is a constraint, a general rule is that a grade such as MS-63 or Proof-63, carefully selected, is ideal for the silver issues from 1932 through 1964, except for certain of the rare issues, which can be obtained in lower grades according to your budget requirements. Most clad issues from 1964 to date are sufficiently plentiful that MS-65 and Proof-65 are within reach of just about everyone.

As for the statehood quarters (1999–2008), MS-65 is a good OCG for circulation strikes and Proof-66 is good for Proofs—and Proofs, carefully made, usually occur in Proof-66 or better.

Abbreviations in the Listings

Breen number—The numbering system of varieties in *Walter Breen's Complete Encyclopedia of U.S. and Colonial Coins*, 1988. In its time this was a leading-edge publication. Since 1988, there have been new finds as well as new analyses of certain of his listings. Still, it remains an excellent basic text. Example: Breen-4285.

FS (Fivaz/Stanton) number—The numbering system in the *Cherrypickers' Guide to Rare Die Varieties* (fourth ed., vol. 2, Whitman Publishing, 2006), by Bill Fivaz and J.T. Stanton. This replaces the old FS system (conversion information is given in the 2006 edition). This is the popular standard guide in the hobby. Example: FS-25-1950-601A.

Grading abbreviations—See the Official American Numismatic Association Grading Standards described in chapter 7 for a complete explanation. Examples: AU-50, MS-65.

OCG (Optimal Collecting Grade)—The pricing point at which a certain grade seems to yield a lot of numismatic value in comparison to the next higher grade priced for much more. In instances in which a very small difference in grade makes a very large difference in price, you may want to opt for the lower grade, here given as the OCG.

RARITY SCALES AND ABBREVIATIONS

Since the 1850s, various systems for describing rarity have been devised. Adjectival descriptions such as "very rare" "I have only seen two in 35 years of experience," "extremely rare," "one of the most elusive varieties," and so on, have little meaning in an absolute sense. We cannot tell if "extremely rare" means just two are known, or 23, or 46.

To simplify matters, rarity scales are based on the number of coins known or estimated to exist by experts in a given series. However, it is likely that for most varieties there are more examples in existence, but which have not been seen by numismatists. By way of analogy, if on a drive through a national park you see 17 elk, there may be 804 more that you haven't seen. If you go to a baseball game and do not see Irene, she may have been there anyway. This concept is very important.

As the popularity of collecting die varieties spreads, more bank-wrapped rolls of coins will be examined, more overmintmarks, doubled dies, and the like will come to light. Paying an extremely high price for a newly discovered variety may be risky, for when it is publicized, chances are excellent that more will be found. It takes time for the rarity of a variety to be evaluated and for prices to stabilize.

The Universal Rarity Scale (URS) is used in the Fivaz-Stanton *Cherrypickers' Guide to Rare Die Varieties*, the several books by James Wiles, and other specialized texts for rarity and is employed in the present book in connection with such varieties:

Universal Rarity Scale

URS-0 = None known	URS-14 = 4,000 to 7,999
URS-1 = 1 known, unique	URS-15 = 8,000 to 15,999
URS-2 = 2 known	URS-16 = 16,000 to 31,999
URS-3 = 3 or 4	URS-17 = 32,000 to 64,999
URS-4 = 5 to 8	URS-18 = 65,000 to 124,999
URS-5 = 9 to 16	URS-19 = 125,000 to 249,999
URS-6 = 17 to 32	URS-20 = 250,000 to 499,999
URS-7 = 33 to 64	URS-21 = 500,000 to 999,999
URS-8 = 65 to 124	URS-22 = 1,000,000 to 1,999,999
URS-9 = 125 to 249	URS-23 = 2,000,000 to 3,999,999
URS-10 = 250 to 499	URS-24 = 4,000,000 to 7,999,999
URS-11 = 500 to 999	URS-25 = 8,000,000 to 15,999,999
URS-12 = 1,000 to 1,999	URS-26+ = same progression
URS-13 = 2,000 to 3,999	

JOHN F. FLANAGAN
(1865–1952)
DESIGNER OF THE WASHINGTON QUARTER

CHAPTER 1

SETTING THE SCENE IN 1932

INTRODUCTION

The Washington quarter dollar was born in the very depths of the Depression, when the nation was struggling for economic survival. The issuance of coins had slowed nearly to a halt the previous year, and the outlook for 1932 was no better. However, the bicentennial of George Washington's 1732 birth was at hand, and Americans wanted to celebrate it. The exposition and world's fair that had been envisioned during the heady times of the Roaring Twenties were set aside in face of reality.

The quarter was created, but not easily.

NEWS AND EVENTS OF 1932
AMERICAN LIFE

The Great Depression had its beginnings in 1928 and 1929, when banks experienced slow repayments on loans, and the momentum of the great boom in real estate, art, and other prices began to slow. The stock market kept rising, and national

Washington quarter struck at the Denver Mint in 1932, the first year of the new design.

focus was on this phenomenon. Behind the scenes, many financiers were worried, but just about everyone proclaimed that the American economy was robust. In commerce, being anything less than optimistic was apt to bring great criticism from one's peers.

In October 1929 the stock market crashed, and banks began to fail at a staggering rate. Production lines in factories slowed nearly to a halt, with total output for the year only a third of what it had been in 1929. More than 20,000 businesses closed their doors. In 1929, more than 5 million motorcars were sold; in 1932 the figure was a fifth of that. The first patent application was filed for a parking meter, but widespread success for the device had to await better times. Route 66, the Main Street of America, connected Chicago to Los Angeles, but paving wouldn't be complete until 1938. Roads and highways were filled with homeless wanderers, some of whom camped in "hobo jungles." Many cities rejected people they considered to be riffraff—in Cheyenne, Wyoming, for example, those who did not leave as requested were apt to be shot at or clubbed.

The Dow-Jones Industrial Average touched bottom at 41.22 on July 28, 1932, the low point for the Depression years. This was in contrast to its record high of 381.17 on September 3, 1929. By 1932, one out of every four persons in the labor force was unemployed. Throngs lined up in breadlines and outside soup kitchens in the cities. Those who were lucky enough to be employed took home an average weekly paycheck of $17, as compared to $28 in 1929. Army privates were paid $17.85 per month. These figures, while interesting enough in themselves, also have a connection to numismatics; they explain why, when Washington quarters were released in 1932, they not widely saved as novelties.

Hobbies and recreation took on a new focus. At home, solving crossword puzzles, playing cards, competing in board games, and fitting wooden jigsaw puzzles together became popular, as did listening to the radio. Fishing, hunting, and enjoying the outdoors took on new meaning. Citizens who had never turned a spade of earth were now planting gardens. Miniature golf courses were a booming business. Libraries had record numbers of books checked out.

In most towns and cities, homes and businesses were being wired for electricity, making both work and play easier—but in many rural areas, where more than 25% of the population resided, the era of electric power and conveniences had not yet arrived. Life down on the farm was not much different in 1932 than it had been in 1929, except that crops now sold more slowly and for lower prices. Tougher times were coming to certain districts, especially in the Midwest, with a prolonged drought forcing farmers to pick up and move. Throughout the decade there was a strong migration from the Dust Bowl to the "Promised Land" of California.

Most Americans lived in small or medium-sized communities and either walked to school and work or used public transportation. Nearly every municipality had a streetcar line connecting local businesses with residential districts and, often, an amusement park on the outskirts of town. Those who could afford an automobile owned one, and in rural areas these became a necessity. Horses were still used to deliver milk and ice along some routes, but motor trucks serviced most regional commerce. The Revenue Act of 1932 provided for the first national tax on gasoline, amounting to 1¢ per gallon.

Travel from city to city was usually done by train. Interurbans (glorified trolley lines), which had flourished in the teens and early 1920s, were still in use in many places. Passenger steamships were still in use in coastal areas, on the larger rivers, and on the Great Lakes, but these were diminishing in importance. Commercial airlines were but a tiny blip on the horizon. In the 1930s, when coin dealer Abe Kosoff flew from New York City to Ohio to buy a coin collection, his picture landed in a city paper as evidence that airlines could be useful for business.

Three Musketeers candy bars reached the market for the first time in 1932, as did Zippo cigarette lighters, Skippy peanut butter, and Fritos cornchips. Breakfast cereals, soaps, and other household products were widely advertised in such magazines as the *Saturday Evening Post* and *Collier's*. Newspapers carried financial and political news and were essential to staying informed, although the radio was beginning to be strong competition. While telephones were in wide use, letters and postcards remained the most popular way to communicate over long distances. The cost to mail a first-class letter increased to 3¢ in July 1932, a rate that would remain in effect for many years afterward.

RULES AND PREJUDICES

In 1932, Prohibition was still in effect, but public support for it was fading fast. "We Want Beer" marches were staged in many cities, including in Detroit, where 15,000 people joined the procession. Meanwhile, alcohol was readily available under the counter in many stores and openly in speakeasies and private clubs.

Segregation of whites and blacks was widespread, especially in the South. In Washington, DC, in 1932, black workers at the site of the new Justice Department building on Pennsylvania Avenue had to walk two miles to find the nearest restaurant that would serve them. A government manual informed readers that "dark-skinned children of the South" were destined for careers in domestic service and manual labor.

Prejudices were often focused on immigrants, Catholics, Jews, and other minorities. Anti-Semitic and anti-black articles, slurs, jokes, and more were often printed in newspapers; and even in the nation's capital, many fine neighborhoods were "restricted." Private country clubs nationwide routinely excluded Jews, and it was not uncommon for a summer resort or hotel to state in a brochure, "Hebrews are not welcome" or "Hebrews will not be comfortable here." As for women of all backgrounds, their "place," per popular philosphy, was in the home, and except in the fields of entertainment and the arts, career-oriented women were often criticized. It was acceptable for a woman to be a teacher, but some districts hired only those who were not married.[1] Thus it was quite a break with tradition when, on January 12, 1932, Hattie W. Caraway became the first woman to be elected to the U.S. Senate.

THE POLITICAL SCENE

Herbert Hoover was president; his vice president was Charles Curtis. The national population was about 125,000,000. Every night when Hoover was at home in the White House, he partook of an elegant seven-course dinner, never mind the hard times. He had considered practicing frugality, including in the kitchen, but stated that it would be "bad for the country's morale." Hoover commented, "Nobody is actually starving. The hoboes, for example, are better fed than they have ever been. One hobo in New York got ten meals in one day." To this, *Fortune* magazine in its September issue called Hoover a liar and stated that the real situation was "twenty-five million people in want."[2] Schoolchildren were chanting:

> *Mellon pulled the whistle,*
> *Hoover rang the bell,*
> *Wall Street gave the signal,*
> *And the country went to hell.*

In July 1932, an estimated 17,000 indigent World War I veterans marched to Washington to plead that their cash bonuses (authorized by the Adjustment Compensation Act of 1924, but not payable until 1945) be paid immediately. Led by a Medal of Honor winner, the "Bonus Army" marched down Pennsylvania Avenue carrying faded American flags. When their pleas were rejected by the Senate, most of the old soldiers and their families went home, having spent two months living in temporary encampments while pursuing the futile effort. Return-transportation aid was offered by the government. However, some elected to stay. It was soon learned that many of those who remained behind were not veterans at all, but were rabble-rousers and agitators.

Herbert C. Hoover, elected to the presidency in 1928 and inaugurated in 1929, grappled with the Great Depression. (American Bank Note Co. vignette)

President Hoover refused to meet with the remaining veterans and characterized them as Communists, hoodlums, and ex-convicts, as, indeed, some were. On July 28, a mob of about 5,000 rioters moved up Pennsylvania Avenue, toward the Treasury Building and the White House. The police were outnumbered and called for federal help. Hoover summoned 600 federal troops, commanded by Army Chief of Staff Douglas MacArthur, to remove the veterans from the city. Major Dwight D. Eisenhower, Major George S. Patton, and others led the soldiers, backed by machine guns, six tanks, and cavalry, and drove the demonstrators back to their Anacostia Flats encampment. MacArthur ordered the military to follow. They broke up the settlement and forcibly removed the remaining veterans and agitators, about 2,000 in number, allegedly killing two babies with tear gas. The camp was torched, perhaps by the bonus marchers themselves, sending flames shooting into the sky.[3]

Front of the camp set up on the Mall, near the Capitol building, by bonus marchers from New York City. (Signal Corps photographer Theodor Horydczak / Library of Congress)

Part of the tent city set up on the Mall by the Bonus Army in Washington in the summer of 1932. (Signal Corps photographer Theodor Horydczak / Library of Congress)

Overall federal spending for 1932 was $4.66 billion. Among proposals for reviving the solvency of American commerce was the federally funded Reconstruction Finance Corporation, approved on January 22, to stimulate banking and business. By year's end, $1.5 billion in loans had been placed, mostly to businesses seeking to restore their former solidity. The average citizen however received nothing. Proposals to give direct aid to the millions of unemployed fell on deaf ears. A proposal by Hoover to create a corps of paid civilian workers for government construction and other jobs was not passed by Congress.

Hoover felt that to dole out funds to the indigent would create an underclass of citizens who would become permanently reliant on the government, as they would have no incentive to work. His comments such as "Prosperity cannot be restored by raids upon the public treasury" and "The sole function of government is to bring about a condition of affairs favorable to the beneficial development of private enterprise" did little to cheer the common man or woman.

ENTERTAINMENT AND LEISURE TIME

The most popular films of 1932 were *Arrowsmith, Bring 'em Back Alive, Business and Pleasure, Delicious, Emma, Frankenstein, Grand Hotel,* and *Hell Divers.* All of these were "talkies"—silent films were now relegated to history. Movie houses were one of the few bright spots in the economy. Typical admission was 25¢ for adults and 10¢ for kids, though prices were sometimes cheaper at matinees.

Though few of the movies of 1932 are remembered today, some if not most of the top 10 songs of the year are apt to be familiar, such as "Night and Day" and "Dinah." The two signature songs of the Depression were "Brother Can You Spare a

Dime?" and "Happy Days Are Here Again," the rousing tune used in 1933 when Roosevelt entered the White House.

The 1932 Olympic Games were held in Los Angeles with great success. Thirty-seven nations participated, with 1,408 athletes in 124 events representing 23 sports. In the World Series the New York Yankees bested the Chicago Cubs 4-0. The now-famous high point of the game took place when Babe Ruth, with two strikes against him, went to bat and was jeered by hecklers. He pointed to the flagpole to the right of the score-board in the distance past center field and hit the next pitch over the wall. Burgoo King won the Kentucky Derby. The Nobel Prize for fiction went to Pearl S. Buck for *The Good Earth*, and for history to John J. Pershing for *My Experiences in World War.* The *Indianapolis News* garnered the prize for public service.

RADIO

This was the age of the radio. In the 1920s, as broadcast stations multiplied and content of commentaries and programs improved, radio receivers evolved from crystal sets to elegant console units. By 1932, just about every family within reach of a radio station had a set, usually in the living room. Unlike movies or theater, radio was free. In numismatics, Texas dealer B. Max Mehl made effective use of the medium, advertising on the air to sell copies of his *Star Coin Book* (also known as the *Star Rare Coin Encyclopedia*, and giving information that could lead to finding a treasure in pocket change) for a dollar each.

On May 2, 1932, comedian Jack Benny's radio program aired for the first time. On November 7, the radio show *Buck Rogers in the 25th Century* had its initial broadcast. Radio audiences grew, casting fear into the hearts of theater owners. *Amos 'n' Andy*, already a favorite comedy show for several years, was a particular threat. In an accommodating move, many movie houses shut down the projector, turned on the lights, and played the program to the audience when it aired, then resumed normal operations. The *Walter Winchell Show* also made its debut at this time. Winchell's advice would be listened to by presidents, and his opinions, including his prejudices, were viewed as fact by many. The *Fred Allen Show*, new on the radio in 1932, would become a longtime comedy favorite.

At Rockefeller Center in New York City, the Radio City Music Hall opened. With the largest Wurlitzer theater pipe organ ever constructed, a huge stage, a 100-piece orchestra, 6,200 seats, and illuminated art deco furnishings, it soon became a focal point for entertainment. At first, the hall featured only stage performances, but the public wanted movies, too. When these were introduced to complement stage acts, the operation turned from red ink to black. The Rockettes chorus line, at first called the Rox-yettes, became famous. The Radio Corporation of America (RCA) demonstrated an improved television set using a better cathode-ray tube, which received broadcasts beamed from the nearby and recently completed Empire State Building.

Radio brought instant news into the living room, as it had been doing for more than a decade. Election results, sports scores, and running commentaries on athletic contests were popular. The next day, any missed details could be found in local papers.

On March 1, Charles A. Lindbergh Jr., the infant son of aviation hero Charles Lindbergh and his wife, Anne Morrow Lindbergh, was kidnapped from his home in New Jersey. Radio coverage was immediate and intense, and 5,000 federal agents were put on the case. Ransom was paid in currency totaling $50,000, with the serial numbers recorded by the authorities and distributed widely. The Lindbergh baby was found dead on May 12. Bruno Richard Hauptmann was arrested for the crime in 1934, convicted in 1935, and executed in 1936. The case against Hauptmann was largely circumstantial, and there was dissention regarding the verdict.

HOOVER VS. ROOSEVELT

In the meantime, attention was focused on the forthcoming presidential election. Hoover, though he was an educated, talented man of many accomplishments, was simply out of his element in dealing with the worst economic depression the nation had ever seen. His prediction for prosperity had not come true, and his wait-and-see policy was wearing thin. Shantytowns where the unemployed and poor tried to eke out an existence were popularly called *Hoovervilles*, and *Hoover blankets* were newspapers under which the destitute huddled for warmth.

Franklin D. Roosevelt was chosen as the Democratic nominee over Al Smith, the 1928 candidate. "I pledge you, I pledge myself, to a new deal for the American people," Roosevelt stated in his acceptance speech. *New deal* later became synonymous with the early Roosevelt administration.

Roosevelt's campaign publicity portrayed him as having ideas to restore prosperity, offering hope to a country with an unemployment rate of about 25%. Hoover tried to paint his opponent as a wild-eyed extremist who would plunge the country into ruin. Hoover did not converse with homeless men in the streets of Washington or console a former executive who was now selling apples for a nickel apiece. The radio could provide a fine forum to reach the people, but Hoover dismissed the idea, apparently as being below his dignity. Instead, he kept up a steady pace of elegant dinners at the White House, often with several dozen guests present. William Allen White, renowned editor of the *Emporia* (Kansas) *Gazette*, wrote: "Without leaders, the people grow blind, and without vision, the people perish."[4]

Matters were not helped for Hoover by his poor relationship with the press. He campaigned by defending his record, suggesting that without him things could have been worse—something difficult for citizens to envision. To this he added constant criticism of Roosevelt, pointing out inconsistencies. Meanwhile, Roosevelt charmed the electorate, offering them hope, not excuses.

To the populace, Roosevelt seemed more promising. On November 8, 56.9% of registered voters went to the polls and elected him president in a landslide victory, tallying 22,821,857 votes, compared to Hoover's 15,761,841.

Thus the Hoover administration soon came to an end. It was a different ballgame after Roosevelt's inauguration on March 4, 1933.

Franklin D. Roosevelt won the November 1932 election in a landslide. (American Bank Note Co. vignette)

NUMISMATICS IN 1932
NEW AND OLD COINAGE OF THE ERA

From the standpoint of new issues, 1932 was a rather barren numismatic year. Production of Lincoln cents was small, and only at the Philadelphia and Denver mints. No nickels, dimes, half dollars, dollars, or commemorative coins were minted. Gold $10 and $20 coins were made, but few people could afford to collect them; even in more prosperous times in the 1920s, fewer than a dozen specialists aspired to keep up with current date and mintmark releases of these denominations.

Coins in general circulation bore dates back into the 19th century. Indian Head cents were common, with most dated from 1878 onward. Liberty Head nickels were plentiful, and well-worn Shield nickels were seen on occasion. All varieties of Indian Head / Buffalo nickels were in pocket change, although the earlier years from 1913 onward were apt to show extensive wear. Mercury and Barber dimes were the order of the day in the ten-cent series, with some earlier Liberty Seated issues seen now and then. Quarters and half dollars dated back to the 1870s as a rule.

Silver dollars, not popular with collectors, were available from banks or through the Federal Reserve System. Many of the coins dated back as early as 1878, the first year of the Morgan design, and many were in brilliant Mint State preservation. They had been stored for decades (as backing for Silver Certificates) because people did not like using them in commerce. The availability of certain dates and mintmarks was erratic for the few who sought them. Carson City coins were seldom encountered, and certain San Francisco issues seemed rare.

Gold coins were available through banks and included five-, ten-, and twenty-dollar coins dated as early as the 1840s and 1850s, including five-dollar coins minted at Charlotte and Dahlonega. Gold dollars and three-dollar coins were not to be seen, for dealers such as New York City's Thomas L. Elder had been paying small premiums to bank officers and tellers for any they could find. Quarter eagles, minted as recently as 1929, were not available for face value either, but could be bought for a small premium, such as 25¢, from tellers who received them in the course of business.

Most gold coins were held by the government. Official gold-related figures for the year, as issued by the Treasury Department, are as follows:

Gold coins minted in 1932 ($10 and $20 coins)—$66,665,000; these consisted of 4,463,000 $10 coins and 1,101,750 $20 coins, all struck at Philadelphia.
Gold coins held by the Treasury Department—$964,795,000.
Gold coins in Federal Reserve Banks—$410,760,000.
Gold coins in National Banks—$12,753,000.
Other gold coins in the United States—$455,726,000.
Total gold coins held domestically—$1,844,034,000; including bullion: $4,513,001,000.
Gold coins imported in 1932—$196,539,282.
Gold coins exported in 1932—$163,863,560.

A TREASURY BONANZA

The Treasury Department in Washington, DC, endeavored to be helpful to numismatists, as it had been for many years. Examples of current coinage were available for face value plus a handling charge. In 1932, Charles W. Foster, librarian and curator of the American Numismatic Association (ANA), issued a notice to all coin collectors and dealers, detailing how to request new coins from the Mint. He emphasized the need to include not only the price of the coins but also the price of postage, including separate postage if the applicant wanted coins from different mints. Foster also detailed the holdings of each mint:

> *Denver Mint coinage:* 1907 half eagles, 1909 half eagles, 1914 eagles, 1921 Morgan silver dollars, 1922 Peace dollars, 1925 double eagles, 1926 double eagles, Peace dollars, 1927 double eagles, 1928 quarters, 1929 halves, quarters, dimes, nickels, 1930 cents, 1931 double eagles, dimes, cents, 1932 cents.
>
> *Philadelphia Mint coinage:* 1921 Morgan and Peace dollars, 1924 Peace dollars, 1925 Peace dollars, 1926 Peace dollars, 1927 Peace dollars, 1928 Peace dollars, 1929 half eagles, quarters, dimes, nickels, cents, 1930 quarters, dimes, nickels, cents, 1931 double eagles, dimes, cents, 1932 double eagles, eagles, cents.
>
> *San Francisco Mint coinage:* 1921 Morgan dollars, 1922 Peace dollars, 1923 Peace dollars, 1924 Peace dollars, 1925 double eagles, Peace dollars, 1926 double eagles, Peace dollars, 1927 double eagles, Peace dollars, 1928 Peace dollars, quarters, 1929 halves, quarters, dimes, nickels, cents, 1930 double eagles, eagles, quarters, dimes, nickels, cents, 1931 dimes, nickels, cents.

This list yields delights for present-day readers and also gives insights as to coin-holding policies of the Treasury Department. Silver dollars and gold coins were stored as backing for Silver Certificates and Gold Certificates. The 1927 Denver double eagle, available in any quantity desired in 1932, would prove to be a rarity to a later generation of collectors. Official records state that just 110 coins were paid out. This issue, and most other Denver double eagles of the 1920s, were melted in the 1930s. Very few were ever released into circulation.

Among Philadelphia Mint coins, the gold double eagles would prove to be rare and valuable, but in 1932 there was little demand for them. The large quantities of copper, nickel, and silver coins from San Francisco reflected merely a backup of supply. With no call for these coins in circulation, they were simply held by the Treasury Department until needed. Soon, the low-mintage 1931-S cents and nickels would be recognized as potential rarities, and Treasury supplies would be cleaned out. The pleasing result is that both of these issues are plentiful in Mint State today.

The stock of quarter dollars at all three mints indicates why no new coins of this particular denomination had been struck in 1931.

COLLECTING COINS

Numismatics remained a strong hobby in 1932. Prices weakened for certain rare and expensive coins, simply because few people had money to buy them. Interest remained intense for affordable coins, including commemorative half dollars dating back to 1892 and dates and mintmarks of current low denominations.

M.L. Beistle of Shippensburg, Pennsylvania, had marketed a line of coin album pages since 1928, and these had become popular. However, most collectors kept their coins in 2x2-inch paper envelopes or in coin cabinets, with envelopes being preferred. Information about each coin was written or typed on the face, and the envelopes were then sorted in order, often in long, cardboard, piano-roll-style boxes. These were easy to store.

There were no regularly issued guides to prices, although Wayte Raymond, who conducted the Coin Department of Scott Stamp & Coin Co. in New York City, produced a slim guide with meager information, which was a predecessor to the *Standard Catalogue of United States Coins* (a larger, more elaborate production that created a sensation when it was launched in 1934). Raymond also sold Beistle's album pages, soon developing them into an extensive line under the National name.

The American Numismatic Society (ANS), New York City, had lapsed into a fairly quiet mode, with curators and members concentrating on ancient and world coins, with little interest in the American series. This was due in large part to the collecting preferences of its major benefactor, Archer Huntington, who had paid for its new building in 1908 and its expansion two decades later. The once-dynamic *American Journal of Numismatics* had evolved into a series of occasional, specialized monographs, and lacked mainstream interest for U.S. collectors.

In the meantime, the ANA, founded in 1891, was the main focus group in the hobby. Its magazine, *The Numismatist*, was the only monthly numismatic periodical in 1932 and was the main source for auction, convention, and other information. Coin clubs were active in many towns and cities, and reports of their activities were published each month.

In New York City, the Chase National Bank Collection of Money of the World continued to be a prime tourist attraction, introducing many to the hobby. The curator was Farran Zerbe, who had sold the collection to the bank several years earlier.

Frank Duffield, editor of *The Numismatist*, discussed trends and changing preferences in the hobby in the September 1932 issue. He included this passage:

> Collectors of all series of coins cannot fail to have noted the increasing number of those who collect the small United States cents in the higher grades of preservation and the consequent advance in prices of Uncle Sam's humble coin. Much of this is probably due to an increase in the number of collectors who began a few years ago to form collections of cents from coins found in circulation, many of whom later became dissatisfied with the condition of their coins after they had been obliged to purchase a few of the rarer dates in a high state of preservation, and finally accepted Uncirculated or Proof as their standard.

Wooden Nickels and Commemoratives

A nationwide fad was started in the small town of Tenino, Washington. The local bank had closed its doors, and there was a shortage of small change. The Chamber of Commerce intervened and produced its own money—"coins" of thin wooden veneer cut into the size of silver dollars. Though they were imprinted with denominations of 25¢, $1, $5, and $10, they were called *wooden nickels*.

Local merchants agreed to accept the "nickels," and normal business was soon restored. Word of the novelty spread nationwide through newspaper accounts, and the townsfolk were offered up to twice face value for any they wanted to sell. The genie was out of the bottle, and since that time many towns, businesses, and coin clubs have issued their own styles of wooden nickels.

No new commemorative coins had been issued since 1928, when Hawaiian and Oregon Trail half dollars were struck. The Hawaiian halves sold out, but the Oregon Trail Memorial Association had a glut of unsold 1926 coins on hand and did not release the 1928-dated pieces. In 1932 there was a call by collectors for these 1928 coins. The association said it would keep the 1928s in reserve until thousands of the unwanted 1926 coins found buyers.

It was Treasury policy in the 1920s to mint commemorative coins for committees and organizations that had received congressional permission to sell the issues. The Treasury charged face value plus a die-making charge and shipping—but the commissions could charge whatever they wanted to. As can be imagined, there were many abuses. Production of the Oregon Trail coins, considered by collectors to be very beautiful, recommenced in 1933 and did not wind down until 1939. The deceptions practiced by their sellers prompted Congress to curtail any later commemorative coins. No more were made until 1946.

THE AMERICAN NUMISMATIC ASSOCIATION

The grading of coins was a hot topic in 1932, just as it remains today. In the June issue of *The Numismatist*, Frank Duffield stated that ever since 1907, descriptions of coin conditions had been controversial. Although it had been suggested that the ANA prepare a list of official grading standards, this would not solve the problem.

> The difficulty is not in preparing such a standard classification, because there is very little difference of opinion among collectors on this point. The apparently insurmountable objection to it is that no one would feel compelled to adhere to it once adopted. Many dealers and cataloguers who have been selling coins for years have their own standards, which they have been using for years and which they honestly believe to be fair and just to all concerned. . . .

Duffield concluded by agreeing with a recent correspondent that the best policy would be to get to know the dealers, after which "the customers will soon learn where to send for Uncirculated and Proofs when they get what they order." At the time, many "Uncirculated" coins were what might be called About Uncirculated today. The lure was that these bore cheaper prices.

In 1932 the annual convention of the ANA was held in Los Angeles from August 20 to 26. The Biltmore Hotel served as the headquarters for the gathering of 50 collectors. It was generally agreed that if the show had been held in the East, more would have attended. George J. Bauer, a highly regarded dealer from Rochester, New York, was president. At the convention, votes in the recent ANA election were reported, and Alden Scott Boyer, a Chicago manufacturer of chemicals and cosmetics, was announced as the incoming president.

Affairs of the ANA were in good order, with strong finances and only a small dip in membership. "The general business depression has affected *The Numismatist* only slightly," Duffield reported. "With renewed interest in collecting with the coming of fall and more hopeful conditions in the business world, the outlook for the coming year is bright."

AMONG THE DEALERS

Reflective of hard times worldwide, the advertisement of Spink & Son of London in the January issue of *The Numismatist* included this wording:

> A Happy and Prosperous New Year is the wish we extend to all numismatists the world over, and, although it is an old, old wish, we believe it will be said with greater sincerity than ever this year.
>
> Times are difficult, and have been for some months, but we feel sure that the old adage, "Hope springs eternal in the human breast," is still true, and that with the advent of the New Year we are all looking forward with renewed optimism to a general if gradual improvement in world affairs.
>
> But if we are to expect this improvement we must be ready and eager to put our shoulders with yet greater energy to the wheel, whatever our sphere of life, and, as the work may become harder, we venture to say that numismatics will prove still further that it is unsurpassed as a hobby and a relaxation from the daily round.
>
> We should therefore like to offer our services and experience to all numismatists, old or young, novices or experts, in furthering their interest and researches in this fascinating pursuit.

B. Max Mehl, of Fort Worth, Texas, basking in the great sales of his dollar-priced *Star Rare Coin Encyclopedia*, was accounting for more than half of the incoming mail at the post office in his city. He was also occupied with more serious numismatic matters, including the sale on consignment of the large and valuable coin collection formed by Waldo C. Newcomer, a Baltimore banker. In January, Mehl took 75 of the most impressive coins and made them available for members of the Dallas Coin Club to examine and discuss. In gratitude, William A. Philpott, representing the club, presented Mehl with a leather album of Fractional Currency specimen notes originally made by Spencer M. Clark, of the National Currency Bureau, for President Andrew Johnson.[5]

Early in the year, William Hesslein, a prominent dealer in Connecticut for many years, but then located in Boston, absconded with coins and other property belonging to his clients, leaving behind a string of debts and a bewildered family.

The numismatic estate of Virgil M. Brand was being disposed. The collector had died in 1926, leaving more than 350,000 coins, including multiple specimens of many rarities. His brothers Armin and Horace were the sole heirs, and soon became involved in wrangling. Large quantities of high-denomination gold and paper money were cashed in for face value. The rare material was appraised by dealers Henry Chapman, of Philadelphia, and Burdette G. Johnson, of St. Louis. In 1932, much of the paper money was sold to B. Max Mehl. Other segments of the estate would be filtered into the market through the 1980s.

During the year, more than 30 mail-bid and auction sales of American numismatic items were conducted. Sellers included J.C. Morgenthau & Co. (a division of Scott Stamp & Coin; the sales were cataloged by James G. Macallister and Wayte Raymond), Wayte Raymond (separately), Barney Bluestone, B. Max Mehl, Thomas L. Elder, M.H. Bolender, and several others.

Bluestone, a newcomer to the auction field, held four sales in 1932, none of particular note. M.H. Bolender, a schoolteacher who dabbled in coins in his spare time, ran eight mail-bid sales (again, none of lasting memory). The Morgenthau sales comprised five offerings, notable among them being a consignment from Waldo C. Newcomer (patterns, an original 1861 Confederate cent, and colonial paper money) and the collection of William Festus Morgan, containing remarkable large copper cents. Raymond's standalone sale included outstanding world coins from the G.P. Morosini Collection. Mehl held just two mail-bid sales, both unimportant.[6] Elder announced that his New York City business was for sale and began to wind down his affairs. No buyers were forthcoming, so in 1932 Elder renewed his business interest, including auctions. He was also a frequent correspondent to various publications such as *Hobbies* magazine, which had a special section for coins.

Visit Your One-Stop Shopping Source!

LittletonCoin.com
Easy-to-Use, Secure Site!

- **Search** America's widest variety of coins & paper money all day, every day
- **Discover** how to sell your collection – top prices paid!
- **Sign up** to receive our FREE newsletter full of exclusive offers and insightful information, or a FREE catalog
- **Every purchase** backed by our 45-Day Money Back Guarantee of Satisfaction
- **We reward you** with 10 Profit Shares for every dollar spent – redeemable for coins and supplies!

- **Check out** our buyers' newest acquisitions and featured items
- **Get** valuable collecting tips and answers to frequently asked questions
- **Always** safe & confidential shopping
- **Check out** just-released state quarters and pre-order future releases

✓ **Add LittletonCoin.com to your Favorites today!**

Littleton Coin Company
1309 Mt. Eustis Road
Littleton NH 03561-3735
1-800-645-3122

B4J945

Over 60 Years of Friendly Service to Collectors

©2006 LCC, Inc.

CHAPTER 2

EARLY QUARTER DOLLARS

BACKGROUND
"TWO-BIT" PIECES

Today, *two bits* remains a nickname for quarter dollars, including the newest Washington state-reverse varieties. The term has been in use for more than two centuries, a remarkable record of endurance.

In the early days, before U.S. quarter dollars were first minted (in 1796), many if not most monetary transactions were denominated in Spanish-American coins. The Continental Currency paper issues of 1775 to 1779 were payable in Spanish milled dollars. There was no federal monetary system yet in place.

The Spanish-American coins, minted of silver and gold mined in Mexico, Central America, and South America, were denominated in *reales* and escudos. Silver coins of one *real* were valued at 12-1/2¢ and were familiarly called *bits*. The 8-*real* piece was called a *dollar*, or *Spanish dollar*, and became the foundation of the federal system when it was established in 1792 (but in revised form, with decimal equivalents).

Most popular of the smaller denominations was the 2-*real* coin, or *two bits*, worth 25¢; these were also called *quarters*. It was logical that when Uncle Sam began making his own twenty-five-cent pieces, people would call them two bits. Other popular Spanish-American silver coins included the 1/2-*real*, called a *medio*, worth 6-1/4¢; and the four-*real* piece.

Certain of these foreign silver and gold coins remained legal tender in the United States until the passage of the Act of February 21, 1857, even though federal coins had been produced for more than six decades. This legislation provided for the legal-tender status to expire in two years, later extended for a further six months.

Quarter dollar, 24 cents

Two reals, 20 cents

2 reils, 16 cents

2 reals, 22 cents

¼ dollar, 22 cents

Two reals, 22 cents

A selection of silver coins, which are about the size of a quarter dollar, in circulation in the United States in 1850. The illustrations are from *The Coin Chart Manual* of that date, with exchange values printed below each (only one side is shown of each coin). Bankers and merchants kept charts and guides on hand to aid in transactions when foreign coins were tendered for payment.

EARLY U.S. QUARTERS

The Mint Act of April 2, 1792, provided for the establishment of a federal coining facility. The legislation also established a monetary system based on dollars and the decimal system, and gave weights and finenesses for various issues from the copper half cent to

The first United States quarter dollars were made in 1796, and only to the extent of 6,146 pieces. Many were saved as novelties, with the result that several hundred high-grade examples exist today. Due to their status as a one-year type, such coins today are expensive and highly sought-after.

The Draped Bust obverse design was combined with the Heraldic Eagle reverse to coin quarters from 1804 to 1807, including the 1805 shown here.

Quarter dollar of the Capped Bust type, motto on reverse, large diameter, of the style made from 1815 to 1828.

Quarter dollar of the Capped Bust type, no motto, reduced diameter, as made from 1831 to 1838.

the gold $10 coin, or eagle. Although the act authorized the quarter dollar, no coins of this denomination were made until 1796, the same year that the silver dime and gold $2.50 quarter eagle made their debut.

George Washington was president of the United States but would soon leave the office. After his inauguration in 1789, he lived in New York City for a year until the seat of the federal government was moved to Philadelphia. The Federal City, known today as Washington, DC, was still in the planning stages.

In this era the Mint did not coin silver or gold coins for its own account. Instead, when depositors brought precious metal to the Mint, they specified what denominations they wanted. For silver coins, this usually meant dollars, as they were more popular for export and large transactions than were equivalent values in half dimes, dimes, quarters, or half dollars.

An 1870 Liberty Seated quarter dollar. In various modifications, Liberty Seated quarters were minted from 1838 to 1891.

The first quarter dollar of 1796 featured the Draped Bust obverse in combination with the Small Eagle reverse. Only 6,146 were made, after which no more of this denomination were struck until 1804. In that year a new reverse was employed, the Heraldic Eagle style, modeled after the Great Seal of the United States. Coins of this design were produced through 1807. As demand for this denomination was low, and depositors continued to request larger coins, no more quarters were made until 1815, when a new motif was used: John Reich's Capped Bust style in combination with a perched eagle on the reverse. Coinage was intermittent until a modification to the design was made in 1831, after which quarters of this type were made continuously until 1838.

Liberty Seated and Barber Quarters

The Liberty Seated quarter, designed by Christian Gobrecht, was introduced in 1838 and made continuously through 1891 with several modifications to the weight and design details. In 1866 the motto IN GOD WE TRUST was added. Until 1838, all U.S. coinage had been made at the Philadelphia Mint. In that year, branches opened at Charlotte, North Carolina; Dahlonega, Georgia; and New Orleans, Louisiana. Charlotte and Dahlonega struck only gold coins, each with a C or D mintmark, respectively; these mints made no quarter dollars. Silver and gold coins were produced at New Orleans. In 1854 the San Francisco Mint opened for business. Coins made there had an S mintmark. The next branch mint was Carson City (mintmark CC), which operated from 1870 to 1893.

A 1907 quarter of the Barber design, made from 1892 to 1916.

In 1862, the second year of the Civil War, the outcome of the conflict was uncertain, and the public hoarded coins of all kinds, including quarters. It was expected that silver coins would become abundant in circulation after the war ended. In April 1865 the Confederate States of America surrendered, but coins remained in hiding. Due to political and economic uncertainties, plus a large flood of Legal Tender Notes and other paper money that the public considered to be of less value than coins, quarter dollars and other silver pieces continued to be hoarded. It was not until April 20, 1876, that coins began to circulate in large quantities once again, although beginning in 1873, small numbers were seen in larger cities and elsewhere. Federal Legal Tender Notes and other paper currency sold at discounts in relation to gold and silver coins.

In 1892 the Liberty Head design by Chief Engraver Charles E. Barber made its debut. Known as Barber quarters today, these were produced until 1916. The Denver Mint began operations in 1906 and used a D mintmark.

Standing Liberty Quarters

In 1916 the silver dime, quarter, and half dollar denominations were redesigned. For this dramatic event, artists in the private sector submitted designs—their submissions constituted a first in these denominations, for it had been the responsibility of Mint engravers to routinely create designs. The Standing Liberty quarter dollar motif by artist Hermon A. MacNeil became the new standard and was described by the Mint in an official press release on the afternoon of May 30, 1916:

> The design of the twenty-five cent piece is intended to typify in a measure the awakening of the country to its own protection. The law specified that on the obverse of the coin not only the word "liberty," but a representation of Liberty shall be shown.
>
> In the new design Liberty is shown as a full length figure, front view, with head turned toward the left, stepping forward to the gateway of the country, and on the wall are inscribed the words "In God We Trust." The left arm of the figure of Liberty is upraised, holding the shield in the attitude of protection, from which the covering is being drawn. The right hand bears the olive branch of peace. On the

Standing Liberty quarter dollar of 1917. This is the Type I design made in 1916 and early 1917. In 1917 the Mint modified the design by encasing Miss Liberty in a suit of armor and rearranging the stars on the reverse.

A 1920-S quarter of the modified design used from 1917 to 1930.

field above the head is inscribed the word "Liberty," and on the step under her feet, "1916."

The reverse of this coin necessitates by law a representation of the American eagle, and is here shown in full flight with wings extended, sweeping across the coin. Inscription "United States of America" and "E Pluribus Unum" and "Quarter Dollar" below. Connecting the lettering above on outer circle are olive branches with ribbon that is stirred by the breeze as the bird flies.[1]

The coins distributed later in the year differed slightly from that just described (a pattern version) in that there were neither olive branches nor a ribbon.

Quarters of the Standing Liberty design were made continuously from 1916 to 1930, with the exception of 1922. In 1931, no quarter dollars were minted, as in this Depression year there was no call for them. Thus was set the stage for the Washington quarter dollar of 1932.

THE ISABELLA QUARTER

In 1892 the first American silver commemorative coin was created, a half dollar to be issued in conjunction with the World's Columbian Exposition. At the beginning this and other commemorative issues were officially designated *souvenirs* (the *commemorative* nomenclature became popular later). The World's Columbian Exposition inspired the production not only of half dollars dated 1892 and 1893, but of the first and only commemorative twenty-five-cent piece, the 1893 Isabella quarter, which was made at the behest of society matron Mrs. Potter Palmer.

The Isabella quarters were sold for $1 each in the Woman's Building at the World's Columbian Exposition. (From a stereoview published by J.F. Jarvis)

The Isabella quarters had a late start. An act of March 3, 1893, specified that the production of these quarters would not exceed 40,000 and that the pieces would be of standard weight and fineness. Like the Columbian half dollars, the quarters would be made from metal taken from uncurrent silver coins held by the Treasury Department.

For the obverse, a depiction of Queen Isabella of Spain was suggested, for King Ferdinand and Queen Isabella furnished the financing for Columbus's voyage of discovery, Isabella vowing to pledge her crown and jewels if necessary (according to popular legend). In April 1893 the Treasury Department responded by submitting its own two obverse designs to the Board of Lady Managers; one sketch (the one eventually chosen) showed Isabella as a young queen, while the other depicted a facing head of Isabella in later years. Thus the Isabella quarter was the first legal-tender U.S. coin to depict a foreign monarch. The sketch for the reverse design depicted a woman kneeling, holding a distaff, signifying woman's industry, although an alternative suggestion was that an illustration of the Woman's Building at the fair would be appropriate. The models and dies for the Isabella quarter were prepared by Chief Engraver Charles E. Barber, who also designed the obverse of the Columbian half dollar.

Production of the coins began at the Philadelphia Mint on June 13, 1893. Soon afterward they were placed on sale in the Woman's Building at the exposition. Priced at $1 each, they drew little attention, for the 1892 and 1893 Columbian half dollars at the same price seemed to be a better value. Sales languished, and even considering 10,000 coins bought by Mrs. Palmer Potter, only 24,214 were distributed. Quantities remained on the numismatic market through the 1920s. Today, they are widely dispersed, popular, and in strong demand.

AMERICAN NUMISMATIC
RARITIES

Offers Over 250 Years of Numismatic Experience

IF YOU ARE ASSEMBLING A GREAT COLLECTION, it's time you discovered American Numismatic Rarities. From copper and nickel issues to silver and gold rarities, our staff members offer experience with every series. Whether you are building a cabinet of Morgan dollars by date and mint, a set of United States coins by design type, or a collection of Washington or State quarters, American Numismatic Rarities can be of service to you.

WHEN YOU DECIDE TO SELL YOUR COLLECTION, consider American Numismatic Rarities. During their numismatic careers, members of our staff have worked with many of the finest collections ever assembled, including those of Louis E. Eliasberg, Sr., Ambassador and Mrs. R. Henry Norweb, Walter H. Childs, Harry W. Bass, Jr., Haig A. Koshkarian, the Garrett family, and many others. To this experience we add a commitment to make the sale of your numismatic material easy and financially rewarding.

IF YOU HAVE NOT DONE BUSINESS WITH US BEFORE, we offer a free trial subscription to our publications, including our auction catalogues, *Numismatic Sun* magazine, and *Numismatic Perspective* newsletter. Visit our website at www.anrcoins.com to take advantage of this offer. Contact us today and discover why American Numismatic Rarities is your headquarters for all your numismatic needs!

Q. David Bowers	Christine Karstedt	Dr. Rick Bagg	John Pack	Frank Van Valen	John Kraljevich	Melissa Karstedt
Numismatic Director	President	Consignments	Consignments	Senior Numismatist	Numismatic Research	Numismatic Sales

TRUSTED NAMES, FAMILIAR FACES, DYNAMIC RESULTS!

P.O. Box 1804 • Wolfeboro, NH 03894 • Toll-free: 866-811-1804
603-569-0823 • Fax: 603-569-3875 • auction@anrcoins.com

www.anrcoins.com

CHAPTER 3

THE LIFE OF GEORGE WASHINGTON

GENTLEMAN AND PLANTER

The subject of the new quarter, George Washington, was born on February 11, 1732,[1] on a farm later known as Wakefield, in Westmoreland County, Virginia. An ancestor, John Washington, had settled in Virginia in 1657. His descendants followed farming, real estate, milling, iron founding, and other trades, generally with success. The family was viewed as prosperous. George's father, Augustine Washington, had four children in a previous marriage and six with George's mother, Mary Ball. From 1735 to 1738 the family lived at Little Hunting Creek, later the site of Mount Vernon. In 1738 the Washingtons moved to Ferry Farm, on the Rappahannock River opposite Fredericksburg. His father died when George was 11, leaving an estate that included several farms. George's half-brother, Lawrence, inherited the Mount Vernon tract, where he built the main part of what would become a famous mansion. Wakefield went to another half-brother, Augustine, and Ferry Farm was kept by George's mother (after her death it passed to George).

General George Washington as engraved for the *National Portrait Gallery of Distinguished Americans*, by Asher B. Durand, 1834.

In comfortable circumstances, young George went to local schools but never had an advanced education. At an early age he was trained in the manners and morals of a gentleman of the era. He learned the trade of a surveyor by age 15, and at age 16 he was hired to survey the Shenandoah Valley for Thomas, Lord Fairfax. He was a skilled traveler on horseback and was familiar with life in the wilderness. In 1749 he took his first job in public service, as surveyor for Culpeper County. In 1751 and 1752 he went with his half-brother and mentor, Lawrence, to Barbados, where the latter sought relief from his tuberculosis. George was infected with smallpox, which permanently scarred his face. Lawrence, in failing health, died shortly after their return. Mount Vernon was leased by George Washington in 1754, and 1761 it became George's by inheritance after the passing of Lawrence's widow, Anne Fairfax Lee.

In 1753, Governor Robert Dinwiddie of Virginia sent Washington and a small group to Fort Le Boeuf, in Waterford, Pennsylvania, to confront French troops stationed there and, in so doing, to assert Britain's claim to the district. Washington returned to report that the French commander had no intention of backing down. His description of the wilderness and his winter travels to and from the French fort solidified his reputation as a man of strength and courage. In 1754 he was commissioned as a lieutenant colonel and then colonel in the militia, and he saw action in the early skirmishes of the conflict that evolved into the French and Indian War. Disillusioned with British military practices, he resigned in 1754 and went back to Mount Vernon. He reentered military service with the courtesy title of colonel in 1755, as an aide to General Edward Braddock. In that service he narrowly escaped with his life several times: four bullets tore his coat, and two horses were shot from under him. For his bravery, he was rewarded with his colonelcy and command of the militia forces in Virginia. He resigned his commission in 1758. His war experience to this point was, in the balance, unsatisfactory, with confused instructions and criticism from his British superiors and a lot of political intervention.

Washington returned to manage the farming lands around Mount Vernon, overlooking the Potomac River. On January 6, 1759, he married Martha Dandridge Custis, a widow with two children, whom George adopted: George Washington Custis, age four, called Jacky; and Eleanor Parke Custis, age two, called Patsy. The couple never had children of their own.

He became a member of the Virginia House of Burgesses in 1758, which necessitated lengthy stays away from home, and served until 1774. His main crop on the Mount Vernon lands was tobacco. As a producer of raw goods, Washington was forced to deal with British regulations on exports that required him to buy all finished goods from Britain. The imbalance between imports and exports with Britian increased Washington's distaste for that country. Increasingly, he thought of himself as an American, not a citizen under British authority. He turned to other activities. With slave labor, he turned cloth into finished goods.[2] He raised wheat and operated a gristmill. His commercial fishery on the Potomac proved to be profitable. Many of his products were exported to the West Indies, one of the most active maritime trading areas in the New World. Real estate transactions brought additional profits.

THE REVOLUTIONARY WAR

In the meantime, Great Britain levied increasing restrictions on commerce and conduct in the Virginia colony, without the advice or consent of the population. The Townshend Revenue Act, the Stamp Act, and other offensive decrees were enforced by British troops in America, some of whom stayed in private homes as uninvited guests. Washington and others felt that the self-rule of the colonies was being eroded, and that America would soon be subjected to outright tyranny. By the early 1770s, most political figures in Virginia were anti-British. In May 1774, Washington joined other burgesses in Virginia to propose the establishment of a continental congress to further the rights of citizens. In September, he was a Virginia delegate to the First Continental Congress in Philadelphia. Returning to Virginia, he helped organize independent military companies that could possibly be used to fight the British.

In other colonies the fires of revolution were burning as well, with Massachusetts being the focal point after the Boston Massacre of March 5, 1770; the Boston Tea Party; and the citizens' continuing resentment of British troops. On February 2, 1775, the British House of Commons declared Massachusetts to be in rebellion. British Army troops took charge of Boston, but were encircled by American militiamen on the outskirts.

After convening in Philadelphia on May 20, 1775, the Second Continental Congress elected Washington as commander in chief of the Continental Army on June 17. In Cambridge, Massachusetts, on July 3, he assumed command of his troops, most of whom had plenty of patriotic spirit, but little in the way of

To finance the Revolution, the Continental Congress issued vast amounts of paper money. This $1 note of January 14, 1779, is representative.

formal training. On August 3, King George III signed the Royal Proclamation of Rebellion and charged Washington with treason, subject to punishment. Although certain members of the Continental Congress hoped for appeasement and formation of a satisfactory arrangement with Britain, Washington felt that the colonies had no choice but to become independent. In the summer of 1776 the Declaration of Independence was signed.

For six years, until the surrender of British General Cornwallis at Yorktown, Virginia, in 1781, General Washington overcame many adversities, losses, and tragedies, which were punctuated by triumphs. The story of the Revolution is beyond the scope of the present numismatic text but is easily found elsewhere. Washington's first victory was the ouster of British troops from Boston in March 1776.

Perhaps the low point was the winter at Valley Forge in 1777 and 1778 as the war raged on. In February 1778, France joined as an ally, providing troops, naval vessels, and equipment. At first vastly outnumbered by British troops and warships, but later gaining strength and achieving notable victories, Washington secured the independence of the united colonies, soon called the United States of America. In 1783, Congress voted to give officers of the Revolution full back pay. As a postscript to history, during the bicentennial celebrations in 1976, Congress voted to designate Washington as a six-star general, so that he would permanently rank over all of his successors.

Jean Antoine Houdon's bust of George Washington. Many copies of this sculpture were made in bronze, marble, and plaster.

Washington went back to Mount Vernon, where he hoped to continue life as a gentleman farmer. The main house was enlarged and other improvements were made. At the request of Benjamin Franklin and Thomas Jefferson, in October 1785, French sculptor Jean Antoine Houdon (1741–1828) visited Mount Vernon, took a life-mask impression, and spent two weeks modeling a marble bust. Afterward, he went back to Paris, where the bust was completed years later. In 1796 it was installed in the state capitol in Richmond, Virginia. In 1786, Pierre Simon Duvivier used the work, not yet completed by Houdon, to model the Washington Before Boston medal authorized by the United States Congress.[3] The Duvivier depiction was copied by many others, most notably Charles Cushing Wright in the 19th century. From 1775 to 1789, Houdon sculpted the busts of many well-known figures in Europe and America, including Jefferson (the bust used on the

Portrait of General Washington, painted from life by Charles Willson Peale, 1784. (Nassau Hall, Princeton University)

1801 Indian peace medal, the 1903 commemorative gold dollar, and the 1938 nickel five-cent piece) and Franklin (the bust used on the 1963 half dollar).

WASHINGTON AS PRESIDENT

With a constant eye on the political situation, George Washington realized the fledgling government had problems operating under the Articles of Confederation. He became a prime mover in the formation of the Constitutional Convention held in Philadelphia in 1787. When the Constitution was completed and ratified, the Electoral College elected him as the first president of the United States.

On April 30, 1789, on the balcony of the Federal Hall on Wall Street, New York City, George Washington took his oath of office. In 1790 the seat of the government was moved from New York to Philadelphia, where it remained for the ensuing decade.

The first American medals bearing an authentic portrait of Washington were sold in 1790 by J. Manly & Co. in Philadelphia, and by Peter Rynberg in Wilmington, Delaware. Struck on cast planchets from dies cut by Samuel Brooks, these were offered for $2 in a brass composition and $4 in silver. Gold strikings were also available, priced according to weight. The brass version proved to be immensely popular.

The Manly medal, 1790, features the earliest true portrait of Washington on a medal made in America.

In 1792, Washington was reelected president unanimously by electoral vote. In the same year, residing in Philadelphia, he may have participated in the groundbreaking for the Mint on July 31. Earlier in the same month he is thought by some to have furnished silver for the striking of 1,500 half dismes, the first circulating coins made by the government. Equipment was on hand for the new Mint, but it was stored in local craftsman and saw-maker John Harper's coach house, where the coins were struck.

Washington contended with many challenges during his administration. England and France were at war, and each side sought the alliance of the United States. Washington issued a proclamation of neutrality on April 22, 1793. Matters became tense, and a war with England seemed imminent, due to British interference with American shipping and the impressing (kidnapping) of American sailors. The treaty of November 19, 1794, signed in London by American emissary John Jay, soothed matters with the British, but angered the French. The latter engaged in attacks on and seizures of American ships in 1799 and 1800 in the so-called Undeclared War with France. Decades later, in the 1830s, reparations by France brought large quantities of gold coins to the Philadelphia Mint. Washington successfully guided the expansion of the western frontier, trade on the Mississippi River (involving negotiations with Spain), the forging of relationships and policies between the states and the federal government, and other dynamic challenges. He worked with Congress to establish and define the new executive office of the government, to establish an effective judiciary system, and to put a diplomatic corps in place.

In 1789, as a unification measure, he traveled throughout the Northeast, and in 1791 through the South, often staying at private residences. The "George Washington slept here" phrase arose mainly from these trips.

In his farewell address of September 17, 1796, the president urged elected officials to support the Constitution and federal laws, to strengthen and support the public financial system, to avoid entangling alliances with foreign countries, to maintain friendship with other nations, and to discourage political parties favoring a certain section of the United States. Washington left the office in 1797. His vice president, John Adams, was elected the next president of the United States.

RETIREMENT

George Washington returned to Mount Vernon, where he enjoyed his surroundings and received many visitors. One of these was Daniel Eccleston, an Englishman who some years later, in 1805, produced a large medal with his portrait.

In 1798 he agreed to command an American army should a war with France erupt, but hostilities remained limited to maritime commerce in the aforementioned Undeclared War. In the same year he opposed the Virginia and Kentucky Resolutions, which sought to supersede the Constitution with certain laws of their own.

In December 1799 Washington caught a cold, which worsened. He went to bed, and blood was drawn from him by the use of leeches (a common practice at the time). On December 14, 1799, he died, following an illness of two days.

FATHER OF HIS COUNTRY
MEMORIALS

George Washington's passing, a national loss, was widely mourned. In Newburyport, Massachusetts, silversmith and inventor Jacob Perkins struck a series of silver medals, about the diameter of a copper cent, with the inscription HE IS IN GLORY, THE WORLD IN TEARS on the obverse. The reverse gives life dates and events in abbreviated form, with a funeral urn at the center. In Massachusetts, the *Essex Journal*, January 10, 1800, printed this notice (dated January 7):

A gold funeral medal honoring Washington, made by Jacob Perkins and sold in 1800. The hole permitted it to be hung by a cord or ribbon. (Dwight N. Manley)

Commemorative pitcher made in Liverpool, England, 1800, with designs similar to those on the Perkins medal. (Larry Stack)

Washington memorial funeral procession on High Street in Philadelphia.

Jacob Perkins takes leave to inform the public that he will now be able to answer orders for the medals in memory of the late illustrious Gen. WASHINGTON, from any part of the continent, and to any amount, executed in gold, silver, or white metal, with punctuality and dispatch—from 3 to 5 thousand can be made daily. A liberal discount will be made to those who purchase quantities to sell again.

These funeral medals (as numismatists refer to them today) were holed at the top for suspension on a cord or ribbon. Many were worn at memorial services held in January 1800, and in parades held on the anniversary of Washington's birthday, February 22, 1800. In 1832, the centennial of his birth, there were extensive celebrations and remembrances, and several varieties of medals were struck.

WASHINGTON HONORED

From 1804 to 1807, *The Life of George Washington*, by John Marshall (famed as chief justice of the Supreme Court), was published in five volumes, followed in 1843 by a work of the same title by Jared Sparks. The latter's main source was 10 folio volumes of Washington's collected correspondence. After extracting what he wanted, Sparks distributed many pages and documents to friends and acquaintances, without making copies first. A later generation of historians lamented the action.[4]

In 1824 and 1825, Marquis de LaFayette, French hero of the American Revolution, revisited America and toured each of the states. Congress honored him as "The Nation's Guest." Many souvenirs depicting Washington were made in connection with this event, perhaps the most famous being the Washington/Lafayette counterstamps applied to current coins, mostly copper cents and silver half dollars.

In the early 1850s a group of women organized under the leadership of Ann Pamela Cunningham; they would come to be known as the Mount Vernon Ladies Association of the Union. In 1858 the association, for about $200,000, payable in installments, acquired Mount Vernon and 200 acres. A campaign was mounted to raise the necessary funds.

Edward Everett, famous Massachusetts legislator and orator, became the champion of the cause. He traveled widely and gave nearly 200 speeches on the subject. In the meantime, Benson J. Lossing's two-volume *Pictorial Field-Guide of the Revolution*, published in 1852, went through multiple printings. Superbly illustrated by hundreds of engravings, the work showcased the leadership of Washington and depicted most of the Revolutionary War battle sites with accompanying narrative.

Other publishers hastened to issue books about the Revolution and the president. Prints of Washington achieved wide sale. His portrait was featured on many notes issued by state-chartered banks, and his life was a popular subject for articles in illustrated weekly magazines, an innovation of the decade.

NUMISMATICS TO THE FOREFRONT

The Act of February 21, 1857, eliminated the copper large cent and half cent, provided for the phasing out of foreign coins as legal tender, and authorized the copper-nickel small cent. On May 25 the first of the new cents, with a flying eagle design, were released into circulation.

A wave of nostalgia swept across America. The familiar, warm copper "pennies" of childhood would soon be gone. Thousands of citizens checked their change, looked in drawers, and hunted elsewhere in an effort to collect as many different dates as possible. It was soon realized that a well-worn cent of 1793 or 1799 could be sold for several dollars, that and certain other dates had value as well. Numismatics became a popular hobby. Inquiries about the value of old coins were published in newspapers, and *Historical Magazine* published articles on old money. Jewelers, art dealers, and others found that a few old coins on display found ready sale.

In early 1858 the Philadelphia Numismatic Society—the first such club in America—was formed. In March of the same year, the American Numismatic Society was organized by Augustus B. Sage (a teenager at the time) and his collector-friends. Auctions of coins soon drew wide interest and participation.

THE MINT CABINET

Numismatics, formerly the purview of a few hundred collectors scattered across the United States, now encompassed thousands. The Philadelphia Mint received increasing inquiries for Proofs, patterns, and other items. Mint Director James Ross Snowden was happy to comply, at first selling or exchanging pieces with most applicants.

A numismatist himself, Snowden contemplated adding Washington medals to the Mint Cabinet, to build a first-class display. The cabinet had been formed in June 1838, and since that time had been augmented with yearly coinage—interesting pieces obtained from bullion and exchange offices and by trade with collectors. However, only a few Washington medals had been acquired.

With all of the current interest in the life of George Washington and his times, a great demand arose for the medals that had been produced over the years, dating back to the Manly medal of 1790 and the even earlier Voltaire medal, the latter with a fictitious portrait of Washington (as in France his actual appearance was not known).

The Voltaire medal of Washington, struck in Paris in 1778, bore an imaginary portrait of the American general as no image was on hand. This is believed to be the earliest of the medals relating to Washington, initiating a series that would eventually comprise hundreds of different versions of his likeness in the coming century.

The Georgivs Triumpho token dated 1783 was likely made in Birmingham, England. As to whether it applies to George Washington of America or to King George III of England is a matter of debate. Likely, Washington was intended, despite the imaginary portrait, as 1783 is the year that the peace treaty was signed, and it was George Washington who was triumphant (Triumpho) in the Revolution. The reverse shows Britannia (a figure used on contemporary British halfpence) restrained by a grate of 13 vertical bars, a significant number. The fleur-de-lis emblems at the corners of the grate represent France, which aided America in the conflict. These tokens were made in large numbers and are readily available today.

Director Snowden contemplated the possibilities, but rued that the Mint Cabinet had so few pieces. In 1859 Snowden began placing medallic memorials of Washington in the cabinet of the National Mint. At first he knew of 20 Washington memorials, but investigation soon ascertained that at least 60 different such medals existed. By the time the collection was formally inaugurated on February 22, 1860, 138 pieces resided in the cabinet.[5]

WASHINGTONIANA

In the late 1850s and early 1860s, many new Washington medals were struck to accommodate the increasing demand. George H. Lovett, of New York City, was perhaps the most prolific engraver of dies of such pieces. His brother, Robert Lovett Jr., of Philadelphia, also turned out many. A half dozen or more other diesinkers added to the supply. Inscriptions on certain of these are wonderful to contemplate today, and reflect the esteem in which Washington was held. Some of the more innovative include *How Abject Europe's Kings Appear by the Side of Such a Man*; *Freedom's Favorite Son*; *Hail Immortal Washington*; *Time Increases His Fame*; *George the Great Whom All Do Honor*; *While We Enjoy the Fruit Let Us Not Forget Him That Planted the Tree*; *Though Lost to Sight to Memory Dear*; *Hero of Freedom*; *Emancipator of America*; and *Providence Left Him Childless That the Nation Might Call Him Father*.

Copper store card (advertising token) issued by Augustus B. Sage, New York City, in 1859, from dies by George H. Lovett. Sage, a teenaged dealer and collector, was instrumental in founding the American Numismatic Society in March 1858. The obverse of the medal is based on the Houdon bust, but with Washington draped with the top of a toga, in classic Roman style.

Shown enlarged (actual size 19.05mm).

Of course, Jacob Perkins started it all in 1800, with his HE IS IN GLORY, THE WORLD IN TEARS funeral medal.

In the auction salesroom, Washington tokens and medals led the market. Collectively known as *Washingtoniana* (or, in modern times, often shortened to *Washingtonia*), the coins, medals, prints, books, and other items relating to the first president found ready sale.

In the meantime, Director Snowden authorized the restriking of many rare coins, the making of curious patterns and die combinations, and the creation of other special pieces for the numismatic trade. While some were used in trade for Washington pieces needed for the Mint Cabinet, most were sold into the coin market. The latter activity was done in secret, with the profits going to the Mint officials involved. No records were kept, and inquiries were met with denials or false information. In the process, thousands of rare coins were made; these constitute most of the existing pattern issues of that era.

On February 22, 1860, the Washington Cabinet section of the Mint Cabinet was dedicated in a special ceremony. A large and handsome medal was struck for the occasion, in copper and silver, from dies by Anthony C. Paquet.

In the 1860s, pattern two-cent pieces and nickel five-cent pieces were made with Washington's portrait, but no circulating coinage materialized. Federal paper money was issued in quantity, beginning with the Demand Notes of 1861, followed by other issues, including Legal Tender Notes. From that era to the present, Washington's portrait has been a popular subject for currency, and is today on the $1 bill.

Washington Cabinet medal by Anthony C. Paquet, 1860. The obverse features Houdon's bust as adapted by DuVivier on the 1776-dated Washington Before Boston medal. The reverse depicts Washington tokens and medals on display.

In 1885, *Medallic Portraits of Washington*, by W.S. Baker, was published. By that time the market for Washingtoniana had diminished, and many prices were lower than they had been in the late 1850s and early 1860s. Still, the book sold widely.

The centennial of Washington's inauguration, 1889, saw the production of many new medals. Over a period of years, Washington's was a popular portrait on many tokens and medals, aggregating into hundreds of different interpretations by the early 20th century. Although the investment-and-speculation fever of the late 1850s and early 1860s was never regained, Washington pieces remained a popular specialty through the 1920s and into the early 1930s, when the Washington quarter was created.

Pattern nickel five-cent piece of 1866 (variety Judd-473). The obverse portrait is an adaptation of the familiar Houdon bust.

Waffled State Quarters
The New, Hot Collectible!!

Waffled Coins have sold for hundreds of dollars on Ebay.

Indiana State Quarter

State Quarters are among the most popular coins with collectors but only a select group of people will be able to get State Quarters that contained an error or imperfection and had to be waffle cancelled by the U.S. Mint.

All Waffled Coins are available NGC Certified or sonically sealed in an attractive Global Certification Services holder, which contains a photo of the coin and tells the story of "Waffle Coins", the Millenium's hottest collectable.

As seen in the 2006 Redbook, CoinAge, the Numismatist and Coin World

2002 P Indiana 25C
WAFFLE CANCELLED
BRILLIANT UNCIRCULATED
GLOBAL CERTIFICATION SERVICES, INC.

GLOBAL CERTIFICATION SERVICES, INC.

Other waffle coins available in 2006 include:

We have the only Waffled Quarters from "The Philadelphia Waffle Hoard"

Kennedy Half Dollar   Missouri   Maine   Illinois (available Fall 2006)

To order online or to see a video presentation about the minting and waffling process, log onto

www.certifiedEnterprises.com

or call (908) 788 2646

Your #1 Source for Waffle Coins

CHAPTER 4

HISTORY OF THE WASHINGTON QUARTER

PLANNING FOR THE WASHINGTON BICENTENNIAL
GETTING READY

In 1924 in America, times were good. The financial recession of 1921 was over, and banks and businesses were taking advantage of growth opportunities. Money flowed freely—to buy elegant automobiles, waterfront estates, and other luxuries of life. The stock market had not yet gone into fever heat, but lots of action was provided by the land boom in Florida—buyers fell all over themselves to stake out options and buy properties across the state. Never mind that some land was swamp, at best.

Ahead on the calendar was 1932, the bicentennial of Washington's birth. How to celebrate the occasion in proper and memorable fashion was anyone's guess. On December 2, 1924, Congress formed the United States George Washington Bicentennial Commission to do some planning. President Calvin Coolidge was on the commission ex officio and was joined by an impressive lineup of other politicos. The private sector was represented by leading citizens, the most prominent being Henry Ford.

After the initial announcements, not much was done—although various statements were made about a commemorative medal and a related half dollar, stamps, and the importance of various sites in Washington's life, such as Mount Vernon and Valley Forge. Some even talked of holding a world's fair, the likes of the Panama-Pacific International Exposition of 1915. However, the Sesquicentennial Exposition held in Philadelphia in 1926 was a financial dud, and thoughts of a similar event in 1932 soon died.

HERBERT HOOVER'S VETO

After his inauguration in 1929, President Herbert Hoover became the chairman of the United States George Washington Bicentennial Commission. While Hoover is not remembered as a numismatist, he did have an awareness of recent commemorative issues, perhaps including the large, still-undistributed quantities of Oregon Trail Memorial half dollars, which had found no buyers.

In early 1930, a commemorative coin bill passed by Congress was presented for his signature. Hoover vetoed it on April 21. In his memorandum to Congress on the matter, the president discussed the number of commemorative coins minted in the previous 10 years, as well as the number of pending bills for coinage and additional requests in earlier stages. His argument against further commemorative coins centered on maintaining the integrity of the U.S. monetary system.

Hoover worried that the minting of commemoratives would lead to more success with passing counterfeit coins. Without standard coinage, the public would be unable to determine which coins were real and which were not. In addition, he pointed out that Congress had already addressed this issue when it provided that "No change in the design or die of any coin shall be made oftener than once in twenty-five years from and including the year of the first adoption of the design, model, die, or hub from the same coin."[1]

Aware that many events deserved the recognition that commemorative coins afforded, Hoover concluded: "The government would be glad to assist such celebrations in the creation of appropriate medals which do not have coinage functions."

In 1930 there was talk about making a commemorative coin to honor the 200th anniversary of Washington's birth. A careful reading of Hoover's veto dashed any hopes on the subject.

BEHIND THE SCENES AT THE TREASURY DEPARTMENT
THE DESIGN COMPETITION FOR A HALF DOLLAR

On February 21, 1930, a new group, titled the George Washington Bicentennial Committee and established by an act of Congress, seemingly took the place of the United States George Washington Bicentennial Commission established in 1924. Associate directors were Lieutenant Colonel U.S. Grant III and Representative Sol Bloom, the latter from New York and with an interest in past expositions, celebrations, and related memorabilia.

In the same year the Bicentennial Commission went into action to create an appropriate *regular-issue* half dollar, not a commemorative, to observe the Washington bicentennial. The half dollar was the logical coin of choice, as the largest regularly circulating silver denomination. Although Peace-type silver dollars were current and had last been minted in 1928, they were not seen in everyday commerce, except in certain Rocky Mountain states.

Following several precedents, it was decided to open a competition for designs that would serve for both a commemorative coin and a medal. Perhaps reflective of the sometimes unfocused motifs used on commemorative coins up to this point, the commission published guidelines specifying the nature of the art, these being under the direction of Secretary of the Treasury Andrew W. Mellon:

> That, subject to the approval of Congress, the coinage of the United States silver half dollars during the calendar year 1932 shall have a commemorative character. That the obverse shall bear a head of Washington based on the Houdon bust at Mount Vernon.
>
> That the design of the reverse is left to the sculptor, with the proviso that it shall be national in conception.
>
> That one sculptor be selected to design both the coin (if Congress shall provide) and the medal (already provided for).
>
> That each competitor shall submit in plaster for one design for each the obverse and reverse of the medal. The designs for the coin will be considered when and if Congress shall so provide.

A copy of the famous Houdon bust, this one in the unusual medium of papier maché made from macerated paper money. (Steve Tanenbaum and Steve Hayden)

Secretary Mellon (1855–1937) was one of America's best-known collectors of art, and no one questioned his choice of the Houdon image.[2] Making this decision as well as approving the final art was his option. Representative Bloom secured a photograph of the Houdon bust and sent copies to artists who expressed interest in the competition. This avoided free-style ideas as to what the Father of Our Country should look like. It was up to the artist to create a reverse design.

The Washington Before Boston medal, copper striking from original dies, Paris Mint. The medal was commissioned by Congress. Pierre Simon DuVivier cut the dies in 1786, using the Houdon bust as a model.

The Houdon bust was already the most familiar coin and medal representation of Washington, having been used on the 1900 Lafayette dollar, 1926 Sesquicentennial half dollar, and hundreds of tokens and medals. On coins and medals dating back as early as the Washington Before Boston medal, the Houdon bust was modified by adding a peruke (wig) of long hair tied by a ribbon. All entries were to be submitted by October 27, 1930, at which time they would be reviewed by the Commission of Fine Arts—an advisory group whose members would make recommendations to the Treasury Department.

A reading of the above reflects that while the design for the half dollar was to be commemorative in nature, the motif was to take the place of the current style (the Liberty Walking design by Adolph A. Weinman, used since 1916) and was to be a circulating issue. Due to the slow economic times, there had been no need for half dollars, and none had been coined since 1929.

In due course, selections were received and reviewed, and one by Laura Gardin Fraser was selected by the Commission of Fine Arts as being the best.

A Quarter Dollar Instead

On February 9, 1931, Representative Perkins introduced HR 16973 to change the design to the *quarter* dollar, instead of the half dollar. From this arose plan B, so to speak. The House of Representatives Coinage Committee issued a memorandum on February 13, 1931, addressing several issues, including the ban on changing design more often than once every 25 years. The proposed legislation was required in order to overcome that prohibition. The memorandum concluded:

> As the new design would replace the present type of quarter dollar, it would be in no sense a "special coin," and the issue thereof would not be contrary to the Department's policy of opposing the issue of "special coins."

> The plan would serve several purposes:

> 1. It would replace an unsatisfactory design now being issued.
> 2. It would be in a popular denomination; and
> 3. It would permit the Treasury Department to contribute a notable feature to the coming celebration.

Present-day numismatists who specialize in Standing Liberty quarters (minted 1916–1930) might not agree with purpose number one above! However, that was the view at the time, and the design was discontinued.

Charles Moore, chairman of the Commission of Fine Arts, wrote to the chairman of the House Committee on Coinage, Weights, and Measures on February 12, 1931, to protest the switch of denominations, stating that his commission plus the George Washington Bicentennial Medal Committee each preferred the half dollar. Moreover, the medal committee had already chosen a design for its medal, and this could just as well be used on a coin also. This had been done by Laura Gardin Fraser, with whom the medal committee had a contract. It seemed natural that she would create a coin to match.

Ignoring the Commission of Fine Arts, on March 4, 1931, Congress authorized a quarter dollar, following the memorandum quoted above. Chairman Moore of the commission would not remain silent, and a letter written on April 21, 1931, by David E. Finley (Treasury Department point person for this situation) for Secretary Mellon's signature, pointed out that the Treasury Department was not a party to any program or any agreements made by the Medal Committee or the Commission of Fine Arts. While the Treasury desired to cooperate, it alone was in charge of the final decision.

A New Competition

To reflect the change of denomination, the Treasury Department decided that a new competition was in order. Mary M. O'Reilly, assistant director of the Mint (a post she had held since 1923), courteously contacted Chairman Moore of the Commission of Fine Arts to ask for recommendations. Moore protested that a competition had already been held, and that another was not necessary. The half dollar designs could be used for quarters just as well, with some changes in the lettering. He was overridden by Secretary Mellon. By June 16, 1931, mimeographed invitations were sent out. The second competition attracted more than 100 entries by 98 artists, a few of whom submitted more than one design, as they were allowed to do.

ABOUT THE COMMISSION OF FINE ARTS

The Commission of Fine Arts, established by Congress on May 17, 1910, had its offices in the Department of the Interior Building in Washington. Members in 1931 included Chairman Charles Moore, Ferruccio Vitale, Benjamin Morris, Adolph A. Weinman, Ezra Winter, John L. Mauran, John W. Cross, and Egerton Swartwout.

The commission, formed of recognized people in the arts and architecture, had been involved in earlier designs, as in the case of the commemoratives for the Panama-Pacific International Exposition in 1915. It was not easy for the commission, due to the extreme resentment that Chief Engraver Charles E. Barber had toward outside artists, including those recommended by the commission. He had assumed that it was his right to design them all. The commission also held design competitions for various national medals, buildings, and federally controlled open spaces.

A decade before the Washington-quarter era, on July 28, 1921, President Warren G. Harding had issued an executive order assigning to the commission the right to pass on all coinage designs. It was not to have a veto power, but still the influence was hoped to be very great for the final design. This action would come to the fore in the design-selection process for the 1932 Washington quarter.

Outside the circle of numismatic historians, the Commission of Fine Arts is little understood today. Through the years, the group has acted as advisers on designs, including the original as well as the state-reverse Washington quarters, but quite often its recommendations were ignored. Some writers (including those on the topic of the Washington quarter), seemingly unaware of the purely advisory nature of the commission, have viewed the nonacceptance of commission guidelines as a travesty or even a minor crime. For a long time, like it or not, the secretary of the Treasury has had the final say in most instances. A pleasing exception is found in the state-quarter program, in which the governor of each state makes the choice; but ultimately that decision must be approved by the secretary of the Treasury.

THE COMMISSION AND THE QUARTER DESIGN

Commission members selected number 56, a model by Laura Gardin Fraser, but noted that it would need some refinement. On November 2, 1931, Secretary of the Treasury Andrew W. Mellon reviewed the submissions, including the commission's favorite, but selected a different model, number 84. The commission asked Mellon whether Fraser could restudy her design and perhaps improve it to the secretary's liking. His response was that if this opportunity were given to one contest entrant, it should be given to all. On November 4, Mellon sent the commission photographs of the models he preferred.

On the same day, Chairman Moore responded, reiterating the strong preference for model number 56 based on specific criteria set by the Commission of Fine Arts and with guidance from renowned American sculptor Adolph Weinman. Mellon again disagreed and advised Chairman Moore accordingly. On November 10, the commission, reluctant to give up on the matter, advised Mellon that its members had reviewed Mellon's further ideas, but they still preferred model number 56.

THE FRASER CHOICE

Accommodatingly, the Treasury sent a letter to Laura Gardin Fraser on November 12, 1931, noting the aspects of her design that did not conform to the requirements for the new coin and inviting her to "submit a restudy of your design, if you so desire."

In her November 14 reply, Fraser readily agreed to comply with the request and set out how she planned to proceed, including a visit to the Treasury to work out the remaining ambiguities. The correspondence between Fraser and Treasury officials continued until her new models were submitted in January 1932.

COMING TO A CONCLUSION

Commission Chairman Moore doggedly pursued his advocacy of model number 56, and on January 20, 1932, wrote a three-page letter to Secretary Mellon, repeating much of what had been sent before, plus expanded praise of model number 56. Then, the matter of Mellon's own favorite (no. 84) was taken up:

> The Commission, however, found in a design [no. 84] which called for detailed examination a lack of simplicity and vigor in the head, and an artistically unfortunate and also an unnatural arrangement of the hair which became conspicuous in the reduced size representing the actual coin. The reverse was pictorial rather than medallic in character. For these reasons the Commission felt that the design lacked those very elements of universality and permanence which the quarter dollar should embody.
>
> The Commission also considered a suggestion that the Saint-Gaudens eagle on the twenty-dollar gold piece be used for the reverse. They considered that to use a design that had been used on another coin would be unfortunate and sure to provoke criticism.[3] Moreover, the eagle as it now appears on the coin has lost that essential quality which Saint-Gaudens gave to it. In reducing the relief vigor has been lost. Now the eagle has the quality of an engraving; it has become a picture instead of an emblem. . . .

Commission wishes notwithstanding, Secretary Mellon persisted with his choice of number 84. Mellon left office on February 12, 1932, to take up an appointment as ambassador to Great Britain.

His successor was Ogden L. Mills, who served as secretary of the Treasury from February 12, 1932, until March 3, 1933.

On March 2, 1932, Secretary Mills had a meeting with O'Reilly in which he was briefed on the whole matter of the new quarter, former secretary Mellon's views, the correspondence with the Commission of Fine Arts, and other documents. David E. Finley, who had worked with and advised Mellon on the project, continued to advise Mills.

On March 8, the Treasury sent John Flanagan, creator of design number 84, a letter requesting minor model alterations on his portrait of Washington. The same letter informed him confidentially that while the final decision had not been made, the secretary of the Treasury preferred Flanagan's design.

Chairman Moore, who was becoming a nuisance to the Treasury by this time, sought to have Mills change the selection to the Fraser design. The matter was ended by a letter from Mills, dated April 11, 1932, in which he noted that while Chairman Moore's concerns prompted him to request changes from the artist, he would adhere to Mellon's decision. He went on to say that "the duty of making the selection falls upon the secretary of the Treasury and not upon the Commission of Fine Arts, the function of that body being purely advisory."

The official choice was made, and on April 16, the name of competition winner John Flanagan was publicly disclosed. John Sinnock, chief engraver at the Mint, prepared the final models needed for the process of creating working dies.

On August 20, Martin, acting superintendent under Superintendent Freas Styer of the Philadelphia Mint, sent this official description of the design to the director of the Mint:

Quarter Dollar

OBV: Portrait head of Washington to left; above, around the border LIBERTY; below the bust, around the border, 1932; in left field, IN GOD WE / TRUST.

REV: Eagle with wings spread, standing on a bundle of arrows; above around the border, UNITED STATES OF AMERICA and within this, E PLURIBUS / UNUM below around the border QUARTER DOLLAR; in lower field, two sprays of olive.

LAURA GARDIN FRASER

In recent generations many comments have reached print to the effect that Laura Gardin Fraser's work was rejected by Mellon because the artist was a *woman*. That concept is difficult to reconcile, inasmuch as during Mellon's tenure as secretary of the Treasury, several fine legal-tender commemorative coins were created by women, including Fraser. Moreover, no correspondence from the Treasury or other contemporary source, nor any published articles of the time, corroborate this theory. It seems to belong in the category of modern numismatic fiction.

The talent of Fraser is unquestioned. With her husband, James Earle Fraser (best known for the 1913 Indian Head / Buffalo nickel and for his sculpture *The End of the Trail*), she created many memorable works, including the 1926 Oregon Trail Memorial half dollar, which years later the members of the Society for United States Commemorative Coins voted as being the most beautiful in that series. On her own, Laura Gardin Fraser designed other coins and medals, including the 1922 Grant commemorative half dollar and gold dollar.

In 1999 the Fraser designs for the 1932 quarter dollar were adapted by Mint sculptor-engraver William C. Cousins to create a commemorative $5 gold half eagle. Sales were modest and totaled 22,511 in circulation-strike finish and 41,693 Proofs.

JOHN F. FLANAGAN
FLANAGAN, MEDALIST

John F. Flanagan (1865–1952), a sculptor and medalist born in Newark, New Jersey, created the winning design for the 1932 Washington quarter. Although the artist seems to have been well regarded in his own time, modern scholars have been less kind. Part of this has been due to a curious circumstance: he has been confused with another sculptor, John Bernard Flannagan (1895–1942), a ne'er-do-well whose art is less than memorable, who had a life of self-inflicted travails, and who died a suicide.[4] Probably, after the present book achieves wide circulation, John Bernard Flannagan will disappear from numismatic listings.

John F. Flanagan was a studio assistant to sculptor Augustus Saint-Gaudens from 1885 to 1890. Flanagan learned from the master the techniques of creating human figures in plaster, metal, and stone. In particular, he worked on the Saint-Gaudens statue of Lincoln that now stands in Lincoln Park, Chicago.

For the World's Columbian Exposition, opened to the public in Chicago in 1893, Flanagan assisted Frederick MacMonnies in the creation of the Columbia Fountain. Alas for MacMonnies, he never created a commemorative or circulating coin. Thus, his name is not familiar in popular numismatics today. However, MacMonnies is well remembered by medal specialists. Importantly, he considered John F. Flanagan to be "the leading medalist of America."[5] In the 1890s, Flanagan lived in Europe and spent most of his time there. In Paris, he became internationally known for his relief work. In 1902 he settled in New York City, where he remained for the rest of his career.

In 1904, at the Louisiana Purchase Exposition, several of Flanagan's works were on display. Working in his New York City studio, Flanagan created many highly acclaimed medals and plaques, including the official award medal for the Panama-Pacific International Exposition. To reduce certain of his models he employed the Janvier portrait lathe, which was owned by the Deitsch brothers, New York City medalists and badge manufacturers, and was considered to be the latest in technology at the time.[6] By use of this pantograph-type machine, an original model in plaster or hardened clay, or a galvano impression of such a model, of large size, could be reduced to create a smaller medal, plaque, or other work of art. At the time, the Philadelphia Mint was making do with a Hill portrait lathe purchased in 1866 and put into service on May 2, 1867. It would be 1906 before the Mint would install its own Janvier device, and 1918 before a Mint engraver would be able to use it properly (when John Sinnock, who later became chief engraver, employed it in making the Illinois Centennial commemorative half dollar).[7]

In 1905, Flanagan went to Cornish, New Hampshire, and modeled a portrait of Saint-Gaudens from life. The art remained unfinished at Saint-Gaudens's death in 1907. In 1920, he resumed work, now with a commission from New York University's Hall of Remembrance for American Artists.

Flanagan joined the American Numismatic Society on November 17, 1909, this being the year after it moved into its well-appointed building on Audubon Terrace on Broadway between 155th and 156th streets. This building was a meeting place for sculptors and artists interested in medals. Victor D. Brenner, creator of the Lincoln cent of 1909, had been a member of the society since 1894.

In 1909, Flanagan created a medal for the Massachusetts Horticultural Society, depicting a kneeling gardener with a greenhouse in the background—evocative of a fine estate. After the sinking of the *Titanic* on April 15, 1912, Congress voted that a gold medal be made to honor Captain Arthur Henry Rostron, whose crew helped

John Flanagan's *Philosopher* statue on view at the 1915 Panama-Pacific International Exposition, San Francisco.

rescue many survivors, and Flanagan won the design competition. In 1915, Flanagan was named as an associate member of the Academy of Design. In the same year, several of his sculptures were on view, by invitation, at the Tower of Jewels at the Panama-Pacific International Exposition in San Francisco. In 1920 he created a medal, *From the People of the United States to the City of Verdun.*[8]

FLANAGAN IN THE 1930s AND 1940s

In the 1920s and 1930s Flanagan's address was 1931 Broadway, New York City. By that time his list of accomplishments was lengthy. For the Library of Congress, he created a monumental clock. For the Knickerbocker Hotel, famous in its time, he sculpted a highly acclaimed marble relief of Aphrodite. A bronze portrait of Samuel Pierpont Langley, aviation pioneer, was made on commission for the Smithsonian Institution.[9] It seems that he was kept continually busy with a stream of public and private projects, at least through the heady economic times extending to the late 1920s. Included were dozens of portrait plaques of artists, notable Americans, and commissioned subjects. After that time, new work became scarce, although many buildings and civic projects authorized before 1930 were carried to completion.

An unadopted entry in the 1932 competition, by Thomas Cremona. The obverse photo is of a modern medal made from the Cremona design by the Patrick Mint. The reverse photo is of the original Cremona design. (Jesse Patrick photographs)

Reduced illustration of an original plaster model by Laura Gardin Fraser for an unadopted reverse of the 1932 quarter, marked on the back, "Oct. 10, 1931." Diameter 10-3/4 inches. (Richard Jewell photograph)

In 1935, Congress authorized the minting of commemorative half dollars to observe the 150th anniversary of the founding of the city of Hudson, New York. Representative Philip A. Goodwin of New York wrote Charles Moore, who was still holding his post as chairman of the Commission of Fine Arts, to ask his advice in the selection of a medalist to create the design. Moore strongly recommended Laura Gardin Fraser, stating that she "stands in the very first rank of medalists," and that she had been involved with several earlier commemoratives. Other of Moore's recommendations included John Sinnock, Chester Beach, Francis H. Packer, and Paul Manship. It can be conjectured that Moore had animus toward Flanagan, perhaps left over from the events of 1931 and 1932. While this was going on, Frank Wise, mayor of Hudson, did his own investigations and concluded that John Flanagan would be the best choice. In the end, however, it was Chester Beach who got the nod.

In 1946, Flanagan resided at 1947 Broadway, New York City. His name was mentioned in connection with the design of two new commemoratives. However, the work for the Iowa Centennial and the Booker T. Washington half dollars went to others.

THE WASHINGTON QUARTER BECOMES A REALITY
THE FINAL DESIGN

Although the Flanagan portrait is usually described as a close copy of the Houdon bust, in fact it is not. The outline of the head is different, as is the treatment of the hair. Flanagan added a heavy roll of curled hair above the neck, artistic license that does not seem to have been widely commented upon at the time, except, perhaps, behind closed doors at the Commission of Fine Arts and in the earlier-quoted correspondence to the Treasury Department.[10] Laura Gardin Fraser's version is much closer to the original. Both the Flanagan and the Fraser portraits show a peruke of long hair tied by a ribbon, similar to that used on many earlier tokens, coins, and medals, whereas the hair on the Houdon bust lacks this feature. The heavy roll of curled hair was distinctive to Flanagan's interpretation, although some early adaptations of Houdon's bust do have a light roll of hair.

The head is well positioned on the new quarter. On the 1932 issue, the letters in the lower left obverse field are not bold (per numismatic terminology, they are in the *Light Motto* style). Early in 1934 (no quarters were made in 1933), after more Light Motto coins were made, the letters were strengthened to create the Heavy Motto, in effect from that time onward.

On the reverse the national bird is depicted as especially bold, with heavy wings opened and extending downward. The eagle is firmly perched on a bundle of arrows. Similar bold eagles in the art deco style were popular as architectural ornaments at the time. A wreath below completes the arc of the eagle's wings and adds a nice effect. Above the eagle's head is the motto E PLURIBUS / UNUM in small letters on two lines. UNITED STATES OF AMERICA is around the top border, and QUARTER DOLLAR is at the lower border.

Mintmarks, D or S, were placed below the wreath on silver issues struck at Denver and San Francisco, respectively, from 1932 to 1964. No mintmarks were used from 1965 to 1967, when the Treasury Department, under Mint Director Eva Adams, sought to "punish" numismatists for supposedly creating a nationwide coin shortage. Later issues, made of clad metal, have a D or S mintmark, later joined by P when the Philadelphia Mint used this letter. The location is on the obverse to the right of the ribbon at the lower part of Washington's hair.

At long last, the Mint had a new coin design that had *no* problems in striking! The heads of Washington and the eagle are both arranged with the relief spread over a large area, with no high-relief points. Accordingly, the vast majority of Washington quarters of the 1932-to-1998 era are well struck. This aspect, although not widely mentioned in numismatic texts, is a blessing for collectors.

MINTING THE COINS

Production commenced in the summer of 1932, but there was no need for more quarter dollars in commerce at that time. None had been made since 1930, when 5,632,000 of the Standing Liberty design were struck at the Philadelphia Mint and 1,556,000 at the San Francisco Mint.

Money was scarce in people's pockets in 1932, and the Mint had no plans for a generous production. By year's end, the Philadelphia Mint had struck 5,404,000 coins, Denver had made 436,800, and San Francisco had produced 408,000. On August 1, 1932, the quarters were released into circulation.

In September, *The Numismatist* printed a report on the new coin. The article reminded readers that it carried a new design to commemorate the 200th anniversary of Washington's birth, and was not a "commemorative" coin in numismatic terms. It pointed out that the Washington quarter corrects the problem of wear that had plagued the design it replaced, and that had earned the Standing Liberty motif "almost universal objection." In conclusion:

> All in all, it is an attractive coin. The bust of Washington stands out in strong relief in contrast to the reverse, which appears somewhat crowded, particularly the part above the eagle's head. But sculptors are better judges of such things than laymen.

THE CONTINUING STORY
THE 1930s AND BEYOND

The supply of 1932 quarters was sufficient that no more were made in 1933. This was the very depth of the Depression. In 1934, coinage of the quarter resumed, with the Philadelphia, Denver, and San Francisco mints producing coins each year for the rest of the decade (except for San Francisco in 1938).

The coinage from each of the three mints continued through 1954, with the exception of San Francisco in 1949. The year 1954 marked the end of making quarter dollars for the San Francisco Mint; and, after coining cents and dimes in 1955, it was announced that the facility would discontinue operations as a mint and would serve only as an assay office and storage facility. From 1955 through 1964, quarters were made each year at the Philadelphia and Denver mints.

In 1936 the Philadelphia Mint offered Proof sets for sale; it was the first such coinage since 1916. Each contained a Lincoln cent, Buffalo nickel, Mercury dime, Washington quarter, and Liberty Walking half dollar. Sets were sold at $1.81 each, and single coins could also be ordered. In the first year, 3,837 Proof quarters were made, in comparison to 5,569 cents. Proof sets continued to be produced through and including 1942, then were discontinued due to the exigencies of World War II. In 1942 the mintage of Proof quarters was 21,123, compared to 32,600 cents.

During this period, quarters were also less popular than the other denominations with regard to collecting circulation strikes. The cent, nickel, and dime were regarded as inexpensive, and the higher-denomination Liberty Walking half dollar was admired for its artistry. Washington quarters fell betwixt and between.

Under the administration of President John F. Kennedy, Eva Adams was director of the Mint. As many (but not all) Mint directors have done, she visited an annual convention of the American Numismatic Association. In 1962 in Detroit she made a good impression and was given a warm welcome, and at the convention banquet she was honored with a one-of-a-kind gold convention medal from the ANA-CNA [Canadian Numismatic Association] and Medallic Arts Company. "When she finally gave her sincere 'Thank you,' all knew it was from a full heart and . . . all rejoiced with and for her."[11] No one predicted that these mutual good feelings would change for the worse.

THE "CHANGING DIMES" OF 1964

In 1964 the Kennedy half dollar was launched. The obverse, designed by Chief Engraver Gilroy Roberts (who soon resigned his position to take an executive post with the Franklin Mint), featured the portrait of the recently martyred president. The reverse was an adaptation of the Great Seal of the United States, by Frank Gasparro, who succeeded to the post of chief engraver after Roberts's departure.

The public went wild when the coins were released. Immediately, supplies given to banks had to be rationed, then they dried up entirely. Those fortunate to have bought quantities could sell them for twice face value or more. Demand was great in other parts of the world. In Europe the going rate was the equivalent of $5. By year's end, more than 400,000,000 had been minted—more than one each for every American citizen—yet no Kennedy halves were to be found in circulation.

At the ANA convention in Cleveland, Ohio, in the summer of 1964, Director Adams gave a talk with the pun title "These Changing Dimes." In that speech, Adams lamented the effect that the leading edge of the baby boom was having on the U.S. coin supply. She alluded to the impact John F. Kennedy's assassination had had, with the reaction to the half dollars minted in his honor. She told of cash-department layoffs at the Federal Reserve because coins were not flowing back to the banks in usual numbers. Adams announced that the Proof program had to be scrapped so all the Mint's efforts could be turned to producing coinage for circulation. With this speech, she began to hold the numismatic community responsible for the shortfall:

> I need not remind you that there are probably 43 billion coins in circulation now, or in your piggy banks or dresser drawers, or wherever they may be. Someday we just won't have a coin shortage; I think it will be very soon. And so I hope none of you are depending on making any tremendous profit on those vaults full of coins. I really don't think any of you here have them, and I hope the people who are doing it will stop.[12]

Increasingly, Director Adams and others in the government blamed coin collectors (numismatists, that is) for hoarding coins. In actuality, relatively few numismatists were interested in squirreling away quantities of current coins that were being produced in immense quantities. The culprits, if they should be called that, were everyday citizens who had learned of the shortages and were seeking to make some profit by buying whatever coins they could.

THE GREAT CONFUSION OF 1965–1967

In 1964, the price of silver was rising on international markets, and was seemingly headed to the point that it would cost more than face value to mint silver dimes, quarters, and half dollars (the higher denominations then being made). The Treasury Department made a sweeping change: beginning in 1965, silver coins would no longer be made, except for half dollars, which would have a sharply reduced silver content. Thus a tradition of minted silver coins that had started in 1794 came to an end. Later, some silver coins would be made for collectors and sold at a premium. In 1971 silver was dropped from the half dollars.

The substitute metal was a clad composition. The planchet was a metal sandwich with an outer layer of copper-nickel (75% copper and 25% nickel, the same alloy used for five-cent pieces) bonded to a core of 100% copper.

In 1965 the public was still agog about coins. Lincoln cents, Jefferson nickels, and all other denominations were being hoarded, especially the lower values. Cents were scarce at supermarkets and stores, and some advertised to pay a few cents' premium for every 100 coins brought to them. In the meantime, Kennedy half dollars continued to be minted, but all were hoarded by the public. For *years* afterward, despite mintages of hundreds of millions of coins, the Kennedy half dollars did not circulate. The quarter dollar became the highest-value circulating coin of the United States.

This was a dynamic change. In time, as new vending machines were developed, and when arcade machines (Pac Man, Donkey Kong, and the like) became a passion for the younger set, their slots took quarters. Half dollars remained out of circulation. To this day they are rarely seen in commerce.

In 1965, Mint Director Eva Adams continued to blame coin collectors for the coin shortage—an erroneous view that was loudly protested by the numismatic press. Numismatists did not cause the problem, the general public did, in combination with sluggishness in the Federal Reserve System's distribution process.

To punish coin collectors, Director Adams, backed by Congress, carried out the decree that Proof sets would no longer be made and that mintmarks (D for Denver) would be removed from coins. Moreover, the Silver Bullion Depository at West Point, on the grounds of the Military Academy (and later called the West Point Bullion Depository), was equipped with coining presses to turn out cents, but without mintmarks. The San Francisco Mint, now known as the San Francisco Assay Office, once again began to produce coins for circulation, its first since 1955 (when it had last made cents and dimes). Adams declared that no mintmark would be used. Included were *silver* quarters dated 1964 and without mintmark. The San Francisco Assay Office / Mint began in 1966 to produce Special Mint Sets (SMS)—quasi-Proofs—that were dated 1965. Special Mint Sets were also made in 1966 and 1967 with dates of those two years.

In 1965, Assistant Secretary of the Treasury Robert A. Wallace visited the ANA convention held in Houston. He gave a mixed message, including this:

> I would like to emphasize one basic point: the Treasury Department is for coin collectors. I won't say that you have not caused us any problems. When there is a coin shortage, any coins held back from commercial transactions cannot help but add to the tightness of our supplies. But in the case of coin collectors, these problems are peripheral even if there are 10 million collectors, and some estimates place the figure this high. If each collector takes one of each coin from each mint this would shrink the supply of coins by 100 million pieces. With an estimated 65 billion coins in circulation this would represent less than two-tenths of one percent of the supply. Of course, 100 million coins is still a substantial number and this is one of the reasons that the Treasury sought and obtained authority to continue the 1964 date on all of our current coins.
>
> Our basic problem last year was not the coin collector but the coin speculator who bought up coins by the roll and by the bag in the

hopes of an increase in their value. If anyone thinks these coins will be valuable because they are rare, let me say that we have made over 10.5 billion of them and we are still going strong. Nor are the coins dated 1961, '62 and '63 particularly rare, there having been from almost three to almost four billion minted in each of those years. . . . We have pretty much put [speculators] out of business by our huge production programs and we hope to keep it that way. . . .[13]

At a subsequent private luncheon with Assistant Secretary Wallace and Mint Director Eva Adams, the ANA board of governors passed a motion suggesting that coin collectors wait several months after new coins were released before adding them to their collections.

In 1966 the report of a joint Treasury–Federal Reserve Board committee expressed this under the heading "Hoarding": "The Treasury consider hiring an outside research group to develop and carry out a proposal for sampling coin dealers and collectors for the purpose of obtaining a representative indication of their holdings."[14]

Despite numerous pronouncements by Treasury officials to the contrary, the numismatic community felt that it was receiving the lion's share of the blame, while virtually nothing was being done to discourage everyday citizens from hoarding coins.

The topsy-turvy mintmarkless and date-mix situation lasted until 1968, when Denver coins got their mintmarks back. In the same year, the mintmark position changed to be on the obverse, at the lower right, opposite the end of Washington's wig. From 1968 onward, the figures in *Mint Reports* reflected where the coins were struck, and, generally, with the date on the coin matching the calendar date.[15]

A peculiar thing then happened with Mint Director Adams. Around 1967 or 1968 she "got religion," became active in the affairs of the ANA, and in time was elected to the board of governors, where she served from 1971 to 1975. To the great puzzlement of many members of the Numismatic Literary Guild (NLG), in 1974 she was given the group's highest honor, the Clemy Award, awarded in recognition of writing skill, a sense of humor, and dedication to numismatics and the NLG. However, no one was or is aware of anything she ever wrote of a numismatic nature—other than routine *Mint Reports*, with even these being written by staff.

In 1975, Adams sought election as ANA vice president, but was beaten by Grover Criswell. Criswell became president in the 1977 election. During his inaugural speech at the ANA convention banquet in August 1977, with ex-director Adams in attendance, Criswell excoriated the Treasury Department and Adams on their actions against and attitudes concerning coin collectors in the 1960s. Many on hand were uncomfortable with the remarks and felt that the forum was inappropriate.

Trying to soothe hurt feelings, at an open meeting with the ANA board held the next day, certain members present offered up a resolution that the board extend a formal apology for Criswell's remarks. In Criswell's opinion, however, he had simply spoken the truth, for indeed there had been a "war" against coin collectors. Those with memories extending back to 1964 and 1965 undoubtedly remembered when collectors were made scapegoats for the coin shortage. However, by 1977 that unpleasant situation had been forgotten by some. Many new ANA members did not even know of it, and relations with the Bureau of the Mint and the Treasury Department had improved greatly.

President Criswell stood by his remarks and called for each member of the board to vote by mail. The resolution died from lack of support. Obviously, the board agreed with what Criswell had said.[16]

THE QUARTER REMAINS DOMINANT

In the late 1960s the price of silver rose, and silver coins in circulation became worth more than face value. The public rushed to sell them to coin dealers, bullion brokers, and others, who sent them to refineries. By the early 1970s, no more were to be seen in commerce. In the meantime, half dollars old and new disappeared from circulation, and the quarter dollar remained established as the largest denomination in wide use.

In 1968, Proof sets were again made. This time they were produced by the San Francisco Assay Office, as it was now called (the term *Mint* was later restored), instead of by the Philadelphia Mint. The Proofs were struck on slow, knuckle-style presses, some of them dating back to the 19th century. Though old, they were very effective for the job. Each coin was struck twice in rapid eye-blink succession, to bring up the details fully. Each coin bore an S mintmark. From that time to the present day, Proof sets with quarters have been issued—a continuous run except for the year 1975.

THE BICENTENNIAL

To observe the Bicentennial of American Independence in 1976 the Treasury Department announced that three coin denominations—the quarter dollar, half dollar, and dollar—would have obverses of regular style, but dated "1776 • 1976" (commonly described in numismatic literature as *1776–1976*), combined with reverses of a commemorative nature.

The National Bicentennial Coin Design Competition was launched, and many professional artists entered. The winner for the quarter dollar was Jack L. Ahr, of Arlington Heights, Illinois, whose motif of a colonial drummer boy was considered by numismatists to be very attractive.

On Wednesday, April 24, 1974, the three winners were hosted at the White House by Anne L. Armstrong, counselor to President Gerald Ford; John W. Warner of the American Revolution Bicentennial Administration; and Mint Director Mary Brooks. Virginia Culver, president of the ANA, was also an invited guest, and signed up the three artists as ANA

Janvier transfer or portrait lathe reducing the galvano with the 1776–1976 obverse for the bicentennial quarter, photographed at the Philadelphia Mint, June 15, 1974, by R.W. Julian with the permission of Mint Director Mary Brooks and Chief Engraver Frank Gasparro. Detail shows the galvano, an epoxy-coated model with its features in relief.

members. After the reception, Secretary of the Treasury William E. Simon presented each of the winners with a $5,000 check. (Brooks, the successor to Director Eva Adams, was from the outset interested in coin collectors.)

Two days later, the artists visited the Philadelphia Mint to meet with the staff of the Engraving Department and view the process of transforming a design to models, then through the Janvier transfer lathe, to smaller size to make hubs. Director Brooks stated that she expected that 1.4 billion quarters, 400 million half dollars, and 225 million dollars would be minted with the new motifs. Clad metal was to be used for coins struck at all three mints, plus silver for special pieces to be made only at San Francisco.

During the following year, 1975, the mints struck regular-design quarters from 1974 as well as many coins with the 1776–1976 date. Thus the mints in 1975 were *re*-striking and *pre*-striking, but were making no quarters dated 1975!

The Bicentennial coins were released in 1976. It was a slump time in the coin market, and sales of Proof coins and silver versions were so sluggish that the Mint had supplies on hand for sale for several years afterward.

LATER ISSUES

The regular Washington quarter dollar design was resumed in 1977. From then until 1998, circulation-strike coinage took place at the Philadelphia and Denver mints, and Proofs were made at San Francisco. Under changing administrations at the Treasury Department and the Bureau of the Mint (later designated the U.S. Mint), relations with the coin-collecting community became warm and friendly, and the Eva Adams era of the mid-1960s was forgotten.

From 1992 through 1998, special silver Proofs were made at San Francisco, these in addition to regular clad Proofs of the same years. In 1999 the 50 State Quarters® Program was inaugurated. For the next 10 years, five states per year would be honored with a special reverse design on the quarter dollar. The order was the same as the sequence in which each acquired statehood, beginning with Delaware. Detailed information about the state quarters is given in chapter 9.

CHAPTER 5

DIE CHANGES AND TECHNICALITIES

INTRODUCTION

Most collectors of Washington quarters aspire to obtain one of each different date and mintmark from the years 1932 to 1998, and one of each of the later state-quarter varieties. Beyond that, there are many different varieties that can be explored. Some are very significant, such as the 1950-D Over S overmintmark and the related 1950-S Over D. Others are subtle, such as slight changes in the obverse or reverse hub.

Whether to collect these varieties is a matter of preference. Many use as a roadmap the issues listed in *A Guide Book of United States Coins* (popularly known as the "Red Book"), these being but a small fraction of the varieties listed in the *Cherrypickers' Guide to Rare Die Varieties*. An attractive aspect of the varieties not listed in the Red Book is that they can often be acquired for no more cost than regular examples of a given date and mintmark. Herbert P. Hicks's study, "The Washington Quarter Reverse: A Die-Variety Bonanza,"[1] *The Numismatist*, gives extensive descriptions of subvarieties, particularly for Variety C (to be discussed shortly). *Walter Breen's Complete Encyclopedia of U.S. and Colonial Coins* (1988) is important as well. James Wiles has issued three copiously illustrated books covering die varieties of certain years of Washington quarters, with more books on the way.

This chapter gives a chronological overview of many of the changes and developments in the Washington-quarter series. All coins are shown enlarged for visibility of details. For specific collecting information and listings as well as specific die varieties, see the entries under the different dates and mints in chapters 8 and 9.

DIE AND OTHER CHANGES, 1932–2001

1932—*Obverse:* All of the quarters of 1932 have IN GOD WE TRUST in faint or "Light Motto" letters. This was per John Flanagan's original design. ***Reverse:*** The Variety A (Breen nomenclature is *Type A;* Hicks nomenclature is

A 1932 Washington quarter, first year of issue. All coins of this year are of the Light Motto style.

Variety I) reverse is from an original design by John Flanagan. The relief is low, and the E and S (in STATES) nearly touch. The border between the field and the edges of the letters and motif is often indistinct. There is only one bold leaf to the left of the arrowheads, and the leaf above the A (DOLLAR) is very weak and hardly visible. This reverse was used on circulation strikes from 1932 to 1958 and on Proofs of 1936. See comments under 1937.

Generally, the issues from 1932 through 1935 have wider rims, which better "frame" the design, than do later issues.

1934—*Obverse:* There were two obverse hub changes this year, the "Medium Motto" and the "Heavy Motto." The Medium Motto was used for just a short time in 1934, then for all coinage of 1935. The Heavy Motto was introduced in June 1934 and was used on 1934 and 1934-D coins, and in 1936. Later it became the standard. Light,

Medium, and Heavy Motto varieties exist for 1934. Medium and Heavy Motto varieties exist for 1934-D.

- *Light Motto*—The central peak of the W (in WE) is *lower* than the sides. The letters and field blend without strong differentiation of the letter edges. Used for 1932, 1932-D, 1932-S, and some 1934 coins.

The first style of 1934 quarter, with Light Motto as used on all quarters of 1932. Close-up details the motto. CH 05-1020c.

- *Medium Motto*—The central peak of the W (in WE) is *lower* than the sides. It has the same style as the Light Motto, but the letters are stronger and are not faded into the field. This was used for some 1934 and 1934-D coins and all 1935 coinage.
- *Heavy Motto*—The central peak of the W (in WE) is *higher* than the sides, and the letters are heavier (thicker) than the those on the other 1934 varieties. This was used for some 1934 and 1934-D coins; then it became standard beginning in 1936.

Reverse: David W. Lange writes

The second style of 1934 quarter, with Medium Motto. This style was used only in this year. Close-up details the motto.

> A fact I've never seen mentioned in print and which may have escaped observation to this point is that the original reverse hub of 1932 was never used after that date. It featured a much higher border that shielded the reverse from the rapid wear typical of all later issues through the end of silver coin production. This distinction is very difficult to discern from the Uncirculated coins that most collectors seek, yet it becomes readily apparent when studying worn pieces. [The] 1932 quarters from all three mints wear quite evenly front and back, while silver issues 1934 and later

Close-up of the Heavy Motto. Note that the center peak of W (WE) is higher than either side. The Heavy Motto became the standard in 1935.

will still show complete obverse borders long after the reverse border is worn deeply into the lettering. This is true even of the 1934 Light Motto quarters. [2]

1937—*Reverse:* Variety B (Breen Type B, Hicks Variety II) was introduced this year. The relief was strengthened by a lowering of the field. In this variety, the E and S (STATES) appear distinctly separated. There are two bold leaves to the left of the arrowheads; the stronger leaf touches or nearly touches top of the A (DOLLAR). The leaf touches on some Proofs, and nearly touches on dies that were more extensively relapped. Stronger than on Variety A. Certain letters and the edges of feathers were retouched. This reverse was used on Proofs of 1937 to 1964 and on circulation strikes from 1959 to 1964. Details on the Proofs are sharper than on circulation strikes.

Herbert Hicks writes:

> High-relief dies are not desirable for business strikes because of production problems, including greatly shortened die life, difficulty in bringing up the full relief, and stacking problems.
>
> However, these same dies, with their ability to withstand repeated polishing, would outlast low-relief dies on the Proof line and produce a much more attractive coin. Extra pressure and double striking brought up full relief with all the design showing. Thus began the modern Mint system of using different artwork for Proof and circulation strikes.[3]

Reverse Variety B (top) was introduced on the 1937 Proof quarter and was continued on Proofs through 1964. Reverse B was employed on circulation strikes from 1959 to 1964. Compare to Reverse A (bottom).

1938—*Obverse:* The profile details of Washington were strengthened slightly.

The 1938 obverse.

The 1944 obverse.

The 1945 obverse.

1944—*Obverse:* The profile details of Washington were strengthened slightly and minor changes were made in the peruke and ribbon. The initials of the designer, JF, became slightly distorted.

1945—*Obverse:* The initials JF were corrected.

1964—*Reverse:* Variety C (Breen Type C, Hicks Variety III) was introduced this year. It is similar to Type A (see 1932) in general relief. Leaf details include the centers for the first time. The leaf above the A (DOLLAR) is short and does not touch the letter. This variety was probably made in anticipation of the clad coinage that commenced in 1965, but it is known on some of the silver 1964-D coins.

Reverse C (shown here on a Proof 1973-S quarter) was first used for circulation on certain 1964-D quarters.

Herbert Hicks describes the difference:

> The new reverse variety . . . was the clearest design to date, although it is the lowest in relief. You can think of it as a two-dimensional drawing rather than a three-dimensional sculpture. Leaf centers have detail for the first time. These quarters also have stacking problems: they will teeter when two obverses meet.[4]

1965–1967—*Obverse:* In 1965, a new obverse hub was introduced for the clad coinage. The relief was slightly lower than on the earlier silver issues. *Reverse:* Variety C (described under 1964) was introduced for regular coinage.

The 1974 obverse.

Obverse and reverse of the 1965 quarter. Close-up shows motto style used from 1965 onward, somewhat similar to the Medium Motto of 1934. Note that the center of the W (WE) is lower than the sides.

The 1776 • 1976 Bicentennial quarter (a 1976-S Proof is illustrated).

In the three years from 1965 to 1967, the Mint did not issue Proofs for collectors, but instead made Special Mint Sets containing coins that were struck from lightly polished dies, but were not deeply mirrored.

1974—*Obverse:* In 1974, a new obverse hub was introduced, with a slight lowering of the relief and sharpening of some details.

In 1977 the obverse and reverse were altered slightly, a style continued until 1983. A 1981-S Proof quarter is illustrated.

The 1983 obverse.   The 1987 obverse.   The 1988 obverse.   Obverse of a 1992-S Washington quarter.

1976—*Obverse:* Another new obverse hub was introduced, with a slight lowering of the relief and sharpening of some details. The double date "1776 • 1976" was used for this year. ***Reverse:*** The Bicentennial motif of a colonial drummer boy was used only this year.

1977—*Obverse:* In 1976, Mint engraver Matthew Peloso reworked certain details of the quarter dollar obverse, including a lowering of the relief. ***Reverse:*** The reverse relief was lowered and the lettering and feathers were sharpened. The revised dies were first used in 1977.

1982–1983—*Obverse:* The diameter of the design elements (but not of the coin itself) was reduced slightly, as elements on the periphery had "migrated" closer to the rim. The details were sharpened slightly.

It had been the practice of the Mint to sell *Mint Sets*, or sets of circulation-strike coins, each year, so collectors could maintain their collections. The Mint was busy starting its new program of commemorative coins, beginning with the Washington half

The 1993 reverse.   By the time of the 1994 obverse modification, the hair details were quite different from those on the first quarter dollars of 1932.   Obverse, 1999 to date.

dollar in 1982 and expanding to include Olympic Games coins in 1983. In 1982 and 1983, no Mint Sets were sold. Accordingly, high-grade Mint State coins of these two years are scarcer than are those of the surrounding years.

1987—*Obverse:* The hairline and curls were sharpened.

1988—*Obverse:* The hairline and curls were sharpened further.

1992—*Obverse:* The hairline and curls were sharpened even further. The border of the coin was widened slightly, and the relief was slightly reduced.

1993—*Reverse:* The relief of the reverse was lowered and the lettering and feathers were sharpened.

1994–1998—*Obverse:* The relief was further lowered ever so slightly and at intervals during the next several years, and the hairline and curls were sharpened.

1999—The obverse was redesigned in 1999, when the individual state reverses were introduced (these are discussed at length in chapter 9). The date was moved to the reverse.

2000—At the Philadelphia Mint, an undated obverse die for the Washington state-quarter coinage was combined with an undated Sacagawea "golden dollar" flying-eagle reverse. Examples were struck on a dollar press using regular manganese-brass clad-dollar planchets. Likely, they were struck in April or May 2000. It may have been that some strikings were from an accidental muling (putting an incorrect front and back together) of two unrelated dies. At least three die pairs were involved.

The first specimen that came to light is believed to have been from an unintentional error at the Mint. It was discovered in late May of 2000 by Frank Wallis, who found it in a roll of Sacagawea dollars he bought for face value from the First National Bank & Trust in Mountain Home, Arkansas. This coin was auctioned in 2001 by Bowers & Merena for $29,900. Another was found in a roll in September 2000 by Greg Senske, a Missouri collector. Interest increased, and transactions as high as $70,000 took place later.

Some of the mulings, but not the two mentioned above, were made secretly by Mint employees, and two coining-press operators were arrested. One pleaded guilty to a federal charge, and the other became a fugitive. The charge was not for minting the coins, as this was not proved, but for selling such coins for their private profit. The sentence for the man with the guilty plea was restitution of $5,000—the price he had received for a coin—and five years' probation.

By now, the media have publicized 10 such coins, some of which seem to be from the illegal actions of the two Mint employees. Eight of these are owned by Tommy Bolack, a New Mexico collector. According to Paul Gilkes, *Coin World* has information that others are in private hands but have not been marketed for fear that they may be confiscated. The Treasury Department has issued no policy on the subject.[5]

2001—New Schuler presses were brought into service. These, plus the use of riddler machines (circular sieves), dramatically reduced the number of misstruck and other error coins that left the mints. The 2001 Rhode Island quarter is the first for which relatively few off-center strikes and other oddities are known.

CHAPTER 6

THE MINTING OF WASHINGTON QUARTER

DIE-MAKING: FROM MODEL TO WORKING DIE

After John F. Flanagan made plaster models of the obverse and reverse of the Washington quarter in 1932, these were sent to the Philadelphia Mint. All of the features were in raised relief. The models, each probably about 10 inches or so in diameter, were used by Chief Engraver James R. Sinnock to make new models and finesse the details.

The finished plaster models were lightly coated with oil; plaster was then poured on top of them, creating versions with the features incuse, or intaglio. From these were made copper electrotypes called *galvanos*, with the features in relief once again.

THE MASTER HUB (POSITIVE, FEATURES IN RELIEF)

The finished galvanos were examined by Sinnock, and any roughness was smoothed or cut away. The metal model was then placed in a Janvier transfer lathe (a.k.a. portrait lathe); as the model slowly rotated, its surface topography was traced by a stylus that was connected with a pantograph arm to a tiny cutting head. The cutting head worked on a soft steel master hub that rotated in synchrony with the model, creating a small version of the model known as a *master hub*. The process usually took more than a day, sometimes two. All of the features on the master hub were raised, as on the larger version.

The small version in soft steel was examined and, if necessary, touched up. It was then heated to a high, sustained temperature, after which it was suddenly quenched to harden the crystalline structure. After being examined again and finessed to remove any further scaling or debris, the master hub, with most (but not all) of the design elements, was now finished.

THE MASTER DIE (NEGATIVE, FEATURES INCUSE)

The next step was to press the master hub into a soft shank of steel to create the master die, with the features incuse, or recessed. When this soft master die was completed, the engraver punched the numerals of the date into the surface (if the die was for an obverse). In the first year of the Washington quarter these were the digits 1, 9, 3, and 2. The undated master hub was then placed in storage for use in later years.

THE WORKING HUB (POSITIVE, FEATURES IN RELIEF)

In a repeat of the transfer process, the working hub was created in soft steel—in relief, a copy of the finished coin with all details. The obverse working hub was complete with the date. After hardening, the working hub was used to make as many working dies as needed.

THE WORKING DIE (NEGATIVE, FEATURES INCUSE)

Going through the process again, the hardened working hub was impressed into many working dies of soft steel, one at a time. Often, two or more blows were required to bring up the detail. If the later blow was slightly off register, a *doubled die* was created—with doubled outlines to certain of the features. This happened only occasionally.

Unhardened working dies for the Denver and San Francisco mints were taken to the Engraving Department of the Philadelphia Mint, where a staff member punched a D or S mintmark into each, using a punch about the size of a short pencil. D and S punches of various sizes were kept on hand. Sometimes different-size or style punches were used within a given year, creating varieties of interest to numismatists. It required two or more taps of a small hammer to impress the mintmark into a reverse die. If the punch slipped before the second tap, a *repunched mintmark* was created. This happened often in the Washington quarter series. Beginning in 1968, the mintmarks, now including a P for Philadelphia, were punched into the obverse die at the lower right. There was no jig to position the mintmark punch, although a sketch on the wall outlined the general area in which the mintmark was to be placed on each die. The punch was set visually by a trained engraver.

After this, the working dies for use at the Philadelphia Mint were hardened by the usual process, and then dressed by grinding or lapping of the field. For Proof coins, such dies were given a high polish. The dies were then ready for coining use. Unhardened dies were shipped to Denver and San Francisco. At the branch mints the hardening and finishing process took place in the machine shop.

Each die was heated to a cherry red and maintained for a time at that temperature, after which it was plunged into cold water or oil to harden it. After the quenching, the surface of the die was apt to have some scale or irregularities, so it was finished by grinding or basining (grinding with a circular motion). This resulted in tiny lines in the die, called *striae*. On Washington quarters these tiny, raised, parallel striae are most often seen in the open areas of the obverse field. For Proofs, the polishing process by basining removed the striae.

Changes in the process were made in the 1990s. The P, D, and S mintmarks were added to the master die. This ended the era of repunched mintmarks and other variations. A die shop was opened at the Denver Mint to share some of the work done formerly at Philadelphia.

THE COINING PROCESS
PREPARING THE PLANCHET

Quarter dollars as well as other coins are struck on planchets—circular discs of slightly smaller diameter than the finished coins. To make planchets for quarters, Mint workers first cut blanks out of long strips of silver alloy (90% silver and 10% copper), much as a cookie cutter would punch out pieces of dough. After 1964, the quarters were made of a clad composition, in which the strip has a solid copper core with a layer of copper-nickel (75%-25%, respectively) bonded to each side. In time, the process whereby blanks were cut one at a time from single strips of alloy gave way to a more efficient system, in which wider strips and gang punches are used to stamp out multiple blanks in one blow. This is a very noisy operation, as is coining, and visitors to the Mint must wear ear coverings.

In the early years of the Washington quarter, silver strips were made at the various mints from metal refined on the premises. Today, strips for the clad quarters are purchased in large coils from outside contractors.

Each individual blank must be of a specified diameter and with a weight of 96.45 grains, with a maximum 1.5-grain variation allowed (or, put another way, with a variation of plus or minus about 1.5%, totaling 3% overall).

After the circular blank is ready, it is put into a milling or upsetting machine and run at high speed between a roller and an edge, in an area in which the diameter decreases slightly, forcing the metal up on ridges on both sides of the coin. This process creates what is called a *planchet*. The resultant planchet is blank on both sides but has raised rims.

Although processes have varied, in the past it has been customary to anneal the planchets by heating, followed by slow cooling, to soften the metal. Afterward they are cleaned in a soapy or acidic mixture (dilute sulphuric acid), rinsed, and then dried by tumbling in sawdust or corncobs or by exposure to currents of air. Once dry, the planchets are ready for coining. Tumbling around in a cleaning machine imparts countless nicks and marks to both sides. It is hoped that these will be obliterated during the squeezing and compression of the planchet in the coining press. In practice, many times the dies did not come completely together in the coining press, and the deepest areas of the dies—representing the highest areas on the finished coins—were not completely struck, with the result that marks from the original planchets were still visible in these areas. On Washington quarters this is much more obvious on the clad coins from 1965 to date than on the earlier silver pieces, as silver metal flowed more readily into the die recesses.

STRIKING THE COINS

The working dies are fitted to a coining press powered by an electric motor that is either fitted to the press, as with new equipment, or connected by shafts and pulleys, on older presses. Today's presses use gang dies and spew out coins at a rapid rate. Old-style presses, driven by connection to an electric motor, are still in use at the San Francisco Mint for the striking of Proofs. These use single pairs of dies.

An old-style press, used to make the early silver issues in the Washington series as well as Proofs today, is vertical with a more-or-less elliptical frame. An open area at the center holds the dies. The hammer (top) and anvil (bottom) dies can be removed at will when they become worn or damaged. The hammer die is fixed to a matrix that moves up and down as the flywheel on the press rotates and actuates a cam. This general type of press is called a *knuckle press*.

An old-style coining press.

On a single die-pair press used years ago, the blank planchets were placed into a receptacle at the front, and mechanical fingers fed them one by one into a circular collar just above the anvil die. This collar, the size of a finished coin, was vertically reeded on the inside. After placing the blank, the fingers retracted automatically, and the hammer die came down, stamping the obverse and reverse of the coin and forcing the metal to the edge of the collar, the reeded pattern of which was impressed on the coin's edge. The finished coin, measuring 19/20" (or 24.3 mm) in diameter, was then forced from the collar and ejected by the mechanical fingers. At that point, the coin went down a slide at the back of the press and dropped into a little hopper or bin. Presses of this type were brought back into service and used during the coin shortage of the 1960s. Later, more-automated processes were developed. Proof coins are made with a slightly different process, which will be described later.

In recent times, a "riddler" machine—essentially a sieve with openings slightly larger than a quarter—has been used to check the finished coins. Oversized pieces will not fall through; thus many double-struck coins and certain other types of mint errors are caught. These errors are mutilated by being run through a press, creating so-called waffle coins.

Allowing for Variances

It was and still is the intention of the Philadelphia, Denver, and San Francisco mints to produce the largest number of quarter dollars in the least possible time and with the least possible effort. There was and is no consideration whatsoever to please the numismatists who might later collect such coins.

The sharpness of a finished Washington quarter depends on the technician who adjusts the press as well as on the weight of the planchet and how it is prepared. If the dies are fit precisely the right distance apart, and a planchet is of precisely the correct weight and has been annealed to the proper softness, a coin with every detail as sharp as on the original engraver's model will be the result. This represents the idea situation.

Bear in mind, however, that a 3% latitude in weight is permitted by law, and that problems will occur if an overweight planchet is introduced. If a too-heavy (though still legal) planchet is fed into the press, the excess metal will have nowhere to go into the dies and will be forced out the edge, creating a wire rim (called a *fin* in mint jargon) and wearing out the die in the process, or worse, cracking the die.

The obvious answer is to space the dies slightly farther apart than optimum, so that slightly overweight planchets can be accommodated and coined at high speed without attention. Under this arrangement, only overweight planchets will produce perfectly struck coins, while correct-weight and underweight planchets will create coins with areas of weakness. This fact has played havoc with most other 20th-century coins. Lincoln cents are often weak on Lincoln's shoulder; Indian Head / Buffalo nickels are nearly always without full details on the bison's head and shoulder; Jefferson nickels often lack full steps on Monticello; Mercury dimes sometimes are weak at the center of the reverse and also near the date; Standing Liberty quarters rarely have full details on the head and shield; Liberty Walking halves are usually lightly struck at the obverse center; and Franklin halves sometimes lack full bell lines.

The original Washington quarter design, used from 1932 to 1998, was in low relief at the high points. As a result, it is the rule, not the exception, that Washington quarters of this period show all of the few details intended. Any lightness in the striking process is compensated for by the lack of details on the original design. This was an ideal situation for the Mint—but one that, curiously, is not mentioned in any reports or other publicity I have seen. Not so with the state quarters, as certain features with fine details are significantly raised on the coin. Many 2004-D Michigan quarters have areas of light striking on the reverse. No sooner did the 2005 California quarters come out than it was noticed that, on some coins, one leg of John Muir was not fully struck-up. In addition, the hardness of improperly annealed planchets, poor metal flow, and design peculiarities can contribute to weakness.

Incidentally, the Roosevelt dime, minted since 1946, is similar to the Washington quarter in that its design permits some tolerance in the coining process, and still yields excellent coins. Similarly, the lack of detail on the portrait of Franklin on the 1948 to 1963 half dollar masks any lightness of striking.

OTHER ASPECTS OF QUALITY

While it has been and still is a general rule that planchets should be bright and clean, sometimes defective planchets with stains, flakes, or the like have been used. In the nickel five-cent piece series, discolored planchets are common, especially for the 1950s and 1960s, but nearly all silver quarter-dollar planchets have been of high quality as to brightness. It is not unusual to see a mint-fresh clad metal quarter—1965 to date, including the state-reverse issues—with many nicks in the obverse field from the original planchet.

After the box receiving newly minted quarters at the back of the coining press is filled, it is taken by an attendant and dumped into a hopper and mixed with other coins. Afterward the coins, still mixed together, are run through the "riddler" or sieve, then mixed together again and taken to a mechanical counting machine. Next, they are put into cloth bags and tossed into a vault in bags heaped on the floor, later to be shipped away by truck. At no time, past or present, has any care been taken to prevent nicks and marks on planchets, nor has any effort been made to reduce damage during the storage, riddling, bagging, shipping, and delivery processes.

The result of this is that very few production-run quarter dollars ever emerged as Mint State–65 or higher quality when they finally reached the user. A banker viewing a bag of quarters might find few coins any nicer than MS-63 to MS-64 or so. As illogical as it might seem now, decades ago, few numismatists cared if a coin had numerous nicks. The vast majority of surviving Mint State examples of the two rarest regular varieties, the 1932-D and 1932-S, have nicks and marks, usually most prominent on the obverse.

Many of the later clad quarters, including state issues, that are certified in higher grades such as MS-66, 67, and even 68, are apt to have at least a few obvious marks, including (especially on the obverse) marks remaining from the original planchet. There seems to be some looseness in grading interpretations.

PRODUCING PROOF QUARTERS

Proof coins have been and are still being made in a different manner from the process used to make circulation strikes. The die-production steps are essentially the same, except that the face of each Proof from 1936 to date has been given a high degree of polish to create brilliant or mirror surfaces. Exceptions are certain

The 1936 Proof quarter was the first Proof of this denomination struck for collectors since 1915, the last year of Proof Barber quarter coinage.

early 1936 Proofs, which are not as mirrorlike as those made later in the same year.

A pair of dies was fitted into a hand-fed press of the old knuckle-action style located in the Medal Department of the Philadelphia Mint. A planchet was placed into the collar by an attendant in front of the press, the press actuated, and a coin struck. In some years, including in the present generation, the press struck each coin twice in quick succession to bring up all details sharply. The finished coin was then removed by hand and a new planchet inserted. These old presses, once used for high-speed regular coinage, are operated slowly when Proofs are struck.

In the early era of Washington quarters, planchets for Proof coins were always inspected (although sometimes not carefully) to be sure they did not have chips, flakes, discoloration, or damage. After annealing, they also went through a special cleaning process, after which they were dried.

Beginning in 1968, the making of Proofs was transferred to the San Francisco Mint. In addition, Special Mint Sets were made at the San Francisco Mint from 1965 through 1967; these bore no mintmark. At the San Francisco Mint in the 1970s, when I took a tour, camera in hand, the finished Proof coins of each denomination were carefully stacked on top of each other in small piles in a tray. Most Proofs made since 1968 have frosty or "cameo" designs set against deeply mirrored backgrounds. Cameo-style Proofs for certain earlier Washington quarters are very rare.

Today, the quality of Proof coins is superb. Nearly all can be graded PF-68 to PF-70 with cameo contrast. The packaging is very attractive as well.

In 1968 the making of Proof coins was transferred to the San Francisco Mint. From that point onward, Proofs display the S mintmark on the obverse, as on this 1981-S.

MINTS AND THE DISTRIBUTION OF QUARTERS
QUANTITIES MINTED

Quarter dollars cost less than face value to produce, and, accordingly, they have always been a source of profit for the Mint. The profit margin soared when silver was eliminated, beginning in 1964. The profit, called *seignorage*, has contributed heavily to the operating profits of the various mints and, accordingly, the production of such pieces has been highly encouraged. This was quite unlike the situation for silver and gold coins in the early days, when gold was of full intrinsic value, and for a long time (until 1873) silver was likewise, resulting in little if any profit for the Mint.

After the initial production of Washington quarters in 1932, no more were struck until 1934, as in this Depression era enough coins were already on hand. In fact, quantities of Standing Liberty quarters from the 1920s still were in bank vaults, awaiting distribution. As the economy pulled out of its slump in the late 1930s, demand for quarters increased. At the time, half dollars were the highest-denomination silver coins regularly used in circulation. Dollars were plentiful at banks, but circulated widely only in the Rocky Mountain district.

During World War II, mintages of all coins increased sharply. After the war, quantities remained high, but not at the levels of the early 1940s. By this time, quarters increasingly replaced half dollars in circulation, although the latter remained plentiful.

It seemed more convenient to have a pocketful of quarters than of halves. In many ways, this was and is a coin of ideal size for handling.

The advent of the Kennedy halves in 1964 was the beginning of the end of the half dollar denomination. Later Kennedy halves were mostly hoarded, and even today they are hardly ever seen in commerce. I have not received one in change for several years. The rise in the price of silver in the late 1960s made half dollars profitable to melt down. The result was that, by the 1970s, there were very few halves in circulation.

The quarter dollar became the largest coin of the realm to see active use. When arcade machines, turnpike toll machines, and other devices became popular, they were fitted to take quarters. Today, the quarter remains secure as the highest-value coin normally seen, despite occasional challenges, such as the Eisenhower, Anthony, and "golden" dollars, none of which have ever been popular. The reasons for this are simple: paper dollars are also current. Eliminate the paper dollars and dollar coins will circulate. Further, most coin-operated machines will not accept dollar coins.

THE PHILADELPHIA MINT

By the time Washington quarters were first made, in 1932, the Philadelphia Mint had been relocated in the third facility to bear that name, in a building first occupied in autumn 1901. Much new equipment had been installed, and operations, some of which had been conducted by steam power earlier, were now electrified. This structure remained in use until the fourth Philadelphia Mint was inaugurated in 1967.

The third Philadelphia Mint in the early 20th century. Within its walls the Washington quarter designs were finalized and dies were made.

During these transitions the Philadelphia Mint remained the center for creating designs and making dies. Later, in the 1990s, some die-making was assigned to the Denver Mint. The Engraving Department was and is headquartered in Philadelphia. The facility is staffed with talented sculptor-engravers, as they are known, but has lacked a chief engraver since Elizabeth Jones departed in 1992.

THE DENVER MINT

Construction of the Denver Mint began in 1904, and in 1906 it struck its first coins, these being in silver and gold. It was not until 1911 that the first cents were made there and not until 1912 that nickels were first struck.

The Denver Mint, opened in 1906, has produced Washington quarters nearly continuously since 1932.

When Washington quarters were inaugurated in 1932, the Denver Mint coined an allotment, as it has ever since.

The facility was enlarged in 1937. Today, the same structure is in use, although with many improvements in technology. In recent years, limited die-making operations have been set up there, but they do not involve the design process.

THE SAN FRANCISCO MINT

The San Francisco Mint joined the other two mints in producing Washington quarters in 1932. Afterward it produced them nearly continuously. At that time, the facilities were located in the second building to bear that name—an impressive structure nicknamed the Granite Lady, in which operations had commenced in 1874. In 1937 a new facility, a modern fortress-like structure, was occupied on Duboce Street in the same city.

The second San Francisco Mint—nicknamed the Granite Lady—opened in 1874 and remained in use until 1937.

In 1955 the Treasury Department announced that the San Francisco Mint would close its coining operations forever, and designated it the San Francisco Assay Office. In that particular year, 1955-S Lincoln cents and Roosevelt dimes were made, but no Washington quarters, the last being the 1954-S. Later, the San Francisco Mint did resume coinage of some lower denominations, but not quarters, except for special silver-content and Proof coins sold at premiums to collectors and others. It also got back its Mint designation.

CHAPTER 7

SECRETS OF BEING A SMART BUYER

COLLECTING AND THE MARKETPLACE
IN THE EARLY YEARS

In 1932, there was little collector interest in Washington quarters. Economic times were difficult, and while the public saved many as souvenirs, they spent most of them once the novelty passed. A quarter could buy a meal in a typical restaurant, or furnish an evening's entertainment at a movie or vaudeville show.

Collecting coins by date and mintmark was not popular. M.L. Beistle of Shippensburg, Pennsylvania, had launched a series of coin album pages that had circular openings, faced on each side with cellulose acetate slides, but they were not yet widely popular. There is no recorded instance in which any collector or dealer set aside a quantity of coins for investment, although some dealers routinely added them to inventory. William Pukall was particularly active. Since about 1914 had he acquired multiple rolls of each date and mintmark in the quarter series.[1] Tatham Stamp & Coin Co., in Springfield, Massachusetts, also squirreled rolls away in the early period of Washington quarters.

The date-and-mintmark syndrome had yet to occur. In 1932, Standing Liberty quarters were not widely collected, either, and no one cared that, for example, the 1927-S had a very low mintage.

CHANGES OF 1934 AND 1935

In 1934, that all changed. Wayte Raymond, a leading New York City dealer, obtained a license to sell the Beistle album pages, which he did with great publicity. Raymond's first issue of the *Standard Catalogue* came out this year as well. Hobbies were a nationwide fad, and coin collecting caught on rapidly. A catalyst was the low-mintage 1931-S cent, affordable to just about everyone. In Neenah, Wisconsin, J.K. Post began selling "penny boards" made for him by Western Publishing Company of Racine. Later, Post's interest was bought by Western through a subsidiary, Whitman Coin Products—the precursor to today's Whitman Publishing, LLC, maker of the *Guide Book*.

While cents and nickels were the most popular series to collect, quarters soon developed a following. With an eye on the future, many dealers, collectors, and investors stashed away bank-wrapped rolls. However, these were saved in smaller quantities than were lower-value cents, nickels, and dimes. In autumn 1935 the great commemorative craze began with wild speculation in the 1935-D and S Daniel Boone Bicentennial half dollars with a small 1934 on the reverse; these coins had multiplied in value by year's end. The low-mintage Hudson Sesquicentennial and Old Spanish Trail halves of 1935, with mintages of 10,000 each, quickly sold out and rose sharply in value.

The *Numismatic Scrapbook* made its debut in 1935 under the brilliant editorship of Lee F. Hewitt, of Chicago. Hewitt was a collector and had a keen sense of what the public wanted. This magazine, written with human-interest items, fillers, and the like, quickly surpassed *The Numismatist*, the official magazine of the ANA, which was considered to be quite dull in comparison. (Today, the magazine known simply as *Numismatist* is a showcase of interesting articles and excellent graphics.)

When I first started dealing in rare coins as a teenager in 1953, the typical Washington quarter set owned by an advanced collector was housed in Raymond "National" album pages. All coins from 1932 to date were typically in Uncirculated grade, except for 1932-D and S, which were usually About Uncirculated (AU). The latter two grades were what people would have found in circulation when the coin-hobby boom started in a large way in 1934. Many of the large-mintage 1932-P coins were readily available from pieces kept as souvenirs. For some reason, the 1932-D slipped through the cracks. Few were saved, and from the outset this was considered the key to the series.

In addition, and even more popular in numismatics in 1953, were sets currently taken from circulation and housed in blue Whitman folders. Such coins usually included well-worn examples from the early 1930s, increasing in quality as the years progressed, with recent dates in Uncirculated and About Uncirculated grades. All could be found in circulation, although the 1932-D and S were scarce. In 1953, bank-wrapped rolls of quarters could be found in dealers' stocks with ease for all dates except 1932, 1932-D, 1932-S, 1934-D, and 1936-D. The 1932 Philadelphia coins were very common, but usually came in groups other than rolls.

INTO THE 1940S

The production of Washington quarters slipped into a routine in the 1930s—Philadelphia, Denver, and San Francisco minted coins each year, with the exception of 1938, when San Francisco did not participate. There was never an investment boom, promotion, or razzle-dazzle. The series was quietly collected by those who wanted to maintain continuing sets of current coinage. Dealers with good over-the-counter or mail-order retail trade stowed rolls away in quantity, and investors continued to do so as well.

In 1936, Proofs were struck for the first time since 1916. These were available singly as well as in sets. Quarters were the least popular of the five denominations included. Proofs were not minted after 1942, due to the war efforts.

In July 1939, Wayte Raymond offered quarters for sale in *The Numismatist*. A complete date run of Proof quarter dollars of the Liberty Seated and Barber issues from 1858 to 1915 cost $125, a complete set of Uncirculated Barber quarter dollars except the 1901-S cost $200, a complete set of Uncirculated Standing Liberty quarters cost $275, and a complete collection of Washington quarters from 1932 to date cost $12.50. Today, to replicate all of these sets in gem Mint State and Proof would cost more than $500,000, and the $12.50 set of Washington quarters from 1932 to 1939 would cost several tens of thousands of dollars, mainly because of the 1932-D.

In June 1944, the Bebee Stamp & Coin Company of Chicago offered a complete set of Uncirculated Washington quarters of 1932 through 1944 for $30. In the 1950s I met Aubrey and Adeline Bebee, who by that time had moved to Omaha. Later, I handled much of their personal collection and inventory in a series of auctions. It was the policy of the Bebees to maintain a minimum stock of 100 coins in popular series from the 1930s onward. For Washington quarters they did this, except for 1932-D, which they were always scrambling to find.

THE 1950S AND 1960S

In January 1953, M. Hirschhorn, of Long Island City, New York, listed Uncirculated 40-coin rolls of Washington quarters of many dates. Sample prices include these: 1935, $42.50; 1936-S, $60; 1937-D, $34; 1937-S, $90; and 1939-S, $50.

Prices continued to rise, but gradually. In June 1954, Chicago dealer Ruth Green offered an Uncirculated set of Washington quarters from 1932 to date for $140. The

Greens and the earlier-mentioned Bebees were among the dealers who delivered good quality. Some others fudged a bit, and a 1932-D or S quarter that was offered as Uncirculated might upon examination be found to have friction. In all instances, even the top-rated dealers sold what they could find in rolls. Accordingly, the typical set would grade MS-63 to MS-65 by today's standards.

From the 1930s through the 1950s, coins were simply graded as Uncirculated, period. No numbers, no differentiation in price between bagmarked coins and those we would call gems today. Similarly, a Proof was simply a Proof. There were no grading standards or regulations, as a perusal of the advertisements in *The Numismatist* or the *Numismatic Scrapbook* from the 1940s would show. Often, buffed or chrome-plated circulation-strike quarters would be offered as "Proofs," with an enticing low price. Then as now, bottom-feeders and bargain hunters usually ended up with the poorest quality.

In 1950, Proofs were again struck at the Philadelphia Mint. Most quarters from this year are not as deeply mirrorlike as those of later times. Soon, Proof sets became very popular for investment purposes. Proof coins were no longer offered singly. Production increased, and the Mint placed restrictions on how many sets could be ordered. Prices rose dramatically, a set of 1936 Proof coins going from the $300 or so to a peak of $600 in 1956. Then the market crashed; there were many sellers, but few buyers. In time, interest revived, and by 1960 Proofs were popular once again.

From 1960 through 1964 there was a tremendous boom in the rare-coin market, ignited by the great excitement over the 1960 Small Date Lincoln cent (bags of $50 face value soared to $12,000 or more) and the launching of *Coin World*, the first weekly numismatic publication. The Teletype system connecting dealers added to the enthusiasm, as did the *Coin Dealer Newsletter*, first published in 1963.

The market then slumped, and it remained in the doldrums for several years. Not all series suffered—tokens, medals, colonials, and many other series remained as popular as ever, and even grew. Washington quarters were never prominent in any of these cycles, but they did go up and down with the tide.

LATER TIMES

The market became hot again in the early 1970s, this time spurred by the rising price of gold. In mid-decade it slumped. The 1976 bicentennial coincided with a slack period in investment interest. For this reason, special Proofs and silver strikings laid a big fat egg. The Mint had unsold quantities on hand for several years afterward.

In the late 1970s the rising price of silver and gold bullion carried rare-coin prices along with it, but the market slumped in early 1980. Again, Washington quarters were not darlings of the market or the subject of any special interest, but were carried along with the rest. In 1992, a new product—*silver* strikings of quarter dollars—was added to the Mint menu of things offered to collectors. Similar to current Proofs, these were struck at the San Francisco Mint.

In the meantime, commercial grading services took hold in the market, the first big player being the American Numismatic Association Certification Service (ANACS) launched in the late 1970s, with Tom DeLorey running the division. Coins were split-graded, with a separate number assigned to each side, based on the new *Official American Numismatic Association Grading Standards for United States Coins*. Photographs were taken, and the coin and a photograph certificate were returned to the submitter.

The venture was so profitable that the ANA had an embarrassment of riches—as a nonprofit organization. The money was put to good use, with an expansion of the head-quarters building in Colorado Springs and other expenditures beneficial to the hobby. Later, ANACS was sold to Amos Press, parent company of *Coin World*, and still later to Anderson Press, which today is also the parent of Whitman Publishing.

During the early years of ANACS, numerical grading increased in popularity, with Uncirculated now called Mint State and divided into several categories, finally into 11, from MS-60 to 70 (see the expanded discussion under "Official ANA Grading Standards" later in this chapter).

In 1986, the Professional Coin Grading Service (PCGS) revolutionized commercial grading by promoting and popularizing sealed plastic holders. In 1987, the Numismatic Guaranty Corporation of America (NGC) went into the same business. Soon, ANACS played catch-up and adopted holders as well. Then, in 1999, the new state-reverse quarters changed everything. All of a sudden, and for the first time in their entire history, Washington quarters were hot! Now, finally, attention was being paid to the scarcer early dates. In addition, a great demand arose for any Washington quarter—common or rare—that was in an ultra-high grade certified by a leading service. This popularity extends to the present day.

WAYS TO COLLECT WASHINGTON QUARTERS

BY TYPE

Since 1932 there have been many different types of quarters produced, the "many" being the result of all of the different state types since 1999. The basic types are these:

1932 to 1964—Silver content, regular design. Additional silver strikes were made for sale to collectors from 1992 to 1998.

1965 to 1998—Clad quarters of the regular design, except for 1976.

1976—Bicentennial coins dated 1776–1976 in clad metal.

1976—Bicentennial coins dated 1776–1976 in silver.

1999 onward—50 different state quarters.

ONE OF EACH VARIETY

This is the most deluxe way to go. Such a collection includes one of each date and mint-mark from 1932 to 1998, plus Proofs of the various issues. Special Mint Set coins of 1965 to 1967 are part of such a set. In addition, the silver-content quarters of 1992 to 1998 are included.

The state quarters from 1999 to date are an essential element, including circulation strikes from the Philadelphia and Denver mints and Proofs in clad metal and silver from the San Francisco Mint.

In the aggregate, the preceding includes hundreds of different dates, mintmarks, and other variations, to which five new state quarters are being added each year through 2008, each with four varieties—or a total of 20 new coins annually.

A set such as the preceding is extensive and impressive.

STATE QUARTERS

State quarters can be collected on their own, and many people do just that. Such a set commences with 1999 and is kept current each year. The circulation strikes can be collected from pocket change, or purchased inexpensively. Sets of the Philadelphia and Denver Mint issues are the most popular—anyone can collect them, and easily. The clad and silver Proofs made in San Francisco play to a different and more dedicated audience, defined in numbers by about 3 million or so of each clad issue and slightly less than a million of each silver issue.

In sharp contrast to the limited-edition Proofs and silver issues, the clad-metal circulation strikes seem to be popular with just about everybody. At the launch ceremony for the 2005 California quarter, Mint Director Henrietta Holsman Fore stated that 140 million citizens were collecting them—wow!

CHOOSING WHAT IS RIGHT FOR YOU
FACTORS AFFECTING PRICE

What at first glance seems to be a simple pursuit—obtaining one of each of the quarters you desire—is actually quite challenging and, in some aspects, complex. In the simpler world of, say, the 1950s, basic rarity determined price. In the Washington quarter series, the 1932-D and 1932-S were the most expensive, because they had the lowest mintages and, across all grades, were the hardest to find.

There was one—just one—notable exception: the high-mintage 1936-D was expensive, but only in Uncirculated condition. Worn examples were very common. Although saving bank-wrapped rolls was a popular thing to do from 1934 onward, the 1936-D was overlooked by most dealers and investors. It did not seem to be rare in 1936, and focus was on buying commemorative coins, the hot spot of the market at the time. A few years later, collectors and dealers looked around and, surprisingly, found that rolls of 1936-D quarters were very rare—while both 1936 Philadelphia and 1936-S could be bought by the dozens of rolls, simply by writing a check.

Thus was introduced the concept of *condition rarity* in the Washington series. A variety could be common and of low value in one grade, but could be rare and expensive in a high grade.

Today, Uncirculated and Proof grades are each divided into 11 categories. In Mint State, these range from MS-60 continuously through MS-70. A Washington quarter can be worth a dollar or two in MS-60, but be priced in the hundreds of dollars, or even far more, if approaching MS-70 when few others are certified at that level.

Today, basic rarity affects price. However, condition rarities sell for very high prices if they are in high grades. Condition rarity is the hot ticket for now. If someone were to mention on an Internet forum that he owned a 1932 Philadelphia quarter in the ultimate MS-70 grade there would be lots of buzz. A mention that he had an MS-64 1932-D would attract no attention at all! Personally, basic rarity appeals more to me—perhaps because that is the way I grew up in the hobby. I would rather have a whole collection of silver Washington quarters in MS-63 grade than a single common date that grades as the only known MS-69 or 70, this being valued at the same price. I am in the minority in my view. High-grade coins are where the action is at the moment, basic rarity not being as important.

CHOICES

One of the first things to do when contemplating purchases is to review market prices. This book gives an excellent overview, which can be supplemented by current listings in the weekly coin papers and elsewhere.

Evaluate the depth of your interest as well as your budget. For me—and I say again that I may not be typical in the current market—I see excellent value in obtaining all of the varieties in MS-65 and Proof-65. By their very nature, the more recent Proofs will be graded higher than that, due to improved manufacturing and quality-control procedures.

This set will cost several tens of thousands of dollars, with the 1932-D being the key issue, and the 1932-S and 1936 Proof being expensive as well.

On second thought, I would probably critique my plan a bit more carefully, to see what a set in MS-64 and Proof-64 would cost for the silver issues. The price would fall off sharply. Being a careful buyer by training and tradition, and having some patience in the matter, I am confident that by cherrypicking for quality, my "64" set would be as good as if not nicer than a collection put together quickly by simply buying holders labeled 65.

Other variations suggest themselves, such as buying all the scarcer early dates in MS-63 grades, and the other silver issues in MS-64 or 65. It doesn't cost much to have the clad issues from 1965 to date in MS-65. Such a set would be far less than $10,000.

There is also the aspect of how you want to spend your money. If I had $100,000 to spend, I would still go for an MS-65 and Proof-65 set, and use the leftover amount to buy something else—a set of silver commemoratives, or a type set of gold, or whatever.

In chapters 8 and 9, for each variety among the various entries for dates and mints, I have listed the Optimal Collecting Grade (OCG)—my opinion of a high grade that offers special value for the price paid, usually meaning that the OCG is one point less than a higher grade that costs *much* more.

Grading by the Numbers
Grading Washington Quarters

The grade of a Washington quarter or other coin reflects the amount of handling or wear it has received. Most collectors, dealers, and commercial grading services use the book published by Whitman: *Official American Numismatic Association Grading Standards for United States Coins*. Another fine guide is *Photograde*, by James F. Ruddy (1970). PCGS, NGC, and *Coin World* have each issued information-filled grading texts.

The ANA standards were codified in 1977 by Kenneth E. Bressett and Abe Kosoff, with input from many hobby leaders and the ANA board of governors.[2] I wrote the introductory material. The most recent edition, the sixth, was published in 2005, with Bressett doing the descriptions for each series (including Washington quarters), while I wrote the narrative. Many collectors and professionals provided information and suggestions.

OFFICIAL ANA GRADING STANDARDS
WASHINGTON QUARTER DOLLARS, 1932 TO DATE

The following standards are from the sixth edition of the *Official American Numismatic Association Grading Standards for United States Coins*, edited by Kenneth Bressett, with narrative by Q. David Bowers (Atlanta: Whitman Publishing, 2005).

MINT STATE

Absolutely no trace of wear.

MS-70 • A flawless coin exactly as it was minted, with no trace of wear or injury. Must have full mint luster and brilliance or light toning.

MS-67 • Virtually flawless, but with very minor imperfections.

Washington quarter obverse and reverse, MS-63.

MS-65 • No trace of wear; nearly as perfect as MS-67 except for some small blemishes. Has full mint luster but may be unevenly toned or lightly fingermarked. May be weakly struck in one small spot. A few barely noticeable nicks or marks may be present.

MS-63 • A Mint State coin with attractive mint luster, but noticeable detracting contact marks or minor blemishes.

MS-60 • A strictly Uncirculated coin with no trace of wear, but with blemishes more obvious than for MS-63. May lack full mint luster, and the surface may be dull, spotted, or heavily toned.

ABOUT UNCIRCULATED

Small trace of wear visible on highest points.

AU-58 (*Very Choice*) • Has some signs of abrasion: high points of cheek, hair in front and back of ear; tops of legs and details in breast feathers.

AU-55 (*Choice*) • OBVERSE: Only a trace

Washington quarter obverse and reverse, AU-55.

of wear shows on highest points of hair in front and back of ear. REVERSE: A trace of wear shows on highest spots of breast feathers. SURFACE: Nearly all of the mint luster is still present.

AU-50 (*Typical*) • OBVERSE: Traces of wear show on hair in front and in back of ear. REVERSE: Traces of wear show on legs and breast feathers. SURFACE: Three-quarters of the mint luster is still present.

EXTREMELY FINE

Light wear on most of the highest points.

EF-45 (*Choice*) • OBVERSE: Slight wear shows on high points of hair around ear and along hairline up to crown. Hair lines are sharp and detailed. REVERSE: High points of legs are lightly worn. Breast feathers are worn

Washington quarter obverse and reverse, EF-40.

but clearly defined and fully separated. SURFACE: Half of the mint luster is still present.

EF-40 (*Typical*) • OBVERSE: Wear shows on high points of hair around ear and at hairline up to crown. REVERSE: High points of breast, legs, and claws are lightly worn, but all details are clearly defined and partially separated. SURFACE: Part of the mint luster is still present.

VERY FINE

Light to moderate even wear. All major features are sharp.

Washington quarter obverse and reverse, VF-20.

VF-30 (*Choice*) • OBVERSE: Wear spots show on hair at forehead and ear, cheek, and jaw. Hair lines are weak but have nearly full, visible details. REVERSE: Wear shows on breast but some of the details are visible. All vertical wing feathers are plain. Most details in the leg are worn smooth.

VF-20 (*Typical*) • OBVERSE: Three-quarters of the lines still show in hair. Cheek lightly worn but bold. Some hair details around ear are visible. REVERSE: Wear shows on breast but a few feathers are visible. Legs are worn smooth. Most details on the wings are clear.

FINE

Moderate to considerable even wear. Entire design is clear and bold.

F-12 • OBVERSE: Details show only at back of hair. Motto is weak but clearly visible. Part of cheek edge is worn away. REVERSE: Feathers on breast and legs are worn smooth. Leaves show some detail. Parts of wings are nearly smooth.

Washington quarter obverse and reverse, F-12.

VERY GOOD

Well worn. Design is clear but flat and lacking details.

VG-8 • OBVERSE: Entire head is weak, and most details in hair are worn smooth. All letters and date are clear. Rim is complete. REVERSE: About half of the wing feathers are visible. Breast and legs are only outlined. Leaves show very little detail. Rim is flat in spots but nearly complete.

Washington quarter obverse and reverse, VG-8.

GOOD

Heavily worn. Design and legend are visible but faint in spots.

G-4 • OBVERSE: Hair is well worn with very little detail remaining. Half of motto is readable. LIBERTY and date are weak but visible. Rim merges with letters. REVERSE:

Washington quarter obverse and reverse, G-4.

Eagle is worn nearly flat but is completely outlined. Leaves, breast, and legs are worn smooth. Legend is all visible but merges with rim.

ABOUT GOOD

Outlined design. Parts of date and legend are worn smooth.

AG-3 • OBVERSE: Head is outlined with nearly all details worn away. Date is readable but worn. Traces of motto are visible. Legend merges into rim. REVERSE: Entire design and lettering are partially worn away. Rim merges into legend.

Washington quarter obverse and reverse, AG-3.

Notes

- The obverse motto is always weak on coins of 1932 and early issues of 1934.
- The obverse rim is especially thick on coins of 1932 through 1935, protecting the obverse and often resulting in split grades (e.g., VG/AG) on well-worn examples.
- The reverse rim and lettering tend to be very weak, particularly on coins dated 1934D, 1935-D and S, 1936-D and S, 1937-D and S (especially), 1938-S, 1939-D, 1940-D and S, 1941-S, 1943-S, and 1944-S.
- Clad pieces are often weakly struck in spots.
- Bicentennial and statehood coins can be graded by obverse and surface quality.[3]
- The mintmark on many of the earlier issues tends to be filled.

SIGNIFICANCE OF GRADING NUMBERS

Grading numbers are simply shorthand for the rating that one person, group of people, or commercial certification service assigns to a particular coin at a particular time. The system is highly subjective, not scientific. For a rare 1932-S Washington quarter for which a small difference in grade can mean a large difference in price, Grader A might call it MS-64. Grader B may be more liberal and suggest MS-65. Grader C may consider it to be MS-63.

Differences of a point or two among experts are not unusual. In fact, via the practice of *resubmission*, many numismatists send certified coins back to the same services that graded them, and often the coins are returned with higher grades. This verifies that grading is a matter of opinion—an art, not a science. If it were scientific, the rules would be easy to follow, and all grading services would assign precisely the same number to a given coin, as would a collector or dealer using the grading descriptions. Under a scientific system, anyone with a copy of the ANA Grading Standards, a good light, and a good magnifying glass could come to precisely the same grade as that assigned by a commercial service.

In my opinion, it is easy to learn to grade Washington quarters. The ANA Standards given here are an outline. For a reality check, you need to examine coins in person. The best way to do this is to visit a coin convention or a friendly local coin dealer, and look at the coins on display. Most sellers are happy to "talk coins" and give you some advice. It is courtesy to buy a few coins or a few books from the person who helps you.

After an hour or two of immersion, examining certified as well as "raw" coins, you will be able to evaluate Washington quarters on your own.

Certification Services

Over the years, many companies, generally called *certification services* or *grading services*, have been established to assign grades to coins that are submitted. Since 1986, the year PCGS was established, more than 100 have been set up. Most have faded from the scene. PCGS was the first to make a large, successful business by encapsulating coins in tamper-resistant holders. ANACS began a large trade in the late 1970s, but did not use sealed holders until the late 1980s.

In alphabetical order, the four leading grading services today are ANACS, Independent Coin Grading (ICG), Numismatic Guaranty Corporation of America (NGC), and PCGS. There are other grading services as well. Many collectors and dealers have preferences. Before selecting a favorite, it would be good to ask around for advice. Some are services stricter than others.

In very high grades, opinions can vary widely, and you should proceed with caution. One person's MS-67 can be another's MS-69. If you are contemplating paying a high price for a condition rarity—an otherwise common Washington quarter in MS-65 or 66, but very expensive in MS-69—it would be wise to show the coin to others and seek opinions. Also read about market trends and fads, perhaps by borrowing or buying a copy of my 2005 book, *The Expert's Guide to Collecting and Investing in Rare Coins.*

However, within a certain range, the leading services are very good. If you sent the same Washington quarter to the four mentioned previously, you might get opinions such as these: MS-65, 65, 66, and 66. It is highly unlikely that you would get an MS-62, if three called the coin MS-65 or 66. Before the advent of such services, there were many overgraded, processed, cleaned coins advertised as "choice," "gem," or the like, often with the sellers assigning ANA numbers. Traps such as chrome-plated pseudo-Proofs are easily caught by the services, but might fool you in the beginning stages of your knowledge.

Among Washington quarters, the majority of dates and mintmarks are inexpensive. The result is that it costs more to have a coin certified than the coin is worth. This is particularly true of issues from the 1940s onward, including the state quarters. In addition, the hundreds of holders needed for a full set would weigh many pounds and take up a lot of space. Probably a good compromise is to buy certified examples of the rarer issues, but to acquire "raw" specimens of the usual inexpensive varieties. To do the latter you will either need to learn grading on your own, or buy from a trustworthy dealer. To store and display a high-grade, expensive set, a notebook-type album with plastic pages permitting a mix of certified holders and plain plastic holders may be a good way to go.

Population Reports Vs. Mintages and Values

ANACS, NGC, and PCGS publish population reports listing each date and mintmark of Washington quarters (and other coins), with a number signifying how many times a variety has been certified in a given grade. As it usually costs $10 or more to have a Washington quarter certified by a leading service, the population reports are distorted in that common, inexpensive coins can appear to be very rare, as not many have been submitted for grading. As one of hundreds of examples, an extremely common 1965 quarter in MS-63 grade has a market price of only a dollar or so. Accordingly, population reports indicate that very few have been certified. The unknowing reader may assume incorrectly that such a coin is hard to find. In contrast, the rare 1932-D and 1932-S have many certified as MS-63, because they are expensive, and certification helps sell the coins and gives buyers assurance. The following examples from the combined population reports of ANACS, NGC, and PCGS as of late 2005 with prices from *Coin Values*, April 3, 2006,[4] will suffice to illustrate the situation.

The distribution for 1932 is unusual in the series in that two of the issues, the 1932-D and 1932-S, are scarce and valuable even if well worn. On the other hand, a worn 1932 Philadelphia coin is of little interest or value to intermediate or advanced collectors, as an MS-60 can be obtained for $30. Using the certification numbers alone it thus appears that the 1932 Philadelphia is the *rarest* of the trio, with just 15 certified, as opposed to 1,225, which must be common by comparison. The reason, of course, is that a well-worn 1932 is worth just $10 in VF-20 in *Coin Values*, while comparable 1932-D and S coins are worth $200 and $175, respectively. It makes no economic sense to certify a Very Fine 1932, whereas such an expenditure is justified for the branch-mint coins.

At the MS-65 level and higher, each of the three is fairly expensive, ranging (in MS-65) from $425 for the 1932 to $24,000 for the 1932-D, and $6,750 for the 1932-S. At the MS-66 level the three coins are $1,400, $90,000, and $27,000, respectively.

Therein lie great opportunities. The same grading service can certify a coin as MS-65 on one pass and MS-66 on another. That is what the resubmission game is all about. Some people make their living by doing just that. Take the 1932-S: 137 have been certified in MS-65, and the coin is priced at $7,000; compared this to just nine certified in MS-66 and a much higher price of $25,000. A connoisseur or cherrypicker will do this—first, examine as many MS-65 coins as possible, until a very nice or high-end example is seen. Then buy it. Then send it to the same grading service to see what happens. Send it in five times, eight times, or whatever. A California dealer sent a rare, 20th-century silver coin to a leading grading service 24 times without success, but on the 25th try the coin gained a point in grade and thousands of dollars in value. This is a quid pro quo game for all involved: the owner of the coin reaps a windfall profit just by having a sharp eye, and the grading service gets a lot of business from a single coin! The corollary is that if you are in the market for an MS-65, and if you have patience and know what to look for, chances are great that you can buy an MS-64 that will look just as nice as an MS-65. Or, you can buy an MS-62 that looks just as nice as an MS-63.

Of course, you want a "nice" 1932, 1932-D, and 1932-S in whatever grade you can afford, combined with a good value for the price paid.

While the preceding comments make sense, most people are not aware of such considerations and are surprised when their condition rarity proves not to be so rare after all. These are the things to think about before investing significant funds in Washington quarters or anything else.

Table 7.1 Comparison of Population Reports, Mintages, and Values for Washington Quarters of 1932

Year and Mintmark	G–VF [a]	EF & AU [b]	MS-60–MS-62 [c]	MS-63	MS-64	MS-65	MS-66	MS-67	MS-68
1932 (5,404,000 minted)									
Number certified	15	354	317	636	768	673	148	3	0
Price	$6	$10	$25	$50	$90	$425	$1,400		
1932-D (436,800 minted)									
Number certified	1,225	2,852	1,046	755	619	78	1	0	0
Price	$185	$285	$1,100	$3,200	$7,500	$24,000	$90,000		
1932-S (408,000 minted)									
Number certified	870	2,789	1,319	1,175	1,330	137	9	0	0
Price	$170	$215	$500	$1,400	$2,750	$6,750	$27,000		

[a] Prices in this column are for coins graded F-12.
[b] Prices in this column are for coins graded EF-40.
[c] Prices in this column are for coins graded MS-60.

BEING A SMART BUYER

If you've read some of my other books you know that buying coins in some series can be very complex. Washington quarters, for a change, are straightforward.

STEP 1: THE NUMERICAL GRADE

Following my earlier advice, look at market listings and determine what grades you would like to buy for each of the coins you need. This will be a combination of your budget plus the desire to obtain good value for your money. The OCG given for each issue later in this book may furnish some ideas. Generally, this means that if the next-higher grade of a coin is multiples of the price, it may not be a good value.

If you are typical, you will probably have a high grade in mind for most if not all issues from the 1960s onward, and perhaps slightly lower grades for earlier, more expensive varieties. Make up a want-list with each variety and the hoped-for grade, and cross off each as you acquire it. Except for the handful of rare issues, a first-class collection can be made with MS-64 and 65 coins for the dates before 1940, and MS-65 and 66 after 1940. As to the 1932-D and S, contemplate these separately and form a buying plan.

If your budget calls for an MS-60 1932-D, and if you are at a coin show, ask to see pieces in the MS-60 category. There is no particular point in asking for an MS-64 or EF-40. Consider the offered coin and the grade assigned to it. If you can do so, verify with your own knowledge, or ask to show it to a friend, to be sure it is correct. Most dealers welcome outside consultation when making a sale. Better yet, spend an hour or two learning how to grade coins on your own, as mentioned earlier. Then with confidence you can buy most of the pieces you need. It would be advisable, however, to seek an experienced friend's opinion on the more valuable pieces if they are not certified.

Immediately, you can see if the coin at hand is in the numerical grade you are seeking and qualifies for further consideration. Otherwise, hand it back and look at something else. It is likely that most of the Washington quarters you are offered will not be certified, but most will have grading numbers assigned to them.

If you see an offering on the Internet or a catchpenny printed advertisement of "a nice gem," or "a really choice Mint State," ask the buyer to translate that into ANA numbers. If he or she won't, you should walk. There are lots of other coins around.

STEP 2: EYE APPEAL AT FIRST GLANCE

At this point take a quick glance at the coin. Is it "pretty"? Is the toning (if present) attractive, or is it dark or blotchy? Is the coin stained? If it is brilliant, is it attractively lustrous, or is it dull and lifeless?

For all the Washington quarters you will be considering for your collection, there are many opportunities in the marketplace. It is not at all necessary in any instance to compromise on eye appeal! Even the rarest of the rare 1932-D can be found with excellent eye appeal with just a little bit of patience.

If it is not attractive, then reject it and go on to look at another. An ugly coin graded as MS-65 is still ugly, and if it were my decision I would not buy it for half of the current market price! Avoid price-bargains; most are overgraded, lack eye appeal, or have some other problem. The market for quality Washington quarters is very strong, and there is no such thing as "below wholesale" for a problem-free coin. If the coin is attractive to you, then in some distant future when you sell it, the piece will be attractive to other buyers. Among Washington quarters from the 1940s to date, *most* have good eye appeal—a situation not at all true for many other series (Jefferson nickels, for example). For modern Proof coins 1968-S to date, including the state issues, you can almost buy with your eyes closed—the quality is that nice!

STEP 3: EVALUATING SHARPNESS AND RELATED FEATURES

At this point you have a coin that has excellent eye appeal and that you believe to be in the numerical grade assigned. The next step is to take out a magnifying glass and evaluate its sharpness. In 90% of silver issues from 1932 to 1964 there will be no problem. For clad coins 1965 to 1998, there can be some weakness that often manifests itself by the presence of tiny nicks and marks on the high parts of the portrait, while the surrounding fields are essentially mark-free. The marks on the high areas are marks on the original planchet that did not become obliterated by striking pressure at that deep point in the die.

State quarters are usually well struck, but some are not. Check the high parts of Washington's portrait for planchet marks. Also check the points in highest relief in the reverse design. If you need a reference point for state quarters, examine a Proof of the same variety—these are nearly always needle-sharp in detail, and you can tell which design features should be present.

As part of step 3, look at the planchet and surface quality. Silver issues usually pass with flying colors, but clad coins can be dull, or have a lot of nicks from the original planchet, particularly on the obverse. Take your time, even when buying inexpensive issues.

In other instances, coins were struck from "tired" dies that had been used in some instances to strike more than 200,000 pieces, and may show graininess or metal flow. This can be problematic with quarters of the 1932-to-1998 era, but is less so for the state quarters.

Examine your prospective coin carefully, and reject it if there are any problems with the surface or planchet. No compromise of any kind need be made.

STEP 4: ESTABLISHING A FAIR MARKET PRICE

For starters, use one or several handy market guides for a ballpark estimate. This book is a handy guide, but should be verified with one of the weekly or monthly listings, such as those in *Coin Values*, the "Coin Market" feature of *Numismatic News*, or the *Coin Dealer Newsletter*. Nearly all Washington quarters in grades up to MS-65 have standard values and trade within certain ranges. There will be more variation with such scarce varieties as the 1932-D, 1932-S, and high-grade examples of 1936-D.

If the coin is common enough in a given grade, with sharp strike, with fine planchet quality, and with good eye appeal, then be sure the coin is offered for about the going market price. If the going price is $25, and you are at a convention or coin shop and are offered a nice one for $27, buy it anyway—your time and the opportunity have value. If it is priced at $40, you can wait. If it is offered for $15, better look at it more carefully!

The state quarters are so plentiful that they are almost a commodity. Probably a good way to get all or most is to pick a dealer you like, with reasonable prices, and buy as many as you can from this single source—then fill in any open spaces later.

WASHINGTON QUARTERS 1932–1998

1932–1964: SILVER ISSUES

Specifications:
Composition: 90% silver; 10% copper • *Diameter:* 24.3 mm • *Weight:* 96.45 grains • *Edge:* Reeded

1932 WASHINGTON QUARTER
Circulation-Strike Mintage: 5,404,000
OCG: MS-64

The 1932 Philadelphia Mint Washington quarter has always been popular as the first year of issue.

1932 • Market Values • Circulation Strikes

EF-40	AU-50	MS-60	MS-63	MS-64	MS-65	MS-66
$10.	$15.	$25.	$50.	$90.	$425.	$1,400.

1932 • Certified Populations • Circulation Strikes

Good to AU	MS-60 to MS-62	MS-63	MS-64	MS-65	MS-66	MS-67	MS-68
369	317	636	768	673	148	3	0

Key to Collecting: The 1932 Philadelphia Mint Washington quarter has always been popular as the first year of issue. Mint State coins are readily available, but are certainly scarce in comparison to dates after 1934. The typical coin graded at MS-63 or higher is apt to be lustrous and have good eye appeal. Quite a few are around in About Uncirculated and lower Mint State grades. When marks are present, they are usually most noticeable on the portrait and the left obverse field.

Numismatic Notes: All 1932 quarters are of the Light Motto variety with the edges of the letters in the motto IN GOD WE TRUST blending into the field.

Quarters of this new design were released into circulation on August 1, 1932. There was considerable interest at first, and many were saved as souvenirs. However, in this deep Depression year few bank-wrapped rolls or other quantities were saved by anyone. Later, Mint State examples would prove to be plentiful on the numismatic market, but they were usually offered one or a few at a time, never in quantity.

In the July 1980 issue of *Coin Dealer Newsletter Monthly Supplement*, Allen Harriman wrote, "Of all the P-mints, this is the one most often encountered in AU-55 'slider' and MS-60 condition." Such pieces represent coins saved by the public at the time of release, but spent afterward when the novelty had passed.

All quarters of this date have a higher rim on the reverse than do later silver quarters issued 1934 to 1964.

1932-D Washington Quarter
Circulation-Strike Mintage: 436,800
OCG: MS-64

The Denver Mint issue of the year is far and away the
key issue of the series.

1932-D • Market Values • Circulation Strikes

EF-40	AU-50	MS-60	MS-63	MS-64	MS-65	MS-66
$285.	$500.	$1,100.	$3,200.	$7,500.	$24,000.	$90,000.

1932-D • Certified Populations • Circulation Strikes

Good to AU	MS-60 to MS-62	MS-63	MS-64	MS-65	MS-66	MS-67	MS-68
4,077	1,046	755	619	78	1	0	0

Key to Collecting: Although the mintage figure of the 1932-D is slightly higher than for 1932-S (408,000), in grades of MS-63 or better the 1932-D is at least 5 to 10 times rarer than the 1932-S. As such, it is far and away the key issue of the series. In the dawn days of rare-coin activity on the Internet (in the 1990s), Elliot Goldman, who operated All-state Coin Co. in Tucson, Arizona, specialized in Washington quarters. He and I conversed often on the 1932-D, as we both recognized their rarity and recommended them to clients (many of whom couldn't figure out why we would be excited about such an inactive series!). Today, with collectors' interest catalyzed by the state quarters, the classic 1932-D in a grade such as MS-63 or MS-64 (never mind the even rarer MS-65) is a magnet for bidders in an auction sale.

When the 1932-D was minted and distributed, no effort was made to handle the coins gently. As a result, most pieces saved in Mint State in 1932 and surviving to the present day are apt to be in MS-60 to MS-62 grades. As with other coins in the series, nicks and marks are most obvious on the portrait and in the left obverse field. Such marks generally get lost on the reverse and are not distracting there.

In worn grades, the 1932-D is available in proportion to its mintage and is seen about as often as is the 1932-S. Examples in such grades as Good and Very Good were occasionally found in circulation in the early 1950s, after which they disappeared almost entirely. Due to the high price of Mint State coins, circulated examples enjoy a wide market. Many fakes with D mintmarks added to Philadelphia Mint coins do exist. Seeking the advice of an expert when buying one is good practice; better yet, purchase a specimen that has been certified by one of the leading services.

Numismatic Notes: All 1932-D quarters are of the Light Motto variety with the edges of the letters in the motto IN GOD WE TRUST blending into the field. The D mintmark on genuine coins is often small and in high relief, and is sometimes filled at the center. The small D had been the standard for the entire Standing Liberty quarter production at the Denver Mint from 1917 to 1929. A ghost outline of a larger D, an artifact of machine damage doubling, is seen north and east of the final D.

All quarters of this date have a higher rim on the reverse than do later silver quarters issued 1934 to 1964.

1932-S WASHINGTON QUARTER
Circulation-Strike Mintage: 408,000
OCG: MS-64

The S-Mint quarter ranks right behind the 1932-D
as a key to the series.

1932-S • Market Values • Circulation Strikes

EF-40	AU-50	MS-60	MS-63	MS-64	MS-65	MS-66
$215.	$240.	$500.	$1,400.	$2,750.	$6,750.	$27,000.

1932-S • Certified Populations • Circulation Strikes

Good to AU	MS-60 to MS-62	MS-63	MS-64	MS-65	MS-66	MS-67	MS-68
3,659	1,319	1,175	1,330	137	9	0	0

Key to Collecting: In *worn grades* the 1932-S is slightly scarcer than the 1932-D, as evidenced by finds in circulation decades ago. However, the 1932-D is priced higher (makes no sense!). There are many About Uncirculated 1932-S quarters around—pieces that were plucked from circulation in 1932 and 1933, then spent in the days just before collecting dates and mintmarks became wildly popular, starting in 1934.

Among Mint State coins, most are in lower grades, again representing pieces saved by the public. Quite a few of the About Uncirculated and lower Mint State level 1932 quarters from each of the mints have yellowish toning and/or black specks and freckles, why I don't know. This coloration is not often seen among later dates. Perhaps it is because most of the later ones were taken from bank-wrapped rolls, whereas the 1932 coins were saved one at a time. Mint State 1932-S quarters are more available than are those of 1932-D.

With the 1932-D, the 1932-S is a key to the series—far outranking any other later dates and mints.

Numismatic Notes: All 1932-S quarters are of the Light Motto variety with the edges of the IN GOD WE TRUST letters blending into the field.

All quarters of this date have a higher rim on the reverse than do later silver quarters issued 1934 to 1964.

1934 WASHINGTON QUARTER
Circulation-Strike Mintage: 31,912,052
OCG: MS-64

1934 • Market Values • Circulation Strikes

EF-40	AU-50	MS-60	MS-63	MS-64	MS-65	MS-66
$7.	$9.	$22.	$35.	$45.	$120.	$225.

1934 • Certified Populations • Circulation Strikes

Good to AU	MS-60 to MS-62	MS-63	MS-64	MS-65	MS-66	MS-67	MS-68
223	133	269	833	916	485	103	1

Key to Collecting: The 1934 quarter is readily available in Mint State, although hardly common. Years ago there were only a few bank-wrapped rolls on the market at any given time, and the issue was ranked as quite scarce in comparison to later Philadelphia coins. Most coins have a distinctive satiny finish and are very attractive (the same satin is seen on Peace dollars of this date and mint, but not on other issues of this year). There are several varieties of this date listed below. While most collectors are satisfied with a single example to illustrate the date, the Light Motto, Heavy Motto (easy to find), and Doubled-Die Obverse are sought by many. The Medium Motto is not as popular.

The Light Motto style of the 1934 quarter.

The Medium Motto style of the 1934 quarter.

- *1934 Light Motto (FS-25-1934-401; URS-13)*—This variety was made through the first part of 1932, but was not widely saved (see Numismatic Notes). The same Light Motto style was used for all the coinage of 1932. The center of the W (in WE) is lower than the sides. As this variety is not widely noticed, there is ample opportunity for cherrypicking.

The Heavy Motto style of the 1934 quarter.

- *1934 Medium Motto (FS-25-1934-402; URS-22)*—This variety has the same general letter font as the 1932 with center of the W (in WE) is lower than the sides and somewhat blunt (not pointed as in the Light Motto), but in higher relief. It has thin letters compared to the 1934 Heavy Motto.

FS-25-1934-101.

- *1934, Heavy Motto (FS-25-1934-403; URS-21)*—New obverse with thick, heavy letters in the motto. The center of the W (in WE) is higher than the sides.

- *1934, Doubled-Die Obverse (FS-25-1934-101, Breen-4272; URS-12)*—Prominent doubling, especially at the motto (Medium Motto). The reverse is slightly doubled, one of just a few doubled dies listed in the Red Book. Fivaz-Stanton state that this is "one of the strongest and most popular of all Washington quarter varieties. . . ." Quite a few have been run through the certification services, with the current population totaling over 500 pieces, mostly in circulated grades, but with MS-60 to 62: 37; MS-63: 44; MS-65: 47; MS-65: 22; and MS-66: 16.

Numismatic Notes: Notice of the motto differences was published by Edward S. Horowitz, as part of an article, "The Washington Quarter," in *The Numismatist*, October 1944:

> The records of the Philadelphia Mint, which is the only one using the low relief die in 1934, show that on June 30, 1934, working dies were delivered to the Coining Department with the motto "In God We Trust" in higher relief, prepared on order of the director of the Mint. The records there further show that up to June 30, 6,432,000 pieces had been coined that year, all in May and June; and that 25,480,052 were coined from July to December inclusive.

Today, certain of the certification services are attributing 1934 quarters by the three motto differences, but the vast majority in population reports are simply listed as 1934.

1934-D WASHINGTON QUARTER
Circulation-Strike Mintage: 3,527,200
OCG: MS-64

1934-D • Market Values • Circulation Strikes

EF-40	AU-50	MS-60	MS-63	MS-64	MS-65	MS-66
$25.	$85.	$250.	$350.	$575.	$1,500.	$2,700.

1934-D • Certified Populations • Circulation Strikes

Good to AU	MS-60 to MS-62	MS-63	MS-64	MS-65	MS-66	MS-67	MS-68
475	310	479	785	342	96	6	0

Key to Collecting: Mint State coins are scarce in relation to most later issues, but enough are around that you will find one without difficulty. The luster is of a pleasing but unusual matte-satiny finish, as also used on Peace silver dollars of this year and mint. Dies were prepared at the Philadelphia Mint and shipped unhardened to Denver, where they were hardened and finished for use. Some special process must have been used for quarters and dollars of this date (but not cents, dimes, or nickels).

Medium and Heavy Motto varieties exist, but are not widely known or collected. Most numismatists are content to have just one example of this date and mint. See illustrations under 1932.

Although the 1934-D was minted to the extent of several million coins, this was a year deep in the Depression, and few were saved. This and the 1932-D are the only quarter dollars that I have never handled in roll quantities. I have always considered this to be a sleeper, but not many agree with me, as the published mintage figure is so generous.

- *1934-D, Medium Motto*—This variety has the same general letter font as the 1932, with the center of the W (in WE) is lower than the sides, but in higher relief. It has thin letters compared to other varieties of the year. Opinion is divided as to whether the Medium Motto is scarcer than the Heavy Motto, or vice versa. In his 1988 *Encyclopedia* Walter Breen estimated the production as 1,000,000 Medium Motto and 2,500,000 Heavy Motto, but in the marketplace the Medium Motto is seen more often. David W. Lange of NGC suggests that Breen's estimates should be reversed.[1] Estimated mintage for this variety is 2,000,000. Certification service data are not of much use, for most 1934-D quarters have not been attributed as to the motto style.

FS-25-1934D-501.

- *1934-D, Heavy Motto*—New obverse with thick, heavy letters in the motto. Center of W (WE) higher than the sides. Estimated mintage: 1,500,000.
- *1934-D, Heavy Motto (FS-25-1934D-501; URS-3)*—Small, heavy mintmark as on 1932-D, presumably from a leftover die.

Numismatic Notes: On a minority of coins the D mintmark is small and heavy, similar to that used on 1932-D. On most a large mintmark is seen.

1935 WASHINGTON QUARTER
Circulation-Strike Mintage: 32,484,000
OCG: MS-64

1935 • Market Values • Circulation Strikes

EF-40	AU-50	MS-60	MS-63	MS-64	MS-65	MS-66
$7.	$9.	$22.	$35.	$40.	$120.	$220.

1935 • Certified Populations • Circulation Strikes

Good to AU	MS-60 to MS-62	MS-63	MS-64	MS-65	MS-66	MS-67	MS-68
124	96	193	737	1,123	921	168	1

Key to Collecting: Beginning this year, bank-wrapped rolls were saved in quantity of all Washington quarters except 1936-D. The 1935 is plentiful today, but in view of the demand for such coins they are no longer seen in quantity. The typical coin is well struck and richly lustrous. An MS-65 coin, selected for eye appeal, will be just right for the advanced collector.

Numismatic Notes: All 1935 quarters from each of the mints are of the Medium Motto variety, even though the Heavy Motto had been created in 1934 and would become the standard from 1936 onward.

1935-D WASHINGTON QUARTER
Circulation-Strike Mintage: 5,780,000
OCG: MS-64

1935-D • Market Values • Circulation Strikes

EF-40	AU-50	MS-60	MS-63	MS-64	MS-65	MS-66
$20.	$125.	$250.	$300.	$350.	$900.	$1,650.

1935-D • Certified Populations • Circulation Strikes

Good to AU	MS-60 to MS-62	MS-63	MS-64	MS-65	MS-66	MS-67	MS-68
319	170	290	843	530	200	15	0

Key to Collecting: The 1935-D is easily enough available in an absolute sense, but is at least five times more elusive than the 1935 Philadelphia issue in choice and gem Mint State, MS-63 and above. Examples usually have rich frost and good eye appeal.

Numismatic Notes: All 1935 quarters from each of the mints are of the Medium Motto variety.

1935-S WASHINGTON QUARTER
Circulation-Strike Mintage: 5,660,000
OCG: MS-64

1935-S • Market Values • Circulation Strikes

EF-40	AU-50	MS-60	MS-63	MS-64	MS-65	MS-66
$15.	$38.	$100.	$135.	$165.	$350.	$650.

1935-S • Certified Populations • Circulation Strikes

Good to AU	MS-60 to MS-62	MS-63	MS-64	MS-65	MS-66	MS-67	MS-68
286	191	363	817	621	289	39	0

Key to Collecting: The 1935-S is similar to the 1935-D, but seen more often. Years ago, rolls of the 1935-S were easily found, while those of 1935-D required some searching. High-grade examples usually have excellent frost and good eye appeal.

Numismatic Notes: All 1935 quarters from each of the mints are of the Medium Motto variety.

1936 WASHINGTON QUARTER
Circulation-Strike Mintage: 41,300,000
OCG: MS-64
Proof Mintage: 3,837
OCG: PF-64

In 1936, Proofs of Washington quarters first became available.

1936 • Market Values • Circulation Strikes and Proof Strikes

EF-40	AU-50	MS-60	MS-63	MS-64	MS-65	MS-66	PF-63	PF-64	PF-65	PF-66
$5.	$10.	$21.	$32.	$40.	$100.	$180.	$850.	$1,150.	$1,800.	$4,000.

1936 • Certified Populations • Circulation Strikes and Proof Strikes

Good to AU	MS-60 to MS-62	MS-63	MS-64	MS-65	MS-66	MS-67	MS-68	PF-63	PF-64	PF-65	PF-66	PF-67	PF-68	PF-69	PF-70
94	57	160	647	1,069	553	87	1	251	700	401	225	23	0	0	0

Key to Collecting: This is the first really common date in Mint State, with at least two or three times more known than of the 1935, which itself is plentiful. Occasionally, bags of these traded in the early 1950s, this being the earliest Washington quarter I ever encountered in this quantity. Today, millions of collectors later, such hoards have been dispersed and like most Washington quarters of the 1930s, the 1936 is usually seen singly or on small groups. Most are brilliant, lustrous, and attractive. Proofs are often seen on the market, but are the scarcest of any issue from this year to the present.

FS-25-1936-101.

- *1936, Doubled-Die Obverse*—With very noticeable doubling in the motto, especially at the uprights of I (IN) and the first T in TRUST. Fivaz-Stanton write: "This very rare variety is always in very high demand." Only 76 examples have been certified, including MS-60 to 62: 11; MS-63: 12; MS-64: 8; MS-65: 1; MS-66: 2; MS-67: 1. This is a good variety to cherrypick, as most 1936 quarters have not been checked for this feature.

Numismatic Notes: Beginning in this year the Heavy Motto variety (used for some 1934 and 1934-D coinage) became the standard. Proofs were offered as part of five coin sets (cent, nickel, dime, quarter, half dollar) for $1.81 or could be purchased singly. This method of ordering prevailed through 1942.

1936-D WASHINGTON QUARTER
Circulation-Strike Mintage: 5,374,000
OCG: MS-64

1936-D • Market Values • Circulation Strikes

EF-40	AU-50	MS-60	MS-63	MS-64	MS-65	MS-66
$45.	$250.	$550.	$900.	$1,250.	$1,650.	$3,200.

1936-D • Certified Populations • Circulation Strikes

Good to AU	MS-60 to MS-62	MS-63	MS-64	MS-65	MS-66	MS-67	MS-68
574	305	420	781	370	172	14	0

Key to Collecting: The 1936-D quarter has always been scarce in Mint State, but common in worn grades. Rolls of 1936-S were saved in quantity, but not 1936-D. Finding a lustrous, attractive 1936-D will take some doing, but will hardly be a problem, as at any given time there are examples on the market. Circulated coins are common, but in my opinion overpriced (see notes below).

Breen's *Encyclopedia* lists a 1936-D, D over horizontal D (Breen-4285). The D mintmark was first punched into the die with the rounded part facing down, 90° to the right of normal. A correct D was then overpunched. Little has reached print about this variety. Bill Fivaz commented, "I do not believe this exists. It is not listed in the James Wiles book, nor have J.T. Stanton and I included it in the *Cherrypicker's Guide to Rare Die Varieties.*"[2]

Numismatic Notes: In 1936 at the Denver Mint, 5,374,000 Washington quarters were produced, certainly a common coin by any consideration. Thus, numismatists did not bother to save them. Moreover, many were busy with the great commemorative coin craze. A number of years later, according to Lee F. Hewitt, founder and editor of the *Numismatic Scrapbook Magazine,* when Wayte Raymond's "National" holders had been popular for a few years and when Whitman and other holders became available in quantity, it was discovered that Uncirculated examples of this "common" variety were relatively scarce. Today, the 1936-D remains a key issue in Mint State. However, worn pieces are not at all difficult to find. They exist in proportion to their original mintage. There is no logical reason why a worn 1936-D in a grade such as Very Fine, Extremely Fine, or About Uncirculated should be priced more than a worn 1936-S. The only reason this has happened is that those who know that *Mint State* are scarce, assume *all* are scarce.

1936-S WASHINGTON QUARTER
Circulation-Strike Mintage: 3,828,000
OCG: MS-64

1936-S • Market Values • Circulation Strikes

EF-40	AU-50	MS-60	MS-63	MS-64	MS-65	MS-66
$15.	$50.	$120.	$150.	$200.	$425.	$550.

1936-S • Certified Populations • Circulation Strikes

Good to AU	MS-60 to MS-62	MS-63	MS-64	MS-65	MS-66	MS-67	MS-68
116	84	287	982	940	300	32	0

Key to Collecting: Many rolls of 1936-S were saved in and around the year of issue, making quantities plentiful on the market until the 1960s, when the expansion of the hobby caused most rolls to be broken apart and distributed. The typical 1936-S is lustrous and attractive.

The 1936-S, Repunched Mintmark (URS-2) has the final S dramatically punched over a previous S to the south-southeast and was discovered by Jose Cortez. A few pieces have been noticed by the certification services. Although this variety is not in great demand, if you want one, simply look through regular 1936-S quarters until you locate an example

1937 WASHINGTON QUARTER
Circulation-Strike Mintage: 19,696,000
OCG: MS-64
Proof Mintage: 5,542
OCG: PF-64

1937 • Market Values • Circulation Strikes and Proof Strikes

EF-40	AU-50	MS-60	MS-63	MS-64	MS-65	MS-66	PF-63	PF-64	PF-65	PF-66
$5.	$18.	$25.	$35.	$40.	$90.	$250.	$345.	$485.	$750.	$875.

1937 • Certified Populations • Circulation Strikes and Proof Strikes

Good to AU	MS-60 to MS-62	MS-63	MS-64	MS-65	MS-66	MS-67	MS-68	PF-63	PF-64	PF-65	PF-66	PF-67	PF-68	PF-69	PF-70
62	42	98	496	632	470	98	0	146	507	682	476	153	11	1	0

Key to Collecting: The 1937 is plentiful in all Mint State categories up through 66, but somewhat scarcer above that. Most quarters of this date have not been run through a certification service, so be careful when contemplating paying a high price for a condition rarity. In the future, more will be certified.

Proofs of this year are the second scarcest date from 1936 to the present. The mintage of 5,542 coins was the lowest for any Proof denomination of the 1937 year.

- *1937, Doubled-Die Obverse (FS-25-1937-101, Breen-4287; URS-7)* This variety has very noticeable doubling at the bases of the letters in the motto and at the date. Listed in the Red Book, most known pieces are in circulated grades. Gem Mint State coins are rare. Fivaz-Stanton say this is "considered one of the most important varieties in the series."

- *Reverse B*—This variety was introduced on Proofs in 1937. The relief was strengthened by lowering the field, and the ES (STATES) became distinctly separated. *Two bold leaves to left of arrowheads. Stronger leaf touches or nearly touches top of A (DOLLAR).* Leaf touches on some Proofs; nearly touches on dies which were more extensively relapped. Stronger than on Variety A. Certain letters and the edges of feathers were retouched. Used on Proofs of 1937 to 1964 and circulation strikes from 1959 to 1964. Details on the Proofs are sharper than on circulation strikes.

FS-25-1937-101, showing doubling on the date and motto.

- *Reverse B*—Circulation strikes have the Variety A reverse; Proofs have the Variety B reverse (see chapter 5) used on Proofs 1937 to 1964.

1937-D WASHINGTON QUARTER
Circulation-Strike Mintage: 7,189,600
OCG: MS-65

1937-D • Market Values • Circulation Strikes

EF-40	AU-50	MS-60	MS-63	MS-64	MS-65	MS-66
$15.	$30.	$70.	$85.	$120.	$155.	$360.

1937-D • Certified Populations • Circulation Strikes

Good to AU	MS-60 to MS-62	MS-63	MS-64	MS-65	MS-66	MS-67	MS-68
82	83	206	775	822	291	37	0

Key to Collecting: The 1937-D is another date from the 1930s that was saved in roll quantities. The typical specimen is very lustrous and with good eye appeal.

1937-S WASHINGTON QUARTER
Circulation-Strike Mintage: 1,652,000
OCG: MS-65

1937-S • Market Values • Circulation Strikes

EF-40	AU-50	MS-60	MS-63	MS-64	MS-65	MS-66
$35.	$95.	$150.	$205.	$275.	$350.	$625.

1937-S • Certified Populations • Circulation Strikes

Good to AU	MS-60 to MS-62	MS-63	MS-64	MS-65	MS-66	MS-67	MS-68
118	110	269	920	713	243	35	0

Key to Collecting: With its enticingly low mintage the 1937-S has always been high on the list of collectors' favorites. Mint State coins, while somewhat scarce, are available in the marketplace. Most are lustrous and very attractive. In the context of quarters of the 1930s, circulated coins are elusive.

Numismatic Notes: This is the third-lowest mintage issue in the series (after 1932-S and 1932-D). However, many were saved in roll quantities. James F. Ruddy and I sought to buy all the rolls we could find of these, circa the late 1950s, and were able to find only a few dozen. In contrast, it would have been possible to purchase hundreds of rolls of 1937 (in particular) and 1937-D.

In an article, "Investing in Washington Quarters," in *The Numismatist*, October 1944, Edward S. Horowitz included this: "Two later dates of Washington quarters are probably underrated, and may stage a surprise some day. They are the 1937-S quarter, with a total coinage of only 1,652,000, and the 1939-S quarter with a coinage of 2,628,000. In comparison with other recent coins of greater coinage, they are behind the market."

David W. Lange comments:

> Aside from its scarcity, there is something else that sets the 1937-S quarter dollar apart from every other issue in this long running series. For reasons now forgotten, the obverse rim of the 1937-S quarter was raised above the normal level. . . . It isn't really noticeable on Uncirculated coins. Since most collectors of the Washington series don't bother with worn examples, it's easy to overlook this phenomenon. Still, the obverse rim of 1937-S quarters is clearly higher than on other dates, a fact that becomes quite apparent when examining heavily worn coins. On all Washington quarters, the reverse typically wears more rapidly than the obverse. The inadequacy of the reverse rim in protecting this side from wear is a hallmark of the series. But on the 1937-S quarters the discrepancy in wear is almost ludicrous. The typical coin of this date grading Good on its reverse will grade anywhere from Very Good to Fine on its obverse. One grading as low as About Good on its reverse will still show a complete obverse rim.[3]

1938 WASHINGTON QUARTER
Circulation-Strike Mintage: 9,472,000
OCG: MS-65
Proof Mintage: 8,045
OCG: PF-64

1938 • Market Values • Circulation Strikes and Proof Strikes

EF-40	AU-50	MS-60	MS-63	MS-64	MS-65	MS-66	PF-63	PF-64	PF-65	PF-66
$15.	$45.	$95.	$105.	$150.	$215.	$425.	$160.	$250.	$450.	$575.

1938 • Certified Populations • Circulation Strikes and Proof Strikes

Good to AU	MS-60 to MS-62	MS-63	MS-64	MS-65	MS-66	MS-67	MS-68	PF-63	PF-64	PF-65	PF-66	PF-67	PF-68	PF-69	PF-70
96	75	155	488	634	375	74	1	191	672	881	651	139	11	0	0

Key to Collecting: The 1938 in Mint State has always been scarce, the key issue among Philadelphia Mint quarters in the series. The reason may be that as Proofs were available, not many rolls were saved. In the early 1950s, when roll and bag quantities of Uncirculated Washington quarters often traded among dealers, single rolls of the 1938 were hard to find. The typical coin is lustrous and attractive.

Proofs exist in proportion to their mintage, with probably 7,000 or so surviving from the original distribution of 8,045.

Numismatic Notes: Circulation strikes have the Variety A reverse; Proofs have the Variety B reverse (see chapter 5) used on Proofs from 1937 to 1964. Allen Harriman, writing in the *Coin Dealer Newsletter, Monthly Supplement,* July 1980, commented: "This low mintage issue is by far the scarcest of all the P-mint Washington quarters." I do not dispute this statement.

1938-S Washington Quarter
Circulation-Strike Mintage: 2,832,000
OCG: MS-64

1938-S • Market Values • Circulation Strikes

EF-40	AU-50	MS-60	MS-63	MS-64	MS-65	MS-66
$20.	$55.	$105.	$130.	$180.	$265.	$400.

1938-S • Certified Populations • Circulation Strikes

Good to AU	MS-60 to MS-62	MS-63	MS-64	MS-65	MS-66	MS-67	MS-68
91	63	186	788	991	509	58	1

Key to Collecting: The 1938-S is on the scarce side by virtue of its low mintage. Because of this it is a long time favorite. As is true of most other quarters of the era, Mint State coins are apt to be lustrous and with good eye appeal.

1939 Washington Quarter
Circulation-Strike Mintage: 33,540,000
OCG: MS-64
Proof Mintage: 8,795
OCG: PF-64

1939 • Market Values • Circulation Strikes and Proof Strikes

EF-40	AU-50	MS-60	MS-63	MS-64	MS-65	MS-66	PF-63	PF-64	PF-65	PF-66
$4.	$12.	$15.	$25.	$30.	$60.	$100.	$160.	$225.	$400.	$500.

1939 • Certified Populations • Circulation Strikes and Proof Strikes

Good to AU	MS-60 to MS-62	MS-63	MS-64	MS-65	MS-66	MS-67	MS-68	PF-63	PF-64	PF-65	PF-66	PF-67	PF-68	PF-69	PF-70
71	37	107	478	971	1,111	375	5	153	482	830	804	227	12	0	0

Key to Collecting: Plentiful by virtue of its large mintage. Choice and gem Mint State examples abound. Proofs are scarce, but when found are usually of choice or gem quality.

Numismatic Notes: Circulation strikes have the Variety A reverse; Proofs have the Variety B reverse (see chapter 5) used on Proofs 1937 to 1964.

1939-D WASHINGTON QUARTER
Circulation-Strike Mintage: 7,092,000
OCG: MS-64

1939-D • Market Values • Circulation Strikes

EF-40	AU-50	MS-60	MS-63	MS-64	MS-65	MS-66
$11.	$20.	$40.	$50.	$65.	$115.	$225.

1939-D • Certified Populations • Circulation Strikes

Good to AU	MS-60 to MS-62	MS-63	MS-64	MS-65	MS-66	MS-67	MS-68
80	54	184	587	962	596	82	0

Key to Collecting: Easily available in any grade desired.

Numismatic Notes: Some have a heavily punched mintmark with the center opening small, others have a lighter mintmark with the opening larger. Several varieties of repunched mintmarks are described by James Wiles.

1939-D/S WASHINGTON QUARTER
Circulation-Strike Mintage: Small part of
   1939-D mintage.
OCG: MS-65

FS-25-1939D-501.

1939-D/S • Market Values • Circulation Strikes

EF-40	AU-50	MS-60	MS-63	MS-64	MS-65	MS-66
$100.	$125.	$250.	$350.	$525.	$650.	—

1939-D/S • Certified Populations • Circulation Strikes

Not recorded by the grading services.

Key to Collecting: This is a very rare variety. If you opt to include overmintmarks as part of your date and mintmark collection, this will be a great challenge. The open center of the D mintmark shows the center curve of a previous S, and part of the left upper curve of the S can be seen to the left of the upright of D. Listed by Fivaz and Stanton as URS-2, indicating great rarity. However, as this overmintmark is not widely known, here is an opportunity for cherrypicking. Check all of the regular 1939-D quarters you can find. Fivaz and Stanton designate this variety as FS-25-1939-D-501.

Numismatic Notes: As the Fivaz-Stanton text points out, this is the *real* 1939-D/S. Some repunched D 1939-D coins have been illustrated as "1939-D/S."

1939-S Washington Quarter

Circulation-Strike Mintage: 2,628,000
OCG: MS-64

1939-S • Market Values • Circulation Strikes

EF-40	AU-50	MS-60	MS-63	MS-64	MS-65	MS-66
$20.	$60.	$95.	$135.	$210.	$325.	$450.

1939-S • Certified Populations • Circulation Strikes

Good to AU	MS-60 to MS-62	MS-63	MS-64	MS-65	MS-66	MS-67	MS-68
102	70	166	563	741	393	41	0

Key to Collecting: Although the 1939-S has the fourth lowest mintage figure in the series (after 1932-S, 1932-D, and 1937-S), many were saved in roll quantities, and on an absolute basis they are not *rare*. However, in the context of the several hundred varieties of Washington quarters made from 1932 to date, it is one of the scarcer issues.

Numismatic Notes: See 1937-S.

1940 Washington Quarter

Circulation-Strike Mintage: 35,704,000
OCG: MS-64
Proof Mintage: 11,246
OCG: PF-64

1940 • Market Values • Circulation Strikes and Proof Strikes

EF-40	AU-50	MS-60	MS-63	MS-64	MS-65	MS-66	PF-63	PF-64	PF-65	PF-66
$4.	$6.	$17.	$35.	$45.	$60.	$90.	$120.	$175.	$350.	$400.

1940 • Certified Populations • Circulation Strikes and Proof Strikes

MS-63	MS-64	MS-65	MS-66	MS-67	MS-68	PF-63	PF-64	PF-65	PF-66	PF-67	PF-68	PF-69	PF-70
39	194	514	695	208	1	133	564	989	971	304	18	0	0

Key to Collecting: Easily available, a comment that pertains to all other standard date and mintmark issues from this point forward. Proofs are slightly scarce, per the mintage.

Numismatic Notes: Circulation strikes have the Variety A reverse; Proofs have the Variety B reverse (see chapter 5) used on Proofs 1937 to 1964.

1940-D WASHINGTON QUARTER
Circulation-Strike Mintage: 2,797,600
OCG: MS-65

1940-D • Market Values • Circulation Strikes

EF-40	AU-50	MS-60	MS-63	MS-64	MS-65	MS-66
$24.	$65.	$120.	$165.	$240.	$315.	$500.

1940-D • Certified Populations • Circulation Strikes

MS-63	MS-64	MS-65	MS-66	MS-67	MS-68
166	717	777	430	53	1

Key to Collecting: In the context of quarters of the decade the 1940-D is slightly scarce. See the following notes.

- *1940-D, Doubled-Die Obverse (FS-25-1940D-101; URS-6)*—With light doubling, most notable at the bases of the letters in the motto (more prominent on the motto). Fivaz-Stanton state: "This is a very attractive doubled die!"

FS-25-1940D-101.

- *1940-D, Dramatically Repunched Mintmark (FS-25-1940D-501; URS-3)* The Final D mintmark is separated from and punched to the east of an earlier, lighter D. Fivaz-Stanton comment: "This is one of about 10 known repunched mintmarks [across all United States coin series] that are totally separated." Also see 1941-D from the same reverse die. Discovered by Lee Hiemke in recent times, this dramatic variety was overlooked by a generation of earlier collectors.

FS-25-1940D-501.

Numismatic Notes: In "Grading Insights," *Coin World,* Randy Campbell commented:

The 1940-D Washington quarter dollar, with a mintage of about 2.8 million, has always been popular with collectors and dealers. The typical 1940-D Washington quarter dollar displays a wide range of luster quality. Full gems will have blazing, original, mint frost. However, many examples of this date exhibit substandard luster that is impaired by cleaning, overdipping or improper storage. A significant percentage of 1940-D Washington quarter dollars will have worse than average surface abrasions. Those that are moderately contact marked tend to grade in the MS-63 to MS-64 range. Those with heavy contact marks usually grade MS-60 to MS-62 (if they are still Uncirculated).[4]

1940-S WASHINGTON QUARTER
Circulation-Strike Mintage: 8,244,000
OCG: MS-65

1940-S • Market Values • Circulation Strikes

EF-40	AU-50	MS-60	MS-63	MS-64	MS-65	MS-66
$8.50	$16.	$21.	$32.	$45.	$65.	$125.

1940-S • Certified Populations • Circulation Strikes

MS-63	MS-64	MS-65	MS-66	MS-67	MS-68
58	362	903	751	158	3

Key to Collecting: A popular and easily available variety.

1941 WASHINGTON QUARTER
Circulation-Strike Mintage: 79,032,000
OCG: MS-65
Proof Mintage: 15,287
OCG: PF-64

1941 • Market Values • Circulation Strikes and Proof Strikes

EF-40	AU-50	MS-60	MS-63	MS-64	MS-65	MS-66	PF-63	PF-64	PF-65	PF-66
$4.	$6.	$8.	$14.	$22.	$37.	$85.	$100.	$135.	$250.	$300.

1941 • Certified Populations • Circulation Strikes and Proof Strikes

MS-63	MS-64	MS-65	MS-66	MS-67	MS-68	PF-63	PF-64	PF-65	PF-66	PF-67	PF-68	PF-69	PF-70
49	297	1,443	1,177	227	35	159	722	1,231	1,125	297	20	0	0

Key to Collecting: Plentiful in Mint State. Proofs of this era usually show light gray or hazy toning unless they have been dipped.

- *1941, Doubled-Die Obverse (FS-25-1941-101; URS-7 / FS-25-1941-102)* With light doubling, most notable at GOD WE and UST in the motto. Several other doubled-die obverses exist for 1941.

FS-25-1941-101.

Numismatic Notes: Circulation strikes have the Variety A reverse; Proofs have the Variety B reverse (see chapter 5) used on Proofs 1937 to 1964.

FS-25-1941-102.

1941-D Washington Quarter
Circulation-Strike Mintage: 16,714,800
OCG: MS-65

1941-D • Market Values • Circulation Strikes

EF-40	AU-50	MS-60	MS-63	MS-64	MS-65	MS-66
$7.	$13.	$32.	$58.	$63.	$68.	$200.

1941-D • Certified Populations • Circulation Strikes

MS-63	MS-64	MS-65	MS-66	MS-67	MS-68
63	273	641	487	112	1

Key to Collecting: A popular and readily available issue.
- *1941-D, Dramatically Repunched Mintmark (FS-25-1941D-801; URS-7)*—Final D mintmark separated from and punched to the east of an earlier, lighter D. Reverse die used for 1940-D as well.

1941-S Washington Quarter
Circulation-Strike Mintage: 16,080,000
OCG: MS-65

1941-S • Market Values • Circulation Strikes

EF-40	AU-50	MS-60	MS-63	MS-64	MS-65	MS-66
$5.	$11.	$28.	$55.	$60.	$65.	$150.

1941-S • Certified Populations • Circulation Strikes

MS-63	MS-64	MS-65	MS-66	MS-67	MS-68
103	449	761	516	90	0

Key to Collecting: Readily available in choice and gem preservation.

Numismatic Notes: Large and small mintmark varieties per the Red Book and Breen *Encyclopedia*. The elusive Large S was used on at least four dies. The lower left serif is called the "trumpet tail" due to its shape. Some have the upper loop of the S filled. The *Cherrypickers' Guide to Rare Die Varieties* gives illustrations and details.

1942 Washington Quarter

Circulation-Strike Mintage: 102,096,000
OCG: MS-65
Proof Mintage: 21,123
OCG: PF-64

1942 • Market Values • Circulation Strikes and Proof Strikes

EF-40	AU-50	MS-60	MS-63	MS-64	MS-65	MS-66	PF-63	PF-64	PF-65	PF-66
$3.	$4.	$6.	$9.	$15.	$35.	$180.	$75.	$115.	$250.	$300.

1942 • Certified Populations • Circulation Strikes and Proof Strikes

MS-63	MS-64	MS-65	MS-66	MS-67	MS-68	PF-63	PF-64	PF-65	PF-66	PF-67	PF-68	PF-69	PF-70
73	244	587	490	101	0	269	1,051	1,723	1,437	313	20	0	0

Key to Collecting: Circulation strikes are plentiful. Proofs, while scarce in comparison to those of the 1950s and later, have the highest mintage of the early years, 1936 to 1942. No further Proofs were made until 1950.

- *1942, Doubled-Die Obverse (FS 25-1942-101; URS-5)*—This variety doubles on the motto, especially on GOD and TRUST, and is listed in the Red Book.

Numismatic Notes: Circulation strikes have the Variety A reverse; Proofs have the Variety B reverse (see chapter 5) used on Proofs 1937 to 1964. Doubled-Die Reverses are known to exist for 1942 and are described in the *Cherrypickers' Guide to Rare Die Varieties.*

1942-D Washington Quarter

Circulation-Strike Mintage: 17,487,200
OCG: MS-65

1942-D • Market Values • Circulation Strikes

EF-40	AU-50	MS-60	MS-63	MS-64	MS-65	MS-66
$5.	$10.	$17.	$20.	$25.	$38.	$125.

1942-D • Certified Populations • Circulation Strikes

MS-63	MS-64	MS-65	MS-66	MS-67	MS-68
86	215	650	732	172	2

Key to Collecting: Popular and readily available wartime issue.
- *1942-D, Doubled-Die Obverse (FS 25-1942-D-101; URS-9)* Doubling on LIBERTY, the date, and the motto, this coin is one of just a few doubled-die varieties to be listed in the Red Book. Fivaz-Stanton praise the coin as "one of the 'Top 10' Washington quarter varieties."

FS-25-1942D-101.

1942-S WASHINGTON QUARTER
Circulation-Strike Mintage: 19,384,000
OCG: MS-65

1942-S • Market Values • Circulation Strikes

EF-40	AU-50	MS-60	MS-63	MS-64	MS-65	MS-66
$15.	$20.	$70.	$115.	$150.	$165.	$325.

1942-S • Certified Populations • Circulation Strikes

MS-63	MS-64	MS-65	MS-66	MS-67	MS-68
216	713	705	393	78	1

Key to Collecting: Popular and readily available wartime issue.

Numismatic Notes: Breen distinguishes between sharp-serif and knob-tailed S mintmarks.

1943 WASHINGTON QUARTER
Circulation-Strike Mintage: 99,700,000
OCG: MS-64

1943 • Market Values • Circulation Strikes

EF-40	AU-50	MS-60	MS-63	MS-64	MS-65	MS-66
$3.	$4.	$5.	$9.	$15.	$40.	$90.

1943 • Certified Populations • Circulation Strikes

MS-63	MS-64	MS-65	MS-66	MS-67	MS-68
60	259	946	1,112	294	4

Key to Collecting: Easily available high-mintage issue. Beginning in this year, collectors, dealers, and investors set aside bank-wrapped rolls in much larger quantities than for earlier times. The Michael Higgy sale (Abe Kosoff, September 1943) saw record prices realized for scarce and rare coins of many denominations. This focused attention on current coins as well, resulting in an acceleration of investing interest. In addition, in this wartime period cash was plentiful and consumer goods were scarce. Current coins were a good place to park available funds.

FS-25-1943-102.

- *1943, Doubled-Die Obverse (FS-25-1943-102; URS-2)*—Doubling on LIBERTY, the motto, and the date, this coin is . one of just a few doubled-die varieties to be listed in the Red Book.

1943-D WASHINGTON QUARTER
Circulation-Strike Mintage: 16,095,600
OCG: MS-65

1943-D • Market Values • Circulation Strikes

EF-40	AU-50	MS-60	MS-63	MS-64	MS-65	MS-66
$8.	$15.	$28.	$39.	$43.	$50.	$125.

1943-D • Certified Populations • Circulation Strikes

MS-63	MS-64	MS-65	MS-66	MS-67	MS-68
53	221	681	726	165	0

Key to Collecting: Easily available in choice and gem Mint State. As a general rule for this era, the branch mint coins were saved in smaller quantities than were Philadelphia quarters. However, enough were set aside that all are plentiful today.

- *1943-D, D over horizontal D (Breen-4321)*—D first punched into the die with rounded part facing up, 90° to the left of normal. A correct D was then over-punched.

1943-S WASHINGTON QUARTER
Circulation-Strike Mintage: 21,700,000
OCG: MS-65

1943-S • Market Values • Circulation Strikes

EF-40	AU-50	MS-60	MS-63	MS-64	MS-65	MS-66
$9.	$13.	$26.	$42.	$44.	$50.	$125.

1943-S • Certified Populations • Circulation Strikes

MS-63	MS-64	MS-65	MS-66	MS-67	MS-68
55	382	894	817	174	2

Key to Collecting: Plentiful and popular. Although quality is usually not a problem with quarters of the 1950s through 1964, cherrypicking for nice luster and eye appeal is worthwhile.

- *1943-S Doubled-Die Obverse (FS-1943S-1-101)*—One of just a few doubled-die varieties to be listed in the Red Book.

FS-25-1943S-1-101.

1944 WASHINGTON QUARTER

Circulation-Strike Mintage: 104,956,000
OCG: MS-65

1944 • Market Values • Circulation Strikes

EF-40	AU-50	MS-60	MS-63	MS-64	MS-65	MS-66
$3.	$4.	$5.	$9.	$15.	$35.	$75.

1944 • Certified Populations • Circulation Strikes

MS-63	MS-64	MS-65	MS-66	MS-67	MS-68
49	201	1,100	1,344	299	1

Key to Collecting: One of the most common issues of the era.

Numismatic Notes: All 1944 quarters show doubling on the earlobe and nostril from doubling of the master hub or master die.

1944-D WASHINGTON QUARTER

Circulation-Strike Mintage: 14,600,800
OCG: MS-65

1944-D • Market Values • Circulation Strikes

EF-40	AU-50	MS-60	MS-63	MS-64	MS-65	MS-66
$7.	$10.	$17.	$19.	$21.	$38.	$85.

1944-D • Certified Populations • Circulation Strikes

Good to AU	MS-60 to MS-62	MS-63	MS-64	MS-65	MS-66	MS-67	MS-68
15	23	59	219	928	1,178	501	4

Key to Collecting: Choice and gem Mint State coins are readily available. As is true of most other quarters of this era, the typical Uncirculated coin taken from a bank-wrapped roll is apt to be MS-63 or MS-64.

Numismatic Notes: All 1944 quarters show doubling on the earlobe and nostril from doubling of the master hub or master die.

1944-S WASHINGTON QUARTER
Circulation-Strike Mintage: 12,560,000
OCG: MS-65

1944-S • Market Values • Circulation Strikes

EF-40	AU-50	MS-60	MS-63	MS-64	MS-65	MS-66
$7.	$10.	$14.	$20.	$21.	$35.	$80.

1944-S • Certified Populations • Circulation Strikes

MS-63	MS-64	MS-65	MS-66	MS-67	MS-68
36	225	902	1,146	289	5

Key to Collecting: Choice and gem Mint State coins are readily available.

- *1944-S, Doubled-Die Obverse (FS-1944S-101)*—This variety is also listed in the Breen *Encyclopedia*.

Numismatic Notes: All 1944 quarters show doubling on the earlobe and nostril from doubling of the master hub or master die.

FS-25-1944S-101.

1945 WASHINGTON QUARTER
Circulation-Strike Mintage: 74,372,000
OCG: MS-65

1945 • Market Values • Circulation Strikes

EF-40	AU-50	MS-60	MS-63	MS-64	MS-65	MS-66
$3.	$4.	$5.	$8.	$15.	$38.	$175.

1945 • Certified Populations • Circulation Strikes

MS-63	MS-64	MS-65	MS-66	MS-67	MS-68
47	207	803	529	96	4

Key to Collecting: Choice and gem Mint State coins are readily available.

- *1945, Doubled-Die Obverse (FS-1945-101)*—This variety is also listed in the Breen *Encyclopedia*.

FS-25-1945-101.

1945-D WASHINGTON QUARTER
Circulation-Strike Mintage: 12,341,600
OCG: MS-65

1945-D • Market Values • Circulation Strikes

EF-40	AU-50	MS-60	MS-63	MS-64	MS-65	MS-66
$8.	$12.	$18.	$25.	$30.	$42.	$90.

1945-D • Certified Populations • Circulation Strikes

MS-63	MS-64	MS-65	MS-66	MS-67	MS-68
37	158	555	640	130	1

Key to Collecting: Choice and gem Mint State coins are readily available.

1945-S WASHINGTON QUARTER
Circulation-Strike Mintage: 17,004,001
OCG: MS-65

1945-S • Market Values • Circulation Strikes

EF-40	AU-50	MS-60	MS-63	MS-64	MS-65	MS-66
$5.	$7.	$9.	$13.	$19.	$35.	$90.

1945-S • Certified Populations • Circulation Strikes

MS-63	MS-64	MS-65	MS-66	MS-67	MS-68
54	229	801	750	177	1

Key to Collecting: Choice and gem Mint State coins are readily available.

Numismatic Notes: There are trumpet-tailed and knob-tailed S varieties.

1946 WASHINGTON QUARTER
Circulation-Strike Mintage: 53,436,000
OCG: MS-65

1946 • Market Values • Circulation Strikes

EF-40	AU-50	MS-60	MS-63	MS-64	MS-65	MS-66
$3.	$4.	$5.	$9.	$17.	$42.	$165.

1946 • Certified Populations • Circulation Strikes

MS-63	MS-64	MS-65	MS-66	MS-67	MS-68
32	179	557	420	89	1

Key to Collecting: Although World War II was over, consumer goods remained scarce. Bank-wrapped rolls of quarters continued to be a popular investment. Today, choice 1946 quarters are easily found.

1946-D Washington Quarter
Circulation-Strike Mintage: 9,072,800
OCG: MS-65

1946-D • Market Values • Circulation Strikes

EF-40	AU-50	MS-60	MS-63	MS-64	MS-65	MS-66
$3.	$5.	$6.	$9.	$20.	$43.	$85.

1946-D • Certified Populations • Circulation Strikes

MS-63	MS-64	MS-65	MS-66	MS-67	MS-68
33	263	1,335	1,517	248	1

Key to Collecting: Readily available, although the mintage is low for the era.

1946-S Washington Quarter
Circulation-Strike Mintage: 4,204,000
OCG: MS-65

1946-S • Market Values • Circulation Strikes

EF-40	AU-50	MS-60	MS-63	MS-64	MS-65	MS-66
$3.	$4.	$5.	$9.	$15.	$47.	$85.

1946-S • Certified Populations • Circulation Strikes

MS-63	MS-64	MS-65	MS-66	MS-67	MS-68
65	453	2,981	2,560	350	8

Key to Collecting: The 1946-S was very popular in its time due to the restricted mintage of just 4,204,000 coins. A higher percentage of pieces than usual went to investors who anticipated they would become scarce. Today, the 1946-S is readily available.

Numismatic Notes: There are trumpet-tailed and knob-tailed S varieties.

1947 WASHINGTON QUARTER
Circulation-Strike Mintage: 22,556,000
OCG: MS-65

1947 • Market Values • Circulation Strikes

EF-40	AU-50	MS-60	MS-63	MS-64	MS-65	MS-66
$3.	$5.	$11.	$19.	$27.	$45.	$90.

1947 • Certified Populations • Circulation Strikes

MS-63	MS-64	MS-65	MS-66	MS-67	MS-68
23	147	751	962	233	0

Key to Collecting: Easily available at different levels of Mint State. From this year through the very early 1950s, the interest in hoarding bank-wrapped rolls diminished. Accordingly, although there are enough 1947 quarters to go around, they and others of the next several years are not as common as are those of the earlier part of the decade.

1947-D WASHINGTON QUARTER
Circulation-Strike Mintage: 15,338,400
OCG: MS-65

1947-D • Market Values • Circulation Strikes

EF-40	AU-50	MS-60	MS-63	MS-64	MS-65	MS-66
$3.	$5.	$11.	$17.	$18.	$40.	$80.

1947-D • Certified Populations • Circulation Strikes

MS-63	MS-64	MS-65	MS-66	MS-67	MS-68
31	165	1,349	1,547	607	0

Key to Collecting: Choice and gem pieces are readily available.

1947-S WASHINGTON QUARTER
Circulation-Strike Mintage: 5,532,000
OCG: MS-65

1947-S • Market Values • Circulation Strikes

EF-40	AU-50	MS-60	MS-63	MS-64	MS-65	MS-66
$3.	$4.	$9.	$15.	$16.	$35.	$80.

1947-S • Certified Populations • Circulation Strikes

MS-63	MS-64	MS-65	MS-66	MS-67	MS-68
38	327	2,221	2,752	705	9

Key to Collecting: The rather low mintage for the 1947-S did not attract much attention at the time (unlike 1946-S). Mint State pieces are readily available.

Numismatic Notes: There are trumpet-tailed and knob-tailed S varieties.

1948 WASHINGTON QUARTER
Circulation-Strike Mintage: 35,196,000
OCG: MS-65

1948 • Market Values • Circulation Strikes

EF-40	AU-50	MS-60	MS-63	MS-64	MS-65	MS-66
$3.	$4.	$5.	$9.	$15.	$40.	$75.

1948 • Certified Populations • Circulation Strikes

MS-63	MS-64	MS-65	MS-66	MS-67	MS-68
39	279	1,305	1,401	325	2

Key to Collecting: Choice and gem Mint State coins are readily available. Mintage figures trended upward this year.

1948-D WASHINGTON QUARTER
Circulation-Strike Mintage: 16,766,800
OCG: MS-65

1948-D • Market Values • Circulation Strikes

EF-40	AU-50	MS-60	MS-63	MS-64	MS-65	MS-66
$4.	$7.	$13.	$18.	$22.	$65.	$120.

1948-D • Certified Populations • Circulation Strikes

MS-63	MS-64	MS-65	MS-66	MS-67	MS-68
40	169	652	614	113	0

Key to Collecting: Choice and gem Mint State coins are readily available.

1948-S WASHINGTON QUARTER
Circulation-Strike Mintage: 15,960,000
OCG: MS-65

1948-S • Market Values • Circulation Strikes

EF-40	AU-50	MS-60	MS-63	MS-64	MS-65	MS-66
$3.	$5.	$7.	$13.	$19.	$45.	$80.

1948-S • Certified Populations • Circulation Strikes

MS-63	MS-64	MS-65	MS-66	MS-67	MS-68
59	294	1,297	1,277	281	2

Key to Collecting: Choice and gem Mint State coins are readily available.

1949 WASHINGTON QUARTER
Circulation-Strike Mintage: 9,312,000
OCG: MS-65

1949 • Market Values • Circulation Strikes

EF-40	AU-50	MS-60	MS-63	MS-64	MS-65	MS-66
$10.	$14.	$35.	$47.	$55.	$60.	$135.

1949 • Certified Populations • Circulation Strikes

MS-63	MS-64	MS-65	MS-66	MS-67	MS-68
54	199	618	749	160	3

Key to Collecting: Choice and gem Mint State coins are readily available. This was a slump year in the coin market, a malaise that continued through 1951. Fewer rolls were saved than previously. However, on an absolute basis enough were set aside that they are not scarce today.

1949-D Washington Quarter
Circulation-Strike Mintage: 10,068,400
OCG: MS-65

1949-D • Market Values • Circulation Strikes

EF-40	AU-50	MS-60	MS-63	MS-64	MS-65	MS-66
$4.	$9.	$16.	$38.	$42.	$50.	$150.

1949-D • Certified Populations • Circulation Strikes

MS-63	MS-64	MS-65	MS-66	MS-67	MS-68
38	227	788	755	156	3

Key to Collecting: Choice and gem Mint State coins are readily available.

- *1949-D Over S (FS-25-1950D-501)*—A 1949D/S overmintmark may exist, but it is not distinct and is not widely sought.

1950 Washington Quarter
Circulation-Strike Mintage: 24,920,126
OCG: MS-65
Proof Mintage: 51,386
OCG: PF-65

1950 • Market Values • Circulation Strikes and Proof Strikes

EF-40	AU-50	MS-60	MS-63	MS-64	MS-65	MS-66	PF-63	PF-64	PF-65	PF-66
$4.	$5.	$7.	$8.	$15.	$35.	$80.	$50.	$60.	$70.	$105.

1950 • Certified Populations • Circulation Strikes and Proof Strikes

MS-63	MS-64	MS-65	MS-66	MS-67	MS-68	PF-64	PF-65	PF-66	PF-67	PF-68	PF-69	PF-70
11	111	601	744	205	0	377	741	735	760	64	3	0

Key to Collecting: Choice and gem Mint State coins are readily available. Proofs were made this year for the first time since 1942. The earlier Proof strikings of 1950 are not as mirrorlike as the later ones made this year.

Numismatic Notes: Circulation strikes have the Variety A reverse; Proofs have the Variety B reverse (see chapter 5) used on Proofs 1937 to 1964.

1950-D WASHINGTON QUARTER
Circulation-Strike Mintage: 21,075,600
OCG: MS-65

1950-D • Market Values • Circulation Strikes

EF-40	AU-50	MS-60	MS-63	MS-64	MS-65	MS-66
$4.	$5.	$6.	$9.	$13.	$35.	$80.

1950-D • Certified Populations • Circulation Strikes

MS-63	MS-64	MS-65	MS-66	MS-67	MS-68
33	143	591	633	207	1

Key to Collecting: Choice and gem Mint State coins are readily available.

1950-D/S WASHINGTON QUARTER
Circulation-Strike Mintage: Small part of
   1950-D mintage
OCG: MS-64

The 1950-D, D Over S variety (FS-25-1950D-601).

1950-D/S • Market Values • Circulation Strikes

EF-40	AU-50	MS-60	MS-63	MS-64	MS-65	MS-66
$135.	$185.	$265.	$400.	$1,000.	$3,000.	$6,750.

1950-D/S • Certified Populations • Circulation Strikes

MS-63	MS-64	MS-65	MS-66	MS-67	MS-68
25	43	17	6	1	0

Key to Collecting: This is a very interesting and desirable variety for the specialist. It is scarcer than market prices indicate, as the demand is not great (but is increasing).

Numismatic Notes: Listed widely, including as FS-1950D-501.

1950-S WASHINGTON QUARTER
Circulation-Strike Mintage: 10,284,004
OCG: MS-65

1950-S • Market Values • Circulation Strikes

EF-40	AU-50	MS-60	MS-63	MS-64	MS-65	MS-66
$4.	$8.	$12.	$16.	$20.	$45.	$80.

1950-S • Certified Populations • Circulation Strikes

MS-63	MS-64	MS-65	MS-66	MS-67	MS-68
44	168	634	872	246	2

Key to Collecting: Choice and gem Mint State coins are readily available.

Numismatic Notes: A variety with double-punched S is known.

1950-S/D Washington Quarter
Circulation-Strike Mintage: Small part of
  1950-D mintage
OCG: MS-65

The 1950-S, S Over D variety (FS-25-1950S-501).

1950-S/D • Market Values • Circulation Strikes

EF-40	AU-50	MS-60	MS-63	MS-64	MS-65	MS-66
$150.	$300.	$400.	$475.	$600.	$1,100.	$3,150.

1950-S/D • Certified Populations • Circulation Strikes

MS-63	MS-64	MS-65	MS-66	MS-67	MS-68
6	50	64	43	9	0

Key to Collecting: Another overmintmark that is somewhat scarce, highly interesting, and well worth owning.

Numismatic Notes: Now listed widely, including as FS-25-1950S-501.

1951 Washington Quarter
Circulation-Strike Mintage: 43,448,102
OCG: MS-65
Proof Mintage: 57,500
OCG: PF-65

1951 • Market Values • Circulation Strikes and Proof Strikes

EF-40	AU-50	MS-60	MS-63	MS-64	MS-65	MS-66	PF-63	PF-64	PF-65	PF-66
$4.	$5.	$6.	$8.	$11.	$30.	$80.	$45.	$55.	$60.	$100.

1951 • Certified Populations • Circulation Strikes and Proof Strikes

MS-63	MS-64	MS-65	MS-66	MS-67	MS-68	PF-64	PF-65	PF-66	PF-67	PF-68	PF-69	PF-70
30	107	661	794	229	1	384	455	480	274	62	9	0

Key to Collecting: Choice and gem Mint State coins are readily available. The Proof mintage is higher than that of 1950. The market remained in a slump in 1951, but would awake soon.

Numismatic Notes: Circulation strikes have the Variety A reverse; Proofs have the Variety B reverse (see chapter 5) used on Proofs 1937 to 1964.

1951-D WASHINGTON QUARTER
Circulation-Strike Mintage: 35,354,800
OCG: MS-65

1951-D • Market Values • Circulation Strikes

EF-40	AU-50	MS-60	MS-63	MS-64	MS-65	MS-66
$4.	$5.	$6.	$7.	$11.	$35.	$80.

1951-D • Certified Populations • Circulation Strikes

MS-63	MS-64	MS-65	MS-66	MS-67	MS-68
31	174	835	790	123	0

Key to Collecting: Choice and gem Mint State coins are readily available.
- *1951-D Over S*—A 1951-D/S overmintmark may exist, but it is not distinct and is not widely sought.

1951-S WASHINGTON QUARTER
Circulation-Strike Mintage: 9,048,000
OCG: MS-65

1951-S • Market Values • Circulation Strikes

EF-40	AU-50	MS-60	MS-63	MS-64	MS-65	MS-66
$5.	$7.	$14.	$27.	$32.	$40.	$80.

1951-S • Certified Populations • Circulation Strikes

MS-63	MS-64	MS-65	MS-66	MS-67	MS-68
25	114	583	883	348	10

Key to Collecting: Choice and gem Mint State coins are readily available.

1952 WASHINGTON QUARTER
Circulation-Strike Mintage: 38,780,093
OCG: MS-65
Proof Mintage: 81,980
OCG: PF-65

1952 • Market Values • Circulation Strikes and Proof Strikes

EF-40	AU-50	MS-60	MS-63	MS-64	MS-65	MS-66	PF-63	PF-64	PF-65	PF-66
$3.	$7.	$10.	$12.	$14.	$21.	$80.	$25.	$35.	$50.	$70.

1952 • Certified Populations • Circulation Strikes and Proof Strikes

MS-63	MS-64	MS-65	MS-66	MS-67	MS-68	PF-64	PF-65	PF-66	PF-67	PF-68	PF-69	PF-70
31	118	416	762	197	1	275	674	1,027	894	221	16	0

Key to Collecting: Choice and gem Mint State coins are readily available. Proofs were rapidly catching on with the public, and it was not unusual for dealers and investors to order five or 10 sets instead of just one. The coin market began to strengthen. In Iola, Wisconsin, Chet Krause launched *Numismatic News,* which went on to become the nucleus of the vast Krause Publications empire, a juggernaut by the 1980s.

Numismatic Notes: Circulation strikes have the Variety A reverse; Proofs have the Variety B reverse (see chapter 5) used on Proofs 1937 to 1964.

1952-D WASHINGTON QUARTER
Circulation-Strike Mintage: 49,795,200
OCG: MS-64

1952-D • Market Values • Circulation Strikes

EF-40	AU-50	MS-60	MS-63	MS-64	MS-65	MS-66
$3.	$4.	$5.	$9.	$11.	$40.	$80.

1952-D • Certified Populations • Circulation Strikes

MS-63	MS-64	MS-65	MS-66	MS-67	MS-68
42	120	500	457	32	0

Key to Collecting: Choice and gem Mint State coins are readily available.

1952-S WASHINGTON QUARTER
Circulation-Strike Mintage: 13,707,800
OCG: MS-65

1952-S • Market Values • Circulation Strikes

EF-40	AU-50	MS-60	MS-63	MS-64	MS-65	MS-66
$5.	$6.	$12.	$25.	$30.	$42.	$80.

1952-S • Certified Populations • Circulation Strikes

MS-63	MS-64	MS-65	MS-66	MS-67	MS-68
17	136	663	1,004	437	14

Key to Collecting: Choice and gem Mint State coins are readily available.

1953 WASHINGTON QUARTER
Circulation-Strike Mintage: 18,536,120
OCG: MS-64
Proof Mintage: 128,800
OCG: PF-65

1953 • Market Values • Circulation Strikes and Proof Strikes

EF-40	AU-50	MS-60	MS-63	MS-64	MS-65	MS-66	PF-63	PF-64	PF-65	PF-66
$3.	$5.	$6.	$10.	$11.	$40.	$80.	$20.	$25.	$50.	$60.

1953 • Certified Populations • Circulation Strikes and Proof Strikes

MS-63	MS-64	MS-65	MS-66	MS-67	MS-68	PF-64	PF-65	PF-66	PF-67	PF-68	PF-69	PF-70
23	126	448	587	111	2	212	482	1,003	1,058	521	21	0

Key to Collecting: Choice and gem Mint State coins are readily available. Proofs were ordered in such record numbers that the Mint became alarmed at the prospect. Soon, limits on orders were put in place, which in the next few years only served to fuel demand further. Beginning about this time, interest in saving bank-wrapped rolls of new coins went into high gear. Although most emphasis was on the lower denominations, particularly Lincoln cents, countless thousands of rolls and even bags of new quarters were set aside.

Numismatic Notes: Circulation strikes have the Variety A reverse; Proofs have the Variety B reverse (see chapter 5) used on Proofs 1937 to 1964.

1953-D WASHINGTON QUARTER
Circulation-Strike Mintage: 56,112,400
OCG: MS-64

1953-D • Market Values • Circulation Strikes

EF-40	AU-50	MS-60	MS-63	MS-64	MS-65	MS-66
$3.	$4.	$5.	$7.	$13.	$40.	$80.

1953-D • Certified Populations • Circulation Strikes

MS-63	MS-64	MS-65	MS-66	MS-67	MS-68
67	164	477	328	64	0

Key to Collecting: Attractive choice and gem Mint State coins are readily available.
  • *1953-D, D over horizontal D (FS-25-1953D-502)*—This variety is not widely known and is an excellent cherrypicking opportunity.

1953-D/S Washington Quarter

Circulation-Strike Mintage: Small part of
1953-D mintage
OCG: MS-65

The 1953-D, D Over S (or actually, three D's over
two S's; FS-25-1953D-501, Breen-4367).

1953-D/S • Market Values • Circulation Strikes

EF-40	AU-50	MS-60	MS-63	MS-64	MS-65	MS-66
$35.	$50.	$75.	$150.	$200.	$250.	—

1953-D/S • Certified Populations • Circulation Strikes

MS-63	MS-64	MS-65	MS-66	MS-67	MS-68
17	29	7	2	0	0

Key to Collecting: This curious overmintmark is actually 1953-D, with three impressions of the D punch, over two earlier S mintmarks! This variety is not well known, and thus can be a cherrypicker's delight.

Numismatic Notes: FS-25-1953D-501, Breen-4367.

1953-S Washington Quarter

Circulation-Strike Mintage: 14,016,000
OCG: MS-64

1953-S • Market Values • Circulation Strikes

EF-40	AU-50	MS-60	MS-63	MS-64	MS-65	MS-66
$3.	$4.	$5.	$7.	$13.	$34.	$80.

1953-S • Certified Populations • Circulation Strikes

MS-63	MS-64	MS-65	MS-66	MS-67	MS-68
21	142	1,251	1,320	317	3

Key to Collecting: This variety is easily available in choice and gem Mint State.

1954 Washington Quarter

Circulation-Strike Mintage: 54,412,203
OCG: MS-64
Proof Mintage: 233,300
OCG: PF-65

1954 • Market Values • Circulation Strikes and Proof Strikes

EF-40	AU-50	MS-60	MS-63	MS-64	MS-65	MS-66	PF-63	PF-64	PF-65	PF-66
$3.	$4.	$5.	$12.	$15.	$32.	$80.	$10.	$15.	$25.	$30.

1954 • Certified Populations • Circulation Strikes and Proof Strikes

MS-63	MS-64	MS-65	MS-66	MS-67	MS-68	PF-64	PF-65	PF-66	PF-67	PF-68	PF-69	PF-70
32	216	963	1,015	191	2	144	358	976	1,438	790	59	0

Key to Collecting: Easily available in choice and gem Mint State. Proofs were made in record high quantities, but nothing like the mintage figures of years to come.

Numismatic Notes: Circulation strikes have the Variety A reverse; Proofs have the Variety B reverse (see chapter 5) used on Proofs 1937 to 1964.

1954-D WASHINGTON QUARTER
Circulation-Strike Mintage: 42,305,500
OCG: MS-64

1954-D • Market Values • Circulation Strikes

EF-40	AU-50	MS-60	MS-63	MS-64	MS-65	MS-66
$3.	$4.	$6.	$10.	$13.	$42.	$80.

1954-D • Certified Populations • Circulation Strikes

MS-63	MS-64	MS-65	MS-66	MS-67	MS-68
25	178	625	435	41	0

Key to Collecting: This coin is easily available in choice and gem Mint State.

1954-S WASHINGTON QUARTER
Circulation-Strike Mintage: 11,834,722
OCG: MS-64

1954-S • Market Values • Circulation Strikes

EF-40	AU-50	MS-60	MS-63	MS-64	MS-65	MS-66
$3.	$4.	$5.	$7.	$13.	$36.	$80.

1954-S • Certified Populations • Circulation Strikes

MS-63	MS-64	MS-65	MS-66	MS-67	MS-68
38	364	2,029	1,900	271	3

Key to Collecting: This coin is easily available in choice and gem Mint State. This is the last of the San Francisco Mint silver quarters of the era.

1955 WASHINGTON QUARTER
Circulation-Strike Mintage: 18,180,181
OCG: MS-64
Proof Mintage: 378,200
OCG: PF-65

1955 • Market Values • Circulation Strikes and Proof Strikes

EF-40	AU-50	MS-60	MS-63	MS-64	MS-65	MS-66	PF-63	PF-64	PF-65	PF-66
$3.	$4.	$7.	$8.	$11.	$27.	$80.	$10.	$15.	$25.	$30.

1955 • Certified Populations • Circulation Strikes and Proof Strikes

MS-63	MS-64	MS-65	MS-66	MS-67	MS-68	PF-64	PF-65	PF-66	PF-67	PF-68	PF-69	PF-70
41	198	1,155	1,271	169	0	97	291	727	1,220	240	26	0

Key to Collecting: This coin is easily available in choice and gem Mint State. Proofs attained a record mintage.

Numismatic Notes: Circulation strikes have the Variety A reverse; Proofs have the Variety B reverse (see chapter 5) used on Proofs 1937 to 1964.

1955-D WASHINGTON QUARTER
Circulation-Strike Mintage: 3,182,400
OCG: MS-64

1955-D • Market Values • Circulation Strikes

EF-40	AU-50	MS-60	MS-63	MS-64	MS-65	MS-66
$4.	$5.	$7.	$10.	$17.	$60.	$360.

1955-D • Certified Populations • Circulation Strikes

MS-63	MS-64	MS-65	MS-66	MS-67	MS-68
219	731	794	419	26	0

Key to Collecting: This coin is easily available in choice and gem Mint State, despite a low mintage. The investment potential was widely recognized at the time, and many were saved. Hoarding rolls of all denominations was a passion by this time, driven by the ever-escalating price of the low-mintage 1950-D nickel. The entire market was robust.

1956 WASHINGTON QUARTER

Circulation-Strike Mintage: 44,144,000
OCG: MS-64
Proof Mintage: 669,384
OCG: PF-65

1956 • Market Values • Circulation Strikes and Proof Strikes

EF-40	AU-50	MS-60	MS-63	MS-64	MS-65	MS-66	PF-63	PF-64	PF-65	PF-66
$3.	$4.	$5.	$10.	$17.	$21.	$80.	$8.	$12.	$10.	$25.

1956 • Certified Populations • Circulation Strikes and Proof Strikes

MS-63	MS-64	MS-65	MS-66	MS-67	MS-68	PF-64	PF-65	PF-66	PF-67	PF-68	PF-69	PF-70
27	199	1,178	2,152	520	5	105	204	657	114	1,340	311	0

Key to Collecting: This coin is easily available in choice and gem Mint State. Proofs were especially hot in the market, with much excitement. Those who were lucky enough to have ordered sets under the restrictions in place could sell "futures" at a profit before the coins were delivered. Sol Kaplan, Cincinnati dealer, was in the forefront of the market and posted bid and ask prices, including on a chalkboard at conventions. Some prices for older sets changed *hourly*.

Numismatic Notes: Circulation strikes have the Variety A reverse; Proofs have the Variety B reverse (see chapter 5) used on Proofs 1937 to 1964.

1956-D WASHINGTON QUARTER

Circulation-Strike Mintage: 32,334,500
OCG: MS-64

1956-D • Market Values • Circulation Strikes

EF-40	AU-50	MS-60	MS-63	MS-64	MS-65	MS-66
$3.	$4.	$5.	$7.	$8.	$27.	$80.

1956-D • Certified Populations • Circulation Strikes

MS-63	MS-64	MS-65	MS-66	MS-67	MS-68
63	243	497	566	48	0

Key to Collecting: This coin is easily available in choice and gem Mint State.
- *1956-D, D over horizontal D (Breen-4378)*—The D was first punched into the die with the rounded part facing down, 90° to the right of normal. A correct D was then overpunched. This variety is not listed by Fivaz-Stanton.

Numismatic Notes: Type A and B reverses, see 1937. Variety with D over horizontal D.

1957 WASHINGTON QUARTER

Circulation-Strike Mintage: 46,532,000
OCG: MS-64
Proof Mintage: 1,247,952
OCG: PF-65

1957 • Market Values • Circulation Strikes and Proof Strikes

EF-40	AU-50	MS-60	MS-63	MS-64	MS-65	MS-66	PF-63	PF-64	PF-65	PF-66
$3.	$4.	$5.	$7.	$8.	$27.	$80.	$2.75	$6.	$8.	$25.

1957 • Certified Populations • Circulation Strikes and Proof Strikes

MS-63	MS-64	MS-65	MS-66	MS-67	MS-68	PF-64	PF-65	PF-66	PF-67	PF-68	PF-69	PF-70
26	176	662	1,423	526	5	78	271	602	1,017	714	178	0

Key to Collecting: This coin is easily available in choice and gem Mint State. The Proof mintage crossed the million mark for the first time. However, the market for Proofs crashed by the time most people received their sets from the Mint, placing a damper on all investment in modern coins—Proof sets as well as rolls. Quantities of rolls saved were less from this point, continuing through 1959.

Numismatic Notes: Circulation strikes have the Variety A reverse; Proofs have the Variety B reverse (see chapter 5) used on Proofs 1937 to 1964.

1957-D WASHINGTON QUARTER

Circulation-Strike Mintage: 77,924,160
OCG: MS-64

1957-D • Market Values • Circulation Strikes

EF-40	AU-50	MS-60	MS-63	MS-64	MS-65	MS-66
$3.	$4.	$5.	$8.	$9.	$25.	$80.

1957-D • Certified Populations • Circulation Strikes

MS-63	MS-64	MS-65	MS-66	MS-67	MS-68
37	157	633	1,028	204	5

Key to Collecting: This coin is easily available in choice and gem Mint State.

Numismatic Notes: Type A and B reverses, see 1937.

1958 WASHINGTON QUARTER

Circulation-Strike Mintage: 6,360,000
OCG: MS-64
Proof Mintage: 875,652
OCG: PF-65

1958 • Market Values • Circulation Strikes and Proof Strikes

EF-40	AU-50	MS-60	MS-63	MS-64	MS-65	MS-66	PF-63	PF-64	PF-65	PF-66
$3.	$4.	$5.	$6.	$7.	$20.	$80.	$7.50	$11.	$18.	$25.

1958 • Certified Populations • Circulation Strikes and Proof Strikes

MS-63	MS-64	MS-65	MS-66	MS-67	MS-68	PF-64	PF-65	PF-66	PF-67	PF-68	PF-69	PF-70
43	279	1,258	2,741	683	1	89	255	416	691	483	84	0

Key to Collecting: This coin is easily available in choice and gem Mint State. The mintage of Proofs took a nosedive due to the weak market.

Numismatic Notes: Circulation strikes have the Variety A reverse; Proofs have the Variety B reverse (see chapter 5) used on Proofs 1937 to 1964.

1958-D WASHINGTON QUARTER

Circulation-Strike Mintage: 78,124,900
OCG: MS-64

1958-D • Market Values • Circulation Strikes

EF-40	AU-50	MS-60	MS-63	MS-64	MS-65	MS-66
$3.	$4.	$5.	$6.	$7.	$25.	$80.

1958-D • Certified Populations • Circulation Strikes

MS-63	MS-64	MS-65	MS-66	MS-67	MS-68
47	159	703	1,217	279	6

Key to Collecting: This coin is easily available in choice and gem Mint State.

Numismatic Notes: Type A and B reverses, see 1937.

1959 WASHINGTON QUARTER

Circulation-Strike Mintage: 24,384,000
OCG: MS-64
Proof Mintage: 1,149,291
OCG: PF-65

1959 • Market Values • Circulation Strikes and Proof Strikes

EF-40	AU-50	MS-60	MS-63	MS-64	MS-65	MS-66	PF-63	PF-64	PF-65	PF-66
$3.	$4.	$5.	$6.	$7.	$25.	$90.	$1.75	$5.	$8.	$25.

1959 • Certified Populations • Circulation Strikes and Proof Strikes

MS-63	MS-64	MS-65	MS-66	MS-67	MS-68	PF-64	PF-65	PF-66	PF-67	PF-68	PF-69	PF-70
38	213	892	961	61	0	62	189	527	949	779	159	0

Key to Collecting: This coin is easily available in choice and gem Mint State. Interest in Proofs revived to an extent, and the mintage was more than a million.

Numismatic Notes: Circulation strikes and Proofs have the Variety B reverse (see chapter 5).

1959-D WASHINGTON QUARTER

OCG: MS-64
Circulation-Strike Mintage: 62,054,232

1959-D • Market Values • Circulation Strikes

EF-40	AU-50	MS-60	MS-63	MS-64	MS-65	MS-66
$3.	$4.	$5.	$6.	$7.	$35.	$80.

1959-D • Certified Populations • Circulation Strikes

MS-63	MS-64	MS-65	MS-66	MS-67	MS-68
40	246	960	678	30	0

Key to Collecting: This coin is easily available in choice and gem Mint State.

Numismatic Notes: Type A and B reverses, see 1937.

1960 WASHINGTON QUARTER
Circulation-Strike Mintage: 29,164,000
OCG: MS-64
Proof Mintage: 1,691,602
OCG: PF-65

1960 • Market Values • Circulation Strikes and Proof Strikes

EF-40	AU-50	MS-60	MS-63	MS-64	MS-65	MS-66	PF-63	PF-64	PF-65	PF-66
$3.	$4.	$5.	$6.	$7.	$20.	$80.	$1.75	$5.	$8.	$23.

1960 • Certified Populations • Circulation Strikes and Proof Strikes

MS-63	MS-64	MS-65	MS-66	MS-67	MS-68	PF-64	PF-65	PF-66	PF-67	PF-68	PF-69	PF-70
42	183	601	633	69	0	107	326	798	1,082	902	269	4

Key to Collecting: This coin is easily available in choice and gem Mint State. The coin market was on fire, driven by the advent of *Coin World*, the first weekly publication in the field, and by the excitement of the 1960 Small Date Lincoln cent. All series bene-fited. The Library of Coins album series, marketed widely by the Coin and Currency Institute, proved to be a popular and attractive way to store and display sets of coins.

Numismatic Notes: Circulation strikes and Proofs have the Variety B reverse (see chapter 5).

1960-D WASHINGTON QUARTER
OCG: MS-64
Circulation-Strike Mintage: 63,000,324

1960-D • Market Values • Circulation Strikes

EF-40	AU-50	MS-60	MS-63	MS-64	MS-65	MS-66
$3.	$4.	$5.	$6.	$7.	$20.	$80.

1960-D • Certified Populations • Circulation Strikes

MS-63	MS-64	MS-65	MS-66	MS-67	MS-68
30	119	659	402	16	0

Key to Collecting: This coin is easily available in choice and gem Mint State.

Numismatic Notes: Type A and B reverses, see 1937.

1961 WASHINGTON QUARTER

Circulation-Strike Mintage: 37,036,000
OCG: MS-64
Proof Mintage: 3,028,244
OCG: PF-65

1961 • Market Values • Circulation Strikes and Proof Strikes

EF-40	AU-50	MS-60	MS-63	MS-64	MS-65	MS-66	PF-63	PF-64	PF-65	PF-66
$3.	$4.	$5.	$6.	$7.	$15.	$80.	$1.50	$7.	$8.	$20.

1961 • Certified Populations • Circulation Strikes and Proof Strikes

MS-63	MS-64	MS-65	MS-66	MS-67	MS-68	PF-64	PF-65	PF-66	PF-67	PF-68	PF-69	PF-70
39	186	663	575	26	0	115	268	844	1,387	1,537	384	0

Key to Collecting: This coin is easily available in choice and gem Mint State. Proof mintages continued to climb, and another record was set. The market was dynamic in all series. Interest spread to mint errors, die varieties, tokens, paper money, and other series outside of the mainstream (i.e., not listed in the Red Book).

Numismatic Notes: Circulation strikes and Proofs have the Variety B reverse (see chapter 5).

1961-D WASHINGTON QUARTER

Circulation-Strike Mintage: 83,656,928
OCG: MS-64

1961-D • Market Values • Circulation Strikes

EF-40	AU-50	MS-60	MS-63	MS-64	MS-65	MS-66
$3.	$4.	$5.	$6.	$7.	$15.	$180.

1961-D • Certified Populations • Circulation Strikes

MS-63	MS-64	MS-65	MS-66	MS-67	MS-68	MS-69
30	147	483	299	8	0	0

Key to Collecting: This coin is easily available in choice and gem Mint State. Rolls were hoarded in unprecedented quantities from 1960 through 1964.

Numismatic Notes: Type A and B reverses, see 1937.

1962 WASHINGTON QUARTER
Circulation-Strike Mintage: 36,156,000
OCG: MS-64
Proof Mintage: 3,218,019
OCG: PF-65

1962 • Market Values • Circulation Strikes and Proof Strikes

EF-40	AU-50	MS-60	MS-63	MS-64	MS-65	MS-66	PF-63	PF-64	PF-65	PF-66
$3.	$4.	$5.	$6.	$7.	$15.	$80.	$1.50	$7.	$8.	$20.

1962 • Certified Populations • Circulation Strikes and Proof Strikes

MS-63	MS-64	MS-65	MS-66	MS-67	MS-68	MS-69	PF-64	PF-65	PF-66	PF-67	PF-68	PF-69	PF-70
30	192	696	718	73	1	0	120	416	940	1,386	1,416	812	11

Key to Collecting: This coin is easily available in choice and gem Mint State. Market prices kept rising across the board. Proof production stabilized as slightly over three million, about the level that the Mint found comfortable to produce without having to place other facilities in use.

Numismatic Notes: Circulation strikes and Proofs have the Variety B reverse (see chapter 5).

1962-D WASHINGTON QUARTER
Circulation-Strike Mintage: 127,554,756
OCG: MS-64

1962-D • Market Values • Circulation Strikes

EF-40	AU-50	MS-60	MS-63	MS-64	MS-65	MS-66
$3.	$4.	$5.	$6.	$7.	$15.	$80.

1962-D • Certified Populations • Circulation Strikes

MS-63	MS-64	MS-65	MS-66	MS-67	MS-68	MS-69
31	156	532	293	20	0	0

Key to Collecting: This coin is easily available in choice and gem Mint State.
* *1962-D, D over horizontal D (Breen-4404)*—The D was first punched into the die in a horizontal position. A correct D was then overpunched.

Numismatic Notes: Type A and B reverses, see 1937.

1963 WASHINGTON QUARTER

Circulation-Strike Mintage: 74,316,000
OCG: MS-64
Proof Mintage: 3,075,645
OCG: PF-65

1963 • Market Values • Circulation Strikes and Proof Strikes

EF-40	AU-50	MS-60	MS-63	MS-64	MS-65	MS-66	PF-63	PF-64	PF-65	PF-66
$3.	$4.	$5.	$6.	$7.	$15.	$80.	$1.50	$7.	$8.	$20.

1963 • Certified Populations • Circulation Strikes and Proof Strikes

MS-63	MS-64	MS-65	MS-66	MS-67	MS-68	MS-69	PF-64	PF-65	PF-66	PF-67	PF-68	PF-69	PF-70
38	173	842	1,088	55	0	0	103	359	977	1,690	1,936	1,317	4

Key to Collecting: Mint State coins are available in just about any level desired. The market continued its upward movement. The *Coin Dealer Newsletter* was launched, and included bid and ask prices for rolls and Proof sets.

Numismatic Notes: Circulation strikes and Proofs have the Variety B reverse (see chapter 5).

1963-D WASHINGTON QUARTER

Circulation-Strike Mintage: 135,288,184
OCG: MS-64

1963-D • Market Values • Circulation Strikes

EF-40	AU-50	MS-60	MS-63	MS-64	MS-65	MS-66
$3.	$4.	$5.	$6.	$7.	$12.	$80.

1963-D • Certified Populations • Circulation Strikes

MS-63	MS-64	MS-65	MS-66	MS-67	MS-68	MS-69
30	167	613	362	36	0	0

Key to Collecting: Attractive choice and gem Mint State coins are readily available.

Numismatic Notes: Type A and B reverses, see 1937. Doubled obverse die variety listed in Breen.

1964 WASHINGTON QUARTER
Circulation-Strike Mintage: 560,390,585
OCG: MS-64
Proof Mintage: 3,950,762
OCG: PF-65

The year 1964 was the last in which circulation-strike Washington quarters were solid silver.

1964 • Market Values • Circulation Strikes and Proof Strikes

EF-40	AU-50	MS-60	MS-63	MS-64	MS-65	MS-66	PF-63	PF-64	PF-65	PF-66
$3.	$4.	$5.	$6.	$7.	$12.00	$80.00	$1.50	$7.	$8.	$20.

1964 • Certified Populations • Circulation Strikes and Proof Strikes

MS-63	MS-64	MS-65	MS-66	MS-67	MS-68	MS-69	PF-64	PF-65	PF-66	PF-67	PF-68	PF-69	PF-70
69	285	876	685	34	1	0	70	179	572	1,265	2,360	2,019	36

Key to Collecting: Mint State coins are available in just about any level desired. The market continued its upward movement. *The Coin Dealer Newsletter* was launched, and included bid and ask prices for rolls and Proof sets.

Numismatic Notes: Circulation strikes and Proofs have the Variety B reverse (see chapter 5). Possible Reverse C exists on circulation strikes per Breen "new hub of 1965; 2 leaves touch tops of AR," but this is not confirmed by Fivaz and Stanton.

The Philadelphia Mint continued striking silver 1964-dated quarters in early 1965. The date was not changed, per the "date freeze" mandate of Mint Director Eva Adams. She blamed coin collectors for the current coin shortage and sought to stymie the collecting of new coins. In 1965 the *San Francisco Mint* (then called the San Francisco Assay Office) struck more than 15,000,000 mintmarkless 1964-dated silver quarters in 1965 and a further 4,640,865 in early 1966.[5]

After 1964, solid silver Proof quarters would be discontinued, not to resume again until 1992.

1964-D WASHINGTON QUARTER
Circulation-Strike Mintage: 704,135,528
OCG: MS-64

The year 1964 was also the last in which the Washington quarter mintmark would appear on the reverse.

1964-D • Market Values • Circulation Strikes

EF-40	AU-50	MS-60	MS-63	MS-64	MS-65	MS-66
$3.	$4.	$5.	$6.	$7.	$12.	$80.

1964-D • Certified Populations • Circulation Strikes

MS-63	MS-64	MS-65	MS-66	MS-67	MS-68	MS-69
82	249	906	922	70	0	0

Key to Collecting: Choice and gem Mint State coins are readily available.

- *1964-D Misplaced Mintmark (FS-25-1964D-502; URS-2)*—Fivaz-Stanton states: "On this very dramatic RPM, a secondary D mintmark is evident protruding from the branch above the mintmark area. This is one of the very few totally separated repunched mintmark varieties."

- *1964-D With Rare Reverse C (FS-25-1964D-901; URS-4)*—Fivaz-Stanton: "A very few 1964-D coins are known to have the Type C reverse intended for use starting in 1965. These Type C reverse coins show the leaves above the AR of DOLLAR sharp and almost touching the letters, where the Type-A is weak, and the Type B is bold and the one leaf does touch the A of DOLLAR. Additionally, the leaves below the tail feathers are sharp and barely touch those tail feathers. The leaf in front of the arrow tips comes to a distinct point in front of the arrow tips. On the Type B reverse, this leaf rises above the top arrow tip, and on the Type-A it is very weak."

FS-25-1964D-901.

Numismatic Notes: Type A and B reverses, see 1937. Also rare Type C reverse, see above. The Denver Mint continued striking silver 1964-D quarters through 1965. The date was not changed, per the "date freeze" mandate of Mint Director Eva Adams.[6]

1965–1974: CLAD METAL ISSUES

Specifications:
Composition: Outer layers of copper-nickel (75% copper and 25% nickel) bonded to an inner core of pure copper. The copper can be seen when coins are viewed edge-on • *Diameter:* 24.3 mm • *Weight:* 87.5 grains • *Edge:* Reeded

1965 WASHINGTON QUARTER
Circulation-Strike Mintage: 1,819,717,540 +
2,360,000 (Special Mint Sets)
OCG: MS-65

1965 • Market Values • Circulation Strikes

EF-40	AU-50	MS-60	MS-63	MS-64	MS-65	MS-66
$0.65	$0.75	$1.	$1.	$5.	$9.	$21.

1965 • Certified Populations • Circulation Strikes

MS-63	MS-64	MS-65	MS-66	MS-67	MS-68	MS-69
13	43	65	127	15	0	1

Key to Collecting: Although clad quarters dated 1965 were made in unprecedented quantities, crossing the billion mark for the first time, there was scarcely any interest anymore in saving rolls, for clad metal, unlike silver, faced an uncertain future. For this year through the rest of the decade, very small quantities of quarter rolls were saved in proportion to the mintage figures.

- *1965 Special Mint Sets*—2,360,000 Special Mint Sets of coins dated 1965 were struck *in 1966* at the San Francisco Mint (but with no mintmark) for sale to collectors. These were carefully made and have a satiny, partially mirrored surface. Unless Special Mint Set coins have cameo contrast and are prooflike, they can be indistinguishable from regular issues. Thus they are not priced here.

- *1965 Doubled Die Obverse (FS-25-1965-101; URS-3)*— Fivaz-Stanton says: "The doubling is very strong on all obverse lettering, eye, and the date. This variety is extremely rare, and will sell very quickly at auction."

Numismatic Notes: Examples known on 90% silver planchet.

The mintage of this year set an all-time high record, not equaled since that time. This high figure is explained by the production of 1965-dated quarters into the year 1966, due to the "date freeze" set in place by Mint Director Eva Adams, and by the fact that Denver quarters bore no mintmark in 1965 and thus appeared identical to Philadelphia coins. The Denver Mint did not resume using the D mintmark until 1968.

Strong doubling is obvious on all the obverse lettering of FS-25-1965-101.

Clad quarters were first released into circulation in November 1965.

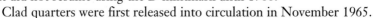

1966 Washington Quarter
Circulation-Strike Mintage: 821,101,500 +
2,261,583 (Special Mint Sets)
OCG: PF-65

1966 • Market Values • Circulation Strikes

EF-40	AU-50	MS-60	MS-63	MS-64	MS-65	MS-66
$0.65	$0.75	$1.	$1.	$4.	$6.	$21.

1966 • Certified Populations • Circulation Strikes

MS-63	MS-64	MS-65	MS-66	MS-67	MS-68	MS-69
5	24	48	138	43	0	0

Key to Collecting: Mint State coins are readily available. Quality of 1966 and other early clad quarters is a different matter, and most coins have extensive marks (including from the original planchets), or striking, or eye appeal, or all of these considerations.

- *1966 Special Mint Sets*—2,261,583 Special Mint Sets of coins were struck at the San Francisco Mint (but with no mintmark) for sale to collectors. These were carefully made and have a partially mirrored surface. Unless Special Mint Set coins have cameo contrast and are prooflike, they can be indistinguishable from regular issues. Thus they are not priced here.

1967 Washington Quarter
Circulation-Strike Mintage: 1,524,031,848 +
1,863,344 (Special Mint Sets)
OCG: PF-65

1967 • Market Values • Circulation Strikes

EF-40	AU-50	MS-60	MS-63	MS-64	MS-65	MS-66
$0.65	$0.75	$1.	$1.	$3.	$5.	$24.00

1967 • Certified Populations • Circulation Strikes

MS-63	MS-64	MS-65	MS-66	MS-67	MS-68	MS-69
14	28	22	240	53	0	0

Key to Collecting: Mint State coins are readily available, but cherrypicking is recommended to obtain quality.

- *1967 Special Mint Sets*—1,183,344 Special Mint Sets of coins were struck at the San Francisco Mint (but with no mintmark) for sale to collectors. These were carefully made and have a partially mirrored surface. Unless Special Mint Set coins have cameo contrast and are prooflike, they can be indistinguishable from regular issues. Thus they are not priced here.

Numismatic Notes: The mintage for this year is the second highest all-time record (1965 is highest).

1968 WASHINGTON QUARTER
Circulation-Strike Mintage: 220,731,500
OCG: PF-65

Philadelphia Mint coins continued to display no
mintmark until 1980.

1968 • Market Values • Circulation Strikes

EF-40	AU-50	MS-60	MS-63	MS-64	MS-65	MS-66
$0.65	$0.75	$1.	$1.	$4.	$5.	$25.

1968 • Certified Populations • Circulation Strikes

MS-63	MS-64	MS-65	MS-66	MS-67	MS-68	MS-69
8	17	64	115	49	2	0

Key to Collecting: Mint State coins are readily available on an absolute basis, although quality can be a problem. Clad coins continued to be ignored by investors.

1968-D WASHINGTON QUARTER
Circulation-Strike Mintage: 101,534,000
OCG: PF-65

Through 1964, the mintmark appeared on the
reverse. From 1965 through 1967, Washington quarters were made only in Philadelphia, and bore no
mintmarks. Beginning with 1968's Denver coinage,
the mintmark appeared on the obverse.

1968-D • Market Values • Circulation Strikes

EF-40	AU-50	MS-60	MS-63	MS-64	MS-65	MS-66
$0.65	$0.75	$1.	$1.	$4.	$5.	$11.

1968-D • Certified Populations • Circulation Strikes

MS-63	MS-64	MS-65	MS-66	MS-67	MS-68	MS-69
5	29	99	363	110	1	0

Key to Collecting: The same comment as for the 1968 Philadelphia quarters. Around this time Ken Bressett, editor of the Red Book, was one of the first to comment that clad coins, ignored by investors, might prove to be scarce someday.

1968-S WASHINGTON QUARTER
Proof Mintage: 3,041,506
OCG: PF-65

The mintmark on Proof Washington quarters of
this period likewise on the obverse.

1968-S • Market Values • Proof Strikes

PF-64	PF-65	PF-66	PF-67	PF-68
$2.50	$4.	$5.	$6.	$7.50

1968-S • Certified Populations • Proof Strikes

PF-64	PF-65	PF-66	PF-67	PF-68	PF-69	PF-70
25	50	131	388	312	93	0

Key to Collecting: Beginning this year, Proofs were packaged attractive hard plastic holders. The quality was better than ever before, and from this point onward, cameo contrast became a feature of many (but not all) Proof coins.

Numismatic Notes: Doubled-die obverse and doubled-die reverse varieties are known and command a strong premium. Listed as FS-25-1968S-101 (URS-3) and 801 (URS-6), respectively.

FS-25-1968S-101.

1969 WASHINGTON QUARTER
Circulation-Strike Mintage: 176,212,000
OCG: MS-65

1969 • Market Values • Circulation Strikes

EF-40	AU-50	MS-60	MS-63	MS-64	MS-65	MS-66
$0.65	$0.75	$1.	$1.	$4.	$5.	$70.

1969 • Certified Populations • Circulation Strikes

MS-63	MS-64	MS-65	MS-66	MS-67	MS-68	MS-69
6	61	62	61	4	0	0

Key to Collecting: Mint State coins are readily available. Cherrypicking for quality is advised. In this era plastic holders, such as those marketed by Capital Plastics, were a popular way to display sets of coins, including Washington quarters.

1969-D WASHINGTON QUARTER
Circulation-Strike Mintage: 114,372,000
OCG: MS-65

1969-D • Market Values • Circulation Strikes

EF-40	AU-50	MS-60	MS-63	MS-64	MS-65	MS-66
$0.65	$0.75	$1.	$1.	$4.	$5.	$20.

1969-D • Certified Populations • Circulation Strikes

MS-63	MS-64	MS-65	MS-66	MS-67	MS-68	MS-69
7	48	82	246	100	36	1

Key to Collecting: Mint State coins are readily available. Cherrypicking for quality is advised. Clad coins continued to be ignored in their own time.

1969-S WASHINGTON QUARTER
Proof Mintage: 2,934,631
OCG: MS-65

1969-S • Market Values • Proof Strikes

PF-64	PF-65	PF-66	PF-67	PF-68
$2.50	$4.	$5.	$6.	$7.50

1969-S • Certified Populations • Proof Strikes

PF-64	PF-65	PF-66	PF-67	PF-68	PF-69	PF-70
20	38	148	359	467	236	0

Key to Collecting: Readily available and with good eye appeal.

Numismatic Notes: Doubled-die obverse listed as FS-25-1969 S-101; URS-4. Doubling on the lettering and date.

FS-25-1969S-101.

1970 WASHINGTON QUARTER
Circulation-Strike Mintage: 136,420,000
OCG: MS-65

1970 • Market Values • Circulation Strikes

EF-40	AU-50	MS-60	MS-63	MS-64	MS-65	MS-66
$0.65	$0.75	$1.	$1.	$3.	$9.	$60.

1970 • Certified Populations • Circulation Strikes

MS-63	MS-64	MS-65	MS-66	MS-67	MS-68	MS-69
7	30	60	115	17	0	0

Key to Collecting: Mint State coins are readily available. Cherrypicking for quality is advised.

1970-D WASHINGTON QUARTER
Circulation-Strike Mintage: 417,341,364
OCG: MS-65

1970-D • Market Values • Circulation Strikes

EF-40	AU-50	MS-60	MS-63	MS-64	MS-65	MS-66
$0.65	$0.75	$1.	$1.	$3.50	$6.	$30.

1970-D • Certified Populations • Circulation Strikes

MS-63	MS-64	MS-65	MS-66	MS-67	MS-68	MS-69
11	47	161	734	206	3	0

Key to Collecting: Mint State coins are readily available. Cherrypicking for quality is advised.

1970-S WASHINGTON QUARTER
Proof Mintage: 2,632,810
OCG: PF-65

1970-S • Market Values • Proof Strikes

PF-64	PF-65	PF-66	PF-67	PF-68
$2.50	$4.	$5.	$6.	$7.50

1970-S • Certified Populations • Proof Strikes

PF-64	PF-65	PF-66	PF-67	PF-68	PF-69	PF-70
9	29	109	352	468	264	0

Key to Collecting: Attractive and of high quality—this is the general rule for coins in the marketplace today. Single Proof quarters are available from sets that have been taken apart.

Numismatic Notes: The writer purchased a 1970-S Proof quarter plainly struck over a 1900 Barber quarter. The coin was publicly offered and was seized by the Treasury Department. Apparently the concoction of a creative Mint employee, the piece somehow escaped into a 1970-S Proof set, no doubt initially baffling its discoverer.

1971 WASHINGTON QUARTER
Circulation-Strike Mintage: 109,284,000
OCG: MS-65

1971 • Market Values • Circulation Strikes

EF-40	AU-50	MS-60	MS-63	MS-64	MS-65	MS-66
$0.65	$0.75	$1.	$1.	$3.	$5.	$55.

1971 • Certified Populations • Circulation Strikes

MS-63	MS-64	MS-65	MS-66	MS-67	MS-68	MS-69
14	70	70	54	3	0	0

Key to Collecting: Mint State coins are readily available. Cherrypicking for quality is advised.

1971-D WASHINGTON QUARTER
Circulation-Strike Mintage: 258,634,428
OCG: MS-65

1971-D • Market Values • Circulation Strikes

EF-40	AU-50	MS-60	MS-63	MS-64	MS-65	MS-66
$0.65	$0.75	$1.	$1.	$2.	$3.	$20.

1971-D • Certified Populations • Circulation Strikes

MS-63	MS-64	MS-65	MS-66	MS-67	MS-68	MS-69
15	6	109	244	54	1	0

Key to Collecting: Mint State coins are readily available. Cherrypicking for quality is advised.

1971-S WASHINGTON QUARTER
Proof Mintage: 3,220,733
OCG: PF-65

1971-S • Market Values • Proof Strikes

PF-64	PF-65	PF-66	PF-67	PF-68
$2.50	$4.	$5.	$6.	$7.50

1971-S • Certified Populations • Proof Strikes

PF-64	PF-65	PF-66	PF-67	PF-68	PF-69	PF-70
15	26	93	243	381	148	0

Key to Collecting: Attractive and of high quality, as usual. The San Francisco Mint set new high standards in production.

1972 WASHINGTON QUARTER
Circulation-Strike Mintage: 215,048,000
OCG: MS-65

1972 • Market Values • Circulation Strikes

EF-40	AU-50	MS-60	MS-63	MS-64	MS-65	MS-66
$0.65	$0.75	$1.	$1.	$3.	$4.	$25.

1972 • Certified Populations • Circulation Strikes

MS-63	MS-64	MS-65	MS-66	MS-67	MS-68	MS-69
4	68	76	108	16	0	0

Key to Collecting: Mint State coins are readily available. Cherrypicking for quality is advised.

1972-D WASHINGTON QUARTER

Circulation-Strike Mintage: 311,067,732
OCG: MS-65

1972-D • Market Values • Circulation Strikes

EF-40	AU-50	MS-60	MS-63	MS-64	MS-65	MS-66
$0.65	$0.75	$1.	$1.	$3.50	$5.	$20.

1972-D • Certified Populations • Circulation Strikes

MS-63	MS-64	MS-65	MS-66	MS-67	MS-68	MS-69
3	41	120	606	183	7	0

Key to Collecting: Mint State coins are readily available. Cherrypicking for quality is advised. As improbable as it may seem in retrospect, there was no emphasis on high quality. Bank-wrapped rolls were Uncirculated, and that was that—no sorting through to find gems. This situation remained in effect for much of the decade.

1972-S WASHINGTON QUARTER

Proof Mintage: 3,260,996
OCG: PF-65

1972-S • Market Values • Proof Strikes

PF-64	PF-65	PF-66	PF-67	PF-68
$2.50	$4.	$5.	$6.	$7.50

1972-S • Certified Populations • Proof Strikes

PF-64	PF-65	PF-66	PF-67	PF-68	PF-69	PF-70
12	14	67	215	416	234	0

Key to Collecting: High quality and beautiful appearance as usual.

1973 WASHINGTON QUARTER

Circulation-Strike Mintage: 346,924,000
OCG: MS-65

1973 • Market Values • Circulation Strikes

EF-40	AU-50	MS-60	MS-63	MS-64	MS-65	MS-66
$0.65	$0.75	$1.	$1.	$3.50	$7.	$25.

1973 • Certified Populations • Circulation Strikes

MS-63	MS-64	MS-65	MS-66	MS-67	MS-68	MS-69
9	41	58	101	11	0	0

Key to Collecting: Mint State coins are readily available. Cherrypicking for quality is advised.

1973-D Washington Quarter
Circulation-Strike Mintage: 232,977,400
OCG: MS-65

1973-D • Market Values • Circulation Strikes

EF-40	AU-50	MS-60	MS-63	MS-64	MS-65	MS-66
$0.65	$0.75	$1.	$1.	$3.	$9.00	$20.

1973-D • Certified Populations • Circulation Strikes

MS-63	MS-64	MS-65	MS-66	MS-67	MS-68	MS-69
14	63	65	115	18	0	0

Key to Collecting: Mint State coins are readily available. Cherrypicking for quality is advised.

1973-S Washington Quarter
Proof Mintage: 2,760,339
OCG: PF-65

1973-S • Market Values • Proof Strikes

PF-64	PF-65	PF-66	PF-67	PF-68
$2.50	$4.	$5.	$6.	$7.50

1973-S • Certified Populations • Proof Strikes

PF-64	PF-65	PF-66	PF-67	PF-68	PF-69	PF-70
8	15	35	102	237	637	0

Key to Collecting: Nice!

1974 Washington Quarter
Circulation-Strike Mintage: 801,456,000
OCG: MS-65

1974 • Market Values • Circulation Strikes

EF-40	AU-50	MS-60	MS-63	MS-64	MS-65	MS-66
$0.65	$0.75	$1.	$1.	$3.50	$5.	$25.

1974 • Certified Populations • Circulation Strikes

MS-63	MS-64	MS-65	MS-66	MS-67	MS-68	MS-69
10	39	67	130	25	0	0

Key to Collecting: Mint State coins are readily available. Cherrypicking for quality is advised. The investment end of the coin market entered a slow period that would reach its nadir in 1976, after which it would become warm, then hot.

Numismatic Notes: Many of the 1974-dated Washington quarters were struck in 1975, pursuant to Public Law 93-531 (December 26, 1974). In 1975 most activities at the mints were in striking the 1776–1976 Bicentennial quarters. Accordingly, while no 1975-dated quarters were made, 1974 quarters were restruck, and 1776–1976 quarters were prestruck.

1974-D WASHINGTON QUARTER
Circulation-Strike Mintage: 353,160,300
OCG: MS-65

1974-D • Market Values • Circulation Strikes

EF-40	AU-50	MS-60	MS-63	MS-64	MS-65	MS-66
$0.65	$0.75	$1.	$1.	$4.25	$11.	$20.

1974-D • Certified Populations • Circulation Strikes

MS-63	MS-64	MS-65	MS-66	MS-67	MS-68	MS-69
6	44	64	162	46	0	0

Key to Collecting: Mint State coins are readily available. Cherrypicking for quality is advised.

1974-S WASHINGTON QUARTER
Proof Mintage: 2,612,568
OCG: PF-65

1974-S • Market Values • Proof Strikes

PF-64	PF-65	PF-66	PF-67	PF-68
$2.50	$4.	$5.	$6.	$7.50

1974-S • Certified Populations • Proof Strikes

PF-64	PF-65	PF-66	PF-67	PF-68	PF-69	PF-70
7	10	24	98	224	1,336	0

Key to Collecting: Beautiful and of high quality.

Numismatic Notes: One variety has a doubled S-mintmark.

EXPOS UNLIMITED

THE place to BUY and SELL
Everything from Coins, Stamps & Paper Money,
to Cigar Label Art, Estate Jewelry, Medals, Tokens,
Casino Chips and much much MORE!

LONG BEACH
COIN, STAMP & COLLECTIBLES EXPO
HELD AT THE LONG BEACH CONVENTION CENTER

Held three times a year since 1964, the Long Beach Expo receives outstanding attendance. There are over 2,000 dealers and 10,000-12,000 public attendees each show from around the world.

HERITAGE
Numismatic Auctions, Inc.
Official Auctioneer of the Long Beach Expo

SANTA CLARA
COIN, STAMP & COLLECTIBLES EXPO
HELD AT THE SANTA CLARA CONVENTION CENTER

Held twice a year since 1978, the Santa Clara Expo receives outstanding attendance. There are over 1,000 dealers and 5,000-8,000 public attendees each show from around the world.

SUPERIOR GALLERIES
Superior Value In Coins...Guaranteed
A STANFORD FINANCIAL PORTFOLIO COMPANY

Official Auctioneer of the Santa Clara Expo

**Free Kids
Treasure Hunt
Saturday 11-2pm**

**Free Daily Gold
Prize Drawings!**

Sponsored by

eBay conducts
Free Seminars on
Fri & Sat at 12:00pm

PLEASE VISIT WWW.LONGBEACHEXPO.COM & WWW.SANTACLARAEXPO.COM
FOR ALL CURRENT & FUTURE SHOW DATES

For more Info, Contact Expos Unlimited: 8 W. Figueroa Street Santa Barbara CA
Ph: (805) 962-9939 Fx: (805) 963-0827 Email: lbexpo@exposunlimited.com

1975–1976 BICENTENNIAL QUARTERS

Specifications of clad coins:
Composition: Outer layers of copper-nickel (75% copper and 25% nickel) bonded to an inner core of pure copper. The copper can be seen when coins are viewed edge-on • *Diameter:* 24.3 mm • *Weight:* 87.5 grains • *Edge:* Reeded

Specifications of special silver coins:
Composition: 90% silver; 10% copper • *Diameter:* 24.3 mm • *Weight:* 96.45 grains • *Edge:* Reeded

1776–1976 WASHINGTON QUARTER
Circulation-Strike Mintage: 809,784,016

Quarters minted in both 1975 and 1976 received the dual dates 1776–1976.

1776–1976 • Market Values • Circulation Strikes

EF-40	AU-50	MS-60	MS-63	MS-64	MS-65	MS-66
$0.50	$0.60	$0.75	$1.	$2.	$6.	$25.

1776–1976 • Certified Populations • Circulation Strikes

MS-63	MS-64	MS-65	MS-66	MS-67	MS-68	MS-69
21	73	127	279	122	1	0

Key to Collecting: Mint State coins are readily available. Cherrypicking for quality is advised. Especially large quantities were saved.

1776–1976-D WASHINGTON QUARTER
Circulation-Strike Mintage: 860,118,839
OCG: MS-65

1776–1976-D • Market Values • Circulation Strikes

EF-40	AU-50	MS-60	MS-63	MS-64	MS-65	MS-66
$0.50	$0.60	$0.75	$1.	$3.50	$6.	$32.00

1776–1976-D • Certified Populations • Circulation Strikes

MS-63	MS-64	MS-65	MS-66	MS-67	MS-68	MS-69
21	62	152	457	158	4	0

Key to Collecting: Common in Mint State, although gems are in the minority. Many were saved.

Numismatic Notes: A doubled-die obverse variety is listed in Breen.

1776–1976-S COPPER-NICKEL CLAD WASHINGTON QUARTER

Proof Mintage: 7,059,099
OCG: PF-65

1776–1976-S • Market Values • Proof Strikes

PF-64	PF-65	PF-66	PF-67	PF-68
$1.	$3.	$5.	$6.	$7.50

1776–1976-S • Certified Populations • Proof Strikes

PF-64	PF-65	PF-66	PF-67	PF-68	PF-69	PF-70
5	9	42	295	418	205	0

Key to Collecting: Easily available due to the extraordinary high mintage. Sales fell short of expectation, and sets were still available from the Mint for several years afterward.

Numismatic Notes: In August 1974 at the American Numismatic Association convention held that year in Bal Harbour, Florida, visitors were given a preview of the Proof coinage. On view were examples of each of the three Bicentennial denominations, but *without* S mintmark. The whereabouts of these coins is not known today.

1776–1976-S SILVER WASHINGTON QUARTER

Circulation-Strike Mintage: 7,000,000
OCG: MS-65
Proof Mintage: 4,000,000
OCG: PF-65

1776–1976-S • Silver • Market Values • Circulation Strikes and Proof Strikes

EF-40	AU-50	MS-60	MS-63	MS-64	MS-65	MS-66	PF-64	PF-65	PF-66	PF-67	PF-68
$1.	$1.	$1.	$30	$4.	$5.	$15.	$2.	$7.	$8.	$10.	$12.

1776–1976-S • Silver • Certified Populations • Circulation Strikes and Proof Strikes

MS-63	MS-64	MS-65	MS-66	MS-67	MS-68	MS-69	PF-64	PF-65	PF-66	PF-67	PF-68	PF-69	PF-70
3	94	165	538	1,372	352	1	17	26	115	467	1,144	5,583	6

Key to Collecting: Choice and gem Mint State and Proof coins are easily obtained, but at a premium due to the silver content.

Numismatic Notes: Demand for the silver strikes was below Mint expectations. By December 31, 1982, only 4,294,000 of the circulation strike (Uncirculated format) coins had been released and only 3,262,970 of the proofs. Some Proofs were struck at the *Philadelphia* Mint before the mintmark was added to the dies.

1977–1998: Normal Design Resumed

Specifications of clad coins:
Composition: Outer layers of copper-nickel (75% copper and 25% nickel) bonded to an inner core of pure copper. The copper can be seen when coins are viewed edge-on • *Diameter:* 24.3 mm • *Weight:* 87.5 grains • *Edge:* Reeded

Specifications of special silver coins (1992-S to 1998-S):
Composition: 90% silver; 10% copper • *Diameter:* 24.3 mm • *Weight:* 96.45 grains • *Edge:* Reeded

1977 Washington Quarter
Circulation-Strike Mintage: 468,556,000
+ 7,352,000 WP) = 475,908,000
OCG: MS-65

1977 • Market Values • Circulation Strikes

EF-40	AU-50	MS-60	MS-63	MS-64	MS-65	MS-66
$0.35	$0.45	$0.60	$1.	$3.50	$6.	$15.

1977 • Certified Populations • Circulation Strikes

MS-63	MS-64	MS-65	MS-66	MS-67	MS-68	MS-69
5	32	49	113	56	0	0

Key to Collecting: Mint State coins are readily available. Cherrypicking for quality is advised, although choice and gem coins are much more available from this era than from the late 1960s and early 1970s.

Numismatic Notes: Includes some examples struck at West Point Mint (designated WP in minage notes).

1977-D Washington Quarter
Circulation-Strike Mintage: 256,524,978
OCG: MS-65

1977-D • Market Values • Circulation Strikes

EF-40	AU-50	MS-60	MS-63	MS-64	MS-65	MS-66
$0.35	$0.45	$0.60	$1.	$2.	$4.	$16.

1977-D • Certified Populations • Circulation Strikes

MS-63	MS-64	MS-65	MS-66	MS-67	MS-68	MS-69
6	29	37	71	31	0	0

Key to Collecting: Choice and gem Mint State coins are common, but they are a minority of the Mint State coins in existence.

1977-S Washington Quarter

Proof Mintage: 3,251,152
OCG: PF-65

1977-S • Market Values • Proof Strikes

PF-64	PF-65	PF-66	PF-67	PF-68
$3.	$4.	$5.	$6.	$7.

1977-S • Certified Populations • Proof Strikes

PF-64	PF-65	PF-66	PF-67	PF-68	PF-69	PF-70
3	9	17	78	121	3,058	34

Key to Collecting: Readily available and of high quality.

Numismatic Notes: Normal- and thin-motto varieties listed by Breen.

1978 Washington Quarter

Circulation-Strike Mintage: 521,452,000
  (+ 20,800,000 WP) = 542,252,000
OCG: MS-65

1978 • Market Values • Circulation Strikes

EF-40	AU-50	MS-60	MS-63	MS-64	MS-65	MS-66
$0.35	$0.45	$0.60	$1.	$2.	$6.	$17.

1978 • Certified Populations • Circulation Strikes

MS-63	MS-64	MS-65	MS-66	MS-67	MS-68	MS-69
11	31	56	109	48	0	0

Key to Collecting: Choice and gem Mint State coins are easily available. The coin market was especially active, driven by rising prices of silver and gold bullion. The market would peak in early 1980. This passion did not extend to saving bank-wrapped rolls of clad quarters.

Numismatic Notes: Includes pieces struck at the West Point Mint.

1978-D WASHINGTON QUARTER
Circulation-Strike Mintage: 287,373,152
OCG: MS-65

1978-D • Market Values • Circulation Strikes

EF-40	AU-50	MS-60	MS-63	MS-64	MS-65	MS-66
$0.35	$0.45	$0.60	$1.	$3.50	$6.	$24.00

1978-D • Certified Populations • Circulation Strikes

MS-63	MS-64	MS-65	MS-66	MS-67	MS-68	MS-69
4	24	32	91	27	0	0

Key to Collecting: Choice and gem Mint State coins are easily available.

1978-S WASHINGTON QUARTER
Proof Mintage: 3,127,781
OCG: PF-65

1978-S • Market Values • Proof Strikes

PF-64	PF-65	PF-66	PF-67	PF-68
$3.	$4.	$5.	$6.	$7.

1978-S • Certified Populations • Proof Strikes

PF-64	PF-65	PF-66	PF-67	PF-68	PF-69	PF-70
0	5	16	82	160	3,782	63

Key to Collecting: High quality and with great eye appeal, as usual.

1979 WASHINGTON QUARTER
Circulation-Strike Mintage: 515,708,000
(+ 22,672,000 WP) = 538,380,000
OCG: MS-65

1979 • Market Values • Circulation Strikes

EF-40	AU-50	MS-60	MS-63	MS-64	MS-65	MS-66
$0.35	$0.45	$0.60	$1.	$3.50	$6.	$18.00

1979 • Certified Populations • Circulation Strikes

MS-63	MS-64	MS-65	MS-66	MS-67	MS-68	MS-69
4	39	39	154	40	1	0

Key to Collecting: Choice and gem Mint State coins are easily available. The American
Numismatic Association Certification Service (ANACS) was active in grading coins for
a fee, popularizing an innovation that would be very profitable to the ANA and create

a lot of attention among dealers and collectors. Coins were returned loose (not encapsulated) with a photographic certification giving the grade separately for each side, such as MS-64/65. From here it was onward and upward in the search for high-grade coins.

Numismatic Notes: Mintage includes pieces struck at the West Point Mint.

1979-D WASHINGTON QUARTER
Circulation-Strike Mintage: 489,789,780
OCG: MS-65

1979-D • Market Values • Circulation Strikes

EF-40	AU-50	MS-60	MS-63	MS-64	MS-65	MS-66
$0.35	$0.45	$0.60	$1.	$2.	$4.	$15.

1979-D • Certified Populations • Circulation Strikes

MS-63	MS-64	MS-65	MS-66	MS-67	MS-68	MS-69
12	25	57	132	23	0	0

Key to Collecting: Choice and gem Mint State coins are easily available.

1979-S WASHINGTON QUARTER
Proof Mintage: 3,677,175
OCG: PF-65

TYPE I
1979-S • Market Values • Proof Strikes

PF-64	PF-65	PF-66	PF-67	PF-68
$4.	$6.	$8.	$10.	$12.

1979-S • Certified Populations • Proof Strikes

PF-64	PF-65	PF-66	PF-67	PF-68	PF-69	PF-70
8	4	13	39	335	4,402	103

TYPE II
1979-S • Market Values • Proof Strikes

PF-64	PF-65	PF-66	PF-67	PF-68
$4.	$6.	$11.	$12.	$15.

1979-S • Certified Populations • Proof Strikes

PF-64	PF-65	PF-66	PF-67	PF-68	PF-69	PF-70
3	5	12	43	227	1,690	42

Key to Collecting: High quality, as expected.

Numismatic Notes: Filled-S (Type I) and Clear-S (Type II) Mintmark varieties are known. The Clear S is the scarcer of the two.

1980-P WASHINGTON QUARTER
Circulation-Strike Mintage: 635,832,000
OCG: MS-65

1980-P • Market Values • Circulation Strikes

EF-40	AU-50	MS-60	MS-63	MS-64	MS-65	MS-66
$0.35	$0.45	$0.60	$1.	$2.	$7.	$12.

1980-P • Certified Populations • Circulation Strikes

MS-63	MS-64	MS-65	MS-66	MS-67	MS-68	MS-69
7	27	89	292	51	2	0

Key to Collecting: Choice and gem Mint State coins are easily available. Early in the year the general coin market went into a slump, where it would remain until the later years of the decade.

1980-D WASHINGTON QUARTER
Circulation-Strike Mintage: 518,327,487
OCG: MS-65

1980-D • Market Values • Circulation Strikes

EF-40	AU-50	MS-60	MS-63	MS-64	MS-65	MS-66
$0.35	$0.45	$0.60	$1.	$2.	$5.	$18.00

1980-D • Certified Populations • Circulation Strikes

MS-63	MS-64	MS-65	MS-66	MS-67	MS-68	MS-69
7	36	58	95	17	0	0

Key to Collecting: Choice and gem Mint State coins are easily available.

1980-S WASHINGTON QUARTER
Proof Mintage: 3,554,806
OCG: PF-65

1980-S • Market Values • Proof Strikes

PF-64	PF-65	PF-66	PF-67	PF-68
$2.	$3.	$4.	$6.	$7.

1980-S • Certified Populations • Proof Strikes

PF-64	PF-65	PF-66	PF-67	PF-68	PF-69	PF-70
2	10	22	50	380	4,563	111

Key to Collecting: Nearly all are of gem quality.

1981-P WASHINGTON QUARTER
Circulation-Strike Mintage: 601,716,000
OCG: MS-65

1981-P • Market Values • Circulation Strikes

EF-40	AU-50	MS-60	MS-63	MS-64	MS-65	MS-66
$0.35	$0.45	$0.60	$1.	$4.	$6.	$21.

1981-P • Certified Populations • Circulation Strikes

MS-63	MS-64	MS-65	MS-66	MS-67	MS-68	MS-69
17	48	81	172	23	0	0

Key to Collecting: Choice and gem Mint State coins are easily available.

1981-D WASHINGTON QUARTER
Circulation-Strike Mintage: 575,722,833
OCG: MS-65

1981-D • Market Values • Circulation Strikes

EF-40	AU-50	MS-60	MS-63	MS-64	MS-65	MS-66
$0.35	$0.45	$0.60	$1.	$5.50	$4.	$11.

1981-D • Certified Populations • Circulation Strikes

MS-63	MS-64	MS-65	MS-66	MS-67	MS-68	MS-69
4	50	84	150	25	0	0

Key to Collecting: Choice and gem Mint State coins are easily available.

1981-S WASHINGTON QUARTER
Proof Mintage: 4,063,083
OCG: PF-65

TYPE I
1981-S • Market Values • Proof Strikes

PF-64	PF-65	PF-66	PF-67	PF-68
$4.	$6.	$8.	$10.	$12.

1981-S • Certified Populations • Proof Strikes

PF-64	PF-65	PF-66	PF-67	PF-68	PF-69	PF-70
3	5	13	53	468	5,463	93

TYPE II
1981-S • Market Values • Proof Strikes

PF-64	PF-65	PF-66	PF-67	PF-68
$4.	$6.	$8.	$10.	$12.

1981-S • Certified Populations • Proof Strikes

PF-64	PF-65	PF-66	PF-67	PF-68	PF-69	PF-70
4	1	10	71	169	859	24

Key to Collecting: Gem quality is the rule.

Numismatic Notes: Two mintmark varieties (Type I and Type II; see 1979-S) mentioned by Breen.

1982-P WASHINGTON QUARTER
Circulation-Strike Mintage: 500,931,000
OCG: MS-65

1982-P • Market Values • Circulation Strikes

EF-40	AU-50	MS-60	MS-63	MS-64	MS-65	MS-66
$0.40	$0.65	$1.25	$3.	$12.	$15.	$45.00

1982-P • Certified Populations • Circulation Strikes

MS-63	MS-64	MS-65	MS-66	MS-67	MS-68	MS-69
20	46	121	100	16	0	0

Key to Collecting: Choice and gem Mint State coins are plentiful, but fewer are around than for recent earlier dates (see notes below).

Numismatic Notes: In 1982 and 1983, "Mint Sets" of current circulation strikes were not sold by the Mint. Accordingly, today the quarters of these two years are slightly scarcer than are others of this era.

1982-D Washington Quarter

Circulation-Strike Mintage: 480,042,788
OCG: MS-65

1982-D • Market Values • Circulation Strikes

EF-40	AU-50	MS-60	MS-63	MS-64	MS-65	MS-66
$0.35	$0.45	$0.75	$1.50	$6.	$10.	$42.00

1982-D • Certified Populations • Circulation Strikes

MS-63	MS-64	MS-65	MS-66	MS-67	MS-68	MS-69
8	31	64	95	19	0	0

Key to Collecting: Choice and gem Mint State coins are plentiful on an absolute basis, but more elusive than for most other issues before and after 1982 and 1983.

Numismatic Notes: In 1982 and 1983, "Mint Sets" of current circulation strikes were not sold by the Mint. Accordingly, today the quarters of these two years are slightly scarcer than are others of this era.

1982-S Washington Quarter

Proof Mintage: 3,857,479
OCG: PF-65

1982-S • Market Values • Proof Strikes

PF-64	PF-65	PF-66	PF-67	PF-68
$2.	$3.	$4.	$6.	$7.

1982-S • Certified Populations • Proof Strikes

PF-64	PF-65	PF-66	PF-67	PF-68	PF-69	PF-70
3	3	9	39	129	2,150	60

Key to Collecting: Gem quality continues to be the rule. Quite a few Proof sets have been broken up, with the result that runs of Proof quarters are available from many mail-order dealers and coin shops.

1983-P WASHINGTON QUARTER

Circulation-Strike Mintage: 673,535,000
OCG: MS-65

1983-P • Market Values • Circulation Strikes

EF-40	AU-50	MS-60	MS-63	MS-64	MS-65	MS-66
$0.50	$1.	$2.	$3.	$25.	$55.00	$285.00

1983-P • Certified Populations • Circulation Strikes

MS-63	MS-64	MS-65	MS-66	MS-67	MS-68	MS-69
30	69	117	81	7	0	0

Key to Collecting: Choice and gem Mint State coins are easily available, but are scarcer than most other issues of the decade.

Numismatic Notes: In 1982 and 1983, "Mint Sets" of current circulation strikes were not sold by the Mint. Accordingly, MS-65 and finer quarters of these two years are slightly scarcer today than are others of this era.

1983-D WASHINGTON QUARTER

Circulation-Strike Mintage: 617,806,446
OCG: MS-65

1983-D • Market Values • Circulation Strikes

EF-40	AU-50	MS-60	MS-63	MS-64	MS-65	MS-66
$0.50	$1.	$2.	$3.	$18.00	$35.00	$70.00

1983-D • Certified Populations • Circulation Strikes

MS-63	MS-64	MS-65	MS-66	MS-67	MS-68	MS-69
7	68	122	62	11	0	0

Key to Collecting: Same comment as 1983-P.

Numismatic Notes: In 1982 and 1983, "Mint Sets" of current circulation strikes were not sold by the Mint. Accordingly, MS-65 and finer quarters quarters of these two years are slightly scarcer today than are others of this era.

1983-S Washington Quarter
Proof Mintage: 3,279,126
OCG: PF-65

1983-S • Market Values • Proof Strikes

PF-64	PF-65	PF-66	PF-67	PF-68
$3.	$4.	$5.	$6.	$9.

1983-S • Certified Populations • Proof Strikes

PF-64	PF-65	PF-66	PF-67	PF-68	PF-69	PF-70
2	9	22	39	117	1,876	52

Key to Collecting: Gem quality is easily available.

1984-P Washington Quarter
Circulation-Strike Mintage: 676,545,000
OCG: MS-65

1984-P • Market Values • Circulation Strikes

EF-40	AU-50	MS-60	MS-63	MS-64	MS-65	MS-66
$0.35	$0.45	$0.60	$1.	$7.	$8.	$60.00

1984-P • Certified Populations • Circulation Strikes

MS-63	MS-64	MS-65	MS-66	MS-67	MS-68	MS-69
13	47	60	63	9	0	0

Key to Collecting: Choice and gem Mint State coins are plentiful.

1984-D Washington Quarter
Circulation-Strike Mintage: 546,483,064
OCG: MS-65

1984-D • Market Values • Circulation Strikes

EF-40	AU-50	MS-60	MS-63	MS-64	MS-65	MS-66
$0.35	$0.45	$0.60	$1.	$5.50	$8.	$32.00

1984-D • Certified Populations • Circulation Strikes

MS-63	MS-64	MS-65	MS-66	MS-67	MS-68	MS-69
15	19	32	54	7	0	0

Key to Collecting: Choice and gem Mint State coins are plentiful.

1984-S WASHINGTON QUARTER

Proof Mintage: 3,065,110
OCG: PF-65

1984-S • Market Values • Proof Strikes

PF-64	PF-65	PF-66	PF-67	PF-68
$3.	$4.	$5.	$6.	$9.

1984-S • Certified Populations • Proof Strikes

PF-64	PF-65	PF-66	PF-67	PF-68	PF-69	PF-70
0	2	11	21	82	1,948	64

Key to Collecting: Easily available in gem preservation.

1985-P WASHINGTON QUARTER

Circulation-Strike Mintage: 775,818,962
OCG: MS-65

1985-P • Market Values • Circulation Strikes

EF-40	AU-50	MS-60	MS-63	MS-64	MS-65	MS-66
$0.35	$0.45	$0.60	$1.	$6.	$15.	$30.00

1985-P • Certified Populations • Circulation Strikes

MS-63	MS-64	MS-65	MS-66	MS-67	MS-68	MS-69
14	37	68	73	4	1	0

Key to Collecting: Choice and gem Mint State coins are plentiful.

1985-D WASHINGTON QUARTER

Circulation-Strike Mintage: 519,962,888
OCG: MS-65

1985-D • Market Values • Circulation Strikes

EF-40	AU-50	MS-60	MS-63	MS-64	MS-65	MS-66
$0.35	$0.45	$0.60	$1.	$3.	$8.	$14.00

1985-D • Certified Populations • Circulation Strikes

MS-63	MS-64	MS-65	MS-66	MS-67	MS-68	MS-69
7	22	96	84	7	0	0

Key to Collecting: Choice and gem Mint State coins are plentiful.

1985-S Washington Quarter
Proof Mintage: 3,362,821
OCG: PF-655

1985-S • Market Values • Proof Strikes

PF-64	PF-65	PF-66	PF-67	PF-68
$2.	$3.	$4.	$6.	$9.

1985-S • Certified Populations • Proof Strikes

PF-64	PF-65	PF-66	PF-67	PF-68	PF-69	PF-70
3	2	6	29	105	2,160	60

Key to Collecting: Gems are readily available from the sets.

1986-P Washington Quarter
Circulation-Strike Mintage: 551,199,333
OCG: MS-65

1986-P • Market Values • Circulation Strikes

EF-40	AU-50	MS-60	MS-63	MS-64	MS-65	MS-66
$0.35	$0.45	$0.60	$1.	$1.	$3.	$11.

1986-P • Certified Populations • Circulation Strikes

MS-63	MS-64	MS-65	MS-66	MS-67	MS-68	MS-69
12	45	46	50	2	0	0

Key to Collecting: Choice and gem Mint State coins are plentiful. The Professional Coin Grading Service (PCGS) was launched, popularizing the grading of coins and encapsulating them in plastic.

1986-D Washington Quarter
Circulation-Strike Mintage: 504,298,660
OCG: MS-65

1986-D • Market Values • Circulation Strikes

EF-40	AU-50	MS-60	MS-63	MS-64	MS-65	MS-66
$0.35	$0.75	$1.	$2.	$6.	$10.	$30.00

1986-D • Certified Populations • Circulation Strikes

MS-63	MS-64	MS-65	MS-66	MS-67	MS-68	MS-69
0	37	81	95	14	0	0

Key to Collecting: Choice and gem Mint State coins are plentiful.

1986-S WASHINGTON QUARTER
Proof Mintage: 3,010,497
OCG: PF-65

1986-S • Market Values • Proof Strikes

PF-64	PF-65	PF-66	PF-67	PF-68
$3.	$4.	$5.	$6.	$9.

1986-S • Certified Populations • Proof Strikes

PF-64	PF-65	PF-66	PF-67	PF-68	PF-69	PF-70
3	2	6	25	82	2,202	77

Key to Collecting: Gems are plentiful.

1987-P WASHINGTON QUARTER
Circulation-Strike Mintage: 582,499,481
OCG: MS-65

1987-P • Market Values • Circulation Strikes

EF-40	AU-50	MS-60	MS-63	MS-64	MS-65	MS-66
$0.35	$0.40	$0.45	$0.50	$6.	$8.	$20.

1987-P • Certified Populations • Circulation Strikes

MS-63	MS-64	MS-65	MS-66	MS-67	MS-68	MS-69
14	44	62	57	12	0	0

Key to Collecting: Choice and gem Mint State coins are easily available. The Numismatic Guaranty Corporation of America (NGC) began business with encapsulated coins and soon acquired a substantial market niche, second to PCGS.

1987-D WASHINGTON QUARTER
Circulation-Strike Mintage: 655,594,696
OCG: MS-65

1987-D • Market Values • Circulation Strikes

EF-40	AU-50	MS-60	MS-63	MS-64	MS-65	MS-66
$0.35	$0.40	$0.45	$0.50	$2.	$5.	$18.00

1987-D • Certified Populations • Circulation Strikes

MS-63	MS-64	MS-65	MS-66	MS-67	MS-68	MS-69
2	33	68	110	16	0	0

Key to Collecting: Choice and gem coins are common but constitute a minority of Mint State coins in existence, this being true of other clad quarters of the era. Many have extensive surface marks, especially prominent on the obverse.

1987-S WASHINGTON QUARTER

Proof Mintage: 4,227,728
OCG: PF-65

1987-S • Market Values • Proof Strikes

PF-64	PF-65	PF-66	PF-67	PF-68
$3.	$4.	$5.	$6.	$9.

1987-S • Certified Populations • Proof Strikes

PF-64	PF-65	PF-66	PF-67	PF-68	PF-69	PF-70
1	0	9	32	106	2,253	72

Key to Collecting: Nearly all are of gem quality. There was an exceptionally high Proof mintage this year. The coin market was heating up, after being sluggish since early 1980.

1988-P WASHINGTON QUARTER

Circulation-Strike Mintage: 562,052,000
OCG: MS-65

1988-P • Market Values • Circulation Strikes

EF-40	AU-50	MS-60	MS-63	MS-64	MS-65	MS-66
$0.35	$0.45	$0.60	$1.	$2.	$14.00	$30.00

1988-P • Certified Populations • Circulation Strikes

MS-63	MS-64	MS-65	MS-66	MS-67	MS-68	MS-69
11	42	52	43	3	0	0

Key to Collecting: Choice and gem Mint State coins are plentiful.

1988-D WASHINGTON QUARTER

Circulation-Strike Mintage: 596,810,688
OCG: MS-65

1988-D • Market Values • Circulation Strikes

EF-40	AU-50	MS-60	MS-63	MS-64	MS-65	MS-66
$0.35	$0.40	$0.45	$0.50	$3.50	$10.	$12.

1988-D • Certified Populations • Circulation Strikes

MS-63	MS-64	MS-65	MS-66	MS-67	MS-68	MS-69
4	30	59	68	11	0	0

Key to Collecting: Choice and gem Mint State coins are plentiful.

1988-S WASHINGTON QUARTER
Proof Mintage: 3,262,948
OCG: PF-65

1988-S • Market Values • Proof Strikes

PF-64	PF-65	PF-66	PF-67	PF-68
$2.	$3.	$4.	$6.	$9.

1988-S • Certified Populations • Proof Strikes

PF-64	PF-65	PF-66	PF-67	PF-68	PF-69	PF-70
0	3	3	22	93	1,446	60

Key to Collecting: Nearly all are gems.

1989-P WASHINGTON QUARTER
Circulation-Strike Mintage: 512,868,000
OCG: MS-65

1989-P • Market Values • Circulation Strikes

EF-40	AU-50	MS-60	MS-63	MS-64	MS-65	MS-66
$0.35	$0.45	$0.60	$0.75	$2.	$15.	$60.00

1989-P • Certified Populations • Circulation Strikes

MS-63	MS-64	MS-65	MS-66	MS-67	MS-68	MS-69
13	32	28	27	9	0	0

Key to Collecting: Choice and gem Mint State coins are plentiful. The coin market was very hot, spurred by much publicity about coins as an investment. Partnerships and funds were set up to invest, including one by Merrill Lynch. "Wall Street money" was said to be descending into the numismatic marketplace, or soon would be.

Numismatic Notes: In this year some Washington quarters were made without a mint-mark, not a die preparation oversight, but due to grease or other material filling the mintmark in a working die. A flurry of media excitement included stories that they were worth $1,000 each. However, after a statement was given by the Philadelphia Mint as to the true nature of the coins, interest faded quickly.

1989-D WASHINGTON QUARTER
Circulation-Strike Mintage: 896,535,597
OCG: MS-65

1989-D • Market Values • Circulation Strikes

EF-40	AU-50	MS-60	MS-63	MS-64	MS-65	MS-66
$0.35	$0.45	$0.60	$0.75	$1.50	$3.	$30.00

1989-D • Certified Populations • Circulation Strikes

MS-63	MS-64	MS-65	MS-66	MS-67	MS-68	MS-69
2	27	44	52	4	0	0

Key to Collecting: Choice and gem Mint State coins are plentiful.

1989-S WASHINGTON QUARTER
Proof Mintage: 3,220,194
OCG: PF-65

1989-S • Market Values • Proof Strikes

PF-64	PF-65	PF-66	PF-67	PF-68
$2.	$3.	$4.	$6.	$9.

1989-S • Certified Populations • Proof Strikes

PF-64	PF-65	PF-66	PF-67	PF-68	PF-69	PF-70
0	0	6	27	99	1,509	54

Key to Collecting: Nearly all are gems.

1990-P WASHINGTON QUARTER
Circulation-Strike Mintage: 613,792,000
OCG: MS-65

1990-P • Market Values • Circulation Strikes

EF-40	AU-50	MS-60	MS-63	MS-64	MS-65	MS-66
$0.35	$0.45	$0.60	$0.75	$2.	$10.	$30.00

1990-P • Certified Populations • Circulation Strikes

MS-63	MS-64	MS-65	MS-66	MS-67	MS-68	MS-69
8	36	41	52	6	0	0

Key to Collecting: The investment market peaked, after which there was a crash in "investment-quality" coins, which were said to include choice and gem silver and gold coins. A set of MS-65 Peace silver dollars would fall to less than 25% of its 1990 high. Mainstream *collectors* were not affected. Wall Streeters who paid record prices were disillusioned. In time, Merrill Lynch liquidated its fund and investors suffered great losses.[7]

1990-D WASHINGTON QUARTER
Circulation-Strike Mintage: 927,638,181
OCG: MS-65

1990-D • Market Values • Circulation Strikes

EF-40	AU-50	MS-60	MS-63	MS-64	MS-65	MS-66
$0.35	$0.45	$0.60	$0.75	$1.50	$3.	$22.00

1990-D • Certified Populations • Circulation Strikes

MS-63	MS-64	MS-65	MS-66	MS-67	MS-68	MS-69
3	32	54	127	20	0	0

Key to Collecting: Choice and gem Mint State coins are plentiful.

1990-S WASHINGTON QUARTER
Proof Mintage: 3,299,559
OCG: PF-65

1990-S • Market Values • Proof Strikes

PF-64	PF-65	PF-66	PF-67	PF-68
$3.	$4.	$5.	$6.	$9.

1990-S • Certified Populations • Proof Strikes

PF-64	PF-65	PF-66	PF-67	PF-68	PF-69	PF-70
4	3	8	22	88	2,609	91

Key to Collecting: Nearly all are gems.

1991-P WASHINGTON QUARTER
Circulation-Strike Mintage: 570,968,000
OCG: MS-65

1991-P • Market Values • Circulation Strikes

EF-40	AU-50	MS-60	MS-63	MS-64	MS-65	MS-66
$0.35	$0.45	$0.60	$0.75	$5.	$12.	$90.00

1991-P • Certified Populations • Circulation Strikes

MS-63	MS-64	MS-65	MS-66	MS-67	MS-68	MS-69
4	21	32	33	9	0	0

Key to Collecting: Choice and gem Mint State coins are plentiful.

1991-D WASHINGTON QUARTER
Circulation-Strike Mintage: 630,966,693
OCG: MS-65

1991-D • Market Values • Circulation Strikes

EF-40	AU-50	MS-60	MS-63	MS-64	MS-65	MS-66
$0.35	$0.45	$0.60	$0.75	$3.	$8.	$18.00

1991-D • Certified Populations • Circulation Strikes

MS-63	MS-64	MS-65	MS-66	MS-67	MS-68	MS-69
6	28	49	43	5	0	0

Key to Collecting: Choice and gem Mint State coins are plentiful.

1991-S WASHINGTON QUARTER
Proof Mintage: 2,867,787
OCG: PF-65

1991-S • Market Values • Proof Strikes

PF-64	PF-65	PF-66	PF-67	PF-68
$2.	$3.	$4.	$6.	$9.

1991-S • Certified Populations • Proof Strikes

PF-64	PF-65	PF-66	PF-67	PF-68	PF-69	PF-70
2	3	4	12	51	1,847	85

Key to Collecting: Nearly all are gems.

1992-P WASHINGTON QUARTER
Circulation-Strike Mintage: 384,764,000
OCG: MS-65

1992-P • Market Values • Circulation Strikes

EF-40	AU-50	MS-60	MS-63	MS-64	MS-65	MS-66
$0.35	$0.45	$0.60	$0.75	$8.	$15.	—

1992-P • Certified Populations • Circulation Strikes

MS-63	MS-64	MS-65	MS-66	MS-67	MS-68	MS-69
9	65	52	63	2	0	0

Key to Collecting: Choice and gem coins are plentiful. By this time PCGS, NGC, and certain other grading services were very popular, but mostly for use in encapsulating earlier coins. There was hardly any interest in having current Mint State quarters certified, due to the high cost of the services in relation to the value of the coins.

1992-D WASHINGTON QUARTER
Circulation-Strike Mintage: 389,777,107
OCG: MS-65

1992-D • Market Values • Circulation Strikes

EF-40	AU-50	MS-60	MS-63	MS-64	MS-65	MS-66
$0.35	$0.45	$0.60	$0.75	$4.	$15.	$225.00

1992-D • Certified Populations • Circulation Strikes

MS-63	MS-64	MS-65	MS-66	MS-67	MS-68	MS-69
12	51	40	34	1	1	0

Key to Collecting: Choice and gem coins are plentiful.

1992-S COPPER-NICKEL CLAD WASHINGTON QUARTER
Proof Mintage: 2,858,981
OCG: PF-65

1992-S • Market Values • Proof Strikes

PF-64	PF-65	PF-66	PF-67	PF-68
$2.	$3.	$4.	$6.	$9.

1992-S • Certified Populations • Proof Strikes

PF-64	PF-65	PF-66	PF-67	PF-68	PF-69	PF-70
1	1	7	9	50	1,707	75

Key to Collecting: Virtually all are gems.

1992-S SILVER WASHINGTON QUARTER
Proof Mintage: 1,317,579
OCG: PF-65

1992-S • Silver • Market Values • Proof Strikes

PF-64	PF-65	PF-66	PF-67	PF-68
$4.	$5.	$6.	$8.	$11.

1992-S • Silver • Certified Populations • Proof Strikes

PF-64	PF-65	PF-66	PF-67	PF-68	PF-69	PF-70
5	4	10	42	88	2,180	44

Key to Collecting: This marked the first year of special Proof coins struck in the old alloy of 90% silver and 10% copper. These are not easily distinguished from the clad examples, except by looking at the coins edge-on to see full silver color. On clad coins, the copper core is seen.

1993-P WASHINGTON QUARTER
Circulation-Strike Mintage: 639,276,000
OCG: MS-65

1993-P • Market Values • Circulation Strikes

EF-40	AU-50	MS-60	MS-63	MS-64	MS-65	MS-66
$0.35	$0.45	$0.60	$0.75	$2.50	$6.	—

1993-P • Certified Populations • Circulation Strikes

MS-63	MS-64	MS-65	MS-66	MS-67	MS-68	MS-69
11	32	57	122	14	0	0

Key to Collecting: Choice and gem coins are plentiful.

1993-D WASHINGTON QUARTER
Circulation-Strike Mintage: 645,476,128
OCG: MS-65

1993-D • Market Values • Circulation Strikes

EF-40	AU-50	MS-60	MS-63	MS-64	MS-65	MS-66
$0.35	$0.45	$0.60	$0.75	$2.50	$6.	—

1993-D • Certified Populations • Circulation Strikes

MS-63	MS-64	MS-65	MS-66	MS-67	MS-68	MS-69
6	27	80	98	8	0	0

Key to Collecting: Choice and gem coins are plentiful.

1993-S COPPER-NICKEL CLAD WASHINGTON QUARTER
Proof Mintage: 2,633,439
OCG: PF-65

1993-S • Market Values • Proof Strikes

PF-64	PF-65	PF-66	PF-67	PF-68
$3.	$4.	$5.	$6.	$9.

1993-S • Certified Populations • Proof Strikes

PF-64	PF-65	PF-66	PF-67	PF-68	PF-69	PF-70
0	1	7	9	34	1,654	61

Key to Collecting: Nearly all are gems.

1993-S SILVER
WASHINGTON QUARTER
Proof Mintage: 761,353
OCG: PF-65

1993-S • Silver • Market Values • Proof Strikes

PF-64	PF-65	PF-66	PF-67	PF-68
$5.	$6.	$7.	$8.	$11.

1993-S • Silver • Certified Populations • Proof Strikes

PF-64	PF-65	PF-66	PF-67	PF-68	PF-69	PF-70
5	3	14	26	93	2,026	23

Key to Collecting: Nearly all are gems. The mintage dropped sharply from that of 1992, primarily because at quick glance the silver coins could not be differentiated easily from the clad coins, unless the edge was inspected.

1994-P WASHINGTON QUARTER
Circulation-Strike Mintage: 825,600,000
OCG: MS-65

1994-P • Market Values • Circulation Strikes

EF-40	AU-50	MS-60	MS-63	MS-64	MS-65	MS-66
$0.35	$0.45	$0.50	$0.60	$6.	$18.00	—

1994-P • Certified Populations • Circulation Strikes

MS-63	MS-64	MS-65	MS-66	MS-67	MS-68	MS-69
14	43	56	57	5	0	0

Key to Collecting: Choice and gem coins are plentiful.

1994-D WASHINGTON QUARTER
Circulation-Strike Mintage: 880,034,110
OCG: MS-65

1994-D • Market Values • Circulation Strikes

EF-40	AU-50	MS-60	MS-63	MS-64	MS-65	MS-66
$0.35	$0.45	$0.50	$0.60	$3.	$8.	—

1994-D • Certified Populations • Circulation Strikes

MS-63	MS-64	MS-65	MS-66	MS-67	MS-68	MS-69
7	40	37	41	3	0	0

Key to Collecting: Choice and gem coins are plentiful.

1994-S Copper-Nickel Clad Washington Quarter

Proof Mintage: 2,484,594
OCG: PF-65

1994-S • Market Values • Proof Strikes

PF-64	PF-65	PF-66	PF-67	PF-68
$3.	$4.	$5.	$6.	$9.

1994-S • Certified Populations • Proof Strikes

PF-64	PF-65	PF-66	PF-67	PF-68	PF-69	PF-70
1	1	6	19	63	2,080	68

Key to Collecting: Nearly all are gems.

1994-S Silver Washington Quarter

Proof Mintage: 785,329
OCG: PF-65

1994-S • Silver • Market Values • Proof Strikes

PF-64	PF-65	PF-66	PF-67	PF-68
$5.	$6.	$7.	$8.	$11.

1994-S • Silver • Certified Populations • Proof Strikes

PF-64	PF-65	PF-66	PF-67	PF-68	PF-69	PF-70
8	6	6	27	73	1,887	27

Key to Collecting: Nearly all are gems.

1995-P Washington Quarter

Circulation-Strike Mintage: 1,004,336,000
OCG: MS-65

1995-P • Market Values • Circulation Strikes

EF-40	AU-50	MS-60	MS-63	MS-64	MS-65	MS-66
$0.35	$0.45	$0.60	$0.75	$6.	$14.00	$36.00

1995-P • Certified Populations • Circulation Strikes

MS-63	MS-64	MS-65	MS-66	MS-67	MS-68	MS-69
7	34	33	66	43	1	0

Key to Collecting: Choice and gem coins are plentiful.

Numismatic Notes: The circulation strikes at the Philadelphia and Denver mint this year crossed the billion mark for the first time since the 1960s.

1995-D WASHINGTON QUARTER
Circulation-Strike Mintage: 1,103,216,000
OCG: MS-65

1995-D • Market Values • Circulation Strikes

EF-40	AU-50	MS-60	MS-63	MS-64	MS-65	MS-66
$0.35	$0.45	$0.60	$0.75	$6.	$12.	$30.00

1995-D • Certified Populations • Circulation Strikes

MS-63	MS-64	MS-65	MS-66	MS-67	MS-68	MS-69
12	15	29	87	36	1	0

Key to Collecting: Choice and gem coins are plentiful.

1995-S COPPER-NICKEL CLAD WASHINGTON QUARTER
Proof Mintage: 2,117,496
OCG: PF-65

1995-S • Market Values • Proof Strikes

PF-64	PF-65	PF-66	PF-67	PF-68
$4.	$10.	$7.	$10.	$15.

1995-S • Certified Populations • Proof Strikes

PF-64	PF-65	PF-66	PF-67	PF-68	PF-69	PF-70
2	0	8	10	46	1,632	49

Key to Collecting: Virtually all are gems.

1995-S SILVER WASHINGTON QUARTER
Proof Mintage: 679,985
OCG: PF-65

1995-S • Silver • Market Values • Proof Strikes

PF-64	PF-65	PF-66	PF-67	PF-68
$5.	$11.	$10.	$12.	$17.

1995-S • Silver • Certified Populations • Proof Strikes

PF-64	PF-65	PF-66	PF-67	PF-68	PF-69	PF-70
5	2	9	28	75	1,847	25

Key to Collecting: Nearly all are gems. Silver Proof quarters continued to generate lukewarm interest in comparison to the clad issues that were part of sets.

1996-P WASHINGTON QUARTER
Circulation-Strike Mintage: 925,040,000
OCG: MS-65

1996-P • Market Values • Circulation Strikes

EF-40	AU-50	MS-60	MS-63	MS-64	MS-65	MS-66
$0.35	$0.45	$0.50	$0.60	$4.	$8.	$12.

1996-P • Certified Populations • Circulation Strikes

MS-63	MS-64	MS-65	MS-66	MS-67	MS-68	MS-69
11	33	58	141	362	54	0

Key to Collecting: Choice and gem coins are plentiful.

1996-D WASHINGTON QUARTER
Circulation-Strike Mintage: 906,868,000
OCG: MS-65

1996-D • Market Values • Circulation Strikes

EF-40	AU-50	MS-60	MS-63	MS-64	MS-65	MS-66
$0.35	$0.45	$0.50	$0.60	$4.	$8.	$12.

1996-D • Certified Populations • Circulation Strikes

MS-63	MS-64	MS-65	MS-66	MS-67	MS-68	MS-69
3	21	48	152	519	30	0

Key to Collecting: Choice and gem coins are plentiful.

1996-S COPPER-NICKEL CLAD WASHINGTON QUARTER
Proof Mintage: 1,750,244
OCG: PF-65

1996-S • Market Values • Proof Strikes

PF-64	PF-65	PF-66	PF-67	PF-68
$4.	$5.	$7.	$10.	$15.

1996-S • Certified Populations • Proof Strikes

PF-64	PF-65	PF-66	PF-67	PF-68	PF-69	PF-70
3	3	5	11	156	1,632	40

Key to Collecting: Nearly all are gems.

1996-S SILVER WASHINGTON QUARTER
Proof Mintage: 775,021
OCG: PF-65

1996-S • Silver • Market Values • Proof Strikes

PF-64	PF-65	PF-66	PF-67	PF-68
$5.	$9.	$10.	$12.	$17.

1996-S • Silver • Certified Populations • Proof Strikes

PF-64	PF-65	PF-66	PF-67	PF-68	PF-69	PF-70
8	5	12	20	77	1,939	40

Key to Collecting: Nearly all are gems.

1997-P WASHINGTON QUARTER
Circulation-Strike Mintage: 595,740,000
OCG: MS-65

1997-P • Market Values • Circulation Strikes

EF-40	AU-50	MS-60	MS-63	MS-64	MS-65	MS-66
$0.35	$0.40	$0.45	$0.75	$9.	$9.	$141.00

1997-P • Certified Populations • Circulation Strikes

MS-63	MS-64	MS-65	MS-66	MS-67	MS-68	MS-69
10	22	49	59	39	0	0

Key to Collecting: Choice and gem coins are plentiful.

1997-D WASHINGTON QUARTER
Circulation-Strike Mintage: 599,680,000
OCG: MS-65

1997-D • Market Values • Circulation Strikes

EF-40	AU-50	MS-60	MS-63	MS-64	MS-65	MS-66
$0.35	$0.40	$0.45	$0.75	$10.	$11.	$35.

1997-D • Certified Populations • Circulation Strikes

MS-63	MS-64	MS-65	MS-66	MS-67	MS-68	MS-69
7	23	23	56	63	10	0

Key to Collecting: Choice and gem coins are plentiful. By this time the certification of current quarter dollars had become popular. Increasingly, collectors were aspiring to own grades beyond MS-65.

1997-S COPPER-NICKEL CLAD WASHINGTON QUARTER
Proof Mintage: 2,055,000
OCG: PF-65

1997-S • Market Values • Proof Strikes

PF-64	PF-65	PF-66	PF-67	PF-68
$6.	$7.	$7.	$10.	$15.

1997-S • Certified Populations • Proof Strikes

PF-64	PF-65	PF-66	PF-67	PF-68	PF-69	PF-70
0	0	6	14	28	1,260	38

Key to Collecting: Nearly all are gems.

1997-S SILVER WASHINGTON QUARTER
Proof Mintage: 741,678
OCG: PF-65

1997-S • Silver • Market Values • Proof Strikes

PF-64	PF-65	PF-66	PF-67	PF-68
$7.	$11.	$10.	$12.	$17.

1997-S • Silver • Certified Populations • Proof Strikes

PF-64	PF-65	PF-66	PF-67	PF-68	PF-69	PF-70
4	4	5	14	62	2,065	48

Key to Collecting: Nearly all are gems.

1998-P WASHINGTON QUARTER
Circulation-Strike Mintage: 896,268,000
OCG: MS-65

1998-P • Market Values • Circulation Strikes

EF-40	AU-50	MS-60	MS-63	MS-64	MS-65	MS-66
$0.35	$0.40	$0.45	$0.75	$7.	$10.	$28.

1998-P • Certified Populations • Circulation Strikes

MS-63	MS-64	MS-65	MS-66	MS-67	MS-68	MS-69
14	66	55	75	70	16	0

Key to Collecting: Choice and gem coins are plentiful. Last of the old-style quarters with the basic obverse and reverse design of 1932.

1998-D WASHINGTON QUARTER
Circulation-Strike Mintage: 821,000,000
OCG: MS-65

1998-D • Market Values • Circulation Strikes

EF-40	AU-50	MS-60	MS-63	MS-64	MS-65	MS-66
$0.35	$0.40	$0.45	$0.75	$10.	$12.	$90.

1998-D • Certified Populations • Circulation Strikes

MS-63	MS-64	MS-65	MS-66	MS-67	MS-68	MS-69
12	45	47	63	12	0	0

Key to Collecting: Choice and gem coins are plentiful.

1998-S COPPER-NICKEL CLAD WASHINGTON QUARTER
Proof Mintage: 2,086,507
OCG: PF-65

1998-S • Market Values • Proof Strikes

PF-64	PF-65	PF-66	PF-67	PF-68
$5.	$7.	$7.	$10.	$15.

1998-S • Certified Populations • Proof Strikes

PF-64	PF-65	PF-66	PF-67	PF-68	PF-69	PF-70
0	2	7	8	66	1,238	24

Key to Collecting: Gem coins are plentiful.

1998-S SILVER WASHINGTON QUARTER
Proof Mintage: 878,792
OCG: PF-65

1998-S • Silver • Market Values • Proof Strikes

PF-64	PF-65	PF-66	PF-67	PF-68
$7.	$8.	$10.	$12.	$17.

1998-S • Silver • Certified Populations • Proof Strikes

PF-64	PF-65	PF-66	PF-67	PF-68	PF-69	PF-70
1	2	3	9	63	2,095	46

Key to Collecting: Nearly all are gems.

THE COLLECTOR'S CHOICE®

ANACS is The Official Grading Service of CONECA,
the world s largest organization of variety and error collectors.

ANACS presents the Clear View™ holder.
For a free ANACS submission form visit www.ANACS.com.

P.O. Box 200300, Austin, TX 78720-0300

800.888.1861

INTEGRITY
ACCURACY
RELIABILITY
SERVICE
TRUST

www.anacs.com

The 50 State Quarters® Program

Introduction

In numismatics, observers have come to expect the unexpected. After the 1776–1976 Bicentennial quarter faded into history, production of this denomination continued routinely. Circulation strikes were made in large quantities at the Philadelphia and Denver mints, and at the San Francisco Mint, Proofs were struck for collectors. Among collectors the series remained fairly humdrum, attracting little attention. Lincoln cents, Jefferson nickels, Roosevelt dimes, and even Franklin half dollars were more popular. Eisenhower dollars came in for their share of attention as well, as did, in time, the Susan B. Anthony mini-dollar of 1979.

Commemorative coins had not been produced since 1954, when the lengthy Carver/Washington half dollar series ended. Unpopular though that series had been, the collecting community soon missed having new issues of commemoratives. Proposals were made, including by spokespeople for the ANA and the PNG. Articles advocating new commemoratives appeared in periodicals. There was no interest on the part of Congress, however, to pass enabling acts, and no encouragement from the Treasury Department.

Finally, in 1982, under the administration of Mint Director Donna Pope, the George Washington 250th Anniversary commemorative half dollars were made, from designs by Chief Engraver Elizabeth Jones. Pieces with frosty or "Mint State" finish were struck at the Denver Mint, to the extent of 2,210,458 coins, and 4,894,044 Proofs were made at San Francisco. The numismatic community gave the new commemoratives a warm reception, but it was more than a year before all were sold.

The 1999 Delaware state quarter, the first issue of a 50-coin series. The obverse has been completely restyled from earlier versions and no longer bears the date.

Other commemorative designs followed. Some issues were of single denominations, such as a silver dollar, while others consisted of several. All were sold at premiums considerably over face value, for amounts often significantly in excess of their metal or intrinsic values. Many complaints were voiced in the coin papers about how expensive it was just to keep current with new issues.

There was a quiet call for a "people's commemorative"—an issue, or issues, that would circulate as regular coinage. I suggested that the reverse of the Kennedy half dollar, a denomination not often seen in circulation, would be an ideal matrix for a series of designs depicting American events. Harvey G. Stack thought that quarter dollars could be made as commemoratives. Other ideas were discussed and written about, as well.

In the summer of 1996, Representative Michael N. Castle (R-Delaware) introduced HR 3793, the 50 States Commemorative Coin Program Act. Under its provisions, the Mint was to produce five new "commemorative" quarter dollars each year, for 10 years, with each coin depicting motifs relating to one of the states. The innovative concept was that these were to be circulating coins, to be placed into the channels of commerce at face value.

The news was greeted with enthusiasm by the numismatic hobby, but with a degree of caution. Memories were still clear regarding the 1979 Susan B. Anthony mini-dollar, publicized as a great innovation in coinage. The program was a flop. The earlier Bicentennial coins—the quarter, half dollar, and dollar with the dates 1776–1976—had not lived up to their expectations, either. Would it be different with the state quarters?

The concept became a reality with the signing by President Bill Clinton of PL 105-124 in December 1997. The U.S. Mint revised the name slightly and launched the 50 State Quarters® Program. This name was registered, and a symbol was used, for in recent times there had been all sorts of private sales organizations—some with minting facilities, but most without—advertising themselves as "mints." Some of these had names suggesting an official or government connection, gulling many buyers into thinking they were buying from the source. The 50 State Quarters® Program was to be the property of the U.S. Mint, and no one else.

In 1994, President Clinton appointed Philip N. Diehl to be director of the Mint, succeeding Donna Pope, who had held the post since 1992. Under Diehl's watch as Mint director, the quarter dollar became the circulating commemorative that so many had wanted. It has also been suggested, from the very inception of the program, some that the 50-state concept be extended to include the District of Columbia and certain territories and possessions. At least two bills have been introduced in the Senate to this effect—but at the time of this writing, both bills remained in committee.

THE PROGRAM PLAN

Under the 50 State Quarters® Program, each year five states of the Union were to suggest designs for the reverse of the quarter dollar, with motifs to depict some aspect of history, tradition, nature, or fame. Prohibitions included busts, state seals, state flags, logotypes, and depictions of living people or of "organizations whose membership or ownership is not universal." Although rules varied over a period of time, these were in effect in 2004:

> Designs shall maintain a dignity befitting the nation's coinage. Designs shall have broad appeal to the citizens of the state and avoid controversial subjects or symbols that are likely to offend. . . . The states are encouraged to submit designs that promote the diffusion of knowledge among the youth of the United States about the state, its history and geography, and the rich diversity of our national heritage.

Generally, citizens were invited to submit art and written suggestions to be reviewed by the governor and advisors, after which up to five semifinal designs would be selected. These would be sent to the Mint, where artists would modify the art to their own specifications. The Mint art would then be submitted to the Commission of Fine Arts and the Citizens Commemorative Coin Advisory Committee (usually referred to as the Citizens Coin Advisory Committee), after which the Mint might make some modifications. In the next step, the state would make a choice among the semifinal motifs. Usually, state citizens would be invited to select their favorites. Sometimes the first-place design would be approved by the governor. In other instances, the governor would have the absolute right to select the motif he or she wanted, regardless of public opinion. The secretary of the Treasury reserved the right to reject any design he or she considered inappropriate, and in all cases would have the final say.

Each year, five quarters have been released in the order in which the states joined the Union (by ratifying the Constitution), with appropriate launch ceremonies attended by Mint officials and dignitaries. The launch times are generally spaced throughout the year. Circulation strikes have been made at the Philadelphia and Denver mints, while at the San Francisco Mint Proofs have been struck for collectors and others, in clad composition as well as silver. The general policy has been to strike coins of a given design, beginning about a month before general release, and continuing until it is necessary to prepare for the next design. Once a design is finished, no additional coins will be made later. However, Proofs are often struck early, so that a year-set of these can be distributed before certain related circulation strikes are released. The quantities of circulation strikes have varied widely, mostly dependent on the general need for new quarter dollars in commerce, not on the popularity of a given state.

Since the inception of the 50 State Quarters® Program in 1999, the Mint has been creative with its marketing (witness the use of Kermit the Frog, of Muppets fame, as the "Mint Spokesfrog"). Many other new ideas have been implemented, among the most recent being the offering of individual issues in rolls and in 100-coin and 1,000-coin bags. Other innovative programs had been devised under the watch of Mint Director Diehl and continued with Jay Johnson. These included the American Spirit Collection of state dolls and related items by Hallmark, promotions with *Reader's Digest* and *National Geographic*, and other entrepreneurial ventures.[1]

From a financial and popularity viewpoint, the entire program has been a spectacular success—absolutely brilliant, in my opinion. And although there have been a few problems involving communication and timely responses,[2] the U.S. Mint has done much in its outreach to collectors in recent years. This includes the administrations of Mint directors Philip Diehl, Jay Johnson, and Henrietta Holsman Fore during the quarters program from 1999 to 2005. Collectors and writers have been warmly welcomed, exhibits have been mounted at conventions, and much information has been supplied to numismatic periodicals, although not all questions have been answered.

DIRECTOR JOHNSON REMEMBERS

Jay Johnson, director of the Mint in 2000 and 2001, shared some reminiscences for readers of this book:

> One of my favorite lines I gave in speeches about the state quarters was that they were both *collectible* coins and *circulating* coins. I used to refer folks (if the audience was old enough to remember) to that old commercial for a breath mint (get it? Mint Director talking about mints!) that said, "Is it a *breath* mint or a *candy* mint? It's both. It's two, it's two, it's two mints in one!"
>
> That's what I used to say of the quarters—as I held a coin in each hand and clicked them together: "Is it a circulating coin, or a commemorative coin? It's both, it's two, it's two coins in one!"
>
> Anyone who remembered the Certs commercial got the connection, and it was an easy way of explaining "circulating" and "commemorative" coins to the non-numismatist.

Non-numismatic audiences also got a smile out of a line I used to use in speeches after talking about the popularity of the 50 state quarters and the numbers of people collecting them. I would add, "Why, these days, practically everybody is calling himself a numismatist!" To many people who couldn't think of even pronouncing *numismatist*, it got a nice smile. Hopefully, it even helped people think about joining the American Numismatic Association.[3]

ARTISTIC INFUSION

In 2004 the U.S. Mint implemented the novel Artistic Infusion Program, an effort to bring the talents of private-sector artists under the wing of the government. Eighteen "master" designers and six "associate" designers were selected from applications received, to create motifs for American coins and medals. Only *one* of the master designers was credited with having any coin experience: Bill Krawczewicz of Severna Park, Maryland, was listed as a bank-note designer, currently with Bureau of Engraving and Printing, and said to be a "designer of U.S. commemorative coins and state quarter dollars."

An orientation meeting was held at the Philadelphia Mint in February of the same year. "Together, we will invigorate the artistry of coin design in America," Mint Director Henrietta Holsman Fore announced.

Each master designer is to receive $1,000 for each sketch submitted, while associates are to receive $500. In contrast, Daniel Carr, a private-sector artist, was paid $2,500 for each of his sketches used on quarters. How this "infusion" will affect the quality of the state quarter program remains to be seen. There is some good news (concerning regular coins and medals) and bad news (state quarters):

The Artistic Infusion Program artists will also receive other new coin and medal assignments as they become available. The initials of both the artists and the engravers will be on all coins and medals, except the 50 state quarters, which will carry only the sculptor-engravers' initials.[4]

Daniel Carr, who designed three of the state quarters and was paid by the Mint for doing so, but whose name did not appear on the coins.

This nonrecognition of private artists who create designs has caused a lot of criticism. The Mint then went a few steps further to ensure internal control of the artwork on the state quarters. Perhaps stung by the Missouri quarter controversy (see pages 213–214), the Mint rewrote the rules to completely eliminate outside art, to be effective with the 2005 designs:

New Rules of 2005

Stage 1: The United States Mint will initiate the formal state design process by contacting the state governor approximately 24 months prior to the beginning of the year in which the state will be honored. The governor, or such other state officials or group as the state may designate, will appoint an individual to serve as the state's liaison to the United States Mint for this program.

Stage 2: The state will conduct a concept selection process as determined by the state. The state will provide to the United States Mint at least three, but no more than five, different concepts or themes emblematic of the state; each concept or theme will be in narrative format. The narrative must explain why the concept is emblematic of the state and what the concept represents to the state's citizens. A narrative that merely describes a particular design is not acceptable.

Stage 3: Based on the narratives, the United States Mint will produce original artwork of the concepts, focusing on aesthetic beauty, historical accuracy, appropriateness and coinability. If the state has not provided at least three concepts, the United States Mint may produce additional concepts for the state.

Stage 4: The United States Mint will contact the state to collaborate on the artwork. The state will appoint an historian, or other responsible officials or experts, to participate in this collaboration to ensure historical accuracy and proper state representation of the artwork. The United States Mint will refine the artwork before forwarding it to the advisory bodies.

Stage 5: The Citizens Coinage Advisory Committee and the U.S. Commission of Fine Arts will review the candidate designs and make recommendations, and the United States Mint may make changes to address such recommendations.

Stage 6: The United States Mint will present the candidate designs to the Secretary of the Treasury for review and approval.

Stage 7: The United States Mint will return to the state all candidate designs approved by the Secretary of the Treasury.

Stage 8: From among the designs approved by the Secretary, the state will recommend the final design through a process determined by the state, within a time frame specified by the United States Mint.

Stage 9: The United States Mint will present the state's recommended design to the Secretary for final approval.[5]

These rules have been viewed by some as taking from the states the right to select art created within that state, and leaving it up to staff artists and engravers at the Mint to create final art from "concepts." From the viewpoint of artistic integrity, things went from bad to worse. In any event, an exception was granted to California for its 2005 quarter dollar.

DIVERSITY IN DESIGNS

If anything, the state-quarter designs are diverse. No two are alike, but closest to being twins are the issues of North Carolina (2001) and Ohio (2002), both of whose motifs include a Wright brothers biplane (though a later plane on the Ohio version). Many include inscriptions familiar only to state citizens or players of Trivial Pursuit. Do you know which state selected "The Crossroads of America"? What about "Foundation in Education," or "Corps of Discovery," or "Crossroads of the Revolution"? I knew none of these until I saw them on the coins (answers, in order: Indiana, Iowa, Missouri, and New Jersey). On the other hand, I and most others know that the Bay State is Massachusetts and the Lone Star State is Texas.

In each and every state, there have been challenges to overcome with regard to the design-selection process. In 2004, when Governor Arnold Schwarzenegger made the final selection for the forthcoming 2005 California quarter, the design featured naturalist John Muir. Among other entries was one depicting an assortment of objects relating to the Gold Rush. When this was rejected, its designer wrote letters to newspapers and otherwise charged that the decision had been unfair. These things happen, and will continue to. Perhaps if a strong central motif, instead of scattered objects, had been suggested, a Gold Rush theme would have won. All's well that ends well, and almost everyone liked the final version when they saw it—a motif with Muir in Yosemite Valley, with Half Dome in the distance and a condor overhead. (The designer, Garrett Burke, contributed the foreword to this book.)

In addition, each and every design has had both its detractors (some more than others) and its fans. In that regard, *Coin World* columnist Michele Orzano wrote this bit of philosophy and opinion:

What would you answer if someone stops you on the street tomorrow and asks, "How would you define the spirit of your state?"

Now think about that question in light of the 26 State quarter dollar designs currently in circulation. The 2004 Michigan design shows the outline of the state and the Great Lakes. There's not an automobile in sight, yet that's what most Americans would probably say is the defining symbol—that of Motown.

Consider the design for the 2002 Mississippi quarter dollar. The design depicts two magnolia blossoms and leaves with the inscription THE MAGNOLIA STATE. But wouldn't many Americans think of riverboats and the tales Mark Twain told in his *Life on the Mississippi*, published in 1883?

Does the image of the Old Man of the Mountain truly define New Hampshire as depicted on its 2000 State quarter dollar? What would archeologists in the future discern from looking at that image? Would they surmise that the folks who populate New Hampshire all have craggy facial features?

The 1999 Georgia quarter dollar features the outline of the state enclosing a peach, with a banner featuring the state motto WISDOM, JUSTICE, MODERATION and a border of live oak sprigs. Does that design capture the full flavor of a state that's given the world and the nation Vidalia onions and the Okefenokee Swamp?

Bottom line: Not everyone is going to be happy with every design. Does that mean the state quarter dollar program is without merit? No. It just means that in a land like America, we're given the privilege to have an opinion and express it. It's clear that no matter the design, collectors are continuing to enjoy the program and will for many years to come.[6]

Well stated, Michele!

COMMENTS ON DESIGNS

Some basic information about the state-reverse quarters has been difficult to find. No single source seemed to have everything—rather surprising, as I thought that details on the launch ceremonies and the creators of the designs or concepts in each state as well as the identities of the Mint artists who made the final sketches and designs would be common knowledge.

What was envisioned as an easy procedure turned into a fairly lengthy search involving the use of numismatic articles, interviews, and comments from those involved, usually adding much to the official information issued by the U.S. Mint.

Concerning my quest for information, and also why some information in print does not reveal what *really* happened, this commentary from *Coin World* editor Beth Deisher may be of interest:

> In the early years, most of the states announced "winners" of their design concept competitions. If that happened, it is reported in news stories. For many of the state quarters, there is no specific person identified as the "concept" designer. Let's use Ohio as an example:
>
> Ohio invited the public to submit design concepts. Although 7,298 were received, none depicted exactly what was finally used on Ohio's quarter. The final design consists of elements selected by the Ohio Quarter Committee that were rendered into a sketch by an artist hired by the committee. Although that artist was introduced at the Ohio launch ceremony, he is not considered the "concept designer" because he did not develop the concept. So officially, *no individual* is credited with the design concept. The most accurate statement is that the Ohio quarter was literally designed by the committee. Proceedings were extensively reported in Ohio daily newspapers, as all meetings of the Ohio committee were open to the public.

It is easier to identify those at the Mint who sculpted the models. The Mint considers the sculptor-engraver who made the model (based on the design concept submitted by the state) to be the designer, and that person's initials appear on the coin.

At the same time, various newspaper articles as well as information on the U.S. Mint web site suggest that for some designs, specific people were indeed involved in creating final sketches before they were submitted to the Mint staff. For example, Daniel Miller, a graphic artist from Arlington, Texas, was identified as the creator of the design selected from about 2,700 others to be used on the 2004 Texas quarter. Much publicity was given to Garrett Burke, designer of the aforementioned 2005 California quarter with the Muir motif. As to whether the limelight for an artist in the private sector is turned on or switched off, that seems to be up to the Mint.

CREDIT WHERE CREDIT IS DUE?

Michele Orzano noted this in one of her *Coin World* columns (excerpted):

Inconsistency Dogs Designer Credit

Future numismatists researching the identities of the designers of the State quarter dollars may get different answers, depending on the sources of their information. Since the beginning of the program in 1999, the U.S. Mint has only credited its staff engravers who created the models for the coins, by placing their initials on the State quarter designs—regardless of whether a state has identified the "designer" or the U.S. Mint paid the designer.

"The policy has been just to have the engravers' initials on the coins because often the design concept is something other people have also submitted," according to Michael White, a spokesman for the U.S. Mint. In many cases, individuals have submitted different versions of the same design theme. . . . The decision to credit only the engravers and none of the original designers, even when their identities are known, is a change for the Mint. In the 20th century, the Mint generally acknowledged artists by placing their initials on the coins.[7]

Indeed, in the early 1980s Mint Director Donna Pope, realizing that for the 1984 Olympic commemorative $10 gold coin, the motif had been designed by one person (James Peed) and the models for dies engraved by another (John Mercanti), sought to recognize both on the coin. Both JM and JP initials appear at the lower left, a double signature, which resulted from a conversation Pope and I had. At the time, I was president of the ANA, and Pope maintained an excellent relationship and continuing dialogue not only with the ANA but with numismatic publications and the entire collecting fraternity. She inquired whether it was accepted practice to include the initials of the designer as well as the engraver, and I cited several examples from history,[8] after which she decided to employ the initials on the 1984 Olympic gold coins.

The current decision not to recognize these artists has cost them an economic opportunity. In the past, retired Mint artist-sculptors (e.g., William Cousins) whose initials appear on regular or commemorative coins have inked profitable contracts by signing holders containing their coins. Some past Mint directors have also inked contracts to autograph coin holders. Those who have designed coins, but whose initials have not appeared, have landed some contracts as well, but their identities are little known to most people. For example, Daniel Carr, an independent artist from Colorado, was paid by the Mint to design the reverses of the 2001 New York and Rhode Island quarters, and was later involved with the 2003 Maine issue—but he received no recognition on the coins and was not featured at launch ceremonies, and Mint publicity does not acknowledge his existence. Garrett Burke, on the other hand, although not allowed to sign his art, was (quite deservedly) feted at the 2005 California quarter ceremony. Would that other artists could have the same honor.

There is one final inconsistency to the whole non-recognition policy. The famous works of old masters are sometimes the source for coin designs. On the 2004 Iowa quarter, the name of Grant Wood, the artist of the *Arbor Day* painting, is displayed in very large letters on the reverse—larger than on any other coin in American history! In contrast, Emmanuel Leutze, painter of *Washington Crossing the Delaware*, receives no credit on the Delaware quarter.

OBVERSE CHANGES

In 1999, to accommodate the creative designs intended for the reverse of the state quarters, the inscriptions UNITED STATES OF AMERICA and QUARTER DOLLAR, were relocated to the obverse above and below the portrait, respectively. LIBERTY and IN GOD WE TRUST were moved to new positions. At the same time, the Mint decided to "improve" the portrait of Washington by adding little curlicue-and-squiggle hair details (apparently, there had been complaints that the portrait details were unclear, and this was the Mint's solution).

In 1999, the name of the Mint engraver who created the new die, William Cousins, was memorialized by the addition of his initials, WC, next to JF (for John Flanagan, the original designer in 1932) on the neck truncation. The initials now appear to run together as JFWC. The W is of unusual appearance and is not very legible.

It is probably correct to call this the Cousins portrait. Perhaps one day the Mint will bring back a classic portrait of Washington—perhaps the 1786 version on the Washington Before Boston medal by Pierre Simon Duvivier (after Houdon, but with peruke added) or the 19th-century portrait by Charles Cushing Wright (after Duvivier).

NUMISMATIC ASPECTS OF STATE QUARTERS

BASIC INFORMATION

Specifications

Clad Issues—Composition: Outer layers of copper-nickel (75% copper, 25% nickel) bonded to an inner core of pure copper. The copper is visible by viewing the coin edge-on. *Diameter:* 24.3 mm. *Weight:* 87.5 grains. *Edge:* Reeded.

Silver Issues—Composition: 90% silver. 10% copper. *Diameter:* 24.3 mm. *Weight:* 96.45 grains. *Edge:* Reeded.

As planned, the various statehood quarters were made in circulation-strike format (Mint State) at the Philadelphia and Denver mints, and in Proof format, both in clad metal and in 90% silver, at the San Francisco Mint. In all instances, circulation-strike mintages have run into the hundreds of millions, clad proofs to the extent of several million, and silver Proofs into the high hundreds of thousands. Accordingly, the four varieties of each issue have been readily available in their years of mintage, and after that time the market supply has been generous.

For each issue described on the following pages, mintage figures are given for circulation strikes and for Proofs. It is normal practice to pay out circulation strikes through banks and the Federal Reserve. Such coins quickly reach circulation all over the United States, not just in the honored state. Proofs are sold at a premium, and at year's end, remaining coins are withdrawn. Usually, the U.S. Mint delays publishing Proof mintage quantities until two years or so after the striking.

Information is also given about the creation of the design, the minting of the coins, and their distribution. Selected information is given about the featured subjects and the state honored. For the states, certain related aspects of numismatic history and interest are given.

Market-price estimates for various grades are given, edited by Lawrence Stack. Population reports represent the combined certification figures of ANACS, NGC, and PCGS as of late 2005. As only a tiny fraction of these coins have been certified, it is likely that these figures will increase over time, perhaps dramatically. Extreme caution is urged in buying a quarter dollar that is common in MS-65 to 68, but for which relatively few have been certified at grades of MS-69 or 70.

In chapter 8, I provided the Optimal Collecting Grade for each issue. For the statehood quarters, there is no need for individual OCGs. A general rule of thumb for these issues is this: for circulation strikes, MS-65 is a good OCG, and for Proofs, Proof-66 (and Proofs, carefully made, usually occur in Proof-66 or better).

Striking and Appearance

Circulation strikes require checking as to sharpness. Planchet quality can vary, and some have marks from the original planchet that did not flatten out during the striking process. For some issues, the obverse can be marked and nicked, while the reverse has fewer such indications. There are so many state quarters around that finding a choice piece will be easy. For a few issues, Denver Mint coins are not sharp in certain areas of the lettering. The 2004-D Michigan quarter usually exhibits lightness, and for this particular issue, cherrypicking is necessary.

Some have interesting die cracks, an example being a 2002-P Tennessee with a large crack from the neck through Q of QUARTER to the border, and another die crack from the forehead through the first S of STATES; others could be cited. Quite a few Mint errors, such as off-center strikings, are available and are interesting to see. Fred Weinberg, a California dealer, has made a specialty of these, and many other professionals have handled them as well. Weinberg advised me that the best time to find significant errors is soon after the coins are released. Not many new discoveries are made in later years.

Nearly all Proofs were well struck and handled with care at the Mint. Grades commonly are Proof-66 and higher, all the way to Proof-70. On some Proofs, over-polishing of dies has eliminated some details, as on part of the WC initials on certain 1999 Delaware pieces. Some Proofs show die cracks. Ken Potter, columnist for *Numismatic News*, has filed a series of stories on these.

FROM CONCEPT TO COIN

California state quarter designer Garrett Burke (pictured here with his wife Michelle, a coin collector) started with a question: "What does California mean to me?"

(a)

(b)

Burke's final contest entry was finessed at the Mint (a). Their final rendering (b) led to the California state quarter (c), one of the most popular coins in the series.

His notes led to rough sketches centering on natural themes, with writer/poet/conservationist John Muir connecting man to Nature.

(c)

California governor Arnold Schwarzenneger (shown with design review committee member Dwight Manley, coin collector Penny Marshall, and wife Maria Shriver) praised the "beautiful, beautiful design."

DELAWARE *1st of 50*

Official Coin Release Date: January 4, 1999.

Mintage Figures:

Circulation strikes (clad) 1999-P: 373,400,000
1999-D: 401,424,000

Proof strikes (clad) 1999-S: 3,713,359

Proof strikes (silver) 1999-S: 804,565

Delaware 1999 • Market Values • Circulation Strikes and Proof Strikes

MS-63	MS-64	MS-65	MS-66	MS-67	MS-68	MS-63	MS-64	MS-65	MS-66	MS-67	MS-68
$1.50	$2.50	$3.50	$4.50	$6.	$7.	$1.50	$2.50	$3.50	$4.50	$6	$7

PF-64	PF-65	PF-66	PF-67	PF-68	PF-64	PF-65
$9	$10	$11	$14	$16	$18	$20

Delaware 1999 • Certified Populations • Circulation Strikes and Proof Strikes

MS-65	MS-66	MS-67	MS-68	MS-69	MS-65	MS-66	MS-67	MS-68	MS-69
701	1,451	491	40	1	519	1,124	231	23	0

PF-65	PF-66	PF-67	PF-68	PF-69	PF-70	PF-65	PF-66	PF-67	PF-68	PF-69	PF-70
2	10	50	335	6,253	23	3	18	77	413	7,305	14

■ Philadelphia Mint circulation strikes ■ Denver Mint circulation strikes

■ San Francisco Mint (clad) Proof strikes ■ San Francisco Mint (silver clad) Proof strikes

SPECIFICS OF THE REVERSE DESIGN

Description: The coin features a rider on horseback headed to the left, with CAESAR / RODNEY near the left border. At the upper right is THE / FIRST / STATE, signifying Delaware's position. The top and bottom border inscriptions are standard.

Designer: Per information given by the Public Information Office of the U.S. Mint in early 1999, the designer was Eddy Seger, an art and drama teacher. However, after reading this statement in *Coin World* (February 15, 1999), certain officials from the state of Delaware stated that no single person deserved the credit, and that at least six different sketches depicted the equestrian Rodney theme.[9] *Mint sculptor-engraver who made the model:* William Cousins. *Engraver's initials and location:* WC conjoined, with the top of the C missing on some impressions due to over-polishing of the die, giving the initials the appearance of "WL." The initials are located to the left, between the horse's extended hoof and the border.

STORY OF THE DESIGN

A Revolutionary War Patriot

The first coin out of the gate, so to speak, was widely appreciated by collectors. Depicted on this coin is Caesar Rodney on horseback, on an 80-mile ride to Philadelphia (then the seat of the Continental Congress). On July 1, 1776, despite severe discomfort and illness, as a delegate from the colony of Delaware he cast the deciding vote that called for independence from England. This bold yet simple design, with the horse and rider quickly catching the eye, is in my opinion one of the best in the entire series. This view is shared by many others. The artistic bar was raised high at the outset, and many later designs could not come up to it.

To start the design-selection process, citizens of the state were invited to send ideas for the design to the Delaware Arts Council, resulting in more than 300 entries. Certain of these were sent to the Mint, where they were converted into drawings. Three concepts were selected, these being Caesar Rodney, an allegorical Miss Liberty, and a quill-and-pen design. The office of Governor Thomas R. Carper conducted a limited email and telephone poll, garnering 1,519 votes, of which 948 were for Rodney, 235 for Miss Liberty, and 336 for the writing materials.

Finally, on December 7, 1998, "Delaware Day" was held at the Philadelphia Mint.[10] On hand were Citizens Commemorative Coin Advisory Committee members, Delaware state officials, and Mint officers and personnel, including Mint Director Philip N. Diehl and U.S. Treasurer Mary Ellen Withrow. All guests were invited to join coining-press operator John Hill in striking their very own Delaware quarters. These were set aside to be mailed to the participants early in 1999, after the official release.

Nearly a month later, on January 4, 1999, the first coins went into circulation.

NUMISMATIC ASPECTS OF THE STATE OF DELAWARE

Colonial era: The state issued many types of currency. *1936:* The Delaware Tercentenary commemorative half dollar was issued.

PENNSYLVANIA *2nd of 50*

Official Coin Release Date: March 9, 1999.

Mintage Figures:

Circulation strikes (clad) 1999-P: 349,000,000
1999-D: 358,332,000

Proof strikes (clad) 1999-S: 3,713,359

Proof strikes (silver) 1999-S: 804,565

Pennsylvania 1999 • Market Values • Circulation Strikes and Proof Strikes

MS-63	MS-64	MS-65	MS-66	MS-67	MS-68	MS-63	MS-64	MS-65	MS-66	MS-67	MS-68
$1.50	$2.50	$3.50	$4.50	$6	$7	$1.50	$2.50	$3.50	$4.50	$6	$7

PF-64	PF-65	PF-66	PF-67	PF-68	PF-64	PF-65
$9	$10	$11	$14	$16	$18	$20

Pennsylvania 1999 • Certified Populations • Circulation Strikes and Proof Strikes

MS-65	MS-66	MS-67	MS-68	MS-69	MS-65	MS-66	MS-67	MS-68	MS-69
561	1,143	477	31	0	437	867	180	6	0

PF-65	PF-66	PF-67	PF-68	PF-69	PF-70	PF-65	PF-66	PF-67	PF-68	PF-69	PF-70
3	7	38	282	6,219	32	6	15	65	393	7,433	20

■ Philadelphia Mint circulation strikes   ■ Denver Mint circulation strikes

■ San Francisco Mint (clad) Proof strikes   ■ San Francisco Mint (silver clad) Proof strikes

SPECIFICS OF THE REVERSE DESIGN

Description: At the center is an outline of the state, with the goddess Commonwealth prominent at the center, holding a standard topped by an eagle. She is elegantly styled and would serve well as a large motif on any coin. At the upper left of the map is a keystone in pebbled bas-relief, representing "the Keystone State," a motto used on license plates and elsewhere. The motto reflects both Pennsylvania's position near the center of the original 13 colonies and, as a Mint release suggests, "the key position of Pennsylvania in the economic, social, and political development of the United States." To the right of the map is a more formal motto, VIRTUE / LIBERTY / INDEPENDENCE, on three lines.

Designer: Concept by Donald Carlucci. *Mint sculptor-engraver who made the model:* John Mercanti. Roland Hinton Perry is deserving of some small part of the credit for his statue of Commonwealth. *Engraver's initials and location:* JM, placed immediately below the bottom border of the state and to the right of the goddess's leg.

STORY OF THE DESIGN

The design of the 1999 Pennsylvania quarter is a small collage of items relating to the state. The design, an outline map, includes a representation of the 14-foot statue from the top of the State Capitol building, a keystone, and a motto, and ties the elements together.

The statue itself was relatively unknown prior to its appearance here, and probably not one in a thousand residents of the state could identify it as Commonwealth, by an obscure New York sculptor. The U.S. Mint gives this information:

> The statue Commonwealth, designed by New York sculptor Roland Hinton Perry, is a bronze-gilded 14' 6" high female form that has topped Pennsylvania's State Capitol dome in Harrisburg, Pennsylvania since May 25, 1905. Her right arm extends in kindness and her left arm grasps a ribbon mace to symbolize justice. The image of the keystone honors the state's nickname, "The Keystone State." At a Jefferson Republican victory rally in October 1802, Pennsylvania was toasted as "the keystone in the federal union."

I am not quite sure what a ribbon mace is, but it sounds important. A keystone is the top stone in an arch, and is the final stone placed during construction.

The design-selection process began when Governor Tom Ridge established the Commemorative Quarter Committee to furnish guidance and solicit designs.[11] More than 5,300 sketches and other submissions were received from residents of the state.

Five final designs were selected by the Pennsylvania Commemorative Quarter Committee; the eventual motif was selected from these five designs.

The First-Ever State-Quarter Launch Ceremony

On March 9, 1999, at the Philadelphia Mint, the official launch ceremony was held. Governor Tom Ridge, U.S. Treasurer Mary Ellen Withrow, Mint Deputy Director John Mitchell, and others were on hand. About two dozen fifth-graders from the General George A. McCall Elementary School were invited guests. Many of those on hand were allowed to push a button to actuate an 82-ton press to strike a quarter.

By the day of the launch ceremony, March 9, millions of Pennsylvania quarters had been struck by both the Philadelphia and Denver mints. On the same day as the ceremony these were released from storage and placed into circulation.

At the launch ceremony on March 9, 1999. Left to right: Govenor Thomas Ridge, Mint engraver-sculptor John Mercanti, and Donald Carlucci.

NUMISMATIC ASPECTS OF THE STATE OF PENNSYLVANIA

Colonial era: The state issued many types of currency. *1775:* Continental Currency was first issued at Philadelphia, the seat of the federal government. It was printed by Hall & Sellers, who also printed bills for colonies and states. *1776:* The Continental Congress is believed to have issued pewter Continental dollars. *1782:* The Bank of North America, the first significant commercial bank in America, was chartered. It issued paper money over a long period of time. *1783:* Nova Constellatio pattern copper and silver coins were made to test coinage concepts for use at the North America Mint; no further action occurred. *1791–1811:* The first Bank of the United States was headquartered in Philadelphia. *1792:* The Philadelphia Mint was established. *Circa 1810–1840:* Philadelphia was the leading center for bank-note engraving and printing. *1816–1836:* The Second Bank of the United States was headquartered in Philadelphia. *1833:* The Second Philadelphia Mint building was occupied. *1858:* The Philadelphia Numismatic Society, the first such organization in the United States, was founded. (It was soon followed by the American Numismatic Society, New York). *1870s:* A vast hoard of silver coins was discovered in the town of Economy. *1901:* The Third Philadelphia Mint building was occupied. *1913:* The Philadelphia Federal Reserve Bank was established under the Federal Reserve Act. Currency issued there bears the letter C. *1926:* A commemorative half dollar and $2.50 piece were issued for the Sesquicentennial Exposition. *1936:* The Battle of Gettysburg commemorative half dollar was issued. *1967:* The Fourth (present) Philadelphia Mint building was occupied. *1990:* Eisenhower Centennial commemorative silver dollars were issued. *1992:* On April 2, a ceremony was held to observe the 200th anniversary of the Mint Act of April 2, 1792. Many numismatists were present.

NEW JERSEY *3rd of 50*

Official Coin Release Date: May 17, 1999.

Mintage Figures:

Circulation strikes (clad) 1999-P: 363,200,000
1999-D: 299,028,000

Proof strikes (clad) 1999-S: 3,713,359

Proof strikes (silver) 1999-S: 804,565

New Jersey 1999 • Market Values • Circulation Strikes and Proof Strikes

MS-63	MS-64	MS-65	MS-66	MS-67	MS-68	MS-63	MS-64	MS-65	MS-66	MS-67	MS-68
$1.50	$2.50	$3.50	$4.50	$6	$7	$1.50	$2.50	$3.50	$4.50	$6	$7

PF-64	PF-65	PF-66	PF-67	PF-68	PF-64	PF-65
$9	$10	$11	$14	$16	$18	$20

New Jersey 1999 • Certified Populations • Circulation Strikes and Proof Strikes

MS-65	MS-66	MS-67	MS-68	MS-69	MS-65	MS-66	MS-67	MS-68	MS-69
419	1,081	296	19		484	1,198	222	14	0

PF-65	PF-66	PF-67	PF-68	PF-69	PF-70	PF-65	PF-66	PF-67	PF-68	PF-69	PF-70
1	2	46	244	6,240	33	7	19	60	378	7,435	20

■ Philadelphia Mint circulation strikes   ■ Denver Mint circulation strikes

■ San Francisco Mint (clad) Proof strikes   ■ San Francisco Mint (silver clad) Proof strikes

SPECIFICS OF THE REVERSE DESIGN

Description: The design features George Washington and accompanying soldiers in a rowboat crossing the Delaware River from Pennsylvania to New Jersey, adapted from an Emmanuel Leutze painting that is now a prized holding of the Metropolitan Museum of Art, New York City. A soldier is seated on the prow and is pushing an ice floe with his foot. The Father of Our Country and at least one other person are standing in the vessel, (seemingly a rather risky thing to do in the dark on a river filled with drifting ice). Moreover, Washington's foot is blocking an oarlock that could be used effectively by the paddler in the bow, who is forced to do without one. Below is the two-line inscription CROSSROADS OF THE / REVOLUTION. The top and bottom border inscriptions are standard.

Designer: Adapted from a painting created by Emmanuel Leutze. *Mint sculptor-engraver who made the model:* Alfred F. Maletsky. *Engraver's initials and location:* AM, located between the end of the boat and the rim on the right. The initials are tiny.

STORY OF THE DESIGN

The 1999 New Jersey quarter furnished the first truly familiar motif on a state coin— the well-known scene taken from the 1851 painting by Emmanuel Gottlieb Leutze (1816–1868), *Washington Crossing the Delaware*, also used in 1976 for 13¢ stamps in connection with the bicentennial. Generations earlier, it was part of the face design for $50 National Bank Notes of the Original Series, Series of 1875, and the Series of 1882. Accordingly, it might have been proper to credit Leutze as the designer of the coin, but this was not done. Mint policy has proved to be erratic in this regard—see the discussion of the 2005 Iowa quarter, which prominently features the name of artist Grant Wood.

The process of creating this design began on November 17, 1997, when the New Jersey Commemorative Coin Design Commission was authorized. This committee of 15 citizens was appointed to review ideas for the quarter design. It is to the everlasting credit of this and many other state committees that experienced coin collectors were invited to join these advisory groups. The 15 advisors settled on five concepts to be sent to the Mint to be developed into drawings. These designs were subsequently reviewed by the Commission of Fine Arts and the secretary of the Treasury, after which three were returned to Governor Christine Todd Whitman, who consulted with her advisors and made the final selection (although she could have made the choice on her own).

NUMISMATIC ASPECTS OF THE STATE OF NEW JERSEY

May 1682: The Legislature made Irish St. Patrick's coinage legal tender in the colony. *Colonial era:* New Jersey issued many types of currency. *1786–1788:* New Jersey coppers were produced under private contract. *1850s:* The Toms River and Cape May areas became centers for fraudulent banks that issued paper money. *2004:* Thomas A. Edison commemorative silver dollars were issued.

GEORGIA 4th of 50

Official Coin Release Date: July 19, 1999.

Mintage Figures:

Circulation strikes (clad)	....	1999-P: 451,188,000
		1999-D: 488,744,000
Proof strikes (clad)	....	1999-S: 3,713,359
Proof strikes (silver)	....	1999-S: 804,565

Georgia 1999 • Market Values • Circulation Strikes and Proof Strikes

MS-63	MS-64	MS-65	MS-66	MS-67	MS-68	MS-63	MS-64	MS-65	MS-66	MS-67	MS-68
$1.50	$2	$3.50	$4.50	$6	$7	$1.50	$2	$3.50	$4.50	$6	$7

PF-64	PF-65	PF-66	PF-67	PF-68	PF-64	PF-65
$9	$10	$11	$14	$16	$18	$20

Georgia 1999 • Certified Populations • Circulation Strikes and Proof Strikes

MS-65	MS-66	MS-67	MS-68	MS-69	MS-65	MS-66	MS-67	MS-68	MS-69
544	927	162	7	0	732	1,131	188	9	0

PF-65	PF-66	PF-67	PF-68	PF-69	PF-70	PF-65	PF-66	PF-67	PF-68	PF-69	PF-70
0	8	47	205	6,241	33	2	12	47	340	7,521	15

■ Philadelphia Mint circulation strikes ■ Denver Mint circulation strikes
■ San Francisco Mint (clad) Proof strikes ■ San Francisco Mint (silver clad) Proof strikes

SPECIFICS OF THE REVERSE DESIGN

Description: An outline map of Georgia with a peach (for Georgia's nickname, "the Peach State") at the center, with a leaf attached to a stem. To the left and right are branches of live oak (the state tree). A loosely arranged ribbon bears the motto WISDOM JUSTICE MODERATION in three sections. Top and bottom border inscriptions are standard.

Designer: Bill Fivaz (peach on the state outline) and Caroline Leake (motto and wreath), sketch by Susan Royal. *Mint sculptor-engraver who made the model:* T. James Ferrell. *Engraver's initials and location:* TJF in italic capitals. Below the lower side of the branch stem on the right.

STORY OF THE DESIGN

The 1999 Georgia quarter features a montage of topics relating to the state, similar in concept to the Pennsylvania issue.[12] An outline map has at the center a peach, the best-known symbol of the state. The official state tree, the live oak, is represented by branches at each side. On a flowing ribbon is the motto WISDOM JUSTICE MODERATION—seemingly good precepts for anyone to observe.

The Georgia Council for the Arts was enlisted to receive and develop motifs. The council brought together a committee consisting of Caroline Leake, executive director of the council; Danny Robinson, then-president of the Georgia Numismatic Association; Bill Fivaz, well-known numismatist and author; and Susan Royal, a local graphic artist who joined the committee at the end to render the designs for submission. The committee met in February and March 1999, choosing five designs, which they narrowed down to four. Governor Roy Barnes selected the winner.

NUMISMATIC ASPECTS OF THE STATE OF GEORGIA

Colonial era: The state issued many types of currency. *1830:* Templeton Reid, assayer and coiner, struck $2.50, $10, and $20 coins at Milledgeville, then at Gainesville. *1838:* The Dahlonega Mint opened and coined gold continuously until 1861. *1913:* The Atlanta Federal Reserve Bank was established under the Federal Reserve Act. Currency issued there bears the letter E. *1925:* The Stone Mountain Memorial commemorative half dollar was issued. *1995:* The Atlanta Olympic Games commemorative half dollar, silver dollar, and $5 gold piece were issued.

CONNECTICUT *5th of 50*

Official Coin Release Date: October 12, 1999.

Mintage Figures:

Circulation strikes (clad) 1999-P: 688,744,000
1999-D: 657,880,000
Proof strikes (clad) 1999-S: 3,713,359
Proof strikes (silver) 1999-S: 804,565

Connecticut 1999 • Market Values • Circulation Strikes and Proof Strikes

MS-63	MS-64	MS-65	MS-66	MS-67	MS-68	MS-63	MS-64	MS-65	MS-66	MS-67	MS-68
$1.25	$2	$2.50	$3.50	$4.50	$6	$1.25	$2	$2.50	$3.50	$4.50	$6

PF-64	PF-65	PF-66	PF-67	PF-68	PF-64	PF-65
$11	$12	$13	$16	$18	$18	$20

Connecticut 1999 • Certified Populations • Circulation Strikes and Proof Strikes

MS-65	MS-66	MS-67	MS-68	MS-69	MS-65	MS-66	MS-67	MS-68	MS-69
686	926	334	28	3	1,136	1,522	409	1,148	0

PF-65	PF-66	PF-67	PF-68	PF-69	PF-70	PF-65	PF-66	PF-67	PF-68	PF-69	PF-70
2	11	33	262	6,487	35	7	15	54	264	3,889	20

■ Philadelphia Mint circulation strikes ■ Denver Mint circulation strikes
■ San Francisco Mint (clad) Proof strikes ■ San Francisco Mint (silver clad) Proof strikes

SPECIFICS OF THE REVERSE DESIGN

Description: A rather bushy-appearing tree, with a small trunk, and leafless (presumably from the frost of winter). Above the ground at the lower left is THE / CHARTER OAK. The top and bottom border inscriptions are standard.

Designer: Andy Jones. *Mint sculptor-engraver who made the model:* T. James Ferrell. *Engraver's initials and location:* TJF in italic capitals, located on the border to the right of M (UNUM).

STORY OF THE DESIGN

The design on the Connecticut quarter is an image of the state's famous Charter Oak—a tree of significance not only to the state of Connecticut but to the nation as well.[13] A United States Mint news release tells of the following:

> If not for the famed "Charter Oak," Connecticut—and this country in general—might be a very different place than it is today! On the

night of October 31, 1687, Connecticut's Charter was put to a test. A British representative for King James II challenged Connecticut's government structure and demanded its surrender. In the middle of the heated discussion, with the Charter on the table between the opposing parties, the candles were mysteriously snuffed out, darkening the room. When visibility was reestablished, the Connecticut Charter had vanished. Heroic Captain Joseph Wadsworth saved the Charter from the hands of the British and concealed it in the safest place he could find—in a majestic white oak.

In 1855, Charles Dewolf Brownell painted the tree from life. By that time, the tree was thought to be more than 400 years old. It had been described by *Niles' Register* (May 7, 1825) as measuring 28 feet in circumference near its base, and about 70 feet in height, with branches extending nearly 40 feet. Such was the gnarled and aged tree depicted by Brownell, and it was his image that was later used on the 1935 Connecticut Tercentenary half dollar, on a commemorative stamp, and elsewhere.

With this gnarled image in mind, many people have found fault with the bushy, youthful-looking tree on the back of the Connecticut quarter. (One numismatist even suggested that it was the *root system* of the Charter Oak being shown, upside down!) Perhaps it illustrates a young Charter Oak, quite unlike the appearance of the same tree when it blew down in a storm in 1856. Whether the image is an accurate representation of the young tree is not known; variations of younger versions appeared on notes of the Charter Oak Bank (Hartford) and in 1859 on a medal issued by coin dealer Augustus Sage. In any case, the design on the state quarter is completely *original*.

The 1935 Connecticut Tercentenary commemorative half dollar, with a rendition of the Charter Oak on the reverse.

When Governor John G. Rowland set up the Connecticut Coin Design Competition, 19 of the more than 100 entries depicted the Charter Oak. Apparently, five were selected from those 19, sent off to the Mint, reviewed, and reviewed again, after which one was picked.

NUMISMATIC ASPECTS OF THE STATE OF CONNECTICUT

Colonial era: The state issued many types of currency. *1737–1739:* The Higley three-pence coins were struck from native metal in Granby. *1785–1788:* The state issued copper coins. *19th century:* Scovill Manufacturing Co., Waterbury, was a major maker of Hard Times tokens, encased postage stamps, and Civil War tokens. *1935:* The Connecticut Tercentenary commemorative half dollar was issued. *1936:* The Bridgeport Centennial commemorative half dollar was issued.

MASSACHUSETTS 6th of 50

Official Coin Release Date: January 3, 2000.

Mintage Figures:

Circulation strikes (clad) 2000-P: 628,600,000
2000-D: 535,184,000
Proof strikes (clad) 2000-S: 4,020,172
Proof strikes (silver) 2000-S: 965,421

Massachusetts 2000 • Market Values • Circulation Strikes and Proof Strikes

MS-63	MS-64	MS-65	MS-66	MS-67	MS-68	MS-63	MS-64	MS-65	MS-66	MS-67	MS-68
$1.50	$2	$2.50	$3	$3.50	$4.50	$1.50	$2	$2.50	$3	$3.50	$4.50

PF-64	PF-65	PF-66	PF-67	PF-68	PF-64	PF-65
$5	$6	$8	$10	$14	$9	$10

Massachusetts 2000 • Certified Populations • Circulation Strikes and Proof Strikes

MS-65	MS-66	MS-67	MS-68	MS-69	MS-65	MS-66	MS-67	MS-68	MS-69
270	1,143	1,525	277	2	319	1,186	637	48	1

PF-65	PF-66	PF-67	PF-68	PF-69	PF-70	PF-65	PF-66	PF-67	PF-68	PF-69	PF-70
3	5	30	168	5,777	51	4	15	55	426	9,617	54

■ Philadelphia Mint circulation strikes   ■ Denver Mint circulation strikes

■ San Francisco Mint (clad) Proof strikes   ■ San Francisco Mint (silver clad) Proof strikes

SPECIFICS OF THE REVERSE DESIGN

Description: An outline map of Massachusetts with a stippled background, and with French's *Minuteman* statue superimposed. The location of Boston is noted by a raised, five-pointed star. At the right, offshore in the ocean, is the three-line inscription THE / BAY / STATE. The top and bottom border inscriptions are standard.

Designer: Two schoolchildren illustrated the famous *Minuteman* statue by Daniel Chester French. Their identities were withheld. *Mint sculptor-engraver who made the model:* Thomas D. Rogers. *Engraver's initials and location:* TDR, located below the bottom left side of the map.

STORY OF THE DESIGN

If you have a 1925 Lexington-Concord commemorative half dollar depicting Daniel Chester French's *Minuteman* statue on the obverse, then you'll recognize the same motif on the back side of the 2000 Massachusetts quarter. The statue itself stands not far from the "rude bridge that arched the flood," evocative of the early days of the American Revolution. On the new coin, the statue is shown with a textured outline map of THE / BAY / STATE (per the legend), complete with such details as Nantucket and Martha's Vineyard islands (among others) and a star indicating the location of Boston.

It was February 1998 when Governor Paul Cellucci began the process leading to the creation of a suitable design, after which more than 100 youngsters provided sketches. Only children were invited (a novel approach and, so far, a unique one in the quarter program). Ten members on an advisory council narrowed the 100 or so entries down to five. In June 1999, Governor Cellucci and Lieutenant Governor Jane Swift announced the winning design.

Considering that the same motif had been used on a commemorative coin, postage stamps, savings stamps, and elsewhere, setting up a 10-member advisory council and engaging in other hoopla may have been wasted effort. But for the two school kids, one in the sixth grade and the other in the seventh, who had the same idea and shared the recognition, the hoopla was welcome. They were featured guests at the official launch ceremony—a heartwarming situation for them and their classmates, all of whom were invited to be on hand at the event in Boston's historic Faneuil Hall. They were illustrated on the Mint web site, but their names were not disclosed.

A 2000-P Massachusetts quarter struck over a 1999-P Georgia quarter! This is the only multistate overstrike known in the state quarter series. (Fred Weinberg photograph)

NUMISMATIC ASPECTS OF THE STATE OF MASSACHUSETTS

1652–1682: The state issued silver coins in the New England, Willow Tree, Oak Tree, and Pine Tree series. *1690:* The state issued the first paper money in the Western World. Many types of colonial currency issued, including some from plates engraved by Paul Revere. *1776:* Pattern copper coins were made. The Washington Before Boston medal also bears this date. *1787–1788:* Copper half cents and cents were minted. *1790s–early 19th century:* Jacob Perkins of Newburyport issued medals and devised the Patent Stereotype Steel Plate for printing paper money. *1860:* The Boston Numismatic Society, today the second oldest society (after the ANS), was founded. *1913:* The Boston Federal Reserve Bank was established under the Federal Reserve Act. Currency issued there bears the letter A. *1920–1921:* Pilgrim Tercentenary commemorative half dollars were issued. *1925:* Lexington-Concord commemorative half dollars were issued.

Various Massachusetts colonial coinage.

From 1652 to 1682 Massachusetts issued silver coins in the NE, Willow Tree, Oak Tree, and Pine Tree series, and in 1690 the colony issued the first paper money in the Western World. In 1787 and 1788 the state minted copper half cents and cents.

(Some coins are shown enlarged.)

MARYLAND *7th of 50*

Official Coin Release Date: March 13, 2000.

Mintage Figures:

Circulation strikes (clad) 2000-P: 678,200,000
2000-D: 556,532,000

Proof strikes (clad) 2000-S: 4,020,172

Proof strikes (silver) 2000-S: 965,421

Maryland 2000 • Market Values • Circulation Strikes and Proof Strikes

MS-63	MS-64	MS-65	MS-66	MS-67	MS-68	MS-63	MS-64	MS-65	MS-66	MS-67	MS-68
$1.50	$2	$2.50	$3	$3.50	$4.50	$1.50	$2	$2.50	$3	$3.50	$4.50

PF-64	PF-65	PF-66	PF-67	PF-68	PF-64	PF-65
$5	$6	$8	$10	$14	$9	$10

Maryland 2000 • Certified Populations • Circulation Strikes and Proof Strikes

MS-65	MS-66	MS-67	MS-68	MS-69	MS-65	MS-66	MS-67	MS-68	MS-69
308	914	831	122	0	416	1,256	734	49	0

PF-65	PF-66	PF-67	PF-68	PF-69	PF-70	PF-65	PF-66	PF-67	PF-68	PF-69	PF-70
1	8	40	185	5,592	42	5	11	65	420	9,477	45

■ Philadelphia Mint circulation strikes ■ Denver Mint circulation strikes

■ San Francisco Mint (clad) Proof strikes ■ San Francisco Mint (silver clad) Proof strikes

SPECIFICS OF THE REVERSE DESIGN

Description: Wooden dome and supporting structure on the Maryland State House in Annapolis, with THE OLD / LINE STATE in two lines, and with branches of white oak to each side. The top and bottom border inscriptions are standard.

Designer: Bill Krawczewicz. *Mint sculptor-engraver who made the model:* Thomas D. Rogers. *Engraver's initials and location:* TDR, located below an acorn and above M (UNUM).

STORY OF THE DESIGN

In the opinion of many collectors, Maryland—the Old Line State, as proclaimed on the coins—laid an egg with the design of this quarter dollar. Featuring the top part of the State House (a "striking dome" in Mint terminology), this supposedly wonderful subject that used up Maryland's once-in-a-lifetime coin opportunity is also "the country's largest wooden dome built without nails." In addition, there are two branches from a white oak—the state tree—complete with a few acorns (but no squirrels).

A Mint news release gave these details of the design-selection process:

> After Governor [Parris N.] Glendening received design concepts from all Maryland residents, including schoolchildren, the 17-member Maryland Commemorative Coin Committee evaluated all of the submissions. The committee narrowed the options down to five selections from which the Governor picked the state house. "In our view, the state house best favors Maryland's rich history, and the unique role the state has played in our nation's history," said Glendening.[14]

But what about the seemingly unfamiliar motto, "the Old Line State"? Lori Montgomery, writer for the *Washington Post*, wrote this in March 2000:

[The] slogan, emblazoned on the tail side of the latest coin in the U.S. Mint's series of 50 state quarters, is raising puzzled brows even in Maryland, the state in question.

. . . [It seems that] Tom D. Rogers Sr., a sculptor and engraver with the U.S. Mint in Philadelphia, found the dome a bit stark. So he added clusters of white oak, the state tree, and "The Old Line State." The words made a nice design, but even Rogers didn't know what it meant. "I pulled it out of a book or off the Internet someplace," he said. "I know I got it somewhere official." . . .

It seems Washington himself bestowed the nickname on Maryland after the Battle of Long Island in August 1776, when a line of Maryland troops held off the British while Washington retreated. Thousands died, and many Maryland soldiers were buried in Brooklyn, said Maryland state archivist Edward C. Papenfuse. Thereafter, Washington referred to Maryland troops as "the old line"—meaning they were always there, reliable, Papenfuse said. . . . [15]

NUMISMATIC ASPECTS OF THE STATE OF MARYLAND

1658–1659: Silver fourpence, sixpence, and shilling coins are struck at the Tower Mint, London, for circulation in the Maryland colony. *Colonial era:* Maryland issued many types of currency. *1783:* Annapolis silversmith John Chalmers issued silver threepence, sixpence, and shilling coins. *1790:* Standish Barry, Baltimore silversmith, issued a threepence coin. In the same era he produced a gold "doubloon" of Spanish-American design.[16] *1934:* The Maryland Tercentenary commemorative half dollar was issued.

SOUTH CAROLINA *8th of 50*

Official Coin Release Date: May 22, 2000.

Mintage Figures:

Circulation strikes (clad) 2000-P: 742,576,000
2000-D: 566,208,000[17]

Proof strikes (clad) 2000-S: 4,020,172

Proof strikes (silver) 2000-S: 965,421

South Carolina 2000 • Market Values • Circulation Strikes and Proof Strikes

MS-63	MS-64	MS-65	MS-66	MS-67	MS-68	MS-63	MS-64	MS-65	MS-66	MS-67	MS-68
$1.50	$2	$3	$4	$5	$6	$1.50	$2	$3	$4	$5	$6

PF-64	PF-65	PF-66	PF-67	PF-68	PF-64	PF-65
$7	$8	$9	$10	$12	$9	$10

South Carolina 2000 • Certified Populations • Circulation Strikes and Proof Strikes

MS-65	MS-66	MS-67	MS-68	MS-69	MS-65	MS-66	MS-67	MS-68	MS-69
314	1,028	1,035	279	1	261	1,392	1,132	160	0

PF-65	PF-66	PF-67	PF-68	PF-69	PF-70	PF-65	PF-66	PF-67	PF-68	PF-69	PF-70
0	8	37	180	5,603	51	3	10	47	432	9,390	45

■ Philadelphia Mint circulation strikes   ■ Denver Mint circulation strikes

■ San Francisco Mint (clad) Proof strikes   ■ San Francisco Mint (silver clad) Proof strikes

SPECIFICS OF THE REVERSE DESIGN

Description: Outline map of South Carolina with a Carolina wren (the state bird) and yellow jessamine flowers (the state flower) to the left; a palmetto (the state tree) with severed trunk is shown to the right. THE / PALMETTO / STATE appears in three lines at the upper left. A raised five-pointed star indicates the position of Columbia, the state capital. The top and bottom border inscriptions are standard.

Designer: Unknown. *Mint sculptor-engraver who made the model:* Thomas D. Rogers. *Engraver's initials and location:* TDR. Below the right side of the palmetto ground.

STORY OF THE DESIGN

The South Carolina Numismatic Society had a hand in picking this design. The motif is the most natural (in the botany and zoology sense) seen to date in the series, what with a palmetto tree, a Carolina wren, and some yellow (we are told) jessamine flowers. These motifs and the motto THE / PALMETTO / STATE are on and around an outline map of South Carolina.[18]

Somebody must have designed this coin, or come up with the concept. Here is what the Mint has stated:

State emblems of South Carolina. (James McCabe Jr., *A Centennial View of Our Country and Its Resources,* 1876)

> Beginning in 1998, the South Carolina Department of Parks, Recreation and Tourism (PRT) accepted quarter design suggestions. Contributions came from PRT's offices, school children and the South Carolina Numismatic Society. From these contributions, PRT compiled five semi-finalist design concepts. The Citizens Commemorative Coin Advisory Committee and the Fine Arts Commission narrowed these five semi-finalist design concepts down to three choices.
>
> Governor Jim Hodges then made his final decision, indicating that the Palmetto Tree represents South Carolina's strength; the Carolina Wren's song symbolizes the hospitality of the state's people; and the Yellow Jessamine, a delicate golden bloom—a sign of coming spring—is part of South Carolina's vast natural beauty.

Perhaps the designer will step forward someday and make a statement. Then, numismatists can wonder if the revelation is fact or fiction.

I am reminded of Irene MacDowell, who, years after the fact, stated that *she,* rather than the usually named Dora Doscher, modeled for the 1916 Standing Liberty quarter dollar. By that time there was no way to check the story, for the others involved were no longer living. We do know that Thomas D. Rogers Sr., a fine engraver at the Mint, made the models for the South Carolina state quarter from designs done by some hitherto unknown person. I consider it very important to learn the identities of the designers of state quarters—such as the school kids who created the Massachusetts quarter motif—before such information becomes lost, and impostors arise to claim the credit.

NUMISMATIC ASPECTS OF THE STATE OF SOUTH CAROLINA

Colonial era: The state issued many types of currency. *1936:* The Columbia Sesquicentennial set of three commemorative half dollars was issued.

NEW HAMPSHIRE 9th of 50

Official Coin Release Date: August 7, 2000.

Mintage Figures:

Circulation strikes (clad) 2000-P: 673,040,000
2000-D: 495,976,000

Proof strikes (clad) 2000-S: 4,020,172

Proof strikes (silver) 2000-S: 965,421

New Hampshire 2000 • Market Values • Circulation Strikes and Proof Strikes

MS-63	MS-64	MS-65	MS-66	MS-67	MS-68	MS-63	MS-64	MS-65	MS-66	MS-67	MS-68
$1.50	$2	$2.50	$3	$3.50	$4.50	$1.50	$2	$2.50	$3	$3.50	$4.50

PF-64	PF-65	PF-66	PF-67	PF-68	PF-64	PF-65
$5	$6	$8	$10	$14	$9	$10

New Hampshire 2000 • Certified Populations • Circulation Strikes and Proof Strikes

MS-65	MS-66	MS-67	MS-68	MS-69	MS-65	MS-66	MS-67	MS-68	MS-69
314	989	1,003	66	0	251	1,051	362	25	0

PF-65	PF-66	PF-67	PF-68	PF-69	PF-70	PF-65	PF-66	PF-67	PF-68	PF-69	PF-70
1	5	22	185	5,620	56	5	16	65	461	9,314	44

■ Philadelphia Mint circulation strikes ■ Denver Mint circulation strikes
■ San Francisco Mint (clad) Proof strikes ■ San Francisco Mint (silver clad) Proof strikes

SPECIFICS OF THE REVERSE DESIGN

Description: The Old Man of the Mountain, a.k.a. the Great Stone Face, on the right side of the coin, extending to the center, gazes upon a field in which the state motto, LIVE / FREE / OR DIE, appears in three lines. Nine stars, representing the state's order of ratifying the Constitution, are at the left border.

Designer: Unknown, one of many traditional versions of the famous icon used in many places, including on a commemorative stamp. Adapted from a quarter-size brass token used until December 31, 2005, on routes I-93, I-95, and the Everett Turnpike in the state. *Mint sculptor-engraver who made the model:* William Cousins. *Engraver's initials and location:* WC, located below the Old Man of the Mountain and above M (UNUM).

STORY OF THE DESIGN

As a resident of the Granite State, I find this quarter is one of my favorites. I was responsible, in a way, for the final design, although I did not create it. By the way, of all state motifs this is one of the most criticized by others—those from out-of-state just don't understand why we like the thing!

Ideas for depictions on the quarter were aplenty. Finally, the choice narrowed down to just two: (1) a wooden spire–topped "meetinghouse" of the type said to have been a forum for town meetings generations ago, and in many New Hampshire communities, still used today; and (2) a covered bridge crossing a stream.

These sketches were sent to Philadelphia, where the ideas were reviewed at the Mint. Committee member Ken Bressett, a long-time friend of mine and editor of the Red Book, sent me copies of several variations of these two final contenders.

I was rather disappointed. To me, the meetinghouse with four spires resembled a standard design for a Baptist church of the old days, not a nonsectarian town hall. As to the covered bridge, while there are dozens in the state, they do not immediately pop to mind as emblematic of the place. Of Vermont, perhaps. Of New Hampshire, no. I mentioned these concerns, then suggested to Ken:

"Why not use the Old Man of the Mountain?"

This referred to the Great Stone Face, as it is (or was) sometimes called—a 40-foot rocky outcrop on Cannon Mountain in Franconia Notch that had been the symbol of the state for a long time. It even attracted the attention of Daniel Webster, who penned a commentary reproduced on a large sign near the site. Ken said that the idea had been considered but the Mint had stated that the motif was too heavy on one side, not balanced. I found this curious, as for years the New Hampshire State Turnpike Commission had been using

A New Hampshire turnpike token (enlarged), the inspiration for the state quarter.

tokens with the Old Man of the Mountain on them—and they were well struck and durable.[19] I sent some of these to Ken, he saw that coining was practical, and soon the Old Man was adopted.

An Inadvertent Commemorative

Unfortunately, on May 3, 2003, the rocky outcrop crumbled to rubble, the victim of thousands of years of weathering—warm summers alternating with icy winters. The Old Man was no more, giving the coin the unwanted distinction of being the first state-reverse quarter that depicted something in existence when the coin was struck, but now, in effect, a *commemorative* of times past, but not forgotten.

NUMISMATIC ASPECTS OF THE STATE OF NEW HAMPSHIRE

Colonial era: The state issued many types of currency. *1776:* Pattern copper coins were made. *1792–1865:* State-chartered banks were among the most sound in America, with very few failures. *1863:* Just one variety of Civil War token was issued in the state, by A.W. Gale of Concord, who operated a restaurant in the Concord railroad station.

Vignette from a New Hampshire bank note.

From 1792 to 1865, the state-chartered banks of New Hampshire were among the most sound in the nation, with very few that failed. This illustration of an Indian Princess is from a $5 note of the Strafford Bank in Dover.

VIRGINIA *10th of 50*

Official Coin Release Date: October 16, 2000.

Mintage Figures:

Circulation strikes (clad)	2000-P: 943,000,000
	2000-D: 651,616,000
Proof strikes (clad)	2000-S: 4,020,172
Proof strikes (silver)	2000-S: 965,421

Virginia 2000 • Market Values • Circulation Strikes and Proof Strikes

MS-63	MS-64	MS-65	MS-66	MS-67	MS-68	MS-63	MS-64	MS-65	MS-66	MS-67	MS-68
$1.50	$2	$2.50	$3	$3.50	$4.50	$1.50	$2	$2.50	$3	$3.50	$4.50

PF-64	PF-65	PF-66	PF-67	PF-68	PF-64	PF-65
$5	$6	$8	$10	$14	$9	$10

Virginia 2000 • Certified Populations • Circulation Strikes and Proof Strikes

MS-65	MS-66	MS-67	MS-68	MS-69	MS-65	MS-66	MS-67	MS-68	MS-69
280	878	952	146	0	243	963	662	22	0

PF-65	PF-66	PF-67	PF-68	PF-69	PF-70	PF-65	PF-66	PF-67	PF-68	PF-69	PF-70
0	5	30	191	5,677	48	1	8	58	421	9,517	41

■ Philadelphia Mint circulation strikes   ■ Denver Mint circulation strikes

■ San Francisco Mint (clad) Proof strikes   ■ San Francisco Mint (silver clad) Proof strikes

SPECIFICS OF THE REVERSE DESIGN

Description: Three ships under sail en route to a destination that would become known as Jamestown. At the upper left is the inscription JAMESTOWN / 1607–2007, and beneath the seascape is the word QUADRICENTENNIAL. The top and bottom border inscriptions are standard.

Designer: Paris Ashton, a graphic artist, was credited by the Independent Coin Grading (ICG) Company as the designer. *Mint sculptor-engraver who made the model:* Edgar Z. Steever. *Engraver's initials and location:* EZS, located on the surface of the ocean at the lower right corner of that feature.

STORY OF THE DESIGN

The center of the 2000 Virginia quarter is graced by a pleasing little flotilla of boats— the *Susan Constant, Godspeed,* and *Discovery*—carrying brave emigrants on their way to what would become Jamestown, the first permanent English settlement in the New World. Under a charter granted to the Virginia Company by King James on April 10, 1606, the vessels left London on September 20 of the same year. On May 12, 1607, the group of 104 men and boys landed on an island in the James River about 60 miles into the Chesapeake Bay from the ocean.

Ruins of an ancient church at Jamestown, Virginia. (Rau Studios, 1920s)

This was 13 years prior to the better-known arrival of the Pilgrims at Massachusetts, far to the north. The Virginia quarter bears legends relating to the 400th anniversary of the event—an observance somewhat premature, but there were no complaints.

To choose a design for the 2000 Virginia quarter, Susan F. Dewey, state treasurer, was appointed as the liaison to the United States Mint. Several different state agencies and offices as well as many citizens joined the effort. Thousands of ideas and sketches were submitted. Finally, Governor James S. Gilmore III made the final selection, and the Treasury Department nodded its approval.

Although the Mint remained mum on the subject, it is generally thought that Paris Ashton (Ashton-Bressler), a graphic designer, created the winning motif. She is a 1985 Bachelor of Fine Arts graduate of the Virginia Commonwealth University, Richmond.

Record Mintage

The mintage figures for Virginia quarters shattered all records, with 943 million for the 2000-P and 651.6 million for the 2000-D. The Mint's dynamic marketing program left no sales opportunity untouched. In print and on television, the state quarters were in view, accompanied by interesting pictures and stories. Congressmen, perhaps not fully aware that the Mint was earning a great profit for the government, squawked about the expenditures, and publicity for the state quarters was cut back dramatically, seemingly costing the Treasury hundreds of millions of dollars in lost revenue.

As to the Virginia production, Paul M. Green contributed this to *Numismatic News* in 2004 as part of a retrospective:

> The massive production that was seen for issues in 2000 and even early 2001 was bound to catch up with the program. The Virginia mintage from Philadelphia represented at least three 2000-P Virginia quarters for every man, woman and child in the United States. No matter how much you love Virginia, that sort of total is on the high side. With over 651 million more from Denver, the combination for just one of the five quarters that year was easily in the range of the normal quarter production in recent times for an entire year. Consequently, there was certain to be something of a backlog at the Mint, especially in an economy that was beginning to slow down.[20]

NUMISMATIC ASPECTS OF THE STATE OF VIRGINIA

Colonial era: Virginia issued many types of currency. *1773:* Copper halfpence of this date were struck in England for distribution in Virginia. *1861–1865:* Richmond was the capital of the Confederate States of America. Most CSA paper money was issued with this imprint. *1936:* The Lynchburg Sesquicentennial commemorative half dollar was issued. *1936:* The Norfolk Bicentennial commemorative half dollar was issued. *1936:* The Roanoke Island commemorative half dollar was issued. *1937:* The Battle of Antietam commemorative half dollar was issued. *1946–1951:* The Booker T. Washington Memorial commemorative half dollar was issued. *1982:* The Washington commemorative half dollar was issued. *1993:* the Bill of Rights commemorative silver dollar was issued. *1993:* The Thomas Jefferson commemorative silver dollar was issued. *1999:* The Dolley Madison commemorative silver dollar was issued.

NEW YORK 11th of 50

Official Coin Release Date: January 2, 2001.

Mintage Figures:

Circulation strikes (clad) 2001-P: 655,400,000
2001-D: 619,640,000

Proof strikes (clad) 2001-S: 3,094,140

Proof strikes (silver) 2001-S: 889,697

New York 2001 • Market Values • Circulation Strikes and Proof Strikes

MS-63	MS-64	MS-65	MS-66	MS-67	MS-68	MS-63	MS-64	MS-65	MS-66	MS-67	MS-68
$1.25	$1.50	$1.75	$2	$2.50	$3	$1.25	$1.50	$1.75	$2	$2.50	$3

PF-64	PF-65	PF-66	PF-67	PF-68	PF-64	PF-65
$9	$10	$11	$14	$16	$9	$10

New York 2001 • Certified Populations • Circulation Strikes and Proof Strikes

MS-65	MS-66	MS-67	MS-68	MS-69	MS-65	MS-66	MS-67	MS-68	MS-69
136	748	1,435	602	13	290	976	385	52	0

PF-65	PF-66	PF-67	PF-68	PF-69	PF-70	PF-65	PF-66	PF-67	PF-68	PF-69	PF-70
0	1	6	92	4,735	49	4	7	25	181	6,747	24

■ Philadelphia Mint circulation strikes   ■ Denver Mint circulation strikes

■ San Francisco Mint (clad) Proof strikes   ■ San Francisco Mint (silver clad) Proof strikes

SPECIFICS OF THE REVERSE DESIGN

Description: Consisting of a textured map of New York State (with apparent topological relief, but not to scale), the design shows a recessed line showing the Hudson River and Erie Canal waterway (at the same level, with no locks in the Erie Canal). The river is shown only to the point at which it joins the canal. The Statue of Liberty is to the left, and to the right, the inscription GATEWAY / TO / FREEDOM. This phrase is not a replacement for the time-honored EXCELSIOR motto, or even for THE EMPIRE STATE, but is seemingly a comment on the fact that New York City harbor, home of the statue, was an entry port for those emigrating from distant lands. Eleven stars are added at the upper left and right borders, past NEW YORK, nicely complementing the design and representing the order in which the state ratified the Constitution. This is the second quarter design to use this symbolism (New Hampshire's was the first).

Designer: Daniel Carr. *Liberty Enlightening the World* was designed by French sculptor Frédéric Auguste Bartholdi, and thus he should get some peripheral credit or at least a slight nod. *Mint sculptor-engraver who made the model:* Alfred F. Maletsky. *Engraver's initials and location:* AM in italic capitals below the left border of the map.

STORY OF THE DESIGN

The first of the 2001 issues, the New York state quarter continued the map concept used for the 1999 Pennsylvania and Georgia and the 2000 Massachusetts and South Carolina issues. The map of the Empire State has some geographical details, including lines added to reflect the course of a waterway using part of the Hudson River and all of the Erie Canal. The Statue of Liberty is on the left side, nicely balancing the heavier map area to the right. However, to some collectors, the statue was a tired motif, in view of its extensive use on 1986 commemorative coins, among other places (including by that time nearly 30 different varieties of postage stamp). This, probably the most famous icon of America, stands on Liberty Island (formerly Bedloe's Island) in the harbor of New York City. It was officially dedicated on October 28, 1886, with President Grover Cleveland doing the honors. At the 1876 Centennial Exhibition in Philadelphia the detached uplifted arm of Liberty had been a great attraction, displaying part of the work in progress.

The Erie Canal at Lockport, New York. (Bartlett, *American Scenery, 1840*)

In keeping with procedures used elsewhere, the governor of the state called for designs from the public, attracting many entries. On June 19, 2000, Governor George E. Pataki unveiled the five semifinal designs as created by Mint artists. These included the aforementioned statue as well as Henry Hudson and his *Half Moon* ship, a scene depicted on the historical *Battle of Saratoga* painting, and the Federal Building on Wall Street, New York City.

Present-day numismatists may know that the 1909 Hudson-Fulton celebration in New York spawned a number of medals with Hudson and the *Half Moon*, but no commemorative coins. The Federal Building is important in numismatic history for its connection with the Treasury Department and the inauguration of George Washington. As to the *Battle of Saratoga*, this is less well known to collectors and probably to state residents as well. However, it was once proposed as the main design for the first Legal Tender Note of 1862 and was used on the back of the rare $500 National Bank Note, Original Series and Series of 1875.

The Statue of Liberty, formally known as *Liberty Enlightening the World*, was dedicated in 1886. (American Bank Note Co. vignette)

Citizens of the state were invited to cast their ballots for their favorite via email or letter to the governor's office. The winner garnered an impressive 76% of responses.

Daniel Carr's design was chosen from among those of 14 artists who were invited to submit proposed designs. The Mint "paid Carr for his work, [but] it did not credit him as designer. The engravers' initials appear on the coins, but not those of Carr. . . ."[21]

The New York state quarters were released in January 2001. At the inaugural ceremony it seems that little-noticed giveaways were New York state quarters in *chocolate*. Numismatist Frank S. Robinson recalled:

> I took my daughter to the launching ceremony here in Albany, they had a bowl full of the chocolate quarters. Some were left behind

untaken at the end, so I took them, and actually sold them on my list (for a very modest sum). I believe I heard somewhere that chocolatizing was repeated elsewhere too.[22]

NUMISMATIC ASPECTS OF THE STATE OF NEW YORK

Colonial era: The state issued many types of currency. *1786:* Nova Eborac and related copper coins were minted. *1786–1787:* Ephraim Brasher, a New York City goldsmith, struck doubloons. *1786–1789:* Machin's Mills in Newburgh made many counterfeit coins that were widely circulated. *1790:* First Presbyterian Church in Albany issued copper "church pennies." *1826:* The Erie Canal medal, by C.C. Wright, was an early product of the famous engraver. *1854:* The New York Assay Office opened. *1858:* The American Bank Note Co. was formed by the consolidation of eight firms, to become world's largest printer of currency. *1858:* The American Numismatic Society was founded by Augustus B. Sage and friends. *1859:* The National Bank Note Co. was founded in New York City. *1862:* The Continental Bank Note Co. was founded in New York City. *1862:* John Gault, New York City, issued encased postage stamps. *1863:* New York City diesinkers produced Civil War tokens in quantity. *1913:* The New York Federal Reserve Bank was established in New York City under the Federal Reserve Act. Currency issued there bears the letter B. *1924:* The Huguenot-Walloon Tercentenary commemorative half dollar was issued. *1935:* The Hudson Sesquicentennial commemorative half dollar was issued. *1936:* the Albany commemorative half dollar was issued. *1936:* the Long Island Tercentenary commemorative half dollar was issued. *1938:* The New Rochelle commemorative half dollar was issued. *1986:* The Statue of Liberty commemorative half dollars and silver and gold $5 pieces were issued. *2002:* The West Point Bicentennial commemorative silver dollar was issued.

NORTH CAROLINA *12th of 50*

Official Coin Release Date: March 12, 2001.

Mintage Figures:

Circulation strikes (clad) 2001-P: 627,600,000
2001-D: 427,876,000

Proof strikes (clad) 2001-S: 3,094,140

Proof strikes (silver) 2001-S: 889,697

North Carolina 2001 • Market Values • Circulation Strikes and Proof Strikes

MS-63	MS-64	MS-65	MS-66	MS-67	MS-68	MS-63	MS-64	MS-65	MS-66	MS-67	MS-68
$1.25	$1.50	$1.75	$2	$2.50	$3	$1.25	$1.50	$1.75	$2	$2.50	$3

PF-64	PF-65	PF-66	PF-67	PF-68	PF-64	PF-65
$9	$10	$11	$14	$16	$9	$10

North Carolina 2001 • Certified Populations • Circulation Strikes and Proof Strikes

MS-65	MS-66	MS-67	MS-68	MS-69	MS-65	MS-66	MS-67	MS-68	MS-69
142	797	1,594	576	7	178	819	560	62	0

PF-65	PF-66	PF-67	PF-68	PF-69	PF-70	PF-65	PF-66	PF-67	PF-68	PF-69	PF-70
0	1	14	89	4,931	46	2	3	23	189	6,726	26

■ Philadelphia Mint circulation strikes ■ Denver Mint circulation strikes

■ San Francisco Mint (clad) Proof strikes ■ San Francisco Mint (silver clad) Proof strikes

SPECIFICS OF THE REVERSE DESIGN

Description: The first manned flight at Kitty Hawk, North Carolina, is depicted as adapted from a famous photograph. The Wright biplane, flying toward the right, has Orville lying on his stomach, operating the controls. Above is FIRST FLIGHT. In the foreground are a bench and the large standing figure of Wilbur Wright (much larger than on the original photograph). The top and bottom border inscriptions are standard.

Designer: Mary Ellen Robinson, "who submitted a drawing based upon the famous photograph," was credited by ICG as the designer.[23] One might also grant posthumous credit to the 1903 photographer, John P. Daniels. *Mint sculptor-engraver who made the model:* John Mercanti. *Engraver's initials and location:* JM, located above the far right side of the ground.

STORY OF THE DESIGN

The 2001 North Carolina quarter depicts the Wright brothers' airplane that, on December 17, 1903, flew a distance of 120 feet among the sand dunes of Kitty Hawk, on the seacoast of the state.[24] Although S.P. Langley, backed by many assertions from the Smithsonian Institution, claimed that he was first in the manned flight of a self-propelled heavier-than-air machine, most historians have credited the Wrights.

The image on the coin is loosely adapted from a contemporary photograph by John P. Daniels, now with the standing figure of Wilbur Wright larger in the foreground, as he observes the historic flight with brother Orville lying flat on his stomach at the controls. Concepts for the plane were developed and the craft constructed in Ohio, home of the Wright brothers, who operated a bicycle shop. Henry Ford, who collected all sorts of things, later bought the shop operated by the Wrights in Dayton, and moved it to Greenfield Village in Dearborn, Michigan, where it can be seen today. Later, in 2002, Ohio also memorialized the Wright brothers on its state quarter, but with a different airplane.

Ideas for the coin design were solicited by the North Carolina Department of Cultural Resources, which set up the North Carolina Commemorative Coin Committee. The resultant publicity drew many submissions. Alternate motifs included the Wright biplane superimposed on an outline map of the state, the Cape Hatteras lighthouse (also on a map), and the same seashore prominence but with a sand dune and seagulls. As Okracoke Inlet, nearby, is famous for its supposed buried treasure, it might have been interesting to add a chest of doubloons.

On June 5, 2000, the Committee and Governor James B. Hunt picked the "First Flight" motif, as it was called—Hunt's choice from three semifinal designs. The FIRST FLIGHT inscription, eventually appearing on the coin, caused some confusion as a slightly different version, FIRST IN FLIGHT, had been used on state license plates since 1981.

NUMISMATIC ASPECTS OF THE STATE OF NORTH CAROLINA

Colonial era: The state issued many types of currency. *1830:* Christopher Bechtler and family opened a private mint and assay office in Rutherfordton to coin $1, $2.50, and $5 pieces. Their mint operated until 1852. *1838–1861:* The Charlotte Mint produced gold coins of $1, $2.50, and $5 denominations.

RHODE ISLAND *13th of 50*

Official Coin Release Date: May 21, 2001.

Mintage Figures:

Circulation strikes (clad) 2001-P: 423,000,000
2001-D: 447,100,000

Proof strikes (clad) 2001-S: 3,094,140

Proof strikes (silver) 2001-S: 889,697

Rhode Island 2001 • Market Values • Circulation Strikes and Proof Strikes

MS-63	MS-64	MS-65	MS-66	MS-67	MS-68	MS-63	MS-64	MS-65	MS-66	MS-67	MS-68
$1.25	$1.50	$1.75	$2	$2.50	$3	$1.25	$1.50	$1.75	$2	$2.50	$3

PF-64	PF-65	PF-66	PF-67	PF-68	PF-64	PF-65
$7	$8	$10	$11	$13	$9	$10

Rhode Island 2001 • Certified Populations • Circulation Strikes and Proof Strikes

MS-65	MS-66	MS-67	MS-68	MS-69	MS-65	MS-66	MS-67	MS-68	MS-69
108	730	799	283	3	118	1,012	686	39	0

PF-65	PF-66	PF-67	PF-68	PF-69	PF-70	PF-65	PF-66	PF-67	PF-68	PF-69	PF-70
0	0	11	80	4,442	45	0	4	25	167	6,776	32

■ Philadelphia Mint circulation strikes ■ Denver Mint circulation strikes
■ San Francisco Mint (clad) Proof strikes ■ San Francisco Mint (silver clad) Proof strikes

SPECIFICS OF THE REVERSE DESIGN

Description: A sailboat shown heading to the left before the wind is the main central feature of the motif. Deck details are visible, but no people are obvious. The boat was modeled after the *Reliance*, the 1903 winner of the America's Cup, a craft built in Bristol, Rhode Island, by the famous Herreshoff Manufacturing Co. In the distance is the Pell Bridge, of the suspension type, with THE / OCEAN / STATE above. The top and bottom border inscriptions are standard.

Designer: Daniel Carr. *Mint sculptor-engraver who made the model:* Thomas D. Rogers. *Engraver's initials and location:* TDR, located at an angle on the surface of the waves at the lower right corner of this feature.

STORY OF THE DESIGN

The Rhode Island quarter of 2001 is inscribed OCEAN STATE, reflecting the importance of the sea, including Narragansett Bay, a vast inlet of the Atlantic.[25] The motif illustrates a vintage sailboat gliding across the waves before the wind, evocative of the America's Cup races centered there for more than a half century. In the distance is the Pell Bridge.

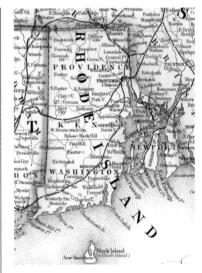

Map of Rhode Island, 1866. (*Mitchell's New General Atlas*)

Governor Lincoln Almond authorized the Rhode Island State Council on the Arts to set up the Coin Concept Advisory Panel. Citizens of the state were invited to submit ideas, and more than 500 were received. The choice was narrowed down to three designs, after which it was open voting via libraries, the State House, and the Internet. Of the 34,566 votes cast, 57% were for the sailboat design. Governor Almond did not use his right to change the results and substitute a favorite. He seconded the will of the voters, and this became a people's coin.

The Mint hired Daniel Carr, the highly talented Colorado artist responsible for the 2001 New York quarter, to create the motif used on the coin, an effort that most numismatists considered to be a great success. For some unexplained reason the Mint did not credit Carr in any way. This coin completed the honoring of the 13 original colonies.

Daniel Carr's sketch for the 2001 Rhode Island quarter as submitted to the Mint, after which the design was modified by a Mint artist. (Daniel Carr photo)

NUMISMATIC ASPECTS OF THE STATE OF RHODE ISLAND

Colonial era: the state issued many types of currency. *1778–1779:* The Rhode Island ship medal bearing this date was struck in Europe. *1805–1809:* The Farmers Exchange Bank of Gloucester issued large amounts of worthless paper money—the first major bank fraud in the United States. *1863–1864:* Many Civil War tokens of a distinctive style were issued, mostly in Providence. *1936:* The set of three Rhode Island Tercentenary commemorative half dollars was issued.

VERMONT *14th of 50*

Official Coin Release Date: August 6, 2001.

Mintage Figures:

Circulation strikes (clad) 2001-P: 423,400,000
2001-D: 459,404,000[26]

Proof strikes (clad) 2001-S: 3,094,140

Proof strikes (silver) 2001-S: 889,697

Vermont 2001 • Market Values • Circulation Strikes and Proof Strikes

MS-63	MS-64	MS-65	MS-66	MS-67	MS-68	MS-63	MS-64	MS-65	MS-66	MS-67	MS-68
$1.50	$1.75	$2	$2.50	$3	$3.50	$1.25	$1.50	$1.75	$2	$2.50	$3

PF-64	PF-65	PF-66	PF-67	PF-68	PF-64	PF-65
$9	$10	$11	$14	$16	$9	$10

Vermont 2001 • Certified Populations • Circulation Strikes and Proof Strikes

MS-65	MS-66	MS-67	MS-68	MS-69	MS-65	MS-66	MS-67	MS-68	MS-69
797	1,371	1,524	686	36	83	1,061	1,094	126	0

PF-65	PF-66	PF-67	PF-68	PF-69	PF-70	PF-65	PF-66	PF-67	PF-68	PF-69	PF-70
0	0	6	84	4,408	65	1	3	16	166	6,690	36

■ Philadelphia Mint circulation strikes ■ Denver Mint circulation strikes

■ San Francisco Mint (clad) Proof strikes ■ San Francisco Mint (silver clad) Proof strikes

SPECIFICS OF THE REVERSE DESIGN

Description: Two maple trees, truncated at the top, stand alone, with an empty field or plain in the distance, beyond which is Camel's Hump, a prominence in the Green Mountain range. A standing man has his right hand at the top of one of four sap buckets in evidence. To the right is FREEDOM / AND / UNITY. The top and bottom border inscriptions are standard.

Designer: Sarah-Lee Terrat. *Mint sculptor-engraver who made the model:* T. James Ferrell. *Engraver's initials and location:* TJF, in italic capitals located above the ground at the far right.

STORY OF THE DESIGN

In 1785 and 1786, Vermont, an independent entity, issued copper coins with the legend STELLA QUARTA DECIMA, or *the 14th star.* Vermont had hoped to achieve statehood by this time, but opposition from nearby New York, with which there were intense boundary disputes, prevented this from happening. Finally, in 1791 Vermont became the 14th star in the flag, as its citizens had hoped.

State emblems of Vermont. (James McCabe Jr., *A Centennial View of Our Country and Its Resources,* 1876)

The 2001 Vermont quarter dollar features a scene of two maple trees in early spring, not in the usual grove, but standing all by themselves. Perhaps the grove is out of sight behind the observer. Maple sugaring is in progress, with sap buckets affixed to trees. Camel's Hump, the eponymous 4,083-foot landmark in the northern part of the Green Mountains range (from which the name Vermont was derived), forms the background. Maple sugar production, earlier done by Native Americans, became an important industry in the state. The theme on the quarter offers a change from motifs earlier seen on Vermont-related coins, including the sun-and-forested-ridge "landscape" design of the aforementioned 1785 and 1786 coppers, and the Ira Allen / catamount design of the 1927 Vermont Sesquicentennial commemorative half dollar.

Governor Howard Dean named the Vermont Arts Council to coordinate the quarter design. This group created five concepts, each including Camel's Hump, after which a casual survey was conducted by radio. Governor Dean made the final choice, based on artwork by Sarah-Lee Terrat (artist and principal owner of YeloDog Design in Waterbury, Vermont), and sent it to the Treasury Department. The identity of Terrat was unknown to viewers of the coins, and only the initials of William Cousins, who altered the motif and made the models, were featured.[27]

NUMISMATIC ASPECTS OF THE STATE OF VERMONT

April 14, 1781: An act authorized the issuance of paper money, eventually amounting to £25,155 in total face value; these are rarities today. *1785–1787:* Vermont copper coins were struck under contract at a private mint on Millbrook, in Pawlet. *1787–1788:* Vermont copper coins were struck at Machin's Mills, Newburgh, New York. *1806:* The Vermont State Bank was authorized, and eventually had four branches. This was the first state-operated bank in the country. *1835:* Gustin & Blake, Chelsea, issued the state's only Hard Times token. *1927:* The Vermont Sesquicentennial commemorative half dollar was issued.

KENTUCKY *15th of 50*

Official Coin Release Date: October 15, 2001.

Mintage Figures:

Circulation strikes (clad) 2001-P: 353,000,000
2001-D: 370,564,000

Proof strikes (clad) 2001-S: 3,094,140

Proof strikes (silver) 2001-S: 889,697

Kentucky 2001 • Market Values • Circulation Strikes and Proof Strikes

MS-63	MS-64	MS-65	MS-66	MS-67	MS-68	MS-63	MS-64	MS-65	MS-66	MS-67	MS-68
$1.50	$1.75	$2	$2.50	$3	$3.50	$1.50	$1.75	$2	$2.50	$3	$3.50

PF-64	PF-65	PF-66	PF-67	PF-68	PF-64	PF-65
$9	$10	$11	$14	$16	$9	$10

Kentucky 2001 • Certified Populations • Circulation Strikes and Proof Strikes

MS-65	MS-66	MS-67	MS-68	MS-69	MS-65	MS-66	MS-67	MS-68	MS-69
104	689	1,416	558	7	128	731	479	43	0

PF-65	PF-66	PF-67	PF-68	PF-69	PF-70	PF-65	PF-66	PF-67	PF-68	PF-69	PF-70
0	0	7	94	4,461	41	4	4	28	178	6,792	45

█ Philadelphia Mint circulation strikes   █ Denver Mint circulation strikes

█ San Francisco Mint (clad) Proof strikes   █ San Francisco Mint (silver clad) Proof strikes

SPECIFICS OF THE REVERSE DESIGN

Description: High on a rise, the two-story Federal Hill house is shown, with 11 five-pointed stars erratically spaced on its sides, either an artistic gaffe on the coin or the result of very sloppy carpentry on the building way back when. In the foreground, a sleek and handsome horse stands behind a wooden fence. Above its head is "MY OLD / KENTUCKY / HOME" in quotation marks, which indicate the inscription as a song title. The top and bottom border inscriptions are standard.

Designer: Seemingly the design is one suggested by Kentucky citizen Ronald J. Inabit, although uncredited. ICG signed a contract with contest entrant Benjamin Blair to sign "slabs" containing the coins, crediting him as the "concept artist."[28] *Mint sculptor-engraver who made the model:* T. James Ferrell. *Engraver's initials and location:* TJF, in italic capitals located below the ground at the far right.

STORY OF THE DESIGN

The 2001 Kentucky quarter dollar illustrates a hilltop mansion with a thoroughbred racehorse behind a fence in the foreground.[29] The U.S. Mint described the design:

> Kentucky was the first state on the western frontier to join the Union and is one of four states to call itself a "commonwealth." Kentucky is home of the longest running annual horse race in the country, the Kentucky Derby. The famous Kentucky bluegrass country is also grazing ground for some of the world's finest racehorses.
>
> Also featured on the new quarter is another prominent symbol of Kentucky, Federal Hill, which has become known as My Old Kentucky Home.

The design shows a side view of the famous Bardstown home where Stephen Foster wrote the state song, *My Old Kentucky Home*.[30]

It may be of numismatic interest to mention that the portrait of Foster is depicted on the obverse of the 1936 Cincinnati commemorative half dollar. The composer roved widely, and called several places home. In 1852 he visited Judge John Rowan (a cousin) in Bardstown, Kentucky, and stayed in his house, built in 1818. While there he wrote the memorable song.

Ideas Invited
Governor Paul E. Patton appointed his wife, Judi, to lead the Kentucky Quarter Project Committee. Designs were solicited, and about 1,800 were received. These were narrowed to 12 final motifs, these being displayed in the Capitol building and shown on the Internet for people to review. By this time the Internet played an important role in disseminating information for states during the design process for their coins. The semifinalists for Kentucky's quarter dollar included "horse behind plank fence in field, house in background," "Birthplace of Lincoln," "My Old Kentucky Home with sunlight surrounding it," "Thoroughbred running with jockey aboard," and "Daniel Boone with long rifle, dog under tree."[31]

More than 50,000 votes were received. The selection was further reduced to just two: one featuring the birthplace of Abraham Lincoln and the other a racing horse. Regarding the Lincoln motif, a spokesperson for the state commented, "The commission threw it out, saying it was artistically unsophisticated."[32]

Confusion and Dissatisfaction
Kay Harrod, who coordinated much of the project, went with other committee members to Washington to visit Mint officials and discuss the racehorse motif. However, the reception proved to be disappointing. In her words:

> They would not look at our drawings. We were just reeling. We thought we had done all the right things. We had been working ourselves to death, our tongues wagging. Why even bother it?
>
> They made up the rules as they went along. The language began to change when we got up there with our design. The word "concept" came up. The words began to change.[33]

An August 22 memo sent by the state, on behalf of the committee, to artists participating in the design took the position that Kentucky would not officially recognize *any* designer, stating:

> The finished art on the coin was done by Mint engraver Jim Ferrell and is a reflection of many entries with horses and *My Old Kentucky Home*. [These] influenced the decision of our committee, Governor Patton and First Lady Judi Patton, who chaired Kentucky's committee. . . .
>
> The art is done by the engravers at the U.S. Mint. In fact, when our committee met with engravers at the Mint in June 1999, the representatives of the Mint did not look at or accept our drawings that we took with us to that meeting, citing legal reasons. Instead they asked our committee members to discuss the look we wanted.[34]

Apparently the "drawings" that the committee took to the Mint were not to be credited to anyone. Bob Farmer, the state's liaison person to the U.S. Mint in matters concerning design selection, cautioned artists from becoming involved with "coin entrepreneurs" who might seek to sell signed coin products crediting particular individuals. In reality, artists as well as former Mint directors profited by making deals with "coin entrepreneurs" to sign holders featuring coins they had created or, in the case of the directors, coins that were made under their administrations (as discussed near the beginning of this chapter).

NUMISMATIC ASPECTS OF THE STATE OF KENTUCKY

1790s: A British Conder token, widely collected in America, is called the *Kentucky token*, as it depicts a pyramid with 15 state abbreviations, with K (for Kentucky) at the top. *1796:* The P.P.P. Myddelton token of this date bears inscriptions for the British Settlement [in] Kentucky and is related to a colonization scheme. These were made at the Soho Mint (England) from dies engraved by Conrad Küchler, were struck in copper and silver, and are rare today. *1934–1938:* The Daniel Boone Bicentennial commemorative half dollar was released

TENNESSEE 16th of 50

Official Coin Release Date: January 2, 2002.

Mintage Figures:

Circulation strikes (clad) 2002-P: 361,600,000
2002-D: 286,468,000[35]

Proof strikes (clad) . . . . 2002-S: 3,084,245[36]

Proof strikes (silver) 2002-S: 892,229

Tennessee 2002 • Market Values • Circulation Strikes and Proof Strikes

MS-63	MS-64	MS-65	MS-66	MS-67	MS-68	MS-63	MS-64	MS-65	MS-66	MS-67	MS-68
$2.50	$3	$3.50	$4	$4.50	$5	$2	$3	$3.50	$4	$4.50	$5

PF-64	PF-65	PF-66	PF-67	PF-68	PF-64	PF-65
$9	$10	$11	$14	$16	$9	$10

Tennessee 2002 • Certified Populations • Circulation Strikes and Proof Strikes

MS-65	MS-66	MS-67	MS-68	MS-69	MS-65	MS-66	MS-67	MS-68	MS-69
52	279	1,291	1,183	54	106	1,010	1,261	127	0

PF-65	PF-66	PF-67	PF-68	PF-69	PF-70	PF-65	PF-66	PF-67	PF-68	PF-69	PF-70
1	5	21	63	4,554	47	2	10	29	160	6,223	49

Philadelphia Mint circulation strikes ■ Denver Mint circulation strikes

San Francisco Mint (clad) Proof strikes ■ San Francisco Mint (silver clad) Proof strikes

SPECIFICS OF THE REVERSE DESIGN

Description: A collage at the center includes a trumpet (this was a year for trumpets, and one would also be used on the 2002 Louisiana quarter, both with errors in the design details), a guitar with five strings (but with six pegs, and intended to be a six-string guitar), a violin (or fiddle), and a music book. Three large, pointed stars are in an arc above and to the sides; below, the inscription MUSICAL HERITAGE is on a ribbon. The top and bottom border inscriptions are standard.

Designer: Shawn Stookey, a teacher at Lakeview Elementary in New Johnsonville, Tennessee, was publicly credited by the Mint for his winning design. Mint sculptor-engraver who made the model: Donna Weaver. Engraver's initials and location: DW, located above the ribbon end at the right.

STORY OF THE DESIGN

The motif of the 2002 Tennessee quarter is a course in the musical history of the state:

> The design incorporates musical instruments and a score with the inscription "Musical Heritage." Three stars represent Tennessee's three regions, and the instruments symbolize each region's distinct musical style.
>
> The fiddle represents the Appalachian music of East Tennessee, the trumpet stands for the blues of West Tennessee for which Memphis is famous, and the guitar is for Central Tennessee, home to Nashville, the capital of country music.[37]

Following the direction of Governor Don Sundquist, a statewide contest for designs was launched in the spring of 2000, with the nearly 1,000 entries being evaluated by the seven members of the Tennessee Coin Commission. That group picked three favorite themes, including Musical Heritage, Ratification of the 19th Amendment, and Sequoyah (the creator of the Cherokee writing system).

On June 28, 2000, these were sent to the U.S. Mint. Nearly a year later, on June 26, 2001, the Mint sent five "approved renditions" of these ideas, from which Governor Sundquist exercised his prerogative and picked the one to be used. The Mint Web site included this desirable information: "The winning design was submitted by Shawn Stookey, a teacher at Lakeview Elementary in New Johnsonville, Tennessee." (Kudos to the Mint for showcasing Stookey!)

A Curious Guitar

After the coin design was released, it was seen that the guitar had six pegs but only five strings. Actually, there are six strings from the tuning pegs to the fretboard, but the sixth string disappears above the sound hole.

There was some controversy about the details of the depicted trumpet, with the bell and leadpipe on the same side as the valves on the instrument. The same error is on the 2002 Louisiana quarter. Errors in design details contribute to the enjoyment of numismatics and are always amusing to contemplate.

NUMISMATIC ASPECTS OF THE STATE OF TENNESSEE

1860s: Civil War tokens were issued by several merchants. Today they range from scarce to rare.

OHIO *17th of 50*

Official Coin Release Date: March 11, 2002 (coins released into the Federal Reserve system).

Mintage Figures:

Circulation strikes (clad) . . . . 2002-P: 217,200,000[18]
2002-D: 414,832,000

Proof strikes (clad) 2002-S: 3,084,245

Proof strikes (silver) 2002-S: 892,229

Ohio 2002 • Market Values • Circulation Strikes and Proof Strikes

MS-63	MS-64	MS-65	MS-66	MS-67	MS-68	MS-63	MS-64	MS-65	MS-66	MS-67	MS-68
$1.50	$2	$2.50	$3	$3.50	$4.50	$1.50	$2	$2.50	$3	$3.50	$4.50

PF-64	PF-65	PF-66	PF-67	PF-68	PF-64	PF-65
$7	$8	$10	$11	$15	$9	$10

Ohio 2002 • Certified Populations • Circulation Strikes and Proof Strikes

MS-65	MS-66	MS-67	MS-68	MS-69	MS-65	MS-66	MS-67	MS-68	MS-69
165	433	1,497	1,660	43	158	907	1,230	298	1

PF-65	PF-66	PF-67	PF-68	PF-69	PF-70	PF-65	PF-66	PF-67	PF-68	PF-69	PF-70
1	4	18	57	4,446	46	2	7	29	163	6,163	40

■ Philadelphia Mint circulation strikes   ■ Denver Mint circulation strikes

■ San Francisco Mint (clad) Proof strikes   ■ San Francisco Mint (silver clad) Proof strikes

SPECIFICS OF THE REVERSE DESIGN

Description: Against an outline map of Ohio, the Wright *Flyer* is shown high in the air with a pilot sitting (or, rather, lying prone) at the controls. BIRTHPLACE / OF AVIATION / PIONEERS appears in three lines below. To the lower right is an Apollo-era astronaut standing in a space suit on the moon, facing forward. The top and bottom border inscriptions are standard. The numismatic community was well represented in the creation of the design.

Designer: Unknown. *Mint sculptor-engraver who made the model:* Donna Weaver. *Engraver's initials and location:* DW, located below the lower left side of the map.

STORY OF THE DESIGN

The history of the 2002 Ohio quarter is especially well documented, as professional numismatist Tom Noe chaired the committee evaluating the designs, and among the members were *Coin World* editor Beth Deisher and Bill Kamb, president of the Columbus Numismatic Society.

Originally, the committee recommended BIRTHPLACE OF AVIATION as the inscription on the coin, this matching what was on Ohio state license plates. On the coin this was changed to BIRTHPLACE OF AVIATION PIONEERS. Mint Director Jay Johnson said that he had no idea why the change was made, and Governor Bob Taft was surprised. Actually, the Commission of Fine Arts had suggested the change, as there was some question as to where aviation itself was actually "born," as the first flight had taken place in North Carolina and had already been depicted on the quarter of that state. Moreover, aviation in the form of lighter-than-air balloons dated back more than a century before the Wright brothers.

This is what the Mint had to say:

> The Ohio quarter, the second quarter of 2002 and seventeenth in the series, honors the state's contribution to the history of aviation, depicting an early aircraft and an astronaut, superimposed as a group on the outline of the state. The design also includes the inscription "Birthplace of Aviation Pioneers."
>
> The claim to this inscription is well justified—the history making astronauts Neil Armstrong and John Glenn were both born in Ohio, as was Orville Wright, co-inventor of the airplane. Orville and his brother, Wilbur Wright, also built and tested one of their early aircraft, the 1905 *Flyer III*, in Ohio.[39]

The *Toledo Blade* reported that the astronaut depicted was created at the Mint by using a photograph taken by Neil Armstrong of Colonel Edwin "Buzz" Aldrin Jr., a native of New Jersey—a clear violation of Mint rules that no living person be used as a motif.[40] Accordingly, an alteration was made. The plane depicted is the Wright *Flyer III* of 1905, although some have mistaken it for the 1903 plane used at Kitty Hawk. Why the original craft was not used was not explained. On the original Mint design there was an error, per this comment from Ohio Governor Bob Taft to Secretary of the Treasury Paul O'Neill, May 11, 2001:

> The designs developed by the Mint show the plane in reverse, which is a common error. What appears to be the tail is actually the front of the aircraft, and the committee feels it is appropriate to show the Wright Flyer emerging from Ohio to show outward growth and progress.

NUMISMATIC ASPECTS OF THE STATE OF OHIO

1913: The Cleveland Federal Reserve Bank was established under the Federal Reserve Act. Currency issued there bears the letter D. *1916–1917:* The McKinley Memorial commemorative gold dollar was issued. *1922:* The Grant Memorial commemorative half dollar and gold dollar were issued. *1936:* The Cincinnati Musical Center commemorative half dollar was issued. *1936:* The Cleveland Centennial commemorative half dollar was issued. *1960: Coin World* was launched in Sidney.

LOUISIANA *18th of 50*

Official Coin Release Date: May 20, 2002.

Mintage Figures:

Circulation strikes (clad) 2002-P: 362,000,000
2002-D: 402,204,000

Proof strikes (clad) 2002-S: 3,084,245

Proof strikes (silver) 2002-S: 892,229

Louisiana 2002 • Market Values • Circulation Strikes and Proof Strikes

MS-63	MS-64	MS-65	MS-66	MS-67	MS-68	MS-63	MS-64	MS-65	MS-66	MS-67	MS-68
$1.50	$2	$2.50	$3	$3.50	$4.50	$1.50	$2	$2.50	$3	$3.50	$4.50

PF-64	PF-65	PF-66	PF-67	PF-68	PF-64	PF-65
$7	$8	$10	$11	$15	$14	$16

Louisiana 2002 • Certified Populations • Circulation Strikes and Proof Strikes

MS-65	MS-66	MS-67	MS-68	MS-69	MS-65	MS-66	MS-67	MS-68	MS-69
37	290	1,369	1,220	45	105	602	683	86	0

PF-65	PF-66	PF-67	PF-68	PF-69	PF-70	PF-65	PF-66	PF-67	PF-68	PF-69	PF-70
0	1	15	82	4,540	58	1	1	16	215	6,034	37

■ Philadelphia Mint circulation strikes   ■ Denver Mint circulation strikes
■ San Francisco Mint (clad) Proof strikes   ■ San Francisco Mint (silver clad) Proof strikes

SPECIFICS OF THE REVERSE DESIGN

Description: A full outline of the contiguous 48 United States is shown, with the Louisiana Purchase Territory represented in a stippled map (with no topological features), in relief slightly higher than the rest of the country. At the bottom of the stippled area, a line separates what is now the state of Louisiana. Above is a trumpet with three musical notes, said by some to have included a design mistake (see commentary under the Tennessee-quarter trumpet) and by others to be simply a "cartoon" illustration of a trumpet. To the right is the inscription LOUISIANA / PURCHASE, and to the lower left is a standing brown pelican, apparently with its beak empty. The top and bottom border inscriptions are standard.

Designer: Unknown. *Mint sculptor-engraver who made the model:* John Mercanti. *Engraver's initials and location:* JM, located in the Gulf of Mexico below the Florida panhandle.

STORY OF THE DESIGN

The 2002 Louisiana quarter features a textured area indicating the Louisiana Purchase as a part of an outline map of the United States, the acquisition having been made for a cost of $15,000,000

The pelican has long served as the state emblem. (Vignette from a stock certificate, Louisiana National Bank of Baton Rouge)

in 1803, during the presidency of Thomas Jefferson.[41] The brown pelican, the state bird of Louisiana, is also depicted on the quarter, as are a trumpet and musical notes—honoring the tradition of jazz in New Orleans. This design was the result of considerable effort, beginning in a significant way when Governor M.J. "Mike" Foster Jr. established the Louisiana Commemorative Coin

Steel-plate engraving of the Mississippi River at New Orleans. (D. Appleton, 1873)

Advisory Commission. The motif was to "be easily understood by both the youth of the state of Louisiana and the youth of other states." In time, the commission reviewed 1,193 design suggestions, about 80% of which were submitted by schoolchildren, paralleling in part the design process for the 2000 Massachusetts quarter. Five concepts were given to the U.S. Mint, which developed designs. Governor Foster made the final choice, not at all his personal preference, which had been "a pelican facing right roosting on a pier piling and a paddlewheel riverboat traveling west over an outline of the state."[42]

Coin World columnist Michele Orzano said the final motif didn't play out very well:

> One design that doesn't "work," or offers a mixed message at best, is the 2002 Louisiana quarter dollar design. The coin features the outline of a map of the United States with a highlighted area designating the Louisiana Purchase and text stating LOUISIANA PURCHASE. That's a message all by itself, but the design gets complicated because a pelican is depicted below the map and a trumpet with musical notes is depicted above the map.[43]

Aesthetic considerations aside, these quarters were avidly sought by numismatists to add to their growing collections, which reflect the diversity of the program.

NUMISMATIC ASPECTS OF THE STATE OF LOUISIANA

1830s: Ten-dollar notes were issued in New Orleans; imprinted DIX (*ten* in French), they are thought to have been the inspiration for the "land of dixes," or Dixie. *1838:* The New Orleans Mint opened; it continued coinage until 1861. *1879:* The New Orleans Mint reopened, and continued operations until 1909.

INDIANA *19th of 50*

Official Coin Release Date: August 2, 2002.

Mintage Figures:

Circulation strikes (clad) 2002-P: 362,600,000
2002-D: 327,200,000

Proof strikes (clad) 2002-S: 3,084,285

Proof strikes (silver) 2002-S: 892,229

Indiana 2002 • Market Values • Circulation Strikes and Proof Strikes

MS-63	MS-64	MS-65	MS-66	MS-67	MS-68	MS-63	MS-64	MS-65	MS-66	MS-67	MS-68
$1.50	$2	$2.50	$3	$3.50	$4.50	$1.50	$2	$2.50	$3	$3.50	$4.50

PF-64	PF-65	PF-66	PF-67	PF-68	PF-64	PF-65
$5	$6	$8	$10	$12	$9	$10

Indiana 2002 • Certified Populations • Circulation Strikes and Proof Strikes

MS-65	MS-66	MS-67	MS-68	MS-69	MS-65	MS-66	MS-67	MS-68	MS-69
50	102	1,168	1,076	30	100	453	728	153	0

PF-65	PF-66	PF-67	PF-68	PF-69	PF-70	PF-65	PF-66	PF-67	PF-68	PF-69	PF-70
1	1	15	71	4,539	48	0	1	15	202	6,212	37

■ Philadelphia Mint circulation strikes ■ Denver Mint circulation strikes

■ San Francisco Mint (clad) Proof strikes ■ San Francisco Mint (silver clad) Proof strikes

SPECIFICS OF THE REVERSE DESIGN

Description: Against the top part of a stippled outline map (without topological features) a powerful Indianapolis 500 racecar is shown, facing forward and slightly right. As Indy 500 racecars and the race itself are commercial, this seems to have been in violation of Treasury rules. CROSSROADS OF AMERICA is below. To the left are 18 stars arranged in a partial circle, with a stray star in the field within, making a total of 19, representing the order of the state's admission to the Union. The top and bottom border inscriptions are standard.

Designer: Josh Harvey. *Mint sculptor-engraver who made the model:* Donna Weaver. *Engraver's initials and location:* DW, located below the lower right of the map.

STORY OF THE DESIGN

The Indiana quarter of 2000 includes 19 stars as part of the motif. The primary image is an outline map of the state, over which is superimposed a racecar of one of the types used in the famous Indianapolis 500 races, held every year from 1911 to date (except during World Wars I and II). The angle and strength of the car image make it appear to almost be speeding toward the viewer—one of the most dynamic visual effects on any state quarter dollar, it violates the Mint rule that no commercial item be used as a motif. The inscription CROSSROADS OF AMERICA reflects the status of the state as a focus of transportation.

Governor Frank O'Bannon asked his wife, Judy, to solicit designs for the quarter, beginning at the Indiana State Fair on August 17, 1999. Eventually 3,737 ideas were received. The Indiana Quarter Design Committee selected 17 of these and submitted them to a referendum of state citizens. After tallying the responses, the committee selected four semifinalists and sent them to the Mint. A news release from the governor's office, May 5, 2000, told the story up to that point:

A basketball player and a racecar superimposed over the state's outline: That's the design Governor Frank O'Bannon recommended today for Indiana's commemorative quarter. The design, created by 17-year-old Josh Harvey of Centerville, was also the first pick among the more than 156,000 ballots cast either online or by mail for the 17 semifinalists in a statewide competition. . . .

O'Bannon is forwarding Harvey's design to the Mint today along with these three others: The state outline with a cardinal, 19 stars and the Crossroads of America logo, submitted by Joan Butler of Rushville; the state outline beside the torch and stars from the state flag, submitted by Seth Fulkerson of Evansville; and Chief Little Turtle, submitted by Zac Shuck of Kokomo.

"Josh did a great job capturing the images that people most identify with Indiana," the governor said. "Our love of basketball and motor racing is world-famous, and I think that when people see our quarter, they'll know immediately that it represents Indiana."

The Mint reviewed the designs, made changes, and sent the revisions back to O'Bannon. On July 18, 2001, the governor made the final choice based on Josh Harvey's design, but now without Harvey's basketball player (in the air or on tiptoe, about to make a shot), with the stars in a different position, and with the racecar from a different perspective. The Commission of Fine Arts recommendation of an entirely different design, one featuring Chief Little Turtle of the Miami Indian nation, was ignored.

An Inside View

Well-known numismatic scholar and historian R.W. Julian was part of the committee to advise the governor about the design. The following account gives certain information that never reached print or official news releases:

Central States Numismatic Society president Ray Lockwood and I were on the Indiana Quarter Dollar Commission. It was our impression that the Treasury banned reference to a private business, which is exactly what was done here. The Indianapolis 500 is a privately owned entity, whose owners contributed to the O'Bannon political campaigns.

The committee preferred a design showing George Rogers Clark wading through the icy water, holding a gun over his head. The committee knew that it was dead in the water when the governor's official representative on the committee looked at it and said "Oh my God, he's carrying a gun!" The other designs were chosen because of pressure from the governor for a sports or Indian design. The public voting on the designs was designed to get votes for the governor in the forthcoming 2000 election; one of his appointees on the committee actually gave stump speeches the first several meetings, stating that a good design would get O'Bannon a lot of votes!

The governor had considered scrapping the racecar and using the Little Turtle design instead (and had called a special meeting of the committee to discuss the point), but this was abandoned when someone on the committee pointed out that Little Turtle's background did not bear close scrutiny. There were some red faces at the governor's office over this incident because, as his representative on the committee never tired of telling us, Indiana history was the governor's favorite pastime reading.[44]

NUMISMATIC ASPECTS OF THE STATE OF INDIANA

Hoosier tame cat became a slang term (ca. 1837–1838) for a bank note originating in Indiana, often worthless.[45] Later, Indiana developed a well-organized state banking system, of which Hugh McCulloch was a vital part. He later became comptroller of the currency for the U.S. Treasury.

MISSISSIPPI *20th of 50*

Official Coin Release Date: October 15, 2002.

Mintage Figures:

Circulation strikes (clad) 2002-P: 290,000,000
2002-D: 289,600,000
Proof strikes (clad) 2002-S: 3,084,245
Proof strikes (silver) 2002-S: 892,229

Mississippi 2002 • Market Values • Circulation Strikes and Proof Strikes

MS-63	MS-64	MS-65	MS-66	MS-67	MS-68	MS-63	MS-64	MS-65	MS-66	MS-67	MS-68
$1.50	$2	$2.50	$3	$3.50	$4.50	$1.50	$2	$2.50	$3	$3.50	$4.50

PF-64	PF-65	PF-66	PF-67	PF-68	PF-64	PF-65
$5	$6	$8	$10	$12	$9	$10

Mississippi 2002 • Certified Populations • Circulation Strikes and Proof Strikes

MS-65	MS-66	MS-67	MS-68	MS-69	MS-65	MS-66	MS-67	MS-68	MS-69
53	449	1,124	547	8	107	645	936	111	0

PF-65	PF-66	PF-67	PF-68	PF-69	PF-70	PF-65	PF-66	PF-67	PF-68	PF-69	PF-70
0	2	15	73	4,513	59	1	8	24	158	6,206	47

■ Philadelphia Mint circulation strikes   ■ Denver Mint circulation strikes
■ San Francisco Mint (clad) Proof strikes   ■ San Francisco Mint (silver clad) Proof strikes

SPECIFICS OF THE REVERSE DESIGN

Description: Magnolia blossoms and leaves dominate the single-subject coin, with *The / Magnolia / State* in italic letters in three lines at the above right. The top and bottom border inscriptions are standard.

Designer: Unknown. *Mint sculptor-engraver who made the model:* Donna Weaver. *Engraver's initials and location:* DW, incuse on the lowest leaf at the right—the first incuse or recessed signature in the statehood series.

STORY OF THE DESIGN

The Mississippi quarter of 2002, with its bold treatment of the state flower and the inscription "The Magnolia State," is simple and effective in its concept—reflecting a tried-and-true symbol. Variety is the spice of life, and the reiteration of familiar motifs is not always desirable, but in this instance the depiction of *Magnolia grandiflora* scored an artistic success, although it is best appreciated when viewed close-up, not at a distance.

Virtually nothing was publicized nationally about the design-creation process. The U.S. Mint gives this:

> In response to the United States Mint's request for design concepts for the Mississippi quarter, Governor Ronnie Musgrove submitted three concepts on June 22, 2000, a Magnolia flower with a branch, a Mockingbird and "Mississippi—The Magnolia State." The United States Mint provided Governor Musgrove with three candidate designs from which he chose "The Magnolia State" on July 3, 2001.[46]

The motif is unusual in that the magnolia is both the state tree (made official on April 1, 1938, by vote of the state legislature) and the state flower (February 26, 1952). The magnolia is not native, but was introduced from Asia. Its name is derived from that of Pierre Magnol, a French botanist.

NUMISMATIC ASPECTS OF THE STATE OF MISSISSIPPI

1862: During the siege of Vicksburg, copper-nickel cents were counterstamped and used as ten-cent pieces.

In 1862, during the Civil War siege of Vicksburg, copper-nickel Indian Head cents like this one were counterstamped and used as ten-cent pieces.

Victors of the siege of Vicksburg. Pictured are Major-General McPherson, of Grant's army, and his chief engineers (from a sketch by Theo. R. Davis, *in Harper's Weekly*, August 1, 1863).

Settling the terms of surrender. *Harper's* illustrated an interview between generals Grant and Pemberton (*Harper's Weekly*, August 1, 1863).

ILLINOIS *21st of 50*

Official Coin Release Date: January 2, 2003.

Mintage Figures:

Circulation strikes (clad) 2003-P: 225,800,000
2003-D: 237,400,000

Proof strikes (clad) 2003-S: 3,408,516

Proof strikes (silver) 2003-S: 1,125,755

Illinois 2003 • Market Values • Circulation Strikes and Proof Strikes

MS-63	MS-64	MS-65	MS-66	MS-67	MS-68	MS-63	MS-64	MS-65	MS-66	MS-67	MS-68
$1.50	$2	$2.50	$3	$3.50	$4.50	$1.50	$2	$2.50	$3	$3.50	$4.50

PF-64	PF-65	PF-66	PF-67	PF-68	PF-64	PF-65
$5	$6	$8	$10	$12	$9	$10

Illinois 2003 • Certified Populations • Circulation Strikes and Proof Strikes

MS-65	MS-66	MS-67	MS-68	MS-69	MS-65	MS-66	MS-67	MS-68	MS-69
150	339	220	33	0	1,871	577	300	12	0

PF-65	PF-66	PF-67	PF-68	PF-69	PF-70	PF-65	PF-66	PF-67	PF-68	PF-69	PF-70
0	1	14	41	6,532	73	0	6	8	57	7,197	52

■ Philadelphia Mint circulation strikes ■ Denver Mint circulation strikes

■ San Francisco Mint (clad) Proof strikes ■ San Francisco Mint (silver clad) Proof strikes

SPECIFICS OF THE REVERSE DESIGN

Description: An outline map of Illinois encloses most of the standing figure of Abraham Lincoln, holding a book in his right hand and a small object in his left.The state motto, *Land / of / Lincoln,* is in three lines to the left, and *21st / State / Century* in three lines to the right, all in upper- and lowercase italic characters. At the upper left of the field is an outline of a farmhouse, barn, and silo. At the upper right is an outline of the Chicago skyline, dominated by the Sears Tower, the last a possibly against-the-rules instance of a commercial icon appearing on a state quarter. At the left and right borders, 21 stars represent the order in which the state was admitted to the Union. The top and bottom border inscriptions are standard.

One of the most famous statues of Abraham Lincoln, not used on the state quarter, is by Augustus Saint-Gaudens and is in Lincoln Park in Chicago. (*Century* magazine, June 1897)

Designer: Tom Ciccelli was important in this regard.[47] *Mint sculptor-engraver who made the model:* Donna Weaver. *Engraver's initials and location:* DW, located to the right of the bottom of the map. On some coins the initials are indistinct.

STORY OF THE DESIGN

An outline map of Illinois sets the background for the design of this state's 2003 quarter.[48] A young Abraham Lincoln, as taken from the statue *The Resolute Lincoln,* by Avard Fairbanks, is seen inside the map, while other motifs, quite diverse, include a farm and the Chicago skyline. Around the border are 21 stars, reflecting the state's sequence in joining the Union on December 3, 1818. The 1918 Illinois Centennial commemorative half dollar also featured Lincoln, but as a facial portrait.

In January 2001, Governor George Ryan launched the Governor's Classroom Contest encouraging youngsters to submit ideas for the quarter. In time, more than 6,000 were submitted, of which about 5,700 were from schoolchildren. A 14-person committee then reviewed the suggestions and narrowed them down to three categories: state history, agriculture and industry, and symbols of the state. The Mint created five different designs from these, from which Governor Ryan made the final decision.

NUMISMATIC ASPECTS OF THE STATE OF ILLINOIS

1891: The American Numismatic Association was formed at a meeting in Chicago. *1892–1893:* The World's Columbian Exposition commemorative half dollar was released. *1893:* The Isabella commemorative quarter dollar was issued. *1913:* The Chicago Federal Reserve Bank was established under the Federal Reserve Act. Currency issued there bears the letter F. *1918:* The Illinois Centennial commemorative half dollar was issued. *1936:* The Elgin Centennial commemorative half dollar was issued.

ALABAMA *22nd of 50*

Official Coin Release Date: March 17, 2003.

Mintage Figures:

Circulation strikes (clad) 2003-P: 225,000,000
2003-D: 232,400,000

Proof strikes (clad) 2003-S: 3,408,516

Proof strikes (silver) 2003-S: 1,125,755

Alabama 2003 • Market Values • Circulation Strikes and Proof Strikes

MS-63	MS-64	MS-65	MS-66	MS-67	MS-68	MS-63	MS-64	MS-65	MS-66	MS-67	MS-68
$1	$1.50	$2	$2.50	$3	$3.50	$1	$1.50	$2	$2.50	$3	$3.50

PF-64	PF-65	PF-66	PF-67	PF-68	PF-64	PF-65
$4.50	$6	$8	$10	$12	$9	$10

Alabama 2003 • Certified Populations • Circulation Strikes and Proof Strikes

MS-65	MS-66	MS-67	MS-68	MS-69	MS-65	MS-66	MS-67	MS-68	MS-69
183	391	127	4	0	1,919	557	363	26	0

PF-65	PF-66	PF-67	PF-68	PF-69	PF-70	PF-65	PF-66	PF-67	PF-68	PF-69	PF-70
1	1	7	34	6,450	72	0	2	13	54	6,896	84

■ Philadelphia Mint circulation strikes ■ Denver Mint circulation strikes
■ San Francisco Mint (clad) Proof strikes ■ San Francisco Mint (silver clad) Proof strikes

SPECIFICS OF THE REVERSE DESIGN

Description: A three-quarters view of Helen Keller seated in a chair, facing to the right, with her fingers on the surface of a Braille book in her lap. SPIRIT *of* COURAGE is on a ribbon below. Her name appears in Braille in the field to the right, with HELEN / KELLER in two lines immediately below it. A long-leaf pine branch is at the left border, and camellia flowers (called a "magnolia branch" by the Mint; see previous narrative). The top and bottom border inscriptions are standard.

Designer: Unknown. *Mint sculptor-engraver who made the model:* Norman E. Nemeth. *Engraver's initials and location:* NEN, placed in the field below SPI (SPIRIT).

STORY OF THE DESIGN

The 2003 Alabama quarter design features Helen Keller (1880–1968), the world-famous author, lecturer, and Radcliffe College graduate (with honors) who lost her sight, hearing, and speech from illness at the age of 19 months. Eventually, an arrangement was made whereby she consulted Alexander Graham Bell, who helped form a relationship between Keller and Anne Sullivan, who remained to work with her for 50 years. The play *Miracle Worker* is based on this partnership. The coin features Keller's name in English as well as in Braille. At the sides are a long-leaf pine branch and mysterious flowers, while a banner inscribed SPIRIT OF COURAGE typifies Keller's life.

The use of Keller as a motif was unexpected to many citizens, who did not consider her to be a recognizable icon to represent the state. This was no reflection on her accomplishments—many numismatists expressed the same surprise. As for the flowers, the Mint calls this part of the design a *magnolia* branch, per a specification in a letter of April 27, 2001, from Governor Don Siegelman. However, six professors of horticulture at the College of Agriculture at Auburn University stated that, in fact, *red camellias* were depicted—not a surprise, since the camellia is the state flower, and Alabama is known as the Camellia State.

Education the Theme

Governor Siegelman called for schoolchildren to create ideas for the quarter dollar, based on the theme "Education: Link to the Past, Gateway to the Future." From the entries received he selected topics including social movements in the state, social and economic history, and Helen Keller. The Commission of Fine Arts and the Citizens Commemorative Coin Advisory Committee both preferred a design featuring the State Capitol in Montgomery, while the choice of the governor was a design "bearing state symbols."[49]

Sketches were produced at the Mint and sent to the governor, who made the final selection, one not among the favorites mentioned earlier. Again, the advisory commissions were ignored.

NUMISMATIC ASPECTS OF THE STATE OF ALABAMA

1861: Montgomery was the first capital of the Confederacy. "Montgomery Notes" in denominations of $50, $100, $500, and $1,000 bear this imprint. *1860s:* White & Swann, in Huntsville, were the only merchants in Alabama to issue Civil War tokens. *1921:* Alabama Centennial commemorative half dollars were issued, two years after the actual centennial.

MAINE *23rd of 50*

Official Coin Release Date: June 2, 2003.

Mintage Figures:

Circulation strikes (clad) 2003-P: 217,400,000
2003-D: 231,400,000[50]

Proof strikes (clad) 2003-S: 3,408,516

Proof strikes (silver) 2003-S: 1,125,755

Maine 2003 • Market Values • Circulation Strikes and Proof Strikes

MS-63	MS-64	MS-65	MS-66	MS-67	MS-68	MS-63	MS-64	MS-65	MS-66	MS-67	MS-68
$0.75	$1	$1.50	$2	$2.50	$3	$0.75	$1	$1.50	$2	$2.50	$3

PF-64	PF-65	PF-66	PF-67	PF-68	PF-64	PF-65
$4	$6	$8	$10	$12	$9	$10

Maine 2003 • Certified Populations • Circulation Strikes and Proof Strikes

MS-65	MS-66	MS-67	MS-68	MS-69	MS-65	MS-66	MS-67	MS-68	MS-69
97	234	170	17	0	1,870	376	208	16	0

PF-65	PF-66	PF-67	PF-68	PF-69	PF-70	PF-65	PF-66	PF-67	PF-68	PF-69	PF-70
0	4	9	33	6,667	44	1	3	12	77	7,030	56

■ Philadelphia Mint circulation strikes   ■ Denver Mint circulation strikes

■ San Francisco Mint (clad) Proof strikes   ■ San Francisco Mint (silver clad) Proof strikes

SPECIFICS OF THE REVERSE DESIGN

Description: On the left, high on the rocky shore, the Pemaquid Lighthouse casts beams to the left and right. At its base is the fenced-in residential compound of the lighthouse keeper. At sea in the distance to the right is the three-masted schooner *Victory Chimes*, with two seagulls nearby. The top and bottom border inscriptions are standard.

Designer: Daniel J. Carr with Leland and Carolyn Pendleton. *Mint sculptor-engraver who made the model:* Donna Weaver. *Engraver's initials and location:* DW, incuse on a shore rock at the edge of the design at lower left.

STORY OF THE DESIGN

The Maine quarter of 2003 was the last for the six New England States. The design shows a lighthouse on the rockbound Atlantic coast.

The Commission on the Maine State Quarter Design was established by Governor Angus King in March 2001. More than 200 sketches and ideas were received. These were narrowed to three and sent to the governor, who added a fourth. The candidates then stood as "Nation's First Light," "Where America's Day Begins," Mt. Katahdin, and the lighthouse at Pemaquid Point.

"Nation's First Light," the suggestion of the governor, depicted West Quoddy Head Light in Lubec, Maine, near the easternmost part of the contiguous 48 states, giving the earliest view of the sunrise. "Where America's Day Begins" was of similar theme, but differently executed, featuring an outline map of the state, with the sun rising above the ocean. The 16 rays of the sun represented the number of counties in the state. To the left of the sun, the North Star—a part of the Maine State Arms—was depicted.

A Beautiful Design and Its Problems

A Mt. Katahdin design, as first submitted by Brian Kent, was one of the most beautiful I had seen thus far in preliminary sketches for the various quarters. A stately pine to the left overlooked a lake with a solitary canoeist, with Mt. Katahdin rising in the distance. In fact, among numismatists who were communicating with me on the subject of state quarters, everyone was enthusiastic—a truly splendid work of coinage art was in the offing!

The Mint made dramatic changes, rendering the design bilaterally symmetrical, more or less, now with the canoe in the center and with five people aboard (an unusually heavy load), pine trees to each side, and a "generic" mountain (not resembling Katahdin) in the distance. The artist found the alterations "disgusting," and the design work "an abomination." Indeed, all of the Mint redoings of the Maine sketches were "so bad they were sent back." By this time a storm of protest had already been mounted by the winning artist of the Missouri quarter (see the following coin description).[51]

Daniel Carr and the Mint Save the Day

More than 100,000 citizens voted on the Maine sketches, and the Pemaquid Lighthouse was the most popular. Daniel J. Carr, a Colorado artist, submitted the lighthouse design. In its original form on the sketch, it appeared as a bold structure on the right side of the coin, with rays streaming to the left and the right, a pine tree to the far right, and at sea to the left a three-masted schooner, *Victory Chimes*, a 170-foot ship in service since 1954. The motif was created in cooperation with Leland and Carolyn Pendleton of Rockland, Maine, the coastal port home of the *Victory Chimes*. This was done in technical conformity to the rules that the motif must be by a Maine resident—and although Carr was from out of state, the "guidelines also indicated that collaborations between groups and individuals were allowed. My submission was a collaboration between the Pendletons and myself."[52] In its final form, as revised by the Mint, the lighthouse is smaller

Daniel Carr's final design, here in the form of a simulated coin, as submitted to the Mint. (Daniel Carr)

and to the left. In my view, *this* Mint version was a great *improvement*, creating one of the finer motifs to date—a splendid blending of Carr's talent with the artistry of Mint engraver-sculptor Donna Weaver.

Again, art is in the eye of the beholder; the *Bangor Daily News* commented, "The Mint's treatment of the original drawing by Daniel J. Carr of this coastal landmark is shabby and inexplicable. Mis-proportion and clutter seem to be consistent elements of Mint style." The paper further suggested that the schooner "resembles Maryland's *Pride of Baltimore II* more than it resembles the *Victory Chimes*." As if that were not enough, the writer went on to state that in real life the Pemaquid Lighthouse is *not* on a rocky cliff![53]

Oh, well!

NUMISMATIC ASPECTS OF THE STATE OF MAINE

1820: Maine, a district of Massachusetts, became a separate state. Banks issuing currency with the Massachusetts imprint afterward issued Maine notes, creating banks that were located first in one state, then in another, without moving an inch! *1840:* The famous Castine hoard of Massachusetts silver and other coins was found. *1863:* Just one merchant—R.S. Torrey, inventor of the Maine State Bee Hive—issued Civil War tokens. *1920:* The Maine Centennial commemorative half dollar was issued. *1936:* The York County Tercentenary commemorative half dollar was issued.

MISSOURI *24th of 50*

Official Coin Release Date: August 4, 2003.

Mintage Figures:

Circulation strikes (clad) 2003-P: 225,000,000
2003-D: 228,200,000

Proof strikes (clad) 2003-S: 3,408,516

Proof strikes (silver) 2003-S: 1,125,755

Missouri 2003 • Market Values • Circulation Strikes and Proof Strikes

MS-63	MS-64	MS-65	MS-66	MS-67	MS-68	MS-63	MS-64	MS-65	MS-66	MS-67	MS-68
$0.75	$1	$1.50	$2	$2.50	$3	$0.75	$1	$1.50	$2	$2.50	$3

PF-64	PF-65	PF-66	PF-67	PF-68	PF-64	PF-65
$4	$6	$8	$10	$12	$9	$10

Missouri 2003 • Certified Populations • Circulation Strikes and Proof Strikes

MS-65	MS-66	MS-67	MS-68	MS-69	MS-65	MS-66	MS-67	MS-68	MS-69
108	292	225	7	0	1,858	849	409	43	0

PF-65	PF-66	PF-67	PF-68	PF-69	PF-70	PF-65	PF-66	PF-67	PF-68	PF-69	PF-70
0	1	6	35	6,258	64	2	3	13	60	7,021	85

■ Philadelphia Mint circulation strikes   ■ Denver Mint circulation strikes

■ San Francisco Mint (clad) Proof strikes   ■ San Francisco Mint (silver clad) Proof strikes

SPECIFICS OF THE REVERSE DESIGN

Description: The Gateway Arch at St. Louis forms the center of the design, with three men in a pirogue in the water in front of it, headed toward the lower left. At each side is a riverbank with trees. Above is the inscription CORPS OF DISCOVERY and the dates 1804 and 2004. The top and bottom border inscriptions are standard.

Designer: Paul Jackson, whose original concept was greatly modified by the Mint. *Mint sculptor-engraver who made the model:* Alfred F. Maletsky. *Engraver's initials and location:* A.M., in script capital letters, located in the field below the ground at the right.

NUMISMATIC ASPECTS OF THE STATE OF MISSOURI

1904: The Louisiana Purchase Exposition (St. Louis World's Fair) saw the issuance of commemorative gold dollars dated 1903, one with McKinley and the other with a Jefferson portrait. *1913:* The St. Louis Federal Reserve Bank was established under the Federal Reserve Act. Currency issued there bears the letter G. *1921:* The Missouri Centennial commemorative half dollar was issued.

STORY OF THE DESIGN

The process for determining the design for Missouri's own coin began in February 2001, when Governor Bob Holden named 12 citizens to the Missouri Commemorative Quarter Design Committee. A statewide competition was announced, and about 3,300 submissions were eventually received. From these, a dozen semifinal motifs were chosen and posted on the Internet for voting. About 175,000 responses were received, the results narrowing the field down to five concepts. Finally, a sketch by Paul Jackson, a Missouri artist, was selected.

In its original form, the Gateway Arch (official name: Jefferson National Expansion Monument) at St. Louis was small in the distance, above center, with a river in the foreground and wooded banks to each side. At the center was a canoe with Lewis and Clark paddling. At the time, the design attracted little admiration in numismatic circles, and many felt its artistic quality would be no better than average, if even that.

This design was altered by the Mint to move the arch to the center, to change the appearance of the riverbank trees, to substitute a heavy rowboat (a pirogue) with six men and an American flag, and to add the inscription CORPS OF DISCOVERY and the dates 1804 and 2004. Controversy erupted when artist Jackson found that the Mint had grossly modified the design without consultation, stating, "Entrants were told that the winning design would appear on the reverse of Missouri's quarter. Now it appears as if the competition was nothing more than a hoax. The United States Mint never intended to use our designs."

The Mint revision was given to the Commission of Fine Arts for review. The Commission members "felt more comfortable with a design featuring a single theme rather than conflicting motifs." Moreover, one member thought that the arch resembled "the handle coming out of an Easter basket."[54] The idea of different elements thrown in, as originally presented in the Jackson art and in different form by the Mint, seemed to please very few people—a double whammy.

Jackson protested the changes and appeared widely to publicize his views, including on the *Morning Edition* program of National Public Radio on August 26, 2002, and on CBS television's *Up to the Minute* news program the next day. According to a story in *Coin World*, by Michele Orzano, Jackson visited the Mint headquarters, but a public-affairs officer would not meet with him. When CBS contacted the Mint for information, "No comment" was the reply. After articles appeared in the *Washington Post* on the 28th and the *Baltimore Sun* on the 29th, the Mint contacted Jackson to finally arrange a meeting.[55]

Although some further changes were made in the design (e.g., the rowboat—somewhat resembling a rubber lifeboat, or, as some said, a bathtub—was revised to have just three men), the Mint's version essentially prevailed. The entire situation was played out at length in the numismatic as well as the public press. The affair was a first-class headache for just about everyone involved, creating a quarter that many observers found to be one of the poorest motifs so far in the series. Mint Director Jay Johnson

The Louisiana Purchase Exposition (St. Louis World's Fair) of 1904 honored the accomplishments of Lewis and Clark, the same theme as used on the 2003 quarter. Shown is a postcard of the Palace of Electricity at that event.

later reminisced, "I still remember the remark that the design looked like three men in a tub rowing between two clumps of broccoli!"[56]

This regrettable controversy was the catalyst for the U.S. Mint's revision of its rules. Future quarter designs for 2005 and later would be created by the Mint itself—

no outside talent wanted. Instead, concepts were to be submitted in writing, and the Mint would do the artistry.

Early in 2005, it was announced that an unknown quantity of misstruck 2004-P Missouri quarters had been run through a crushing machine to disfigure the pieces and make them unfit for circulation.[57] Afterward these were sold as scrap. Rather than going to the melting pot, large quantities ended up in numismatic hands, including many in holders made by NGC. A campaign was mounted to offer these as collectibles, and there was extensive press coverage at the time.

While the Missouri quarter garnered scarcely any praise or admiration, it became part of the series, and today it is especially interesting to contemplate as a reminder of a specific state-quarter project that started going wrong in its early stages. If it is any consolation to Missourians, a few years later the 2005 Westward Journey Nickel Series™ focusing on Lewis and Clark drew unstinted praise from just about everyone.

ARKANSAS *25th of 50*

Official Coin Release Date: October 20, 2003.

Mintage Figures:

Circulation strikes (clad) 2003-P: 228,000,000
2003-D: 229,800,000

Proof strikes (clad) 2003-S: 3,408,516

Proof strikes (silver) 2003-S: 1,125,755

Arkansas 2003 • Market Values • Circulation Strikes and Proof Strikes

MS-63	MS-64	MS-65	MS-66	MS-67	MS-68	MS-63	MS-64	MS-65	MS-66	MS-67	MS-68
$0.75	$1	$1.50	$2	$2.50	$3	$0.75	$1	$1.50	$2	$2.50	$3

PF-64	PF-65	PF-66	PF-67	PF-68	PF-64	PF-65
$4	$6	$8	$10	$12	$9	$10

Arkansas 2003 • Certified Populations • Circulation Strikes and Proof Strikes

MS-65	MS-66	MS-67	MS-68	MS-69	MS-65	MS-66	MS-67	MS-68	MS-69
121	269	207	10	0	1,841	466	454	82	0

PF-65	PF-66	PF-67	PF-68	PF-69	PF-70	PF-65	PF-66	PF-67	PF-68	PF-69	PF-70
0	0	13	30	6,366	82	2	2	9	50	6,945	80

■ Philadelphia Mint circulation strikes   ■ Denver Mint circulation strikes

■ San Francisco Mint (clad) Proof strikes   ■ San Francisco Mint (silver clad) Proof strikes

SPECIFICS OF THE REVERSE DESIGN

Description: A collage of Arkansas-iana greets the eye, with a faceted diamond in the air above a group of pine trees, and with a marsh or lake in the foreground. A mallard duck to the right, with wings upraised, seems to be rising (for its feet are not extended, as they would be if it were about to alight on the water). To the left are stalks of rice. The motif includes no motto or sentiment apart from the required state name, dates, and E PLURIBUS UNUM. The top and bottom border inscriptions are standard.

Designer: Ariston Jacks of Pine Bluff, Arkansas. *Mint sculptor-engraver who made the model:* John Mercanti. *Engraver's initials and location:* JM, incuse on a raised water detail at the lower right.

STORY OF THE DESIGN

The Arkansas quarter of 2003 features a collage of items relating to the state, including a
cut diamond, rice stalks, a lake, and a mallard.[58]
The suite is arranged to be heavy at the sides,
and light at the middle, somewhat distracting
to the eyes of some observers. The Mint commented on the appropriateness of the design
choice, given that Arkansas is "the Natural
State," with abundant waterways; its status as a
prime area fo hunting mallard ducks; its Crater
of Diamonds State Park (with what is said to
be the oldest North American diamond mine);
and its agricultural importance as a rice-grow-
ing state.[59]

The Crescent Hotel in Eureka Springs,
Arkansas. While the state has an abundance of
natural resources as epitomized on the state
quarter, it also has rich scenery and has been a
magnet for tourists, as here. (*Harper's Weekly*,
December 18, 1886)

The search for a design was launched by Governor Mike Huckabee in January 2001
under the name of the Arkansas Quarter Challenge. In two weeks, 9,320 entries were
received. The field was subsequently narrowed to three, whose creators each received
$1,000 in cash, but whose names were not publicized. The Mint then made its own
sketches and submitted them to the governor, who made the final choice. The motif by
Ariston Jacks, modified at the Mint, was the winner.

NUMISMATIC ASPECTS OF THE STATE OF ARKANSAS

1935–1939: The Arkansas Centennial commemorative half dollar was issued. *1936:* The
Robinson–Arkansas Centennial commemorative half dollar was issued.

MICHIGAN 26th of 50

Official Coin Release Date: January 26, 2004.

Mintage Figures:

Circulation strikes (clad) 2004-P: 233,800,000
2004-D: 225,800,000[60]
Proof strikes (clad) 2004-S: 2,761,163
Proof strikes (silver) 2004-S: 1,789,344

Michigan 2004 • Market Values • Circulation Strikes and Proof Strikes

MS-63	MS-64	MS-65	MS-66	MS-67	MS-68	MS-63	MS-64	MS-65	MS-66	MS-67	MS-68
$0.75	$1	$1.50	$2	$2.50	$3	$0.75	$1	$1.50	$2	$2.50	$3

PF-64	PF-65	PF-66	PF-67	PF-68	PF-64	PF-65
$4	$6	$8	$10	$12	$9	$10

Michigan 2004 • Certified Populations • Circulation Strikes and Proof Strikes

MS-65	MS-66	MS-67	MS-68	MS-69	MS-65	MS-66	MS-67	MS-68	MS-69
2,131	204	452	139	1	25	254	830	948	31

PF-65	PF-66	PF-67	PF-68	PF-69	PF-70	PF-65	PF-66	PF-67	PF-68	PF-69	PF-70
1	1	3	14	4,302	64	2	2	20	97	9,537	114

■ Philadelphia Mint circulation strikes ■ Denver Mint circulation strikes
■ San Francisco Mint (clad) Proof strikes ■ San Francisco Mint (silver clad) Proof strikes

SPECIFICS OF THE REVERSE DESIGN

Description: An outline map of the five Great Lakes dominates the center, with the state of Michigan set apart in bas-relief seemingly representing actual topology. GREAT / LAKES / STATE is in three lines to the upper right. The top and bottom border inscriptions are standard.

Designer: Unknown. *Mint sculptor-engraver who made the model:* Donna Weaver. *Engraver's initials and location:* DW, located on the Ohio shore (not indicated as such) on the southern edge of Lake Erie.

STORY OF THE DESIGN

The effort to select a design representative of the state began on November 28, 2001, when Governor John Engler established the Michigan Quarter Commission with 25 members, including numismatists. Residents of the state were encouraged to submit ideas, and 4,300 were received. Four of the semifinalists were "Michigan State Outline, with Great Lakes and State Icons," "Michigan State Outline, with Great Lakes and the Mackinac Bridge," "Michigan State Outline, with the Mackinac Bridge and Automobile," and "Michigan State Outline, with Great Lakes and Automobile."

The fifth was simply the Michigan state outline with the outlines of the Great Lakes, a motif similar in concept to the Cleveland Centennial commemorative half dollar of 1936. Michigan borders on four of these lakes and, per Mint publicity, "Standing anywhere in the state, a person is within 85 miles of one of the Great Lakes."[61] In September 2003, Governor Jennifer Granholm, in consultation with designer Steven M. Bieda, selected this as the winner.

The final design engendered quite a bit of controversy, both in numismatic periodicals and in Michigan newspapers. Among various state designs, it seemed to be among the least pleasing to many people. By this time, critiquing the designs had become a pastime for many citizens, including numismatists. One observer, Ken Anderson, wrote this to *Coin World:*

Plaster mold for the reverse of the 2004 Michigan quarter. (Stephen Bieda photograph)

Daniel Carr's proposal for a Michigan quarter, shown here in the form of a simulated coin. (Daniel Carr)

> I congratulate Governor Jennifer Granholm in regards to the Michigan State quarter design. Her comment of the state outline being the most recognizable characteristic when viewed from space is not justification for portraying only the outline on our quarter.
>
> Out of the first 50 quarters the Michigan quarter is the only quarter that does not depict something of interest within the state, the people of Michigan, or any major accomplishments of its citizens. Next time we are all in space we must remember to look for the outline of Michigan.[62]

There were problems with striking the 2004-D coins, in that the dies were spaced too far apart. Collector Brett Lothrop reported that he had to go through 20 rolls (800 coins) to find *one* that had all of the details sharply defined. As to whether this proportion is true of the whole population of the issue remains to be determined.[63]

NUMISMATIC ASPECTS OF THE STATE OF MICHIGAN

1836: The Gobrecht silver dollar featured 26 stars on the reverse, in anticipation of Michigan's becoming the 26th state. *1837–1838:* Dozens of "wildcat" banks were formed in the state, often by fraudsters with no financial banking. By 1840 most were defunct. *1888:* George F. Heath of Monroe launched *The Numismatist,* later to become the official magazine of the ANA. *1863:* Many merchants in Detroit issued Civil War tokens.

FLORIDA 27th of 50

Official Coin Release Date: April 7, 2004.

Mintage Figures:

Circulation strikes (clad)	2004-P: 240,200,000
	2004-D: 241,600,000[64]
Proof strikes (clad)	2004-S: 2,761,163[65]
Proof strikes (silver)	2004-S: 1,789,344

Florida 2004 • Market Values • Circulation Strikes and Proof Strikes

MS-63	MS-64	MS-65	MS-66	MS-67	MS-68	MS-63	MS-64	MS-65	MS-66	MS-67	MS-68
$0.75	$1	$1.50	$2	$2.50	$3	$0.75	$1	$1.50	$2	$2.50	$3

PF-64	PF-65	PF-66	PF-67	PF-68	PF-64	PF-65
$4	$6	$8	$10	$12	$9	$10

Florida 2004 • Certified Populations • Circulation Strikes and Proof Strikes

MS-65	MS-66	MS-67	MS-68	MS-69	MS-65	MS-66	MS-67	MS-68	MS-69
2,137	182	318	52	1	46	232	453	475	16

PF-65	PF-66	PF-67	PF-68	PF-69	PF-70	PF-65	PF-66	PF-67	PF-68	PF-69	PF-70
0	2	6	17	4,418	48	0	3	32	94	9,653	119

■ Philadelphia Mint circulation strikes   ■ Denver Mint circulation strikes

■ San Francisco Mint (clad) Proof strikes   ■ San Francisco Mint (silver clad) Proof strikes

SPECIFICS OF THE REVERSE DESIGN

Description: The sea is suggested by the presence of a Spanish galleon at the left and a shore with two palm trees to the right. GATEWAY TO DISCOVERY is below. Above the palm trees is a space shuttle at an angle, nose upward, as if coming in for a landing. The top and bottom border inscriptions are standard.

Designer: Ralph Butler, a resident of Bayonet Point, Florida; his design was vastly altered. *Mint sculptor-engraver who made the model:* T. James Ferrell. *Engraver's initials and location:* TJF, in italic capitals, located on the shore below the rightmost palm tree.

Daniel Carr's proposal for a Florida quarter, one of 10 semi-finalists in the competition, shown here in the form of a simulated coin. (Daniel Carr)

STORY OF THE DESIGN

To get the coin project underway, Governor Jeb Bush appointed the nine-person Florida Commemorative Quarter Committee on April 9, 2002.[66] Gary E. Lewis, a collector residing in Cape Coral in the state, was named as chairman. Lewis would later serve as president of the American Numismatic Association, 2003 to 2005.

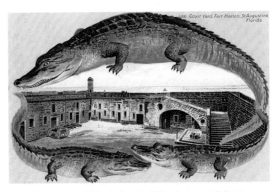

In time, more than 1,500 ideas were received, a field narrowed by the committee to 25, then to 10. These were sent to the governor, who selected five semifinalists. Themes remaining after this cut included "The Everglades," "Gateway to Discovery," "Fishing Capital of the World," "St. Augustine," and "America's Spaceport." The final choice was put to the vote of the citizens, who chose "Gateway to Discovery." Bush had hoped for a great white heron standing in sawgrass, but deferred to his constituents.

Early 20th century "alligator border" Florida postcard showing part of the fort on the coast at Augustine. The old Spanish fort was one motif considered for the state quarter. One of two launch ceremonies was held there.

The art as originally accepted—the galleon on the sea[67] with billowing clouds overhead, two palm trees on the shore to the right, and a somewhat oversize shuttle in the sky—presented a unified picture. However, the design was executed (pun intended) at the Mint, and the three subjects appear disjointed. Perhaps if the sea had been retained, connecting the galleon and the shore, artistic harmony would have been improved. Perhaps an alligator, a bolt of lightning, or some large central theme, a focal point for the eyes, would have helped.

Ralph Butler, designer of the original version of the quarter, signs a souvenir at the Florida United Numismatists convention, January 2005. (Fred Lake photograph)

Public opinion of the design has, predictably, been poor, but at least Ralph Butler, the designer of this quarter (its original scenic version, not the later, scattered-objects version), was publicly acknowledged. Early the next year, at the Florida United Numismatists Convention in Fort Lauderdale, January 2005, he was featured and signed souvenirs for show attendees.

NUMISMATIC ASPECTS OF THE STATE OF FLORIDA

The East Coast of Florida and the Florida Keys have yielded many silver and gold coins sunk when fleets of Spanish galleons encountered hurricanes in the 18th century. *1935:* The route depicted on the map in the Old Spanish Trail commemorative half dollar design began in Florida. *1955:* The Florida United Numismatists (FUN) organization was established. Today it is perhaps the strongest state numismatic club.

TEXAS *28th of 50*

Official Coin Release Date: June 1, 2004.

Mintage Figures:

Circulation strikes (clad)	2004-P: 278,800,000
	2004-D: 263,000,000
Proof strikes (clad)	2004-S: 2,761,163
Proof strikes (silver)	2004-S: 1,789,344

Texas 2004 • Market Values • Circulation Strikes and Proof Strikes

MS-63	MS-64	MS-65	MS-66	MS-67	MS-68	MS-63	MS-64	MS-65	MS-66	MS-67	MS-68
$0.75	$1	$1.50	$2	$2.50	$3	$0.75	$1	$1.50	$2	$2.50	$3

PF-64	PF-65	PF-66	PF-67	PF-68	PF-64	PF-65
$4	$6	$8	$10	$12	$9	$10

Texas 2004 • Certified Populations • Circulation Strikes and Proof Strikes

MS-65	MS-66	MS-67	MS-68	MS-69	MS-65	MS-66	MS-67	MS-68	MS-69
2,154	245	398	107	1	58	213	472	722	29

PF-65	PF-66	PF-67	PF-68	PF-69	PF-70	PF-65	PF-66	PF-67	PF-68	PF-69	PF-70
1	1	4	13	4,280	73	0	5	16	86	9,767	137

■ Philadelphia Mint circulation strikes ■ Denver Mint circulation strikes

■ San Francisco Mint (clad) Proof strikes ■ San Francisco Mint (silver clad) Proof strikes

SPECIFICS OF THE REVERSE DESIGN

Description: Against a stippled map of the state (no topographical features) a bold, five-pointed star, with ridges to each ray, is shown. In the field to the lower left is "The / Lone Star / State" on three lines in upper- and lowercase block letters. Arclike lengths of rope, said to represent a lariat, are placed individually at the left and right. The top and bottom border inscriptions are standard.

Designer: Daniel Miller, a graphic artist from Arlington, Texas. Certain art by Nancy Boren influenced the final version.[68] *Mint sculptor-engraver who made the model:* Norman E. Nemeth. *Engraver's initials and location:* NEN, located in the Gulf of Mexico (to the right of the lower tip of the state).

STORY OF THE DESIGN

The Republic of Texas, which had used the lone-star emblem on its flag beginning in 1839, joined the Union in 1845, becoming the 28th state.[69] Its statehood quarter reflects this tradition, with an outline map of the state, a large single star, and the inscription "The Lone Star State." The two sections of rope around the border represent the cattle-and-cowboy tradition of Texas.

There was no lack of motifs to consider, what with the Alamo, oil wells, longhorn steers, armadillos, tumbleweeds, and chili cookouts! It is an interesting fact that the district has been under the flags of Spain, France, Mexico, Republic of Texas, United States of America, Confederate States of America, and United States of America again, which equates to six *different*, giving rise to the Six Flags amusement park in the late 20th century, which eventually expanded to use the name in other states. The state name is derived from *Tejas*, an Indian word meaning *friends*, a logical connection to the present-day motto "Friendship."

In August 14, 2000, Governor George W. Bush, with his eye on the November presidential election, found time to appoint 15 people to the Texas Quarter Dollar Coin Advisory Committee.

This group wisely enlisted the Texas Numismatic Association to supervise a contest that resulted in the submission of more than 2,500 ideas, these only from natives of the state or those who had lived there for at least a year as of May 11, 2001. The association selected 17 finalists and submitted them to the committee, and five semifinalists emerged. Governor Rick Perry selected the winner, a sketch made by Daniel Miller, a graphic artist from Arlington, Texas.

All in all, the Texas state-quarter design-selection process was a textbook example of a well-run scenario.The program seemed to flow well, the motif was widely appreciated, and the artist was credited in publicity (although not on the coin).

NUMISMATIC ASPECTS OF THE STATE OF TEXAS

1900: B. Max Mehl (1884–1957) began in the rare coin business; in time he became America's most famous dealer. *1836:* The Republic of Texas was formed, and issued paper money. *1913:* The Dallas Federal Reserve Bank was established under the Federal Reserve Act. Currency issued there bears the letter J. *1934–1938:* The Texas Centennial commemorative half dollar was issued. *1935:* The Old Spanish Trail commemorative half dollar was issued.

IOWA 29th of 50

Official Coin Release Date: August 30, 2004.
A ceremonial striking ceremony for the
2004-D quarters was held on July 12, 2004,
at the Denver Mint.[70]

Mintage Figures:

Circulation strikes (clad) .... 2004-P: 213,800,000[71]
.... 2004-D: 251,400,000
Proof strikes (clad) .... 2004-S: 2,761,163[72]
Proof strikes (silver) 2004-S: 1,789,344

Iowa 2004 • Market Values • Circulation Strikes and Proof Strikes

MS-63	MS-64	MS-65	MS-66	MS-67	MS-68	MS-63	MS-64	MS-65	MS-66	MS-67	MS-68
$0.75	$1	$1.50	$2	$2.50	$3	$0.75	$1	$1.50	$2	$2.50	$3

PF-64	PF-65	PF-66	PF-67	PF-68	PF-64	PF-65
$4	$6	$8	$10	$12	$9	$10

Iowa 2004 • Certified Populations • Circulation Strikes and Proof Strikes

MS-65	MS-66	MS-67	MS-68	MS-69	MS-65	MS-66	MS-67	MS-68	MS-69
2,123	196	218	19	0	19	73	299	528	14

PF-65	PF-66	PF-67	PF-68	PF-69	PF-70	PF-65	PF-66	PF-67	PF-68	PF-69	PF-70
1	2	6	15	4,119	70	0	3	9	71	9,767	149

■ Philadelphia Mint circulation strikes ■ Denver Mint circulation strikes
■ San Francisco Mint (clad) Proof strikes ■ San Francisco Mint (silver clad) Proof strikes

SPECIFICS OF THE REVERSE DESIGN

Description: A one-room clapboard schoolhouse is shown at the center and to the left, with a door, two windows, and steps on the front and three windows on the right side. To the right, a teacher in a long flowing dress stands holding the hand of a child with her right hand and the trunk of a tree approximately ten feet tall in her left. The tree, with a very heavy clump of roots, is on the ground, near a hole for it. A kneeling child has both hands on the root clump, while another child is seated, sprawling, on the ground to the right. A fourth child is sitting on the schoolhouse steps. In the distance can be seen a road, a fence, and undulating farmland. The legend FOUNDATION / IN EDUCATION is at the upper right. An oversized inscription, GRANT WOOD, in capitals, is in the field at the lower right. The top and bottom border inscriptions are standard.

Designer: Loosely adapted from *Arbor Day,* a painting by Grant Wood. *Mint sculptor-engraver who made the model:* John Mercanti. *Engraver's initials and location:* JM, located in the field below the lower left of the design.

STORY OF THE DESIGN

In May 2002, Governor Thomas J. Vilsack set up the Iowa Commemorative Quarter Commission, with 16 announced members (number later reduced to 13), to advise on the design of the 2004 quarter dollar. Included were two numismatists: Tom Robertson and Brian Fanton. Libraries, banks, and credit unions were used as information-gathering sources for the designs submitted by citizens—about 5,000 ideas in all. These were narrowed down by the commission to five themes: "American Gothic," "Foundation in Education," "Feeding the World," "Sullivan Brothers," and "Beautiful Land."

Much controversy ensued. The theme concerning the five Sullivan brothers, of Waterloo (who died heroically in November 1942 when their ship, the USS *Juneau,* was sunk), drew fire from critics who said that certain of the brothers had been juvenile delinquents before they went into service. Corn seemed to be a logical—indeed, the one and only—choice for many Iowans, and certainly the "Feeding the World" concept would reflect favor on the state. *American Gothic,* Grant Wood's famous painting that is widely reproduced today, including in parodies, was a strong favorite. The stern-visaged elderly couple with a pitchfork and, behind them, and austere farmhouse symbolized agriculture and hard work.

Daniel Carr's proposal for an Iowa quarter, shown here in the form of a simulated coin. (Daniel Carr)

Vilsack took matters into his own hands, and on May 5, 2003, at PMX Industries in Cedar Rapids (a supplier of certain metal to the mints), he declared that "Foundation in Education" would be the topic.

Arbor Day

To implement the theme of education, the Iowa quarter displays a one-room schoolhouse with a teacher and students planting a *large* tree, a motif based on an obscure and somewhat surrealistic Grant Wood painting, *Arbor Day.* While just about everyone knew about Wood's *American Gothic,* the chosen painting was considered by some to be a strange choice, not on a par artistically with its more-famous counterpart. On the coin, the inscriptions FOUNDATION IN EDUCATION and GRANT WOOD are prominent.

Many details of Wood's painting are altered on the coin: the school outhouse (privy) is ommitted, and the small tree the students were planting has been replaced by a seemingly very large tree (perhaps 10 feet high) with a root clump that must weigh hundreds of pounds—in real life a bit heavy for little school kids to move around! Also missing from the coin are most of the people in the Grant painting, including the driver of a two-horse team who, it seems, could have been helpful in planting the tree. A reviewer in the *Numismatist* took no notice of such things, and gushed about the senti-mental, old-fashioned images depicted on the coin.[73] For my part, I do not think the connection with education seems particularly unique or representative of Iowa, as a cornfield would have been.

What *is* unquestionably unique about this coin, at least so far, is that the name of the artist, GRANT WOOD, on the reverse is the largest inscription of an artist found on any legal tender U.S. coin from 1793 to date! Again, Mint rules for quarter dollars were made to be broken. This contributes to the interesting character of each coin in the series—just about all have some sort of a twist in the stories of their creation and implementation.

NUMISMATIC ASPECTS OF THE STATE OF IOWA

1863: First National Bank of Davenport was the first National Bank to open its doors for business. *1946:* Iowa Centennial commemorative half dollar.

WISCONSIN *30th of 50*

Official Coin Release Date: October 25, 2004.
First-strike ceremonies were held at the
Denver Mint, on October 12.

Mintage Figures:

Circulation strikes (clad) 2004-P: 226,400,000
2004-D: 226,800,000[74]

Proof strikes (clad) 2004-S: 2,761,163

Proof strikes (silver) 2004-S: 1,789,344

Wisconsin 2004 • Market Values • Circulation Strikes and Proof Strikes

MS-63	MS-64	MS-65	MS-66	MS-67	MS-68	MS-63	MS-64	MS-65	MS-66	MS-67	MS-68
$0.75	$1	$1.50	$2	$2.50	$3	$0.75	$1	$1.50	$2	$2.50	$3

PF-64	PF-65	PF-66	PF-67	PF-68	PF-64	PF-65
$4	$6	$8	$10	$12	$9	$10

Wisconsin 2004 • Certified Populations • Circulation Strikes and Proof Strikes

MS-65	MS-66	MS-67	MS-68	MS-69	MS-65	MS-66	MS-67	MS-68	MS-69
2,170	216	158	22	0	1,348	706	307	29	1

PF-65	PF-66	PF-67	PF-68	PF-69	PF-70	PF-65	PF-66	PF-67	PF-68	PF-69	PF-70
0	6	1	18	4,299	63	3	9	19	98	9,669	153

■ Philadelphia Mint circulation strikes ■ Denver Mint circulation strikes

■ San Francisco Mint (clad) Proof strikes ■ San Francisco Mint (silver clad) Proof strikes

SPECIFICS OF THE REVERSE DESIGN

Description: At the left, the head and neck of a cow, wearing a cowbell on a strap, faces right, with its nose nearly touching a large wheel of cheese from which a section has been cut (not very carefully, with the deepest part of the cut noticeably off center). Behind the cheese is an unshucked ear of corn, placed vertically. FORWARD is on a ribbon at the bottom of the design. The top and bottom border inscriptions are standard.

Designer: Adapted from a drawing by Wisconsin resident Rose Marty, who lives on a farm in Monticello. *Mint sculptor-engraver who made the model:* Alfred F. Maletsky. *Engraver's initials and location:* AM, located in the field below D (FORWARD).

STORY OF THE DESIGN

In December 2001, Governor Scott McCallum named 23 people to the Wisconsin Commemorative Quarter Council.[75] Over the allotted period of time for submissions, the council received 9,608 ideas, mostly from schoolchildren, which were narrowed to six.[76] These were further reduced, by a statewide referendum, to three: "Scenic Wisconsin," "Agriculture/Dairy/Barns," and "Early Exploration and Cultural Interaction." Council member Leon A. Saryan had this to say:

> Essentially, the selection process was flawed from the beginning. There is an inherent conflict between, on the one hand, a written design idea (for example, put a cow on the coin), and on the other hand an actual, professionally created piece of artwork (a clear drawing showing how a cow would actually look on a coin). The latter will win every time, because our product, in the final analysis, is not a written dissertation on the glories of this state, but a simple picture, severely limited in size and scope, not more than an inch in diameter.[77]

The preceding commentary is poignant and points out a fatal flaw in the policy of submitting "concepts" rather than actual pictures. Concepts are utterly *meaningless* from an art viewpoint. The *Mona Lisa* is not famous because it is a concept of "woman with scenic background," but because of the *art* involved. To one person, the concept "black-and-white drips and splatters" might conjure an image of a birdcage liner—but to Jackson Pollock it might conjure artwork that would sell for a small fortune.

Far better, in my opinion, is for the state committees to require sketches and other art in the submissions, and for the Mint to faithfully translate this art into coinage. In that way we have Wisconsin art, or Florida art, or whatever. The talent of the Mint's sculptor-engravers could enhance the art submitted to them.

In 2003, Governor Jim Doyle, who had unseated Governor McCallum in the latest election, submitted the three semifinal concepts to voters on the Internet, drawing about 36,000 responses. "Agriculture/Dairy/Barns," a single concept with three elements, was the people's choice.

The governor accepted this referendum. Accordingly, the Wisconsin quarter features the head of a cow and a wheel of cheese, echoing the state motto, "America's Dairyland" (which was not used on the coin, although another motto, FORWARD, was). An ear of corn was also depicted, possibly making Iowans jealous!

The secretary of the Treasury approved the design on October 9, 2003, after which the Mint began design and production plans. Mint sculptor-engraver Alfred F. Maletsky prepared models. This project was his swan song, for he retired on December 31.

Those Curious "Extra Leaf" Varieties

The first "gold rush" in the state-quarter series occurred in January 2005, when word spread of two curious die varieties discovered among 2004-D Wisconsin quarters. As these are the only varieties among state quarters that have thus far captured the fancy of thousands of collectors, I devote extra space to them here.

Ben Weinstein, manager of the Old Pueblo Coin Exchange in Tucson, explained how the varieties were first found. On December 11, Bob Ford brought in two quarters he had found with die breaks. A regular customer in his 70s, Ford often bought loose change to look through for treasure. He showed his latest find to Rob Weiss, the owner, and then to Weinstein. They bought a set of the quarters from Ford and contacted *Coin World* editor Bill Gibbs. By mid-January 2005, their efforts had spread the word to the numismatic community.

Wisconsin state reverse with normal leaves.

It seems that estimates of known pieces are about 2,000 or so of the Extra Leaf Low and about 3,000 of the Extra Leaf High. Distribution of the coins stopped earlier in the year. I am not aware of any significant hoards or new finds. Original distribution seems to have been mainly in Southern Arizona, centered in Tucson, although some turned up at Flagstaff in the north and some in Kerrville, Texas.

Extra Leaf High variety.

On December 20, 2005, J.T. Stanton sent the following excerpt from the manuscript of the *Cherrypicker's Guide to Rare Die Varieties* (fourth edition, vol. 2):

Extra Leaf Low variety.

> It is our belief that the additional lines on this and the next variety of the Wisconsin quarters were deliberately added to the reverse dies. Apparently a tool with a rounded edge was impressed into the working dies to create the images that were not a part of the intended design. Many collectors, dealers, etc. refer to these as an "extra leaf" variety. However, the lines are not the image of a leaf. . . .
>
> It is our belief that someone in the Denver Mint may have been celebrating their retirement (or celebrating something) a little early by intentionally adding an additional image to some dies. The reasons behind our thoughts are as follows:
>
> 1. These additional images are concentric, very similar in appearance, and do appear in a place that would become interesting. The mathematical odds of this occurring totally by accident are too astronomical to be considered.
>
> 2. These concentric lines would have likely been caused by an implement such as a small nut driver or other similar instrument. It would be very easy to make an impression into a working die with such a tool.
>
> 3. These lines would not necessarily be the same length, depending upon the angle and pressure in which the implement was placed against the die.

4. Some error/variety specialists have noted that only a die-room worker could have done this. We totally disagree, as anyone in the Mint with access to the dies at any time could have caused these.

5. The added knowledge of a 2004-D dime with a very similar size and shape mark near the ear is virtually conclusive evidence these were made intentionally as a form of entertainment by a Mint worker.

In our opinion, the lines on the reverse of the Wisconsin quarters in no way appear to be a form of adding a leaf to the corn husk. The location was likely chosen almost at random, yet allowing for the added images to be identified. . . . Our feelings are very simple—if you like the coins as varieties, consider adding them to your collection. If you don't like them, don't consider a purchase. But it's very clear these varieties are here to stay. And if you're wondering, *we love 'em!*

The Mint Police investigated the situation, and concluded that some unknown person or persons "'engaged in a sequence of criminal acts to intentionally alter and/or mutilate an unknown quantity of Wisconsin quarters from the Denver Mint, and in furtherance of their scheme, caused the release of those coins to the public.'"[78]

NUMISMATIC ASPECTS OF THE STATE OF WISCONSIN

1863: State merchants were important issuers of Civil War tokens. *1936:* The Wisconsin Territorial Centennial commemorative half dollar was issued. *1952: Numismatic News* was founded in Iola.

CALIFORNIA *31st of 50*

Official Coin Release Date: January 31, 2005, 12 noon, Eastern Standard Time, 9 a.m. California time.

Mintage Figures:

Circulation strikes (clad) 2005-P: 257,200,000
2005-D: 263,200,000
Proof strikes (clad) 2005-S: 3,262,000
Proof strikes (silver) 2005-S: 1,606,970

California 2005 • Market Values • Circulation Strikes and Proof Strikes

MS-63	MS-64	MS-65	MS-66	MS-67	MS-68	MS-63	MS-64	MS-65	MS-66	MS-67	MS-68
$0.75	$1	$1.50	$2	$2.50	$3	$0.75	$1	$1.50	$2	$2.50	$3

PF-64	PF-65	PF-66	PF-67	PF-68	PF-64	PF-65
$4	$6	$8	$10	$12	$9	$10

California 2005 • Certified Populations • Circulation Strikes and Proof Strikes

MS-65	MS-66	MS-67	MS-68	MS-69	MS-65	MS-66	MS-67	MS-68	MS-69
27	100	140	15	0	68	173	171	20	0

PF-65	PF-66	PF-67	PF-68	PF-69	PF-70	PF-65	PF-66	PF-67	PF-68	PF-69	PF-70
0	0	14	70	7,886	78	0	2	14	28	7,326	106

■ Philadelphia Mint circulation strikes   ■ Denver Mint circulation strikes
■ San Francisco Mint (clad) Proof strikes   ■ San Francisco Mint (silver clad) Proof strikes

SPECIFICS OF THE REVERSE DESIGN

Description: The standing figure of John Muir with a scene of Yosemite National Park in the background showing Half Dome. A California condor, an endangered species, flies overhead. The top and bottom border inscriptions are standard.

Designer: Garrett Burke, with the inspiration of his wife, numismatist Michelle. *Mint sculptor-engravers who made the model:* The design was finessed by Alfred Maletsky at the Mint and was sculpted by Don Everhart II. *Engraver's initials and location:* DE, located at the base of the mountain.

STORY OF THE DESIGN

Much interest centered about the selection of a motif for California's quarter dollar, scheduled to be the first state coin launched in 2005. Although the Mint had announced earlier that no more sketches were wanted—only written concepts—an exception was made for California (a good idea, in my opinion).[79]

Submissions were received by Governor Gray Davis's office in Sacramento from September 9, 2002 (Admissions Day, the anniversary of California statehood in 1850) to November 9. A committee appointed by the governor screened the entries and chose 20 considered to be of special merit. These were presented on an Internet poll from December 31, 2002, to January 31, 2003. After reviewing the results, but not necessarily abiding by them (this being the governor's prerogative), the governor selected five motifs. These were displayed publicly, and comments were invited.

This was a time of political chaos in California. Governor Davis, a Democrat, was charged by some with mismanaging certain of the state's affairs, including the costs of energy. He faced a recall election, and was tossed out of office. Arnold Schwarzenegger, a Republican, was his successor in November 2003.

The five semifinal concepts included the Golden Gate Bridge, a gold miner and implements from the Gold Rush, John Muir and the Yosemite Valley, waves and the sun, and the giant sequoia tree. Public input was invited but, as it turned out, was ignored.

Many numismatists and quite a few others, including the majority of Californians who cast votes for their favorite, supposed that the gold miner would be a shoo-in, a no-brainer. I received much correspondence on this, and while most favored a Gold Rush motif, others said that it had been overdone, and still others said that the semifinal art was more of a group of scattered objects on a plate than a unified artistic scene, not at all on an artistic par with the similarly themed 1925 California Diamond Jubilee commemorative half dollar.

Surprise!

Much to the surprise of many citizens of California, in 2004 Governor Schwarzenegger announced that the forthcoming 2005 state quarter would not feature the Gold Rush at all. Instead, John Muir, a famous naturalist, was to be depicted against a background of Yosemite National Park. It would have been the governor's prerogative to choose a cow jumping over the moon, but in the brouhaha that followed, many people forgot this. History shows that the personal choices of governors for state quarters (and even Treasury Secretary Andrew Mellon's choice for Flanagan's quarter-dollar design in 1932) have been common and proper.

The Sierra Club campaigned intensely for the Muir/Yosemite motif and was backed by a sketch that many found highly artistic. This well-organized effort was viewed as unfair by many who hoped for a Gold Rush motif, although the Gold-Rushers were not organized and mounted no publicity effort at all.

The winning designer was Garrett Burke, whose biography was soon posted on the Web site of the Sierra Club and elsewhere, with a sketch of the design. At the launch ceremony, Schwarzenegger told how he made the final selection:

> We have our landmarks, our discoveries and, of course, all the great achievements, so we couldn't decide. Should it be the Golden Gate Bridge that should be on the coin? Should it be a camera that represents Hollywood, as the entertainment capital of the world? Or should it be the beautiful ocean, the coastline? Should it be the sun, because we have more sunshine than any other place in the world? What should it be? . . .
>
> And the more we went through the five designs, the more we decided that Garrett's design is really the most beautiful one and it says it all. With Yosemite, with the California condor, with John Muir—I thought it was spectacular. A beautiful, beautiful design and a beautiful coin. Muir lit the torch of conservation in our state, and he has inspired generations of Californians to preserve our natural beauty, and this is what makes him so special.[80]

Complaints about the final choice filled many paragraphs of newspapers in California as well as numismatic periodicals, but in the end, this comment from Robert Holbrook, a reader of *Coin World*, is a fair assessment of the matter: "Muir and Yosemite might not 'be California,' but the design is aesthetic. Both are certainly identified with the state by the whole world outside the state and would do the state proud on one of the few tastefully designed coins in the series."[81]

NUMISMATIC ASPECTS OF THE STATE OF CALIFORNIA

1848: The discovery of gold at Sutter's Mill on the American River, by John Marshall, on January 24, was the catalyst for the Gold Rush. *1849–1855:* Private gold coins were minted. Assay offices produced ingots. *1854:* The San Francisco Mint opened. *1874:* The Second San Francisco Mint building opened. *1913:* The San Francisco Federal Reserve Bank was established under the Federal Reserve Act. Currency issued there bears the letter K. *1915:* The Panama-Pacific International Exposition issued five commemorative coins. *1923:* The Monroe Doctrine Centennial commemorative half dollar was issued. *1925:* The California Diamond Jubilee commemorative half dollar was produced. *1935–1936:* The San Diego–California Pacific Exposition commemorative half dollar was produced. *1936:* The San Francisco–Oakland Bay Bridge commemorative half dollar was issued. *1937:* The Third San Francisco Mint building opened. *1983:* The Los Angeles Olympic Games commemorative silver dollar was issued. *1984:* The Los Angeles Olympic Games commemorative silver dollar and $10 gold piece were issued.

MINNESOTA *32nd of 50*

Official Coin Release Date: April 4, 2005.

Mintage Figures:

Circulation strikes (clad) 2005-P: 239,600,000
2005-D: 248,400,000
Proof strikes (clad) 2005-S: 3,262,000
Proof strikes (silver) 2005-S: 1,606,970

"Spiked Head" variety: Certain clad Proof examples of the 2005-S Minnesota quarters have a die break running from the top of Washington's head to the border. Similar cracks are known for Tennessee, Iowa, Florida, and Texas quarters (the Texas crack is in a different location). Such pieces have an additional value.[82]

Minnesota 2005 • Market Values • Circulation Strikes and Proof Strikes

MS-63	MS-64	MS-65	MS-66	MS-67	MS-68	MS-63	MS-64	MS-65	MS-66	MS-67	MS-68
$0.75	$1	$1.50	$2	$2.50	$3	$0.75	$1	$1.50	$2	$2.50	$3

PF-64	PF-65	PF-66	PF-67	PF-68	PF-64	PF-65
$4	$6	$8	$10	$12	$9	$10

Minnesota 2005 • Certified Populations • Circulation Strikes and Proof Strikes

MS-65	MS-66	MS-67	MS-68	MS-69	MS-65	MS-66	MS-67	MS-68	MS-69
12	26	38	135	18	20	114	73	117	1

PF-65	PF-66	PF-67	PF-68	PF-69	PF-70	PF-65	PF-66	PF-67	PF-68	PF-69	PF-70
0	2	13	29	7,852	100	0	6	8	30	6,921	91

■ Philadelphia Mint circulation strikes ■ Denver Mint circulation strikes
■ San Francisco Mint (clad) Proof strikes ■ San Francisco Mint (silver clad) Proof strikes

SPECIFICS OF THE REVERSE DESIGN

Description: Lake scene with a loon in the foreground, a motorboat with two fishermen not far away to the right, and a shore wooded with pines in the distance. Somewhat incongruously, a map of the state is placed vertically in the lake, to the left of the boat, and bears the inscription, LAND / OF / 10,000 / LAKES. The top and bottom border inscriptions are standard.

Designer: Unknown. *Mint sculptor-engraver who made the model:* Charles L. Vickers. *Engraver's initials and location:* CLV (very subtle), located at lower right, at the tip of an islet in front of the loon.

STORY OF THE DESIGN

Minnesota calls itself the *Land of 10,000 Lakes*, a nice motto bespeaking nature and tranquility. As to how many lakes there actually are, the number is 11,842, according to the Minnesota Department of Natural Resources.[83] The U.S. Mint differs and says, "The Land of 10,000 Lakes actually contains more than 15,000 such bodies of water...."[84] Counting the number of lakes is a subjective matter. First, there has to be a definition of the size of a lake—somewhere between a puddle and an ocean. Second, once size is defined, when it is a dry season, some lakes will shrink to below requirements. When it is rainy, some puddles will be definable as lakes. Uncertainties such as this are interesting to contemplate and in a way are reflective of many elements of the state quarter program. In any event, "10,000 lakes" was bound to be a part of the Minnesota quarter theme considerations.

The Minnesota Quarter Dollar Commission was set up in May 2003 to review design ideas for the 2005 quarter. Included was numismatist Bill Himmelwright, of Minneapolis. The group was charged with receiving comments from the public and narrowing the choices to five, to be submitted to the governor. Schools were given lesson plans on the subject from material prepared by the U.S. Mint, but with the proviso that this was only an exercise—the ideas obtained from it were not to be reviewed for consideration. Many of the drawings were posted in a hallway in the State Capitol.[85] Posters encouraged ideas from the public that were to be part of the selection process. The Mint wanted only narratives, not sketches or any other art—with the result that many impossible-to-visualize concepts like "State With Symbols" and "Fisherman Lake Recreation" were submitted.[86] As before, the "concepts-only concept" was roundly attacked by members of the numismatic press, who sought recognition of artists and the preparation of actual art.

State emblems of Minnesota (James McCabe Jr., *A Centennial View of Our Country and Its Resources, 1876*)

In due course, the commission made its choice of five designs. These were sent to the Mint, which rejected one (a depiction of a single snowflake). That left four: (1) a plow, snowflake, and loon superimposed on an outline map of the state; (2 and 3) two versions of a lake with trees and a loon; and (4) the Mississippi River and its headwaters. An exhibit was set up in the huge Mall of America in Burlington so the public could review and comment upon and the semifinalist sketches from the Mint.

On May 14, Governor Tim Pawlenty announced the choice recommended by his commission: a fishing scene on a Minnesota lake as part of the "10,000 Lakes" theme. Depicted was an outline of the state, a forest of pine trees in the distance, and, in the foreground a small motorboat with two fishermen, with a loon swimming in the foreground. (When Canada pictured a loon on its dollar coin, they immediately became called *loonies*. So far, this has not happened to the Minnesota quarters.) The Treasury Department approved of the design on June 15, 2004.

"When people from around the world see our quarter," commented the governor, "they will immediately associate Minnesota with the beautiful woods and waters of our natural resources."[87] Appropriately, the decision was revealed in Baudette, Minnesota, on the eve of the opening day of fishing season there.

NUMISMATIC ASPECTS OF THE STATE OF MINNESOTA

1913: The Minneapolis Federal Reserve Bank was established under the Federal Reserve Act. Currency issued there bears the letter H.

OREGON *33rd of 50*

Official Coin Release Date: June 6, 2005.

Mintage Figures:

Circulation strikes (clad) 2005-P: 316,200,000
2005-D: 404,000,000

Proof strikes (clad) 2005-S: 3,262,000

Proof strikes (silver) 2005-S: 1,606,970

Oregon 2005 • Market Values • Circulation Strikes and Proof Strikes

MS-63	MS-64	MS-65	MS-66	MS-67	MS-68	MS-63	MS-64	MS-65	MS-66	MS-67	MS-68
$0.75	$1	$1.50	$2	$2.50	$3	$0.75	$1	$1.50	$2	$2.50	$3

PF-64	PF-65	PF-66	PF-67	PF-68	PF-64	PF-65
$4	$6	$8	$10	$12	$9	$10

Oregon 2005 • Certified Populations • Circulation Strikes and Proof Strikes

MS-65	MS-66	MS-67	MS-68	MS-69	MS-65	MS-66	MS-67	MS-68	MS-69
14	16	52	35	6	7	82	71	13	0

PF-65	PF-66	PF-67	PF-68	PF-69	PF-70	PF-65	PF-66	PF-67	PF-68	PF-69	PF-70
0	0	17	55	7,955	93	0	3	6	32	6,992	100

■ Philadelphia Mint circulation strikes   ■ Denver Mint circulation strikes

■ San Francisco Mint (clad) Proof strikes   ■ San Francisco Mint (silver clad) Proof strikes

SPECIFICS OF THE REVERSE DESIGN

Description: A panorama of Crater Lake, is shown from the south rim. Pines are in the foreground. In the distance is seen Wizard Island, whose size increases and decreases depending on the water level.

Designer: Unknown. *Mint sculptor-engraver who made the model:* Donna Weaver. *Engraver's initials and location:* DW, located at the lower right near the trunk of the rightmost pine tree.

STORY OF THE DESIGN

In the summer of 2003, Governor Ted Kulongoski received many suggestions for his state's coin motifs: Mount Hood, salmon, beavers, Tom McCall, a woman, Crater Lake, a lighthouse, and Sacagawea, among others (this per his press secretary, Mary Ellen Glynn). In the meantime, he was selecting candidates to sit on the 18-member Oregon Commemorative Coin Commission, "which will include a high-school teacher, a numismatist, a member of an Oregon tribe, a historian, a student, a Republican and a Democrat from both the state Senate and state House, the state treasurer, and the governor himself."[88]

On May 7, 2004, the commission reviewed its past work and the semifinal design submissions. These included Crater Lake, a salmon leaping up a waterfall, Mount Hood, and a historical scene including an Indian village or encampment and a covered wagon. The salmon and historical scene were the first to be eliminated, and Crater Lake defeated Mount Hood 10-8 in the final vote.[89]

On May 24, 2004, Kulogonski endorsed the choice of the commission and announced that Crater Lake would form the motif, and the Treasury approved the design on July 13. An account in *Coin World* told this:

> The Crater Lake design features a view of the lake from the south rim, with conifer trees in the foreground, Wizard Island rising from the lake waters and the opposite rim. Crater Lake is the caldera of a volcano, Mount Mazama; the lake was formed following a cataclysmic eruption approximately 7,700 years ago. The lake is the deepest in the United States and seventh deepest [at 1,949 feet] in the world.[90]

When the mintages were totaled, 720,200,000 circulation strikes had been produced at the Philadelphia and Denver mints—the highest figure since the 2000 Louisiana quarter of 764,205,000. These figures compare to an average of slightly more than 497,000,000 for the issues from 2002 to this point. By this time, the all-time record was held by the 2000 Virginia quarter, with an overwhelming 1,594,616,000 coins. The low point was registered by the 2000 Maine, with just 448,000,000.[91]

The design was widely appreciated by numismatists as one of the finest in the series. The elements were all part of a single scene, giving artistic value to the motif.

NUMISMATIC ASPECTS OF THE STATE OF OREGON

1790: The ships *Columbia* and *Washington* reached and discovered the Columbia River. The vessels carried 1787-dated medals and Massachusetts copper coins; some were distributed to Native Americans. *1820:* The North West Token, which depicted a beaver, was used for trade. *1845:* A.L. Lovejoy and F.W. Pettygrove were pioneers at a settlement but could not decide on a name. Lovejoy, from Massachusetts, wanted to call it Boston, while Pettygrove, from Maine, wanted Portland. An 1835-dated cent was flipped, and Portland was the choice. *1849:* The Oregon Exchange Co. minted $5 and $10 gold coins. *1864:* On July 4, the 38th Congress passed "An Act to establish a Branch Mint of the United States at Dalles City in the state of Oregon for the coinage of gold and silver." To provide for planning and construction, the sum of $100,000 was appropriated. A fine Mint building was constructed, but never used. *1904–1905:* A commemorative gold dollar was issued for the Lewis and Clark Exposition in Portland. *1907:* Gold discs were issued as money in Baker City. At the time, there was a gold rush in the district, centered in nearby Sumpter. *1926–1939:* The Oregon Trail Memorial commemorative half dollar was issued. *2005:* Nickel five-cent pieces in the Westward Journey Nickel Series™ feature the sighting of the Pacific by Lewis and Clark at the mouth of the Columbia River.

KANSAS *34th of 50*

Official Coin Release Date: August 29, 2005.

Mintage Figures:

Circulation strikes (clad) 2005-P: 263,400,000
2005-D: 300,000,000
Proof strikes (clad) 2005-S: 3,262,000
Proof strikes (silver) 2005-S: 1,606,970

Kansas 2005 • Market Values • Circulation Strikes and Proof Strikes

MS-63	MS-64	MS-65	MS-66	MS-67	MS-68	MS-63	MS-64	MS-65	MS-66	MS-67	MS-68
$0.75	$1	$1.50	$2	$2.50	$3	$0.75	$1	$1.50	$2	$2.50	$3

PF-64	PF-65	PF-66	PF-67	PF-68	PF-64	PF-65
$4	$6	$8	$10	$12	$9	$10

Kansas 2005 • Certified Populations • Circulation Strikes and Proof Strikes

MS-65	MS-66	MS-67	MS-68	MS-69	MS-65	MS-66	MS-67	MS-68	MS-69
7	15	12	1	0	7	20	19	0	0

PF-65	PF-66	PF-67	PF-68	PF-69	PF-70	PF-65	PF-66	PF-67	PF-68	PF-69	PF-70
0	2	12	27	8,008	82	2	2	8	39	7,406	68

■ Philadelphia Mint circulation strikes ■ Denver Mint circulation strikes
■ San Francisco Mint (clad) Proof strikes ■ San Francisco Mint (silver clad) Proof strikes

SPECIFICS OF THE REVERSE DESIGN

Description: An American bison, the state animal (chosen in 1955), stands on a small patch of ground, facing forward and slightly to the right. To the left are three large sunflowers. The top and bottom border inscriptions are standard.

Designer: Unknown. *Mint sculptor-engraver who made the model:* Norman E. Nemeth. *Engraver's initials and location:* NEN, located at the lower right in the turf.

State emblems of Kansas. (James McCabe Jr., *A Centennial View of Our Country and Its Resources,* 1876)

STORY OF THE DESIGN

To select a design for the state quarter, Kansas Governor Kathleen Sebelius invited participation from all citizens, including students.[92] Per current Mint policy, no art was welcome, just concepts. More than 1,600 were received by the 16-member Kansas Commemorative Coin Commission. Concepts were varied and included bison, wheat, one or more Indians, the statue atop the state capitol, sunflowers singly and in combination with other objects, and outline maps of the state. One had a sunflower with a banner across it labeled "There's no place like home." Another, with a farmer in overalls standing in a sea of wheat with two children, was flatly rejected by the Mint and was eliminated from final consideration. High-school students voted to select the final motif.

The winning concept for the 2005 Kansas quarter, turned into a design at the Mint, was announced by Sebelius on May 6, 2004. Featured was a standing bison (popularly but incorrectly called a *buffalo* by most Americans) with a group of sunflowers to the left. No special inscriptions beyond the standard were shown on a publicized sketch. The three runners-up all featured sunflowers as well.[93]

On the winning design, the horns of the animal were pointing forward, "but as any bison rancher knows, the horns should be pointing up," one observer commented.[94] Perhaps in Philadelphia there weren't any bison handy for Mint artists to check. State officials suggested some modifications, including raising the bison's head, fixing the horn problem, and making the ground appear more natural.[95] These things were done, preventing the coin from being listed among the design errors in the series.

As to the *bison*-versus-*buffalo* terminology, the correct name of the animal is a bison. A buffalo is a different species and is not the animal of our Wild West. Numismatists call the 1901 $10 Legal Tender issue the "Bison Note," and the 2004 five-cent pieces were called "Bison Nickels" by collectors and the Mint alike. However, collectors love their Buffalo nickels, minted from 1913 to 1938, and never call them Bison nickels. Far and away, *buffalo* is the favorite word Americans use.

NUMISMATIC ASPECTS OF THE STATE OF KANSAS

1860s: Adolph Cohen, a clothier in Leavenworth, was the only Kansas merchant to issue Civil War tokens. *1913:* The Kansas City Federal Reserve Bank was established under the Federal Reserve Act. Currency issued there bears the letter I.

WEST VIRGINIA 35th of 50

Official Coin Release Date: October 14, 2005.

Mintage Figures:

Circulation strikes (clad) 2005-P: 365,400,000
2005-D: 356,200,000

Proof strikes (clad) 2005-S: 3,262,000

Proof strikes (silver) 2005-S: 1,606,9700

West Virginia 2005 • Market Values • Circulation Strikes and Proof Strikes

MS-63	MS-64	MS-65	MS-66	MS-67	MS-68	MS-63	MS-64	MS-65	MS-66	MS-67	MS-68
$0.75	$1	$1.50	$2	$2.50	$3	$0.75	$1	$1.50	$2	$2.50	$3

PF-64	PF-65	PF-66	PF-67	PF-68	PF-64	PF-65
$4	$6	$8	$10	$12	$9	$10

West Virginia 2005 • Certified Populations • Circulation Strikes and Proof Strikes

MS-65	MS-66	MS-67	MS-68	MS-69	MS-65	MS-66	MS-67	MS-68	MS-69
0	5	24	5	2	2	2	1	0	0

PF-65	PF-66	PF-67	PF-68	PF-69	PF-70	PF-65	PF-66	PF-67	PF-68	PF-69	PF-70
0	1	9	25	7,899	93	1	11	9	48	6,741	103

■ Philadelphia Mint circulation strikes ■ Denver Mint circulation strikes

■ San Francisco Mint (clad) Proof strikes ■ San Francisco Mint (silver clad) Proof strikes

SPECIFICS OF THE REVERSE DESIGN

Description: An almost three-dimensional scenic view that features the New River Gorge Bridge and the inscription NEW RIVER GORGE. The bridge abutments or banks are missing at the ends of the bridge. This must have been an oversight.

Designer: Unknown. *Mint sculptor-engraver who made the model:* John Mercanti. *Engraver's initials and location:* JM, located in the waterway at the lower right.

STORY OF THE DESIGN

The governor's office invited citizens to submit ideas for the new quarter. Students at the Governor's School for the Arts were tapped to review more than 1,800 design concepts received.[96] The field was narrowed to include New River Gorge and the related Bridge Day / New River Gorge, River Rafters, Appalachian Warmth, and Mother's Day / Anna Jarvis. Probably, to an outsider, Appalachian Warmth might well reflect the hills, rusticity, and fine people of the state, or as John Denver put it in his "Country Roads" song, "almost heaven."

On March 31, 2004, Governor Bob Wise announced his selection of a motif—a depiction of the New River Gorge and the bridge over it. A sketch showed the river in the foreground and in the distance a steel bridge arching over forested slopes to each side of the waterway. The New River Gorge Bridge, arching 876 feet above the waterway, is the world's second-longest steel span at 3,030 feet. The bridge and gorge are part of the National Park System and are collectively designated the New River Gorge National River. When the bridge was completed in 1977, a 40-mile trip over twisting roads was reduced to one minute.

NUMISMATIC ASPECTS OF THE STATE OF WEST VIRGINIA

After statehood, banks formerly in Virginia had West Virginia addresses, as reflected on changing imprints on currency of banks of the district, similar to the situation in Maine in 1820.

NEVADA *36th of 50*

Official Coin Release Date: January 31, 2006.

SPECIFICS OF THE REVERSE DESIGN

Description: Three galloping mustang horses at the center and to the foreground, representing a species for which the state is known. In the distance is a mountain range with a sun and resplendent rays behind it. To the left and right are sagebrush branches, and THE SILVER STATE appears on a curved ribbon below.

Designer: Unknown. *Mint sculptor-engraver who made the model:* Don Everhart II. *Engraver's initials and location:* DE, located near tip of ribbon at lower right; D and E each lean left.

STORY OF THE DESIGN

In June 2004 it was announced that Nevada State Treasurer Brian Kolicki had been placed in charge of a group with a particularly lengthy name: Great Nevada Commemorative Quarter Quest Advisory Panel. The panel was created to help select the design for the 2006 quarter. Among those appointed was Phil Carlino, a longtime numismatist. Kolicki noted that the decision would not be easy:

The Palace, a saloon and gambling emporium, did a lively business in Reno in 1908. The gambling and entertainment industry, so important to Nevada today, did not figure in motifs selected for the 2006 state quarter.

> There are so many different things in Nevada. The history of mining, railroads, Lake Tahoe, Lake Mead, The Strip, the Biggest Little City in the World [Reno], Yucca Mountain, the good, the bad, the test site, the mushroom cloud, wild horses—you name it. There's so many things that are Nevada and its history and again we have to capture that essence and put it on a small piece of metal.[97]

Once again, no *art* from the state was acceptable. Desired were words. Treasurer

Hoisting works at the Yellow Jacket Silver Mining Co., Gold Hill, Nevada, circa 1880. The Comstock Lode, discovered in 1859, yielded hundreds of millions of dollars in gold and silver in the district centered around Virginia City, giving rise to "The Silver State" motto.

Kolicki's office maintained a Web site to receive concepts and to provide information about the program. Five motifs were posted. In early 2003, votes on the design were solicited until 5:00 p.m. on May 30. The popular choice:

> Residents selected the design called "Morning in Nevada." It depicts the sun behind the Sierra Nevada Mountains with three wild mustangs at center, flanked by sagebrush branches. At the bottom of the design is a ribbon inscribed THE SILVER STATE.[98]

Can a Ram Have a Philosophy?

On January 25, 2004, the Commission of Fine Arts selected a favorite from among five designs done for Nevada by Mint staff. It did not correspond with what the citizens of Nevada preferred. An account in *Coin World* noted:

> CFA Historian Sue Kohler said commission members unanimously selected the design of the bighorn sheep for the 2006 Nevada quarter dollar, but recommended modifications. Kohler said commission members suggested that the image of the ram be reduced in size so that the Sierra Nevada Mountain range could be slightly more prominent in the foreground.[99]

It was also suggested, although the inscription ALL FOR OUR COUNTRY in the left field of the coin design is the Nevada state motto, that it be removed because it makes it appear the ram is espousing that philosophy.

The sheep design follows Nevada's design concept representing "Nevada Wilderness." A close second among the Nevada designs was a design representing the theme "The Silver State." The design features a waist-up portrait of a miner with a pickaxe held in his right hand, a shovel in his left, with elements of a mine in the background and the inscription THE SILVER STATE in the lower left field.

The Nevada designs not selected represented the themes "Morning in Nevada," depicting the sun rising from behind the Sierra Nevada Mountains, three wild mustangs at the center, flanked by sagebrush branches, with a ribbon below inscribed THE SILVER STATE; "Nevada's Early Heritage," showing an outline of the state with American Indian petroglyphs, a Dat-So-La-Lee basket, a tule duck decoy and the inscription NEVADA'S HERITAGE; and "Mother Nature's Nevada," showing crossed miner's axes with a star below for Carson City that separates sagebrush branches, with the sun rising at the center from behind a ribbon inscribed THE SILVER STATE.[100]

The final motif as used on the coin was ramless. The art was arranged more or less symmetrically, with a sun in the distance, over mountains, three galloping wild mustang horses near the center, THE SILVER STATE on a curved ribbon below, and with sagebrush branches to each side. The elements were nicely tied in with each other, with a horse's leg overlapping a sagebrush branch, and the most distant horse against the mountains. Accordingly, the common complaint of collage designs—elements scattered on a background and not connected—was not applicable here. This closely follows a design chosen as the favorite by citizens, but rejected by the Committee of Fine Arts, described above.

Daniel Carr's proposal for a Nevada quarter, shown here in the form of a simulated coin. (Daniel Carr)

NUMISMATIC ASPECTS OF THE STATE OF NEVADA

1870–1893: The Carson City Mint produced silver and gold coins, mostly Morgan silver dollars and gold double eagles. From 1942 to date the structure has housed the Nevada State Museum, which includes a numismatic display. *20th century:* Casino chips become a popular collectible.

NEBRASKA *37th of 50*

Official Coin Release Date: April 3, 2006.

SPECIFICS OF THE REVERSE DESIGN

Description: Historic Chimney Rock to the right, with terrain in the foreground and a covered wagon drawn by two oxen to the left, depicting a scene of pioneers in the 19th century. The sun is in the sky to the left.

Designer: Rick Masters. *Mint sculptor-engraver who made the model:* Charles L. Vickers. *Engraver's initials and location:* CLV, located in the field to the left, below the edge of the terrain.

STORY OF THE DESIGN

Every state quarter has had its procedures, complications, reviews, and so on. Because the scenarios for Nebraska and Colorado are perhaps representative of the others, and because they are the most recent (as of press time), I have chosen the Nebraska scenario for expanded coverage.

In 2003, John Gale, Nebraska secretary of state and chairman of the Nebraska State Quarter Design Committee, posted a notice outlining the quarter program as carried out by other states in the past and suggesting guidelines for the Nebraska issue. He concluded by noting, "This is an opportunity for all Nebraskans to show pride in their state by submitting a design."[101] Actually, the more accurate word would have been *concept.* Again, no *art* was wanted from residents of the state.

The first meeting of the committee was held in the State Capitol two days later. Minutes of meetings were subsequently posted on the Internet, making it possible for anyone to follow the deliberations. The May 30 narrative included this information, giving an excellent overview of the process then in effect. Particularly notable is the comment that a *single motif* is the most desirable:

> *U.S. Mint Guests:* Secretary Gale introduced Gloria Eskridge, associate director sales and marketing and Jean Gentry, deputy chief counsel, both from the Department of the Treasury, U.S. Mint. Ms. Eskridge relayed a little of the history of the program and how the Treasury Department has discovered the importance of working very early and often with the states as they work through the process of their quarter design development. One of the big elements of this program is to educate people across the nation on history in each state. Ms. Gentry stated there are three elements the Mint will be looking for in a design; these are as follows:
>
> 1. Coinability (something that can be reproduced in a large quantity, can be used in vending machines, etc. etc.)
> 2. Historical accuracy (the Mint will work very closely with the state to make sure every element on the design is historically accurate)

3. Appropriateness (should be dignified and not frivolous). Ms. Eskridge and Ms. Gentry gave some general guidelines for elements that should NOT be used on the quarters. One of the things they mentioned is [that] something that is popular now but is only a fad should not be used. It is inappropriate to use any depiction of a religion or a sport. No state flag or seal may be used; however, parts of the flag or seal can be used. No head or shoulders/bust of any person living or dead may be used and no portrait of any living person may be used. There should be no symbol used that can be seen as an endorsement for any commercial product or brand. Even the depiction of a car, tractor, etc., should be completely generic.

It was explained that in submitting concepts in a narrative form, it gets away from setting an expectation from an artist that their design will be reproduced exactly as they had submitted it. It gives the state a lot more latitude in the final design.

They suggested that as a normal rule a simple design is a better design. A single element that stands out usually looks better than several elements in the small space. They did say that wording can be used; and in fact, most quarters do have some wording identifying an element on the coin. The Mint will request source material to support the narrative. Photographs may be used for this.

In time, more than 6,500 concepts were received. Chimney Rock, an icon for Forty Niners on the way to California, was represented. Farming and homesteading motifs, reflective of the early years of the territory that became a state in 1906, included fields, tractors, crops, and sod huts.

Decisions

After the May 1, 2004, deadline, the committee was given until September 30 to select concepts to be forwarded to the U.S. Mint. In the meantime, 25 of the concepts were posted on the Internet, and Nebraskans were invited to vote. From August 20 to the September 30 end date, 138,649 did. The 10 most popular were Chimney Rock and westward migration, Standing Bear, the State Capitol, *The Sower*, the state outline, agriculture, sandhill cranes, frontier travel, transportation and communication, and homesteading.

Numismatic News told what happened next:

On September 28, the Nebraska Quarter Design Committee sent four narratives to the U.S. Mint for rendering for its 2006 state quarter design. Prior to a September 22 meeting, the NQDC had opted for five narratives. However, at the meeting, the design of Chimney Rock with the State Capitol was eliminated.

The committee also slightly altered two other narratives at that meeting. The State Capitol with text "The Unicameral State" was changed to "Home of the Unicameral State," and the Capitol's *Sower* with the text "The Arbor Day State" was changed to the similar "Home of Arbor Day." The designs will now go to Mint sculptor-engravers. Nebraska officials expect the design renderings next spring for final selection.[102]

This narrative from *Coin World* reveals internal processes of the committee, which was struggling with Mint-created art rather than art submitted by Nebraskans—a continuing bone of contention in the state quarter program:

In December [on the 15th] the Nebraska State Quarter Design Committee suggested some minor changes to the first round of U.S. Mint approved designs for its 2006 State quarter dollar. The four design concepts and the committee's recommended changes are:

A depiction of a covered wagon with the Chimney Rock formation in the background and a sun overhead. The text CHIMNEY ROCK appears to the right. Chimney Rock is a naturally occurring rock formation located in the valley of the North Platte River. It is considered one of the state's most famous landmarks and was seen by those traveling along the Oregon Trail. The rock formation stands 325 feet from base to tip. The committee asked the Mint to make the wagon, oxen and family members smaller so Chimney Rock is the more dominant image in the design.

A depiction of the statue *The Sower*, a 19.5-foot bronze sculpture that has stood atop the 400-foot tower of the state Capitol since 1930. The text HOME OF ARBOR DAY appears above and to the right of the image while THE SOWER appears below and to the left of the image and the first initial and last name of the sculptor, Lee Lawrie, appears just to the right and below the depiction of the statue. The committee asked that the name of the sculptor be dropped from the design. The committee also asked that the figure's legs be extended to just below the knee to avoid an amputated look to the legs as on the current Mint designs.

The state Capitol with the text HOME OF THE UNICAMERAL STATE and STATE CAPITOL flank the depiction of the building. The word "unicameral" refers to Nebraska being the only single-house state legislature in the country. The committee requested Mint artists to add details to the north entrance of the Capitol building to show the building's grandeur.

A portrait of Chief Standing Bear of the Ponca tribe with the state's motto EQUALITY BEFORE THE LAW to the right of the portrait and the words CHIEF STANDING BEAR to the left of his portrait. The only change sought by the committee was to increase the size of the state motto and the legend CHIEF STANDING BEAR from 10 to 15 percent.[103]

The Commission of Fine Arts added its commentary:

A desert bighorn sheep ram, state capitol building and grazing bison appear on the designs recommended Jan. 25 by the Commission of Fine Arts for the reverses of the 2006 State quarter dollars. . . .

For Nebraska, commission members selected a design showing the State Capitol building in Lincoln that was designed by renowned architect Bertram Grosvenor Goodhue, who also designed the National Academy of Sciences Building in Washington, D.C. [CFA historian Sue] Kohler said it was recommended that the inscription STATE CAPITOL be moved from the right field on the design to below the building, with the date of completion, 1832, added. There was no mention about retaining or removing the inscription from the left field, HOME OF THE / UNICAMERAL, a reference to Nebraska being the only state with a single-body legislature.

The designs not recommended were a rendition of *The Sower* statue that graces the dome of the State Capitol; a design showing Chimney Rock with a blazing sun rising behind an ox-drawn Conestoga wagon transporting a pioneer family; and a portrait of Standing Bear, a Ponca Indian chief whose 1879 trial in Omaha led to a decision by Judge Elmer Dundy that native Americans are "persons within the meaning of the law" and have the rights of citizenship.[104]

The Final Choice

On June 1, 2005, the governor's office issued this statement:

> Gov. Dave Heineman announced Chimney Rock as his selection for the commemorative U.S. quarter to represent Nebraska. He was joined for the announcement by Secretary of State John Gale.
>
> The Chimney Rock design, which was one of four finalists presented to the Governor last month, features a pioneer family, a covered wagon and Chimney Rock, the clay and sandstone natural wonder that served as a landmark for westward expansion and that today serves as a tourist destination and historical marker. The Governor has forwarded his choice to U.S. Treasury Secretary John Snow for final approval.
>
> "I chose Chimney Rock because I felt it best represented our state's pioneering spirit and cultural heritage," Gov. Heineman said. "It reflected the resolve, persistence and incomparable work ethic that our forbearers brought to the plains."

The Commission of Fine Arts added another item to its long list of rejections of its choices for Washington quarters; the first had been way back in 1932 with the original design. In my opinion, the final design by the Mint is one of the most beautiful in the series—well integrated, with Chimney Rock being the main motif, the covered wagon being subsidiary and a part of the landscape, importantly connected to Chimney Rock by intervening terrain.

An Interview With the Designer

Peter Lindblad contributed "Masters Designs Nebraska Quarter" to *Numismatic News*, December 20, 2005, an interview with the artist:

> Rick Masters is a Midwesterner, born and bred. And that Midwestern upbringing has served him well in his career as an artist, helping Masters come up with the design that will be featured on the 2006 Nebraska state quarter.
>
> "It's still kind of sinking in," said Masters, an associate professor of art and graphic design at the University of Wisconsin-Oshkosh. "It's something I've dreamed of for a long time. It's a one-in-a-million kind of thing. I always thought these kinds of things always happen to other people, not me."
>
> But it did, and for a kid who collected coins while growing up in Sioux City, Iowa, a city near the Iowa-Nebraska border, it's quite an honor. Mas-

ters is the only Midwestern artist in the U.S. Mint's Artistic Infusion Program. He applied for admission to the program in November 2003, when the Mint sent out a call for applicants. He found out about the recruiting plea in *Numismatic News.*

"I was one of the lucky 18, out of the 300 who applied," said Masters. "I think they did most of their advertising on the East Coast. Being a subscriber to *Numismatic News,* that's where I found out about the application process." Applicants were required to have either taught art or worked as a professional artist for five years. Masters was excited to be selected.

"I was one of those typical kids who started out with those blue Whitman folders," said Masters. "Coin collecting was a big phenomenon during the 1960s. I had a paper route, so I was seeing a lot of coins. I remember the transition from silver to clad."

Masters lapsed as a collector until the boom in silver and gold prices. "I became an NN subscriber in 1982 and my interest in the hobby took off," said Masters. After joining the AIP, Masters and the other artists were assigned to work on the 2005 nickels that were part of the Westward Journey Nickel Series. Then, in the fall of 2004, the artists were divided into groups of five to come up with designs for the 2006 state quarters. They were asked if they had any preferences. Immediately, Masters said he wanted to work on the Nebraska design. He talked about how the assignment came about:

"The Mint modified the state quarter process a while back and asked that states not submit artwork for the quarters, but use narratives instead," said Masters. "Those narratives are fairly descriptive about what they want, and Chimney Rock was one thing they'd picked."

Along with Chimney Rock, the state wanted a covered wagon carrying pioneers. "I worked off some historic photographs," said Masters. "I read about Chimney Rock as well, and in the 20th century, Chimney Rock lost a part of its spire. Because of the pioneer family, it had it to be a 19th century image, so 1 wanted it to look like it did in the 19th century."

Masters submitted variations of the same theme. Two of Masters' designs were among the four finalists presented to . . . Heineman. "It was the same subject matter, but it "was kind of like rearranging the stage," said Masters. "There were just different compositions."

While Masters kept Chimney Rock in the same place, he moved the positions of the pioneer family and their wagon. The final design shows the ox-drawn wagon in the left-hand corner with the sun shining directly behind it. It came as a surprise to Masters when his design was picked. "I was not that optimistic," said Masters. "I had an old professor at the University of Iowa who said that if you get selected into the final round of a contest, don't expect to win. It's a matter of luck because you're always at the mercy of the judges, so I didn't get too worked up about it."

That changed when his depiction was selected. "It's been an incredible experience working with the Mint," said Masters, who is currently on sabbatical and working on projects that aren't related to numismatics. "I went out there for two symposiums and the Mint was just a first-class organization."

NUMISMATIC ASPECTS OF THE STATE OF NEBRASKA
The Durham Western History Museum in Omaha houses much of the Byron Reed collection, including an 1804 silver dollar.

COLORADO *38th of 50*

SPECIFICS OF THE REVERSE DESIGN
Description: Landscape scene with pines in the foreground and the Rocky Mountains in the distance. The inscription COLORFUL COLORADO is on a ribbon below.

Designer: No person credited. *Mint sculptor-engraver who made the model:* Norman E. Nemeth. *Engraver's initials and location:* NEN in the branches of a pine tree at the lower right.

STORY OF THE DESIGN
In preparation for the state's turn in the coin lineup, the Colorado Commemorative Quarter Advisory Commission was organized to review and recommend designs.[105]

Residents of the state were then invited to submit written concepts to the governor's office. Art was also allowed, even though art was not to be considered by the Mint. In the early months of 2004, Frances Owens, first lady of Colorado, began a tour to introduce schoolchildren and others to the state quarter concept, inviting designs to be submitted. To listeners in Pueblo she had the following to say:

> "This is an opportunity for you to become a part of history," Mrs. Owens told students in Michael Divelbiss' seventh-grade social studies class. "This is something in your lifetime and my lifetime that the Mint may never do again, so I encourage you to participate. We want your ideas on what you think should be on the Colorado quarter," Mrs. Owens said. "I encourage you to keep it very simple but at the same time design something that you think makes Colorado special."[106]

Reminiscent of the Sierra Club's publicity efforts for the 2005 California quarter design, in Morrison, Colorado, the Friends of Red Rocks, a group supporting the Red Rocks Park and Amphitheatre, began a campaign. A petition was made available for people to sign, and residents of the state were encouraged to write to the governor, proposing Red Rocks Park for the quarter design. The group's Web site proclaimed:

> Red Rocks is the singular icon that differentiates Colorado from all others. Colorado like many other states has amazing mountains and incredible skiing. What does Colorado have that no other state can claim? Creation Rock and Ship Rock, the two majestic red monoliths creating a place so magical and original, that no other place on earth can replicate.

Narrowing the Focus

Design ideas were accepted until May 10, 2004. By this time, more than 1,500 concepts had been submitted. On March 9, 2005, Governor Bill Owens and First Lady Frances Owens unveiled the semifinal concepts, translated into sketches by Mint staff, at a press conference in Denver. The governor commented:

> With a state as beautiful as ours, it is not at all surprising that we have five wonderful designs. Each of these coins uniquely presents the beauty and tradition of Colorado. One of the designs features mountains and foothills behind a large capital C partially encircling the inscription THE CENTENNIAL STATE. A cluster of columbine flowers rests atop a portion of the large C. The columbine is the state flower of Colorado.

Another design features a representation of Mesa Verde's famous Cliff Palace, located in the 52,000-acre site of the Mesa Verde National Park, near Cortez, Colo. From A.D. 600 to 1300, groups of people built stone villages in the alcoves of the canyon walls. These cliff dwellers, as they are known today, eventually disappeared without a trace of explanation, leaving behind their homes.

Daniel Carr's proposal for a Colorado quarter was a semi-finalist, shown here in the form of a simulated coin. (Daniel Carr)

Another design features Pikes Peak, a mountain that has become a Colorado landmark, with a miner's pick and shovel below the central device. The inscription PIKES PEAK OR BUST appears above the date 2006. The mountain peak became the symbol of the 1859 Colorado gold Rush, through that slogan. A trip up the 14,000-plus foot mountain peak by poet Katherine Lee Bates in the 19th century served as the inspiration for her poem "America the Beautiful."

Pikes Peak as photographed in July 1999 from Woodland Park, Colorado.

A third quarter dollar design depicts an alpine soldier skiing downhill with the inscription BIRTHPLACE OF THE 10TH MOUNTAIN DIVISION. A training camp was constructed in early 1942 at Camp Hale, high in the Rocky Mountains near Pando, Colo. The camp became home to the U.S. Army 10th Light Division (Alpine) on July 13, 1943. The Army unit was redesignated the 10th Mountain Division on November 6, 1944.

A fourth design under consideration for the State quarter dollar shows a rugged mountain backdrop above a banner bearing the inscription COLORFUL COLORADO.

Colorado residents submitted more than 1,500 written and visual descriptions of their design concepts. The visual representations were used to help the commission evaluate the written explanations but were not passed along to Mint officials per their request.[107]

The Citizens Coinage Advisory Committee

Citizens Coinage Advisory Committee weighed in with its suggestions. The appointed chairman was Tom Noe, a rare coin dealer from Ohio who had especially strong political ties reaching up to the governor of his state and with connections to the George W. Bush White House.[108] The committee of seven members had been established under PL 108-15 on April 23, 2003, to advise the secretary of the Treasury as to coin designs, suggest events and topics to be commemorated, and to provide estimated coinage levels, among other duties. The same law abolished the Citizens Commemorative Coin Advisory Committee, a predecessor group that had advised on state quarters and certain other coin designs. Concerning the Colorado quarter, Bill McAllister, in an exclusive story filed with *Coin World*, described the inner workings of the committee:

Members of the Citizens Coinage Advisory Committee couldn't agree on whether the mountains on designs for the 2006 Colorado quarter dollar were mountainous enough or whether the coin needs a "the" in the legend THE CENTENNIAL STATE on the proposed design. But in the end, the panel voted overwhelmingly at a March 15 meeting for a design that features that slogan.

Unable to reach a firm consensus on disputed parts of the design, the committee suggested that others will have to decide about the mountains and wording of the state's nickname. The CCAC-favored design, one of five selected by state officials, features a view of the craggy Rocky Mountains rising from a forested valley. It also carries a large letter "C" partially interwreathed with the state flower, the columbine, and bears the nickname THE CENTENNIAL STATE. The design drew 20 out of a possible 30 points in balloting by the 10 members of the panel. Each member could give up to three points for a favored design under the panel's procedures. A design with another view of mountains and the state's other nickname, COLORFUL COLORADO, on a scroll drew 14 points.

A design with a view of Pikes Peak, perhaps the state's best-known mountain, drew 13 points to finish in third place. It carries the slogan PIKES PEAK OR BUST and features two snowflakes and the crossed pick and shovel of a miner. A design that features the cliff dwellings at Mesa Verde

National Park in southwestern Colorado drew only five points with several members complaining the design is too crowded. A design that features a skiing soldier from the Army's famed 10th Mountain Division, a unit formed in the state during World War II, drew no votes at all from the committee members. . . .

Some CCAC members questioned whether the Colorado designs accurately depicted the state's mountains. "It's mountains, mountains, mountains," groused historian Robert Remini, who complained the designs could have represented any mountain state. "Why, Pikes Peak doesn't even have a peak," Remini exclaimed.

But Bill Fivaz, a Dunwoody, Ga., coin collector, responded that the design is "a good representation of the mountain that overlooks the city of Colorado Springs. "It *doesn't* have a peak," he explained. Fivaz has spent much time within view of Pikes Peak.[109] He is a former board member of the American Numismatic Association, which has its headquarters in Colorado Springs. The panel's newest member, Ken Thomasma of Jackson, Wyo., sought to assure the committee that the designs are accurate. "Those mountains look a lot like the mountains of Colorado," said Thomasma, adding he had climbed some of them.

Some panel members clearly liked the designs. Rita Laws called the recommended design "very dramatic" and Mitchell Sanders said "mountains are clearly important" to Colorado. Colorado officials had acknowledged on March 9 when the five designs were disclosed by Governor Bill Owens that they, too, questioned the images of the mountains as created by Mint artists. "They're not used to mountains in Washington," Sean Duffy, Owens's deputy chief of staff, told the *Rocky Mountain News*. "In one drawing the mountain looked like an anthill."

Except for Pikes Peak no specific Colorado mountains were used on the coins, the state officials said. They also said that artists took liberties by showing Mesa Verde National Park with high mountains in the immediate background.[110] That point troubled some members of the CCAC, which gave low marks to that design.

Committee chairman Thomas W. Noe, a coin dealer from Maumee, Ohio, thought that the panel's comments had indicated that most members wanted to drop the word "the" from the phrase "The Centennial State" in an effort to reduce the wording on the coin. Some members also wanted to drop the first C from CENTENNIAL and reduce the size of the large letter "C" from the coin. But the consensus over dropping the word "the" evaporated after Ute Wartenberg, executive director of the American Numismatic Society, suggested that Colorado may have specifically included the "the" to point out that Colorado was the only state to join the Union in the year 1876, the nation's centennial. The Colorado state government's web site reports the state nickname begins with a "the."[111]

The Commission of Fine Arts

The selections went next to the Commission of Fine Arts. Paul Gilkes reported this in *Coin World:*

Two of the final five proposed designs for the 2006 Colorado quarter dollar were approved March 17 by the Commission of Fine Arts, as acceptable, but neither without recommended revisions to simplify the sketches.

CFA historian Sue Kohler said commission members favor the PIKES PEAK OR BUST design that prominently features the 14,110-foot elevation peak outside Colorado Springs. It was recommended that the peak itself be sharpened and be more defined, Kohler said. Commission members also recommended the removal of the PIKES PEAK OR BUST inscription, the flanking snowflake icons, and the crossed miner's shovel and pick axe.

Also considered acceptable was a design featuring mountains looming out of the forest with the inscription COLORFUL COLORADO in a wavy ribbon below. Kohler said it was recommended should this design be chosen, that the ribbon and inscription be removed and the taper at the base of the mountain range be leveled off. Kohler said commission members liked the sharp details of the mountain range as presented.

The commission meeting was attended for the first time by U.S. Mint Director Henrietta Holsman Fore at the suggestion of CFA Chairman David M. Childs. Kohler said Fore introduced herself to CFA members before the meeting and briefly addressed them just before the presentation of the Colorado quarter dollar designs for review. Kohler said Fore discussed the popularity of the State quarter dollar program.[112]

And the Envelope, Please. . . .

On May 31, 2005, Governor Bill Owens announced his personal choice, which became the adopted design. The central motif featured the Rocky Mountains and the inscription COLORFUL COLORADO, the one favored by many Coloradoans and voted as number one by the Citizens Coinage Advisory Committee. The design was of a scenic nature, with all elements tied together—the type of motif that, in my opinion, is most pleasing to the eye.

NUMISMATIC ASPECTS OF THE STATE OF COLORADO

1860–1861: During the gold rush to Colorado, a mint was operated by Clark, Gruber & Co. in Denver, and produced $2.50, $5, $10, and $20 coins, the 1860 versions of the largest two denominations featured a fanciful depiction of Pikes Peak. *1861:* J.J. Conway & Co. in Georgia Gulch produced a small number of $2.50, $5 and $10 gold coins. *1861:* John Parsons & Co. struck a small number of $2.50 and $5 coins near Tarryall. *1862:* The Treasury Department bought the operation of Clark, Gruber & Co. and renamed it the Denver Mint, using that terminology in *Annual Reports.* However, the government did not strike coins there. *1900–1901:* In Victor, Joseph Lesher issued octagonal medals or "Lesher dollars" as a private venture. Most of these bore the advertisements of regional merchants. *1906:* The Denver Mint, in a new building under construction since 1904, opened for business. *1964:* The American Numismatic Association Headquarters was established in Colorado Springs.

NORTH DAKOTA 39th of 50

SPECIFICS OF THE REVERSE DESIGN

Description: Two bison facing left, one running and the other grazing. The top of a mesa is seen in the distance, with a stylized sun outline and rays to the left. *Designer:* None credited. *Mint sculptor-engraver who made the model:* Donna Weaver. *Engraver's initials and location:* DW in the sod at the lower right.

NUMISMATIC ASPECTS OF THE STATE OF NORTH DAKOTA

National Bank Notes from this state are considered by collectors to be especially scarce.

STORY OF THE DESIGN

Serious planning for the state's 2006 quarter began on April 14, 2004, when the North Dakota Quarter Design Selection Commission was formed under Governor John Hoeven. Lieutenant General Dalrymple was chair of the nine-member group composed of historians, state politicians, educators, and tourism officials, per a news release. A Web site was set up to keep interested people abreast of events. North Dakotans were invited to submit written concepts of up to 50 words before the July 1 deadline.

The invitation generated fewer than 400 entries. Chairman Dalrymple sorted them into five thematic categories: agriculture, American Indian culture, Badlands, International Peace Gardens, and landscape.[113] Theodore Roosevelt, one of the few great American presidents not represented on coins (except in miniature in distant view on the Mount Rushmore commemoratives of 1991), did not make the list of finalists. "Rough Rider State," one of North Dakota's nicknames, refers to Roosevelt, who resided there when he was a young man.

Emblems of North Dakota. (*King's Handbook of the United States*, 1891)

These written concepts were sent to the Mint to be turned into art. In December 2004 the commission met to review what they received from the Mint, and suggested several revisions. Three were picked as favorites and returned.

The commission had its say of the three, and selected one with two grazing bison with a backdrop of the sun rising behind Badlands buttes. The commission requested that the two bison be placed farther apart, that the sun be eliminated, and that the buttes made taller.

The ball was then tossed back to the citizens of North Dakota, who were asked to choose from the bison design (with sun remaining in place) and one depicting geese flying over typical terrain of the state with a rising sun in the distance. Governor John Hoeven had the right to make the final choice. On June 3, 2005, he picked the "Badlands with Bison."[114]

SOUTH DAKOTA 40th of 50

SPECIFICS OF THE REVERSE DESIGN

Description: Mount Rushmore flanked by stalks of wheat, with a very large pheasant flying upward and to the left in the foreground.

Designer: None credited. *Mint sculptor-engraver who made the model:* John Mercanti. *Engraver's initials and location:* JM on lower part of rock, below and to the left of Lincoln.

STORY OF THE DESIGN

A five-member committee set up for the South Dakota quarter considered 50 concepts, before settling on five of them. These were: Mount Rushmore framed by two heads of wheat, Mount Rushmore with a bison in the foreground, Mount Rushmore with a pheasant in the foreground, a bison framed by wheat, and a pheasant framed by wheat.[115] These were sent to the Mint to be turned into artwork. Mount Rushmore was considered by numismatists to be a tired motif, for they had a serving of three different Mount Rushmore commemoratives in 1991, none being particularly popular at the time.

Emblems of South Dakota. (*King's Handbook of the United States*, 1891)

The Commission of Fine Arts reviewed the motifs and selected a bison standing on a grassy mound, facing right, with its head slightly toward the viewer. Heads of wheat were to

The boom town of Sherman, South Dakota, shown 12 hours after the first building was erected. (*Leslie's Illustrated Weekly*, March 8, 1890)

each side, somewhat reminiscent of the early design of the Lincoln cent reverse. *Coin World* writer Paul Gilkes said that the CFA was having a "love fest" with bison. One had recently appeared on a commemorative dollar, another on the 2005 Kansas quarter, and still another on the 2005 nickel five-cent piece.[116]

The Citizens Coinage Advisory Commission, met under chairman Tom Noe in Washington, DC, in December 2004. Various commemorative designs and other matters were discussed. Member Rita Laws stated that Native Americans in the state considered Mount Rushmore to be an insult. With this sensitivity in mind, the sculptured mountain design was out, and the winner became the motif with the ring-necked pheasant (the state bird).

The CCAC was required to meet six times a year. To this point, telephone conferencing had been permitted, but no longer. Any member who missed three meetings would now be dropped. Candidates for future appointments, which had been political patronage in the past, now had to include not just one person, but "several" names, so the secretary of the Treasury could make the final choice.[117]

State Special Projects Coordinator John G. Moisan stated soon afterward that residents of the state who learned about Laws's comment had emailed and telephoned his office to protest the possible removal of Mount Rushmore for consideration.[118]

Mount Rushmore, Again

On January 12, 2005, Governor M. Michael ("Mike") Rounds unveiled the Mint staff art for the five final design options. Beginning on this date, public input was requested, until April 15. The governor said he would abide by the people's choice. Residents cast nearly 172,000 votes. The winner with 65,766 votes was a design with Mount Rushmore, a single stalk of wheat to each side, and an out-of-proportion (so it seems) Chinese ring-necked pheasant flying in the foreground. The image was not much different from the 1991 Mount Rushmore commemorative dollar, except for the giant pheasant—suggesting that a lot of time and effort could have been saved by simply modifying that motif.

Coming in second with 49,203 votes was the Mount Rushmore design with bison. This image featured two unrelated subjects—Mount Rushmore and a bison against a plain background (no terrain or connection). Once again, the Commission of Fine Arts' preference was ignored, ditto for the other choice of the Citizens Coinage Advisory Committee, ditto any feelings Native Americans may have had, this time by the voters of the state.

An April 20, 2005, news release from the governor's office included this: "As the state quarter projects across the nation have evolved since the program's inception, states have moved away from a single image or figure representing the state in favor of multiple images highlighting the diversity of the various states." Such a comment flies in the face of what collectors and most people with a sense of art prefer—scenic designs, unified, not scattered objects. On April 27, Governor Rounds picked the "Mount Rushmore and Pheasant" motif.

NUMISMATIC ASPECTS OF THE STATE OF SOUTH DAKOTA

1991: Mount Rushmore Golden Anniversary commemorative half dollars, silver dollars, and $5 gold pieces.

MONTANA *41st of 50*

To Be Issued in 2007

THE DESIGN-SELECTION PROCESS

Montana residents were invited to submit written narratives suggesting motifs for their state quarter, with the deadline set at August 31, 2005. The concepts were to be reviewed by the Montana Quarter Design Commission, after which residents would be allowed to vote for their favorite.

Governor Brian Schweitzer and the commission selected four designs and sent them to the Mint in October 2005. In April 2006, the governor invited the residents to vote for their favorites among the four designs approved by the Mint. One design featured a bull elk at the center with the plains extending back to a rock formation and the sun rising in the distance. A second design featured the skull of a bison at the upper two-thirds of the coin, with plains and distant mountains below and the words BIG / SKY / COUNTRY to the right. A third concept pictured a landscape with a mountain range in the distance, a river, a large expanse of sky with a few clouds, and the inscription BIG SKY COUNTRY in the sky. The fourth design enclosed mountains, plains, and a dramatic sunrise in an outline of the state, with BIG SKY COUNTRY on a ribbon above.

NUMISMATIC ASPECTS OF THE STATE OF MONTANA

The United States Assay Office in Helena was a repository for many Morgan silver dollars that, upon their release in the 1960s, proved to be scarce issues.

The United States Assay Office in Helena was a repository for many Morgan silver dollars that upon their release in the 1960s proved to be scarce issues.

WASHINGTON *42nd of 50*

THE DESIGN-SELECTION PROCESS

To Be Issued in 2007

The Washington State Quarter Advisory Commission invited written suggestions from the public for the design of their state quarter. The deadline was set as July 30, 2005. By that time, the commission had received 1,150 entries. Governor Christine Gregoire planned to select her favorites by September 30, then to submit three to five written concepts for the Mint to turn into art.

This was done, and the five concepts were a salmon; Mount Rainier and an apple within an outline of Washington state; an apple within the outline of Washington state; an outline of Washington State with Mount Rainier centered; a salmon breaching the water with Mount Rainier as a backdrop; and a Northwest Native American stylized orca. It was suggest that the motto *The Evergreen State* be included in at least some of the designs.[119]

After the art was returned by the Mint, a public opinion poll was held. The winning design was that of the salmon breaching at the left of the coin, with Mount Rainier in the background to the right and the motto beneath the mountain.

NUMISMATIC ASPECTS OF THE STATE OF WASHINGTON

1925: The Fort Vancouver Centennial commemorative half dollar was issued.

In 1925, commemorative half dollars were struck to honor the centennial of Fort Vancouver. The coins feature a portrait of John McLoughlin, who built Fort Vancouver on the Columbia River in 1825. They were struck to be sold at $1 apiece, to raise money for the fort's 100-year celebrations. Although they were struck in San Francisco, they do not bear the S mint-mark. The coin's models were prepared by Laura Gardin Fraser, a talented artist whose husband had created the Buffalo nickel design.

(Coin is shown enlarged.)

IDAHO *43rd of 50*

To Be Issued in 2007

THE DESIGN-SELECTION PROCESS

Governor Dirk Kempthorne tapped the Idaho Commission of the Arts to oversee the design-submission process and to review ideas. Citizens of the state were invited to submit written concepts of up to 150 words each until September 9, 2005. To encourage more participation, residents were also invited to submit art, but the governor hastened to say that no art would be sent to the Mint. Multiple submissions from the same person were allowed. To get the ball rolling, he stated:

> Idaho is truly a gem among the states. The spirit of our people is unmatched. Our industrious heritage is rich. The pristine beauty of our mountains, lakes, canyons and rivers is world famous. Idaho shines from the Rocky Mountain bighorns and proud white pines on the high alpine ridges to the crystal clear streams and great sturgeon in our deep desert canyons. Just like our state, the Idaho quarter will stand out among the rest.

State emblems of Vermont. (James McCabe Jr., *A Centennial View of Our Country and Its Resources, 1876*)

Sample submission suggestion: The peaks of the snow-capped Sawtooth Mountains stretch across the top of the coin. A majestic bull elk grazes on the edge of a clear mountain lake in the foreground, his breath steaming in the cold mountain air. Behind the elk, a single tall, straight Western white pine stands on the right side of the coin. In capital, block letters, the words "The Sawtooths" are written in the surface of the lake.[120]

Further, "Simplicity should be emphasized; designs that include too many elements become cluttered and are discouraged."

In late September the governor reported that more than 1,200 ideas had been received. The commission sorted through them and selected 10 to be presented to Governor Kempthorne, who then narrowed the field down to five. These were a peregrine falcon with the state motto ESTO PERPETUA; the Sawtooth Mountains; farmland tapestry showing an aerial view of cropland; two lines from the state song *Here We Have Idaho* flanking an outline of the state; and "bold and distinctive," the latter having the word IDAHO prominently across the center of the coin.[121]

NUMISMATIC ASPECTS OF THE STATE OF IDAHO

Miller's Brewery & Bakery, Idaho City, was the only Idaho merchant to issue Civil War tokens.

WYOMING *44th of 50*

To Be Issued in 2007

THE DESIGN-SELECTION PROCESS

Governor David D. Freudenthal set up the Wyoming Coinage Advisory Committee and appointed *stamp* collector Jack Rosenthal as chairman. Rosenthal had chaired the U.S. Postal Service's Citizens' Stamp Advisory Committee in Washington, DC. News items did not state whether a *numismatist* was anywhere in sight on the committee.

The committee's first meeting was in Cheyenne on January 13, 2005. The goal was to collect and finalize designs by September, at which time no more than five were to be submitted to the Mint, where art would be created—this being the usual process since the 2005 California quarter (the last time that an artist from the honored state was allowed to contribute talent and be recognized).

Residents were allowed to submit words only, up to 50 of them, by completing the statement, "I think the back of the Wyoming quarter should show . . . " The deadline was April 30. More than 1,300 people filled out the form. The committee selected five designs, four of which depicted a bucking horse with rider, with various differences in the background and details. This symbol has been a Wyoming icon for a long time and has been featured on license plates since 1936. The fifth concept was the Old Faithful geyser in Yellowstone National Park, as illustrated on a stamp issued in 1934.

NUMISMATIC ASPECTS OF THE STATE OF WYOMING

1999: The Yellowstone National Park commemorative silver dollar was issued.

In 1999 the Mint struck commemorative silver dollars honoring Yellowstone National Park. The design shows a geyser in full blast, with Yellowstone's park landscape surrounding. (The park has more geysers, hot springs, steam vents, and mud spots than exist in the rest of the world combined.) On the reverse, an American bison—the largest animal in the park's ecosystem—dominates the motif, with mountains and the rising sun in the background. Yellowstone is the nation's first (and the world's oldest) national park; it was dedicated by an act of Congress, signed by President Ulysses Grant, on March 1, 1872. Half the proceeds from the sale of this coin went to support Yellowstone, with the other half assigned to other national parks.

UTAH *45th of 50*

THE DESIGN-SELECTION PROCESS

To Be Issued in 2007

On September 17, 2004, Utah Governor Olene Walker created the Utah Quarter Dollar Commemorative Coin Commission. He appointed as chairman H. Robert Campbell, Salt Lake City numismatist, past president of the ANA, and owner of the All About Coins shop. The commission had just three other members: Frank McEntire, director of the Utah Arts Council; Patti Harrington, superintendent of public instruction of the Utah State Office of Education; and Phil Notarianni, director of the Utah State Historical Society. Three other committees were set up with other connections with the quarter: the Special Events Committee, the Public Affairs Committee, and the Education and Curriculum Committee.[122]

The public were invited to send concepts until March 1, 2005, after which the commission would select five favorites to be submitted to the governor, who would select up to five to send on to the Mint.

The commission presented its five choices to Governor Jon Huntsman on July 29, 2005, this being one of a number of instances in which there were changes of governor during the quarter-dollar design-selection process. Huntsman picked out three designs and sent them to the Mint. One motif illustrated the 1869 transcontinental railroad ceremony at Promontory Point. Another showed a beehive, symbol of industry and long an icon associated with the district, including on the Mormon $5 gold coin of 1860. The third illustrated winter sports, reflecting the state's prominence in that field and its 2002 hosting of the Winter Olympics.

NUMISMATIC ASPECTS OF THE STATE OF UTAH

1849–1850: Mormon gold coinage in denominations of $2.50, $5, $10, and $20 was minted. *1860:* Mormon gold coinage in the $5 denomination was minted. *2002:* The Salt Lake Olympic Games commemorative silver dollar and $5 gold coin were issued.

OKLAHOMA *46th of 50*

To Be Issued in 2008

THE DESIGN-SELECTION PROCESS

A team of individuals from the Oklahoma Centennial Commission was given the duty of reviewing the residents' submitted ideas, which were to be received by March 31, 2006. Perhaps a hint at the final design can be found among the following facts about the state of Oklahoma: *Statehood*—November 16, 1907. *Capital*—Oklahoma City. *Nickname*—Sooner State. *Land area and rank*—68,679 sqare miles (19th). *Largest city*—Oklahoma City. *State motto*—Labor Omnia Vincit (Labor conquers all things). *State flower*—Mistletoe. *State bird*—Scissor-tailed flycatcher. *State tree*—Redbud. *State animal*—Bison. *State song*—"Oklahoma."

NUMISMATIC ASPECTS OF THE STATE OF OKLAHOMA

National Bank Notes from the Territory of Oklahoma, before statehood, are especially highly prized.

NEW MEXICO *47th of 50*

To Be Issued in 2008

THE DESIGN-SELECTION PROCESS

As of press time, little information was available on New Mexico's design-selection process, other than the fact that state residents were given a deadline of May 12, 2006, to submit their written suggestions for the quarter design. Perhaps the following facts about the state of New Mexico hold clues as to what the design will be: *Statehood*—January 6, 1912. *Capital*—Santa Fe. *Nickname*—Land of Enchantment. *Land area and rank*—121,365 sqare miles (fifth). *Largest city*—Albuquerque. *State motto*—Crescit Euondo (It grows at it goes). *State flower*—Yucca. *State bird*—Roadrunner. *State tree*—Piñon. *State song*—"O, Fair New Mexico;" "Asi Es Nuevo Mexico."

NUMISMATIC ASPECTS OF THE STATE OF NEW MEXICO

National Bank Notes from the Territory of New Mexico, before statehood, are especially highly prized.

ARIZONA *48th of 50*

To Be Issued in 2008

THE DESIGN-SELECTION PROCESS

In November 2005, Governor Janet Napolitano of Arizona established a commission to recommend designs for the new state quarter. On December 13, she announced that 22 members had been chosen. The panel was composed of representatives from the State Legislature, historical and art societies, schoolteachers, and members of the general public. By that time, the semiannual Grand Canyon State Poll, conducted over the telephone by Northern Arizona University Social Research Laboratory in Flagstaff, had included the subject in a recent survey. Most respondents preferred a scene from nature, such as the Grand Canyon or a saguaro cactus, instead of state symbols or representations of history.

The commission was charged with selecting up to five concepts to be submitted to the Mint in September 2006; Arizona residents were given a deadline of July 15 to submit their ideas. The following are facts about the state of Arizona; perhaps and element of the eventual design is among them: *Statehood*—February 14, 1912. *Capital*—Phoenix. *Nickname*—Grand Canyon State. *Land area and rank*—111,642 square miles (sixth). *Largest city*—Phoenix. *State motto*—Ditat Deus (God enriches). *State flower*—Blossom of the saguaro cactus. *State bird*—Cactus wren. *State tree*—Paloverde. *State animal*—Ringtail cat. *State song*—"Arizona March Song."

NUMISMATIC ASPECTS OF THE STATE OF ARIZONA

National Bank Notes from the Territory of Arizona, before statehood, are especially highly prized. Superstition Mountain, near Phoenix, is said to be the hiding place for a vast gold treasure.

ALASKA *49th of 50*

THE DESIGN-SELECTION PROCESS

The Alaska Commemorative Coin Commission, established in 2005, was composed of 11 members. The agendas of its meetings, held in Anchorage the first Thursday of each month, were posted on the Internet, as were the minutes. Residents of the state were invited to submit design concepts from January 1 to February 28, 2006; three to five design concepts are due at the Mint in September 2006. Perhaps the following facts about the state of Alaska give clues as to what the design will turn out to be: *Statehood*—January 3, 1959. *Capi-

To Be Issued in 2008

tal—Juneau. *Nickname*—The Last Frontier (unofficial). *Land area and rank*—570,374 square miles (first). *Largest city*—Anchorage. *State motto*—North to the future. *State flower*—Forget-me-not. *State bird*—Willow ptarmigan. *State tree*—Sitka spruce. *State animal*—Moose. *State song*—"Alaska's Flag."

NUMISMATIC ASPECTS OF THE STATE OF ALASKA

1935: Tokens of the Alaska Rural Rehabilitation Corporation were issued; these are listed in the *Guide Book of United States Coins* today.

HAWAII *50th of 50*

To Be Issued in 2008

THE DESIGN-SELECTION PROCESS

Hawaiian residents had until April 30, 2006, to submit written concepts; members of both the Hawai'i State Foundation on Culture and the Arts and the Hawai'i Commemorative Quarter Advisory Commission reviewed the results in May, with a plan to send the final five themes and narratives to Governor Linda Lingle by the end of July. The following facts about the state of Hawaii hint at the final design: *Statehood*—August 21, 1959. *Capital*—Honolulu. *Nickname*—Aloha State. *Land area and rank*—6,423 square miles (47th) *Largest city*—Honolulu. *State motto*—The life of the land is perpetuated in righteousness. *State flower*—Yellow hibiscus. *State bird*—Hawaiian goose. s*State tree*—Kukui (candlenut). *State marine animal*—Humpback whale. *State song*—"Hawai'i Pono'i."

NUMISMATIC ASPECTS OF THE STATE OF HAWAII

1847: Copper cents were issued by King Kamehameha; they were struck in Massachusetts. *1883:* Silver dimes, quarter dollars, half dollars, and dollars (total face value $1 million) were struck in San Francisco (but with no mintmark) for Hawaii. *20th century:* National Bank Notes with territorial address are especially popular with collectors. *1928:* The Hawaii Sesquicentennial commemorative half dollar was issued. *1940s:* $1, $5, $10, and $20 bills with HAWAII overprints were issued during World War II.

AMERICAN
NUMISMATIC
ASSOCIATION

Membership has its perks.

Have **12** issues of *Numismatist* magazine — packed with feature stories, hobby news, collecting tips and ANA updates — delivered to your doorstep.

Learn from the **experts** and join a 33,000-member community.

Borrow books from the
largest numismatic lending library in the world.

Get **consumer awareness** information.

Receive **discounts** on numismatic books and supplies, collection insurance and car rentals.

Submit your coins directly to NGC and NCS for **grading** and **conservation**.

JOIN TODAY!

DISCOVER THE WORLD OF MONEY AND HOW MEMBERSHIP WORKS FOR YOU.

800.514.2646
membership@money.org | www.money.org

Notes

Chapter 1

1. My own mother, née Ruth Eleanor Garrett, married while she was a schoolteacher in Honesdale, Pennsylvania, in the mid-1930s, but had to keep the matter a secret, or she would have been fired. She resigned at the end of the term.

2. William Manchester, *The Glory and the Dream: A Narrative History of America, 1932–1972* (Boston: Little, Brown, 1974), p. 23.

3. Ibid. (p. 16). Seemingly, the Manchester account was either lightly researched or omitted the full story—in particular, the admitted Communist involvement and agitation. For further reading see Douglas MacArthur's *Reminiscences* (New York: McGraw-Hill, 1964), which seems to depict almost a different event!

4. Letter from White to M.F. Amrine, February 4, 1931, reprinted in *Selected Letters of William Allen White, 1899–1943* (New York: Henry Holt, 1947), p. 311.

5. This album later passed to John J. Ford Jr. At the sale of the Ford collection (Stack's) in 2004, it was purchased by a leading Southern currency specialist. A similar album, made by Clark for himself, went to a New England buyer.

6. John W. Adams, *United States Numismatic Literature, Volume II, Twentieth Century Auction Catalogs* (Crestline, California: Kolbe, 1990), passim.

Chapter 2

1. Quotation provided by Roger W. Burdette, from research in the National Archives for the forthcoming book *Renaissance of American Coinage, 1909–1913*.

Chapter 3

1. Old style for February 11, 1731/32. In 1752, the calendar was adjusted by 11 days, making the date February 22; the beginning of the calendar year changed from March 25 to January 1.

2. Washington tolerated slavery and took no action to abolish it. His will specified that his slaves be freed after his wife's death.

3. The medal commemorated Washington's siege that forced the British to evacuate Boston by sea in 1776, preventing their troops from endangering New England.

4. Jared Sparks (1789–1866) served as president of Harvard University from 1849 to 1853.

5. *The Journals and Letters of Samuel Curwen*, as quoted in "Samuel Curwen as a Numismatist," *American Journal of Numismatics* (September 1869).

Chapter 4

1. The current version of the law President Hoover quoted can be found in 31 USC Sec. 5112(d)(2).

2. Biographies of Mellon abound in print and on the Internet. As is true for many other "captains of industry," the facts are hard to find, especially regarding some of the immense legal and tax problems he had (which seemingly diminished with his donation of the National Gallery of Art to the citizens of America).

3. This letter and others (not published here) make it evident that the commission was generally unaware of the traditions of American coinage, and that in an earlier era it was standard practice to use the same designs across many different denominations—as with Liberty Cap, Draped Bust, Capped Bust, Liberty Seated, and other motifs.

4. The Commission of Fine Arts was often casually referred to as the Fine Arts Commission in much correspondence within and outside the Treasury Department.

5. In 2005 the Web site for the North Dakota state quarter gave a detailed overview of the Flanagan-Flannagan confusion, which by that time had spread to hundreds of other Internet

mentions and even a standard numismatic reference book on Washington quarters. Additional errors in print and on the Internet have resulted from numismatists' confusing the year 1932 with 1933. Franklin D. Roosevelt was elected president in November 1932 and was inaugurated on March 4, 1933, by which time the Washington quarter had been created and placed into circulation. Accordingly, the Roosevelt administration had nothing to do with selecting the design.

6. Cornelius Vermeule, *Numismatic Art in America* (Cambridge, Massachusetts: Belknap), p. 177.
7. David T. Alexander, "The Circle of Friends of the Medallion: An Appreciation in American Medallic History." *American Numismatic Association Centennial Anthology* (1991).
8. Roger W. Burdette, communication to the author, December 10, 2005; information from National Archives data.
9. The three medals mentioned in this paragraph are critiqued by Cornelius Vermeule in *Numismatic Art in America*, pp. 124 and 125.
10. One of the great controversies in scientific circles in the early 20th century was the Smithsonian's strong endorsement of Langley as the inventor of powered flight, said to have preceded the accomplishments of the Wright brothers. This stance was finally dropped.
11. Curiously, the Flanagan hairstyle is identical to that on *another* 1785 bust by Houdon, that of Marie-Sébastien-Charles-François Fontaine de Biré, newly appointed treasurer-general under Louis XVI!
12. Jean Bradfield, "The Detroit Story," *The Numismatist*, November 1962.
13. Eva Adams, "These Changing Dimes," transcript of talk, *The Numismatist*, December 1964.
14. Convention report in *The Numismatist*, October 1965.
15. From a February 8, 1966, commentary by Director Adams to Congress, reported in *The Numismatist*, June 1966.
16. Years later, in 1975, quarters dated 1776–1976 (or, more literally, "1776 • 1976"—with a bullet) were *prestruck* at the Philadelphia, Denver, and San Francisco mints.
17. Details from *The Numismatist*, October 1977.

Chapter 5
1. *The Numismatist*, February 1986.
2. Communication with the author, December 19, 2005.
3. Herbert P. Hicks, "The Washington Quarter Reverse: A Die-Variety Bonanza," pp. 249, 251. Walter Breen's description that now two leaves touch the tops of AR in DOLLAR (*Encyclopedia of U.S. and Colonial Proof Coins, 1722–1977*) is wrong; they do not.
4. Hicks, "Washington Quarter Reverse," p. 248.
5. Paul Gilkes, "The 'Mule' Train: Five Years Since Errors Struck," *Coin World*, May 2, 2005. Other sources were also consulted. I was involved in the sale of the Wallis specimen.

Chapter 6
1. David L. Ganz, comments submitted to the author, December 8, 2005.

Chapter 7
1. *Abe Kosoff Remembers* (New York: Sanford J. Durst, 1981) chapter 203 (originally printed April 12, 1967).
2. During the 1970s, governors Virgil Hancock and John J. Pittman were in the forefront of persuading the association to adopt standards. As the manager of ANACS a few years later, Thomas K. DeLorey lent his wisdom and influence to many ANA grading policies.

3. I hasten to add that the standards mentioned previously are those codified by the ANA, not by me. For my money, I would not want to grade Bicentennial and statehood coins without looking at their reverses.

4. Figures rounded to even dollars. *Coin Values* is published by *Coin World.*

Chapter 8

1. Comments to the author, December 19, 2005.
2. Communication to the author, December 14, 2005.
3. David W. Lange, USA Coin Album, *Numismatist*, July 2002.
4. *Coin World*, November 14, 2005.
5. David W. Lange, USA Coin Album, *Numismatist*, November 2002.
6. Ibid.
7. For detailed information on coin-market price cycles see Bowers, *The Expert's Guide to Investing In and Collecting Rare Coins* (Atlanta, Georgia: Whitman, 2005). Few if any of these investment peaks and valleys surprised long-time *numismatists.*

Chapter 9

1. Complete details can be found in *United States Mint 2000 Annual Report.*
2. As an example, no announcement of the California quarter launching in 2005 was sent out in time to be included in the national weekly numismatic newspapers and monthly magazines or in coin club bulletins within California.
3. *Numismatic News*, June 13, 2000.
4. Paul Gilkes, "Sales of Silver Quarter Proof Set End . . . ," *Coin World*, July 5, 2004.
5. Barbara J. Gregory, "In the Wake of Lewis and Clark," *Numismatist*, August 2003.
6. Michele Orzano, "The State Quarters: Define Your State's Spirit," *Coin World*, April 19, 2004.
7. Article by Michele Orzano published in *Coin World*, May 14, 2001.
8. As one of many examples, certain 1783-dated Washington tokens are signed T.W.I. and also E.S. on the reverse. Thomas Wells Ingram was the die engraver who used a design by artist Edward Savage.
9. Article by Michele Orzano published in *Coin World*, May 14, 2001.
10. Selected information is from the U.S. Mint Web site.
11. Certain information is from "Pennsylvania Unveils 'Commonwealth' Quarter," U.S. Mint Web site.
12. Certain information is from "Georgia's Governor Barnes Unveils Peach," U.S. Mint Web site.
13. Certain information is from "U.S. Mint Rounds Out 1999 with New Quarter Honoring Connecticut," October 7, 1999, U.S. Mint Web site.
14. "A New Piece Added to Maryland's History," March 13, 2000, U.S. Mint Web site.
15. Lori Montgomery, "Two-Bit Identity Crisis; Imprint Befuddles the Free—Make That 'Old Line'—State," *Washington Post*, March 14, 2000.
16. First identified and researched by John Kraljevich and featured in the Eliasberg Collection of World Gold Coins sale by American Numismatic Rarities, March 2005.
17. Not included in this figure are these novel coins: At the Denver Mint a die "bearing a South Carolina quarter dollar reverse that was intentionally paired with a 2001-D Sacagawea dollar obverse to strike a mule on a manganese-brass clad dollar planchet," a caper that was detected. However, "it is not known whether specimens . . . escaped the mint facilities. None have been reported in the coin market" (Paul Gilkes, "Mint Made, Caught Additional

Mules, Treasury Reports Reveal Three Double-Denomination Coins," *Coin World*, November 3, 2003).

18. United States Mint Web site, June 2004. Certain other information is from "U.S. Mint Celebrates Summer With the Launch of New South Carolina Quarter," U.S. Mint Web site May 26, 2000.

19. These tokens were retired in 2005 and replaced by E-ZPass.

20. Paul M. Green, *Numismatic News*, November 9, 2004.

21. "Inconsistency Dogs Designer Credit: Not All 'Designers' of State Quarters Gain Recognition," *Coin World*, May 14, 2001.

22. Communication to the author, September 14, 2004.

23. Michele Orzano, "Kentucky Will Not Recognize Artist as Designer of 2001 State Quarter," *Coin World*, September 17, 2001.

24. Certain information is from "North Carolina Quarter Takes Flight," U.S. Mint Web site, March 12, 2001.

25. Certain information is from "Anchors Aweigh for Rhode Island's New Quarter," U.S. Mint Web site, May 21, 2001.

26. From August 6 to August 9, 2001, the Mint had a special 72-hour sale event offering rolls, 100-coin bags, and 1,000-coin bags, resulting in the sale of 10,423,200 coins to collectors and souvenir hunters.

27. Pat Healy, "Quarreling Over Quarters," *Columbia Missourian*, November 17, 2002, p. 1A.

28. Paul Gilkes, "2001-D Kentucky Quarter Circulates: Coin Not Due Until Fall Joins Vermont Coin in Circulation," *Coin World*, June 11, 2001.

29. Certain information is from "Celebrate the Launch of the Kentucky Quarter" and other releases on the U.S. Mint Web site.

30. United States Mint Web site, June 2004.

31. Gwenda Bond, "Quarter Design Finalists Named," office of the governor of Ohio, July 15, 1999.

32. Mike Pulfer, "Quarter Designs Rolling In," *Cincinnati Enquirer*, May 15, 2000, quoting Gwenda Bond, a spokesperson for the governor.

33. Healy, "Quarreling Over Quarters."

34. Orzano, "Kentucky Will Not Recognize Artist."

35. This is the lowest Denver figure to this time. The total of 648,068,000 from both mints was the lowest in the state series to this time, a situation attributed to a slowdown in the national economy and a consequently reduced call for coins in circulation. Unofficially, a drastic cutback in advertising for the program seems to have played an important part.

36. "Spiked Head" variety—Certain clad Proof examples of the 2002-S Tennessee quarters have a die break running from the top of Washington's head to the border. Similar cracks are known for Iowa, Florida, Texas (the Texas crack is in a different location), and Minnesota quarters. Such pieces have an additional value (Ken Potter, "2005-S 'Spiked Head' Proof Seen," *Numismatic News*, May 17, 2005— Potter, who has a special interest in such varieties, reports on them as they are discovered).

37. United States Mint Web site, June 2004. Additional information from "U.S. Hits Right Note With Tennessee Quarter," U.S. Mint Web site, January 14, 2002.

38. This is the lowest quantity for any circulation-strike variety of any statehood quarter, from any mint, to this time. The Philadelphia Mint was closed for nearly six of the normal 10 weeks in the standard production period, to remedy violations pointed out by the Occupa-

tional Safety and Health Administration (Paul Gilkes, "Florida Quarter Dollar Mintages Reverse Recent Downward Trend,"*Coin World*, June 7, 2004).

39. Ken Potter, "2005-S 'Spiked Head' Proof Seen," *Numismatic News*, May 17, 2005.

40. Michele Orzano, "Mint Changes Legend on Ohio 25¢," *Coin World*, July 30, 2001. Fine Arts Commission information from a transcript of the commission meeting regarding the Ohio quarter; also a letter from J. Carter Brown, chairman of the Commission of Fine Arts, to Associate Mint Director Pickens, June 13, 2001: "In regard to the Ohio coin . . . the inscription 'Birthplace of Aviation' still presents a problem because most people will think of the event that took place in North Carolina. As the state of Ohio is honoring Ohioans in aviation rather than events, why not say 'Birthplace of Aviation Pioneers'? There is room for it on the coin as designed, and I would think it would solve the problem to everyone's satisfaction."

41. Certain information is from "The United States Mint Launches Louisiana State Quarter," U.S. Mint Web site.

42. Michele Orzano, "Mint Drops State's Original Choice, Uses Another," *Coin World*, September 3, 2001.

43. Michele Orzano, "Designs that Work," state quarters column, *Coin World*, August 25, 2003.

44. R.W. Julian, communications to the author, December 24 and 27, 2005.

45. William H. Dillistin, *Bank Note Reporters and Counterfeit Detectors, 1826–1866* (New York: American Numismatic Society, 1949), p. 70.

46. United States Mint Web site, June 2004.

47. Paul Jackson, letter to author, August 10, 2004. Jackson, designer of the Missouri quarter dollar, has kept in contact with other artists involved.

48. Certain information is from "United States Mint Unveils Illinois Quarter," U.S. Mint Web site.

49. Paul Gilkes, "2003 State Quarter Designs Under Final Review," *Coin World*, April 8, 2002.

50. The combined mintage of 448,800,000 circulation strikes from these two mints represents the lowest in the statehood series to date, in contrast to 1,594,616,000 circulation strikes for the 2000 Virginia quarters, the high-level record holder to date.

51. Summer Douglass, "Maine Artist Complains About Design," *Coin World*, August 19, 2002.

52. Ibid.

53. Summer Douglass, "Maine Residents Select Design for 2003 State Quarter Dollar," *Coin World*, September 2, 2002.

54. Paul Gilkes, "Fine Arts Panel Pans Design, Rejects Showing Gateway Arch, Lewis and Clark," *Coin World*, July 8, 2002.

55. Michele Orzano, "U.S. Mint Officials May Meet Missouri Quarter Dollar Artist," *Coin World*, September 16, 2002.

56. Conversation with the author, July 28, 2004.

57. Ed Reiter in *COINage*, February 2005: "The machine, manufactured by Kusters Engineering of the Netherlands, contains two rollers which impart corrugated surfaces to coins or planchets by squeezing them at very high pressure. When defective coins are defaced in this manner, portions of the original design may still be visible—but not enough, in the Mint's estimation, to give them any value as minting errors. . . . The U.S. Mint purchased two of the machines—one for the main Mint in Philadelphia and one for the Denver branch. Their rollers squeeze coins and planchets with a force of 26 tons and can process pieces of metal at a rate of 1,000 kilograms per hour. The machines went into regular operation in

mid-2003 and waffled examples are known of all six 2003-dated coin denominations from the Lincoln cent through the Sacagawea dollar."

58. Certain information is from "United States Mint Declares New Arkansas Quarter a Natural Beauty From the Natural State," U.S. Mint Web site, October 28, 2003.

59. United States Mint Web site, June 2004.

60. This is the lowest Denver Mint production to this time for a statehood quarter. Many show lightly struck details.

61. Steven M. Bieda, a state representative from Michigan, designed the reverse of the 1992 Olympic commemorative half dollar (U.S. Mint Web site, June 2004).

62. Michele Orzano, "Cheers and Jeers: Michigan's 2004 State Quarter Design Brings Happiness to Some, Groans to Others," *Coin World,* February 16, 2004.

63. Communication to the author, May 6, 2004.

64. Of the combined production from these two mints, more than 11,000,000 were sold at a premium in the form of rolls, 100-coin mini-bags, and 1,000-coin bags.

65. "Spiked Head" variety—Certain clad Proof examples of the 2004-S Florida quarters have a die break running from the top of Washington's head to the border. Similar cracks are known for Tennessee, Iowa, Texas (with the crack in a different position), and Minnesota quarters. Such pieces have an additional value (Ken Potter, "2005-S 'Spiked Head' Proof Seen," *Numismatic News,* May 17, 2005).

66. Certain information is from "Florida Quarter Launches," by Jim LaFemina, Public Affairs Office, U.S. Mint Web site.

67. Illustrating a Spanish galleon along with other motifs, the 2004 Florida quarter is one of the few to include a distinctly numismatic scene, in this case indirectly. Centuries ago, the Spanish treasure fleet, typically consisting of a dozen or more vessels, returned from possessions in the New World, bearing gold and silver coins and ingots for the royal coffers. The typical homeward route called for a rendezvous at Havana, then passage northward along the east coast of Florida, then into the broad Atlantic. During the time of the equinoctial storms (now known as the hurricane season), certain of these ships—including virtually the entire fleets of 1715 and 1733—perished on the shoals and beaches of Florida. Many coins have been recovered from the remains of these vessels, to the delight of the collecting community.

68. G.C. Carnes, letter to the author, August 10, 2004.

69. Certain information is from "The Eyes of Texas and the Nation Are on Austin as the United States Mint Launches the New Texas Quarter," U.S. Mint Web site.

70. A striking-ceremony for the 2000-D quarters was held at the Denver Mint on July 12, 2004 (*Numismatic News,* July 27, 2004).

71. To this point this was the record-low mintage figure among state quarters, displacing the 2000-P Ohio (217,200,000), the previous record holder.

72. "Spiked Head" variety—Certain clad Proof examples of 2004-S Iowa quarters have a die break running from the top of Washington's head to the border. Similar cracks are known for Tennessee, Florida, Texas (the Texas crack is in a different location), and Minnesota quarters. Such pieces have an additional value (Ken Potter, "2005-S 'Spiked Head' Proof Seen," *Numismatic News,* May 17, 2005).

73. Issue of August 2004.

74. This figure includes an unknown number of the Extra Leaf High and Extra Leaf Low varieties. Of the Extra Leaf High coins, an estimated 2,000 or are so known. The U.S. Mint estimates that just 35,000 to 50,000 of this variety were made. Using the higher (50,000) figure would suggest that this variety is more than 4,500 times more rare than the regular

quarters without an extra leaf. Of the Extra Leaf Low coins, an estimated 3,000 or so are known. The Mint made no estimate of the mintage for this variety, but it was probably slightly higher than for the Extra Leaf High. The estimated populations for both of these varieties are subject to change.

75. Selected information is from "Wisconsin Quarter Launch," J.D. Harrington, external relations, U.S. Mint Web site.

76. Among the submissions was this one—art, not a concept—as described by Leon A. Saryan, from the studio of Daniel Carr (designer of the Maine and Rhode Island quarters and important in the New York scenario): "One of the best submissions in this genre was the Old Abe eagle drawn by a talented out-of-state artist who had already submitted winning designs for other states. The drawing was submitted via a state resident who was a friend of the artist. It was a very professional presentation, a stunningly beautiful numismatic eagle that outclassed almost every other eagle in two centuries of United States coinage. . . . This Old Abe eagle was special. I was immediately attracted to the design, but was a little put off by the fact that it originated from outside the state, since this was against the spirit (if not the ground rules) of the process. . . . I am still haunted by that rendition of Old Abe." Based upon Saryan's description, I can only hope that this majestic depiction of the national bird is used on some other coin in the future!

77. Saryan's article, "Designing the Washington Quarter," *Centinel*, Winter 2004–05, vol. 53 no. 4, was among the information sources used here.

78. *Coin World*, February 6, 2006

79. Michele Orzano, "Patience Is a Virtue," *Coin World*, February 9, 2004.

80. Paul Gilkes, "California Launches Quarter," *Coin World*, February 21, 2005.

81. November 15, 2004.

82. "Spiked Head" variety—Certain clad Proof examples of 2005-S Minnesota quarters have a die break running from the top of Washington's head to the border. Similar cracks are known for Tennessee, Florida, Texas (the Texas crack is in a different location), and Iowa quarters. Such pieces have an additional value (Ken Potter, "2005-S 'Spiked Head' Proof Seen," *Numismatic News*, May 17, 2005).

83. "Thousands Celebrate 'Land of 10,000 Lakes' Quarter," U.S. Mint Web site. Also, *Numismatist*, March 2005.

84. "Minnesota," U.S. Mint Web site.

85. *Numismatist*, March 2005.

86. "Minnesota," U.S. Mint Web site.

87. *Numismatic News*, June 1, 2004.

88. Don Hamilton, "Flip a Coin: Heads—or Salmon? Or Beavers?" *Portland* (Oregon) *Tribune*, August 19, 2003.

89. "Crater Lake Edges Mount Hood," *Numismatic News*, May 25, 2004.

90. "Oregon Selects Crater Lake for 2005 State Quarter Dollar," *Coin World*, June 14, 2003.

91. Paul Gilkes, "Oregon Quarter Mintage Highest Since Louisiana," *Coin World*, August 29, 2005.

92. Certain information is from "Kansas," U.S. Mint Web site, and from "Nation Gets First Buffalo Quarter," U.S. Mint Web site, September 9, 2005.

93. "Kansas to See Quarter September 9," *Coin World*, July 18, 2005.

94. Don Carbaugh, *Numismatist*, August 2004, p. 29.

95. "Mint Green-Lights Alterations Requested for Kansas Design,"*Numismatic News*, June 1, 2004.

96. Certain information is from "West Virginia" and "West Virginia Quarter Celebrates Engineering Triumph," U.S. Mint Web site.

97. Gary Waddell, "Design for Nevada Quarter Begins," www.klastv.com, June 23, 2004.

98. Michele Orzano, "States Select 2006 25¢ Designs," *Coin World*, June 20, 2005.

99. The Citizens Coin Advisory Committee also favored the bighorn sheep design (Bill Fivaz, committee member, communication with the author, December 23, 2005).

100. Paul Gilkes, "Panels Agree on Nevada," *Coin World*, February 14, 2005.

101. Posted on the Internet. The State of Nebraska Web site and the U.S. Mint Web site also furnished much information.

102. "Nebraska Sends Four to Mint," *Numismatic News*, October 12, 2004.

103. "Nebraska," *Coin World*, January 31, 2005.

104. Gilkes, "Panels Agree."

105. Much information is from news releases from the governor's office posted on the Internet.

106. Gayle Perez, "First Lady Frances Owens Seeks Nominations for Colorado's Commemorative 25-Cent Piece," *Pueblo Chieftain* Web site.

107. Michele Orzano, "Colorado Ponders Designs," *Coin World*, March 28, 2005.

108. Tom Noe resigned as chairman in 2005.

109. As Bill Fivaz correctly stated, there is no typical "peak" on Pikes Peak, in the form of a prominent, well-defined top. The mountain is amorphous, and viewed from a dozen different angles, it has a dozen different shapes. Those not familiar with the actual peak are often surprised when they view it in person. The diecutter for the 1860 Clark, Gruber & Co. "Pikes Peak" $10 and $20 gold coins, who is believed to have lived in the East, depicted it as a conical mountain with a pointed top.

110. In reality, Mesa Verde is set in a large opening, low in the face of a vertical cliff.

111. Bill McAllister, "CCAC Makes Quarter Choice," *Coin World*, April 4, 2005.

112. Paul Gilkes, "Review Panel Approves Colorado Coin Designs," *Coin World*, April 4, 2005.

113. *Numismatic News*, July 27, 2004.

114. Michele Orzano, "States Select 2006 25¢ Designs," *Coin World*, June 20, 2005. Certain information also taken from the U.S. Mint Web site.

115. Certain information from the U.S. Mint Web site.

116. Paul Gilkes, "CFA Recommends Another Bison," *Coin World*, October 11, 2004.

117. "CCAC Endorses Pheasant for SD," *Numismatic News*, October 12, 2004.

118. "South Dakota Prepares for Quarter Selection," *Numismatic News*, November 9, 2004.

119. *Numismatic News* Web site, November 12, 2005.

120. News release from Governor Kempthorne's office, July 27, 2005.

121. *Numismatic News* Web site, November 12, 2005.

122. Michele Orzano, "Utah Forms Quarter Panel," *Coin World*, October 11, 2004.

Appendix: Market-Value History

Mint State Coins (1932–1986) and Silver Proofs (1932–1964), by Date

This table shows historical prices for Washington quarters issued from 1932 to 1986. It includes circulation strikes as well as silver Proofs, which were issued through 1964. The following explains the grades used and the sources from which the values were obtained.

1. **1946 column**—Values are from the first edition of *A Guide Book of United States Coins* (the "Red Book"). The grades used were Uncirculated and Proof.
2. **1966 column**—Values are from the 21st edition of the Red Book. The grades used were Uncirculated and Proof.
3. **1986 column**—Values are from the 41st edition of the Red Book. *Circulation strikes* dated 1932 to 1964 are valued in MS-63; later dates are valued in MS-65 (the only grade available for that date range). *Silver Proofs* are valued at PF-65.
4. **2006 column**—Values are from the present text. *Circulation strikes* dated 1932 to 1964 are valued in MS-64; later dates are valued in MS-65. *Silver Proofs* are valued at PF-65.

Circulation Strikes

Date	1947	1967	1987	2007	Increase
1932	$1.35	$15.00	$60.00	$90.00	6,567%
1932-D	17.50	240.00	1,200.00	7,500.00	42,757%
1932-S	10.00	150.00	450.00	2,750.00	27,400%
1934	2.25	16.00	a	45.00	1,900%
1934-D	2.25	75.00	165.00	575.00	25,456%
1935	1.25	13.00	40.00	40.00	3,100%
1935-D	1.75	55.00	160.00	350.00	19,900%
1935-S	2.00	47.50	125.00	165.00	8,150%
1936	1.50	11.00	30.00	40.00	2,567%
1936-D	2.50	285.00	350.00	1,250.00	49,900%
1936-S	1.75	37.50	125.00	200.00	11,329%
1937	1.25	11.00	30.00	40.00	3,100%
1937-D	1.25	17.50	60.00	120.00	9,500%
1937-S	2.00	77.50	140.00	275.00	13,650%
1938	1.00	60.00	75.00	150.00	14,900%
1938-S	1.50	37.50	75.00	180.00	11,900%
1939	1.00	9.00	20.00	30.00	2,900%
1939-D	1.25	12.50	35.00	65.00	5,100%
1939-S	1.50	40.00	70.00	210.00	13,900%
1940	1.00	13.00	20.00	45.00	4,400%
1940-D	1.25	50.00	85.00	240.00	19,100%
1940-S	1.00	9.50	25.00	45.00	4,400%
1941	0.75	3.75	10.00	22.00	2,833%
1941-D	0.75	7.00	25.00	63.00	8,300%
1941-S	0.75	7.50	23.00	60.00	7,900%
1942	0.75	4.00	10.00	15.00	1,900%

1942-D	$0.75	$4.00	$15.00	$25.00	3,233%
1942-S	0.75	27.50	90.00	150.00	19,900%
1943	0.65	1.85	8.00	15.00	2,208%
1943-D	0.65	4.00	18.00	43.00	6,515%
1943-S	0.65	6.75	50.00	44.00	6,669%
1944	0.50	1.75	6.00	15.00	2,900%
1944-D	0.50	4.00	12.00	21.00	4,100%
1944-S	0.50	4.00	13.00	21.00	4,100%
1945	0.40	1.50	5.00	15.00	3,650%
1945-D	0.40	3.00	10.00	30.00	7,400%
1945-S	0.40	2.65	8.00	19.00	4,650%
1946	0.35	1.60	5.00	17.00	4,757%
1946-D	0.35	4.50	7.00	20.00	5,614%
1946-S	0.35	5.75	8.00	15.00	4,186%
1947	0.35	2.00	7.00	27.00	7,614%
1947-D	0.35	2.20	8.00	18.00	5,043%
1947-S	0.35	6.00	6.00	16.00	4,471%
1948		1.60	4.00	15.00	838%
1948-D		2.25	6.00	22.00	878%
1948-S		2.50	6.00	19.00	660%
1949		15.00	27.50	55.00	267%
1949-D		5.00	10.00	42.00	740%
1950		2.75	5.00	15.00	445%
1950-D		2.00	5.00	13.00	550%
1950-D, D/S		n/a	350.00	1,000.00	186%
1950-S		5.00	8.00	20.00	300%
1950-S, S/D		n/a	475.00	600.00	26%
1951		1.50	4.00	11.00	633%
1951-D		1.50	4.00	11.00	633%
1951-S		8.00	9.00	32.00	300%
1952		1.50	4.00	14.00	833%
1952-D		1.30	5.00	11.00	746%
1952-S		3.75	7.00	30.00	700%
1953		3.25	5.00	11.00	238%
1953-D		1.35	3.75	13.00	863%
1953-S		2.00	5.00	13.00	550%
1954		1.15	3.50	15.00	1,204%
1954-D		1.50	3.50	13.00	767%
1954-S		1.75	3.75	13.00	643%
1955		2.00	3.50	11.00	450%
1955-D		6.00	4.00	17.00	183%
1956		0.75	2.75	17.00	2,167%
1956-D		0.85	2.75	8.00	841%
1957		0.75	2.75	8.00	967%
1957-D		0.75	2.75	9.00	1,100%
1958		2.50	2.75	7.00	180%
1958-D		0.65	2.75	7.00	977%

1959	$1.00	$2.75	$7.00	600%
1959-D	0.65	2.75	7.00	977%
1960	0.70	2.75	7.00	900%
1960-D	0.55	2.75	7.00	1,173%
1961	0.60	2.75	7.00	1,067%
1961-D	0.55	2.75	7.00	1,173%
1962	0.50	2.75	7.00	1,300%
1962-D	0.50	2.75	7.00	1,300%
1963	0.50	2.75	7.00	1,300%
1963-D	0.50	2.75	7.00	1,300%
1964	0.50	2.75	7.00	1,300%
1964-D	0.50	2.75	7.00	1,300%
1965	0.50	0.75	9.00	1,700%
1966		0.75	6.00	700%
1967		0.75	5.00	567%
1968		0.75	5.00	567%
1968-D		1.00	5.00	400%
1969		0.50	5.00	900%
1969-D		1.00	5.00	400%
1970		0.50	9.00	1,700%
1970-D		0.50	6.00	1,100%
1971		0.50	5.00	900%
1971-D		0.50	3.00	500%
1972		0.50	4.00	700%
1972-D		0.50	5.00	900%
1973		0.50	7.00	1,300%
1973-D		0.50	9.00	1,700%
1974		0.50	5.00	900%
1974-D		0.50	11.00	2,100%
1966		0.75	6.00	700%
1967		0.75	5.00	567%
1968		0.75	5.00	567%
1968-D		1.00	5.00	400%
1969		0.50	5.00	900%
1969-D		1.00	5.00	400%
1970		0.50	9.00	1,700%
1970-D		0.50	6.00	1,100%
1971		0.50	5.00	900%
1971-D		0.50	3.00	500%
1972		0.50	4.00	700%
1972-D		0.50	5.00	900%
1973		0.50	7.00	1,300%
1973-D		0.50	9.00	1,700%
1974		0.50	5.00	900%
1974-D		0.50	11.00	2,100%
1776-1976, COPPER-NICKEL CLAD		0.50	6.00	1,100%
1776-1976-D, COPPER-NICKEL CLAD		0.50	6.00	1,100%

1776-1976-S, SILVER CLAD	$2.50	$5.00	100%
1977	0.50	6.00	1,100%
1977-D	0.50	4.00	700%
1978	0.50	6.00	1,100%
1978-D	0.50	6.00	1,100%
1979	0.50	6.00	1,100%
1979-D	0.50	4.00	700%
1980P	0.50	7.00	1,300%
1980-D	0.50	5.00	900%
1981P	0.50	6.00	1,100%
1981-D	0.50	4.00	700%
1982P	0.75	15.00	1,900%
1982-D	0.50	10.00	1,900%
1983P	0.50	55.00	10,900%
1983-D	0.50	35.00	6,900%
1984P	0.50	8.00	1,500%
1984-D	0.50	8.00	1,500%
1985P	0.50	15.00	2,900%
1985-D	0.50	8.00	1,500%
1986P	0.50	3.00	500%
1986-D	0.50	10.00	1,900%

[a] Not priced separately.

SILVER PROOFS

DATE	1946	1966	1986	2006	INCREASE
1936	$13.00	$375.00	$1,400.00	$1,800.00	13,746%
1937	5.50	125.00	425.00	750.00	13,536%
1938	4.00	95.00	400.00	450.00	11,150%
1939	3.50	85.00	250.00	400.00	11,329%
1940	3.00	45.00	200.00	350.00	11,567%
1941	2.25	35.00	175.00	250.00	11,011%
1942	2.00	37.50	175.00	250.00	12,400%
1950		32.50	150.00	70.00	115%
1951		20.00	80.00	60.00	200%
1952		10.00	60.00	50.00	400%
1953		9.00	30.00	50.00	456%
1954		5.00	16.00	25.00	400%
1955		6.00	12.00	25.00	317%
1956		5.00	7.00	10.00	100%
1957		2.00	6.00	8.00	300%
1958		4.00	8.00	18.00	350%
1959		2.50	7.00	8.00	220%
1960		2.00	6.00	8.00	300%
1961		1.75	6.00	8.00	357%
1962		1.75	6.00	8.00	357%
1963		1.75	6.00	8.00	357%
1964		2.25	6.00	8.00	256%

Stack's

Synonymous with the finest in the world of numismatics

Whether you are buying, selling or consigning to one of our world famous auctions, you owe it to yourself to deal with the experts. Stack's has conducted more top-quality numismatic auctions than any other American rare coin firm in history. Call Lawrence Stack or Harvey Stack for a consultation.

An original study in plaster by John Flanagan
of an early design proposal for the Washington Quarter.
Owned by Stack's Rare Coins, New York City.

 *Buyers, Sellers and Auctioneers of the*
World's Finest Coins for Over 70 Years.

123 West 57th St. • New York, NY 10019-2280
(212) 582-2580 • FAX: (212) 245-5018
www.stacks.com • or email us at: info@stacks.com
Auctions • Appraisals • Retail • Since 1935

The most respected name in numismatics